Sample Square

Century 21 Academy of R.E. 513 E. Sample Rd.

FLORIDA REAL ESTATE PRINCIPLES, PRACTICES, & LAW

GEORGE GAINES, JR.
and
DAVID S. COLEMAN

FLORIDA REAL ESTATE PRINCIPLES, PRACTICES, & LAW

Printed in the United States of America

Library of Congress Catalog Card Number: 77-84427

First Edition, 1977
Second Edition, 1978

Address inquiries and orders to:

David S. Coleman, Ph.D.
1660 Huron Trail
Maitland, Florida 32751

TABLE OF CONTENTS

other books by Gaines and Coleman:

- FLORIDA REAL ESTATE LAW: A Basic Study
  Sixth Edition, 1977
- FLORIDA SUPPLEMENT
  Prentice-Hall, Inc., 1977
- HOW TO DECIDE . . . HOW TO BUY A HOME
  First Edition, 1978

PREFACE

Perhaps the best reason for writing a book is being urged to do so by a great many people, in this instance, instructors, adult students, administrators, and practitioners of real estate throughout Florida. This indicates several things to the authors, two of which will be mentioned. First, six editions of FLORIDA REAL ESTATE LAW: A Basic Study in four years have been well-received. But secondly, that first book has not been as comprehensive as it might be to suit many student and course needs.

Thus, within the pages of this book, an attempt has been made to bring together the theoretical, practical, and legal aspects of real estate. The authors are fully aware of the difficulty in adequately covering the wide scope of subject matter involved in so broad a topic as real estate. The major objective has been to write and arrange the material to assist the adult learner, regardless of age and time away from formal study, to acquire the maximum amount of knowledge in the minimum amount of time.

In a sense, this book is an expanded version of the first book, but it is much more than that. There are eight entirely new chapters. There is a 125-question practice exam. There is a combination Glossary/Index. The contents (but not the sequence) have been carefully coordinated with the subject areas required by Florida Real Estate Commission Course I. Every effort has been made to incorporate the latest information regarding changes in the law. And, the material in the fifteen chapters of the first book has been retained but consolidated in a more logical and hopefully useful arrangement.

The book is designed as an introductory text for adult students and prospective and functioning real estate practitioners. It can be used for group or independent study, and as a basic textbook in courses for which academic credit is given, for which continuing education units (ceu's) are awarded, or for which noncredit status is assigned.

At the end of each chapter is a series of quizzes. Towards the end of the book is the Practice End-of-Course Exam. These sixteen quizzes and the 125-question exam have been carefully constructed to stress major points and are for the benefit of students and instructors alike as means of testing for understanding. It is the authors' considered opinion that students who will conscientiously test themselves by completing these quiz and exam questions, without referring to any material, should have a benchmark as to their grasp of the knowledge and their readiness for the FREC Course I final examination and the State licensing examination.

The FLORIDA REAL ESTATE COMMISSION HANDBOOK, published by the Florida Real Estate Commission, is the primary reference for real estate law for students and new and existing practitioners. Thus, it has been the primary source for material presented in major portions of this book. Selected references to numbered sections in the HANDBOOK appear in the right-hand margins which are designed as well for making notes. Therefore, this book is to be used, where appropriate, in conjunction with the HANDBOOK so as to provide a bridge of understanding for the layman.

Readers will encounter many instances where certain subjects and terms are repeated. This repetition is intentional for learning purposes and is hopefully not overdone.

Whenever a personal reference to the masculine gender is made, the authors intend it to include the feminine also, unless the context clearly indicates otherwise.

This Preface would be incomplete if the authors failed to acknowledge the critical suggestions received to a draft copy of one of the chapters. The authors, therefore, wish to thank Ford S. Hausman, CFA, Orange County Property Appraiser, for his help in making the chapter entitled "Real Estate Taxes" as accurate and current as possible. Any errors or omissions in the treatment of material in this and all other chapters are the sole responsibility of the authors.

Special acknowledgment must go to the authors' wives for their considerable effort, assistance, and patience. Without them, this book simply could not have become a reality.

To those of you who will use this book as a vehicle to enter the real estate business, the authors wish you well. Real estate is an exciting and rewarding business. It is also very demanding in time, effort, self-discipline, integrity, and continuing study. A solid foundation of knowledge and a firm resolve to maintain ethical standards are two of the most important ingredients in the recipe for success.

A specific effort has been made to elicit suggestions from instructors and students. The Feedback Sheet prior to page 1 can be carefully removed without damaging your book. Please complete, fold, tack, stamp, and send it to the authors. Your comments will be most welcomed at any time. Feedback such as this is what prompted the writing of this book as the first sentence in this Preface indicates.

George Gaines, Jr.
David S. Coleman

August, 1977

Carefully separate this page from the book -- it will not damage your book.
OR, use a plain sheet, but do let us hear from you. We earnestly solicit your help.

fold, tack, and mail

place
stamp
here

TO: Dr. David S. Coleman
1660 Huron Trail
Maitland,
Florida 32751

fold here

from: ______________________
(optional)
____
____

FEEDBACK SHEET

1. I took/gave the real estate course at _______________________.
(name of school or college)

2. I took/gave the course for: _____ college credit hours _____ non-credit hours.

3. I completed the course in ____________ (month), _______ (year).

4. I chose to answer ______ questions on the 125-question Practice End-of-Course Exam.

My score on correct answers was __________ (optional).

5. I found this book to be: (check one)

_____ very helpful

_____ fairly helpful

_____ not very helpful

_____ bad !

6. My suggestions for improving the book are:

7. Other comments:

THANK YOU.

CHAPTER 1

THE REAL ESTATE BUSINESS

Dear Sir:

A real estate salesman showed us a house with an asking price of $52,500. My husband and I wanted to offer the owner $48,500. The salesman refused to write up any offer for less than $50,000. Can a salesman legally keep us from offering what we think is fair?

Peb Public
Homesville, Florida

Dear Sir:

We want to sell our home and move into a condominium. An acquaintance who is a REALTOR tells us she can get a least $46,000 for our house. She says she has a buyer who will pay $7,000 down and take over our $20,000 VA mortgage if we will take back a second mortgage for the remaining $19,000. We would like to sell, but is this advisable?

Cid Citizen
Palmsburg, Florida

How would _you_ answer such questions? They are normal, everyday questions of the type real estate brokers and salespersons encounter routinely. While the average citizen in Florida is developing a greater awareness of and a greater interest in real estate, few are aware of the vast scope of the "real estate industry." Unless they are actively involved in some aspect of real estate, most people have an impression of real estate similar to that of the three blind men in a Hindu fable who were trying to describe an elephant.

One of the blind men in the fable tried to describe the elephant by feeling the elephant's trunk. He said the animal was much like a palm tree. Another, who felt only the tail, thought the beast must resemble a rope. The third blind man measured the side of the elephant with his hands and thought it must surely be very similar to a house. Like the blind men in the tale, the general public seems to view real estate from individual bits and pieces of information which tend to produce conflicting opinions.

This chapter will attempt to isolate and describe the major divisions of the real estate industry. Greatest emphasis will be placed on that division of the business commonly referred to as "agency." This is the division involving all forms of brokerage, management, appraising, property insurance, and counseling. Also, it is the division in which the overwhelming majority of licensed people are active. This would not be true if the activities of unlicensed people who act for themselves by investing, or buying and selling, or working for a regulatory agency of the government were included. However, the concern here is basically with those who are, or will be, licensed practitioners of real estate for compensation in the agency division of the business. That division and the other major divisions of the real estate business with their component activities are shown in the following chart.

MAJOR DIVISIONS OF THE REAL ESTATE BUSINESS

AGENCY	DEVELOPMENT and CONSTRUCTION	INVESTMENT	OPERATIONS	GOVERNMENT SERVICE
A. Sales and Leasing	A. Land Acquisition	Equity	Equity	Acquisition
B. Property Management	B. Subdividing and Development	Mortgages	Mortgages	Building
C. Appraising	C. Construction	Leaseholds	Leaseholds	Conservation
D. Mortgages	D. Marketing	(long-term involvement)	Other	Financing
E. Counseling			(turnover for profit)	Management
F. Property Insurance				Regulation
				Taxation

The letters in front of the activities listed under the Agency and Development/Construction Divisions match the letters which identify the following descriptions of those activities. And, for the purposes of this chapter, only those same two divisions will be examined.

I. The Agency Division

As the foregoing chart indicates, the agency division of the real estate business is composed of those activities which provide a type of specialized service for others in return for compensation, either a commission or a fee. The point to be remembered is that a real estate broker or salesman acts as an "agent" for others. Seldom do they deal with their own inventory of properties. The modern real estate practitioner is paid to handle other people's properties because he or she is considered a specialist, capable of saving a seller or buyer time and money through expertise in at least three areas:

1. Details of Property Transfer. To be worthy of compensation, a professional in real estate must know the economic and legal intricacies associated with the transfer of title, property taxes, financing, and local zoning ordinances. 16.06 16.08

2. Knowledge of the Real Estate Market. The professional knows that the real estate market is never completely static. Is it firming up anticipating a more active market, or is it softening anticipating less activity? Is it rising or is it falling? What types of properties are moving? Where are the most active areas? What values should apply to different properties in different neighborhoods?

   Many brokers and salesmen prefer to select one specific portion of a city and become so expert in that area that it becomes what is called a "farm area." This means that they get to know almost every lot and house in the district. They prepare card files on each property showing when it was built, what it sold for, what resales have produced, what the taxes are, etc. They meet the people in their selected area and make it known that they specialize in only that section of town. The "farm area" soon begins to produce a harvest in the form of listings and sales. A reputation for expertise has been created -- by hard work. When residents in the "farm area" move or decide to sell, they call the expert -- he knows what their property will bring on the market.

3. Knowledge of How to Market Real Estate. It is not enough to know what is happening in the local real estate market. One must also know how to market real estate. The buyer who is interested in purchasing a 300-unit apartment complex cannot be found and sold by using the same methods which produce buyers for a $30,000 house. Even when a brokerage firm specializes in one type of property, each potential buyer must be treated as an individual. The sales presentation most effective with one prospect may be completely ineffective with another.

   Knowledge of how to market also includes expertise in locating prospects. For example, a good broker can locate prospects before they ever arrive in the community. While there may be exceptions, the bulk of evidence and experience available indicates that a property handled by a broker will normally be sold more quickly and with less reduction in the desired sales price than if an owner attempts to sell his property himself.

With the preceding overview of agents as experts who make up the agency division of the real estate industry, an examination can be made of the subdivisions (activities) of real estate under the agency division. All will be dealt with except "leasing" which will be discussed in a subsequent chapter.

A. Sales. As has already been established, a real estate professional's primary asset is specialized knowledge, called expertise. However, to be successful will require that he also be skilled in bringing willing parties together for the purpose of concluding a transaction. In real estate sales, a broker is customarily negotiating with a buyer, on behalf of the seller. Due to the number of dollars involved each year, real estate sales activity has been called the lifeblood of the brokerage business.

Some brokers prefer to sell only residential property because that represents their field of interest and ability. Others specialize in commercial property, in industrial property, or only in agricultural property. Of course, some brokerage firms deal in two or more of the different kinds mentioned. The average real estate brokerage firm, however, consists of three to five licensed people, and numbers alone dictate that their scope of sales specialization must be somewhat less than the larger firms. Regardless of size or type of property handled, the sales transaction is the critical activity to the success or failure of a real estate firm.

The goal of any single real estate sales effort is simple, yet the process is complex and sequential in nature. The simplified flow chart on the facing page depicts the sequence of steps from the first step of listing a property until the last -- recording the new owner's deed.

The sequential steps illustrated on the Real Estate Sale Process flow chart are applicable to all types of sales: residential, commercial, industrial, and agricultural. The steps should be completed in the proper sequence. It would be foolish, for example, to try to close a sale before a listing was obtained and the property was shown to a prospect. Unfortunately, many sales have fallen through because a person did not complete the steps in sequence, one by one. Often, a salesperson will obtain a listing and ignore the need to look for prospects. Someone else then gets the sale, or the listing expires. The four types or categories of sales are briefly described in the paragraphs which follow.

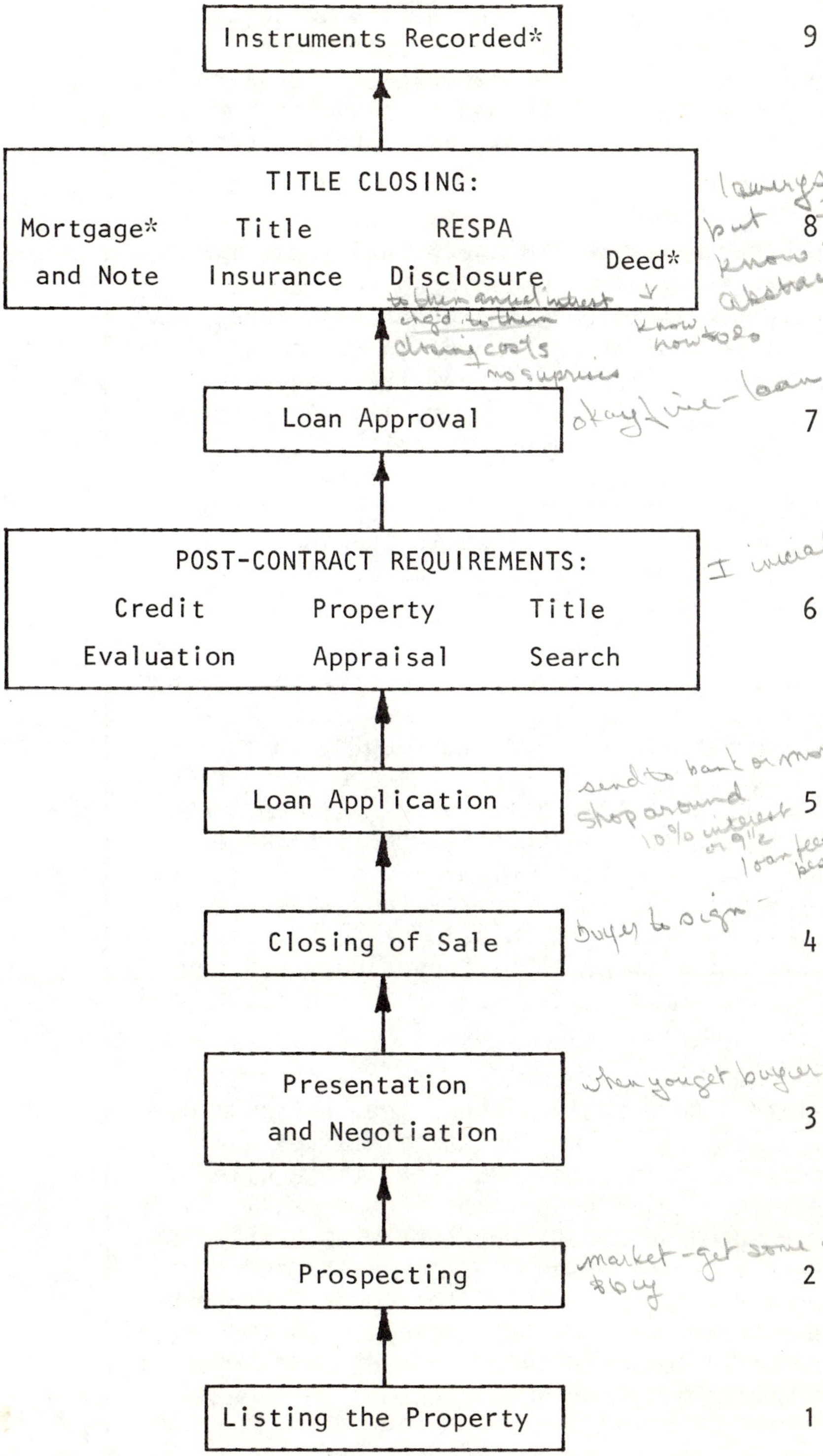

REAL ESTATE SALE PROCESS

Steps: ↑

1. Residential sales. Most licensed individuals in real estate are involved with residential sales. When the average citizen gives his opinion of real estate and the people in it, he is usually voicing an opinion based on his experience with a residential salesperson. It would not be wrong to say that the image and reputation of real estate people as a whole depends to a great extent on the conduct and character of residential real estate salespersons.

To be effective as professionals and to serve their customers well, residential salespersons need specialized knowledge. They should, as soon as possible, acquire a thorough understanding of the strengths and weaknesses of neighborhoods in the area in which they intend to operate. They must know the best access routes and locations of schools, shopping facilities, churches, and recreation facilities. They should also be able to explain property taxes, zoning restrictions, and approximate utility costs in the area. Perhaps the most important aspect of residential sales is knowing how to help prospects obtain financing. All of these items of information will prove useful as the salesperson completes one step after another on the sale flow chart.

2. Commercial sales. The clients who deal with commercial real estate salesmen are normally more sophisticated investor-buyers. For this reason, those who choose to specialize in commercial sales need a broader knowledge, and a greater depth, in their expertise regarding income-producing properties and the various techniques for increasing after-tax cash flow. Apartments, retail stores, office buildings, and shopping centers are examples of income-producing properties which are included in the commercial category. After commercial brokers and salespersons have acquired the expertise necessary to help others to either obtain tax shelters or cash flow or both, they find it is very important to maintain a personal relationship with institutional investors and mortgage lenders.

3. Industrial sales. Industrial properties are a very specialized type of real estate. Comparatively speaking, not as many clients are buying and selling in the industrial market as in the residential or commercial markets. However, those clients wanting to buy or sell industrial properties are generally quite knowledgeable and very specific about what they want. This is a big help to the industrial salesperson. Sales in the industrial field are usually for large amounts. Like the commercial property salesman, the person who decides to specialize in industrial sales will also be required to increase his breadth and scope of knowledge beyond that which might be sufficient to sell residential properties.

The industrial salesperson deals in three types of properties: sites in organized industrial parks or subdivisions, redeveloped industrial parcels in central areas, and industrial acreage. This requires technical knowledge of the many requirements related to different industries, such as industrial transportation requirements, special industrial construction features, unusual utility requirements, and local land-use restrictions affecting industrial properties. More and more industrial brokers are finding it rewarding to develop and sell high quality, beautifully landscaped, and well-conceived industrial subdivisions. Almost every large city in Florida has witnessed the development of such industrial parks. This new aspect of industrial brokerage has done much to increase the prestige and status of a land use which was looked down on formerly.

4. Agricultural sales. In addition to the normal qualifications and skills required of any real estate salesman, one who specializes in the sale of farms and agricultural land must be familiar with the operation of farms and the economic problems peculiar to various types of farming. One of the most important prerequisites is the ability to communicate with farmers. Salespersons who are effective in dealing with farm operators are sincere and knowledgeable about farms and the federal programs affecting farm operations.

In summary of the sales aspect of agency, it certainly is not true that "What you don't know won't hurt you." Not only can practitioners be hurt by what they don't know, but also the sadder fact is that unsuspecting members of the public can be and are hurt every day by what some real estate broker or salesman does not know. The typical real estate transaction involves many details and activities which the layman does not understand. Moreover, the transaction usually involves a large amount of money and is therefore of more than casual importance to the principal or client who must rely on the real estate professional to protect his economic welfare. If for no other reason, persons 16.04
involved in the sale of real estate have a moral and ethical 16.08
obligation to acquire a degree of knowledge and expertise so beneficial to principals and clients that it will prove that money paid for commissions and fees is money well-spent.

B. Property management. Probably in no other real estate activity have rapid growth and increased specialization been more obvious than in the field of property management. Several factors have contributed to the emergence of property management as one of the more important facets of the real estate business. The acceptance of the multi-family apartment building, improvements in structural engineering resulting in high-rise office buildings, and decentralization of retail businesses to surburban neighborhoods have contributed to the increased demand for property managers. Furthermore, the great depression of the 1930's resulted in wholesale foreclosures of income-producing properties which concentrated ownership of large numbers of buildings in the hands of a few institutional owners such as insurance companies, banks, and savings and loan associations. These institutions were forced to place a number of the foreclosed properties under the management of real estate brokers and other professional managers. This resulted in a rapid increase of "absentee owners." A life insurance company with headquarters in New York, for example, might have acquired properties in Florida, California, and Illinois all in a short period of time. Suddenly, the importance of qualified property managers became a critical factor in the planning of institutional owners located in one part of the nation with income-producing properties in another part. Subsequently, individuals desiring to participate in the growth of distant regions have become absentee owners of income-producing properties. So the most important factor in the rapid growth of property management is usually considered to be the increase in absentee ownership.

The term "property manager" should not be confused with "residential manager" or "rental agent." The scope of a property manager's functions go far beyond rent collection, maintenance, and repair. A property manager is the local representative of the owner. His primary task is to produce the greatest possible net income over the longest possible time. This may involve development of plans for modernization, remodeling, or alteration of existing properties. The costs versus benefits must be clearly justified.

As agents of absentee owners, the property manager has a responsibility for improving tenant relations and for advertising and merchandising the type of space he manages. Apartment buildings, condominium developments, shopping centers, and office buildings all require efficient management. The demand for capable managers is growing. Corporations, banks, investment companies, and individuals realize that a trained property manager can usually cope with the intricacies involved in operating income properties better than an owner whose business expertise lies in other areas. This is particularly true for doctors, lawyers, and other professionals who have come to recognize the tax benefits of owning income-producing real estate. Such groups normally hire qualified property managers since they have neither the time nor the desire to become involved in the complexities of property management.

Property managers are compensated in a number of ways. Some work on the basis of a guaranteed base amount, plus a small percentage of rents actually collected. Most prefer to work for a percentage of gross effective income (total income collected) which may vary from 5 to 10 percent depending on region and community.

C. Appraising. As in real estate sales, an appraiser may handle all types of real property or specialize in a particular type of property. Most appraisers gain entry into this specialized field by first appraising single-family dwellings. As they gain experience and broaden their knowledge, they expand into income properties, farms, etc. Appraising requires more training and experience than any other field of real estate, with the possible exception of counseling.

The specialized field of appraising is considered an art. It is one of the most respected phases of real estate. Basically, appraising is estimating the market value of property or some interest in property. Almost anyone can guess at the value of property, but an appraiser carefully analyzes past sales, computes the cost to reproduce a structure, and determines the worth of future income that a property might produce. The calculations are important not only to buyers and sellers but also to mortgage lenders and insurance companies. Various levels of government also use appraisers to arrive at a value for properties condemned in order to build roads, highways, and expressways. Individual investors have learned the value of obtaining appraisals before investing.

Appraisers are paid a fee, not a commission, in order to reduce the possibility of any conflict of interest. If an appraiser were to be paid a percent of whatever value he might estimate, there is a possibility that the temptation to exaggerate might prove irresistible. To preclude this from happening, all of the major professional organizations to which appraisers belong require that compensation be a fee based on the responsibilities, the difficulties, and the expenses involved in doing the work.

In an attempt to maintain the high standards of appraising, a number of professional societies have been formed. The more widely recognized are listed at the end of this chapter along with other professional organizations. The requirements for membership in these organizations are demanding. For example, the requirements to qualify for the designation MAI (Member, Appraisal Institute) are:

1. Be at least 30 years of age
2. Have at least five years of appraisal experience
3. Have a degree from an accredited four-year college, or the equivalent
4. Submit and have accepted two narrative appraisals on different types of property
5. Pass two written examinations.

D. Mortgages. If sales are the lifeblood of real estate, financing can be regarded as the lifeblood of sales. The large amounts of dollars involved in real estate transactions require more than 90 percent of all purchases to be financed to some degree. A knowledge of how financing is arranged and the many ways in which financing problems can be solved are essential to success in real estate. The broker or salesperson who can show a prospect how he can afford to buy has a tremendous advantage over the individual who can only show houses. However, real estate brokers or salespersons are not allowed to act as mortgage brokers or mortgage bankers unless properly licensed to do so.

Lenders of mortgage funds use mortgage specialists to arrange loans for the financing of real estate purchases. Mortgage specialists are commonly divided into two separate categories: mortgage brokers and mortgage bankers. Both have a role to play in the creation of a typical real estate mortgage. Both the mortgage broker and the mortgage banker are called "middlemen" because they are the agents, or go-betweens, bringing together a borrower and a lender. The difference between the two is that the mortgage banker operates on a much higher level than the mortgage broker.

A mortgage broker will normally have a working arrangement with one or more mortgage bankers who have authority to approve or reject loan applications. The mortgage broker will first obtain a loan application from a hopeful borrower. Then he will shop it around to different mortgage bankers, savings and loan associations, or banks until he gets the loan approved or is forced to give up. If the loan application is approved, the mortgage broker has earned a "finder's fee" of about one percent and drops out, from that point on, of the loan arrangement. The mortgage banker or some other lender will provide the loan to the borrower. Usually the mortgage banker will be lending the money for a mutual savings bank or a life insurance company which will have authorized the mortgage banker to approve or reject loans. When the loan is arranged, the mortgage banker will often service the loan for the lending institution. The relationship of mortgage brokers, mortgage bankers, and institutional lenders (the real source of mortgage funds) is shown in the chart below.

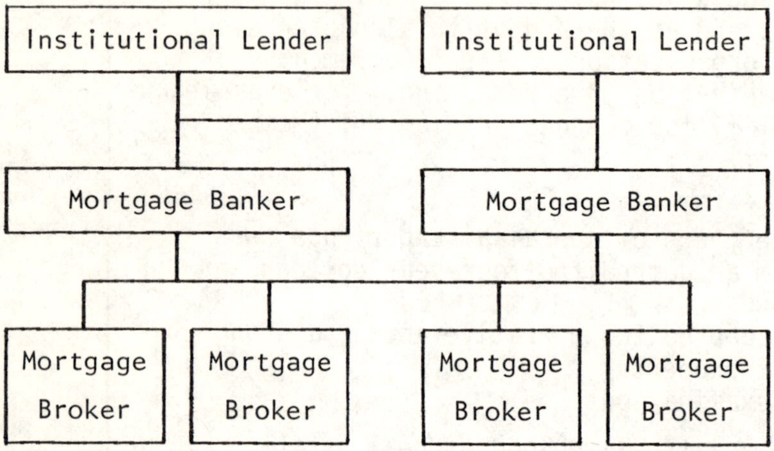

E. Counseling. The function of a real estate counselor is to analyze existing or potential problems and recommend courses of action. A counselor is usually only required for large properties or complex problems. The amount of data related to the property and the counselor's judgment are important factors in finding solutions. A counselor is paid a fee whether the client takes his advice or not. Few people have the education, experience in real estate, knowledge of investing, and tested judgment required to be a qualified counselor; consequently, they are few in number. Our expanding economy, the increasing complexity of problems associated with real estate, and the need for professional counseling services (a legitimate business deduction) all indicate that counseling will grow as a specialized area of the real estate business. Their services are already in demand by developers, investors, corporations, and large-scale buyers and sellers.

F. Property insurance. The value of hazard insurance for improved property is now almost universally accepted. Practically every property owner buys insurance for the structures on his property. In the past, many real estate brokers also found it advantageous to be licensed to sell property insurance. Recently, however, many brokers have found that the increasing requirements for maintaining a current license in the insurance field are just too time-consuming. As a result, the number of real estate brokers active in the property insurance business has been declining. Larger brokerage firms continue to provide this service.

The previously discussed subdivisions (activities) of real estate are all part of the agency division of the business. The next and final major division for discussion is development and construction.

II. The Development and Construction Division

This second major category of the real estate industry is closely related to the agency division, especially in the first phase (land acquisition) and the last phase (marketing). This close relationship is attested to by the increasing number of real estate brokers who, at one time or another, become involved in development and construction.

A. Land acquisition. Developers and builders are involved in the business of improving real estate for profit. They may acquire agricultural land and convert it into a subdivision, shopping center, or an industrial park. The acquisition phase of development may be by outright purchase, or the seller may grant an option to the developer in order to reduce the developer's investment until adequate financing can be arranged. In any case, the developer must acquire control of the land before subsequent phases of developing and construction can proceed.

B. Subdividing and development. Technically, the subdividing phase of the development process involves nothing more than a survey of the tract, drawing lines on the survey to designate individual lots, then placing markers or stakes on the land to locate lot boundaries. However, most communities in Florida have had experience with fly-by-night subdividers who sold lots to the public without improving the property beyond the point of subdividing, as described above. Today, county governments require that subdividing be accompanied by the recording of a plat, that paved roads be included in the proposed subdivision, and that arrangements be made for sewage disposal. County subdivision ordinances have, in effect, combined the subdividing function with the development function. Subdividing alone does not require any physical change to the land except placement of marker stakes.

Development of land is now an extension of the subdivision phase as a result of county subdivision ordinances. This combining of two previously separate functions has resulted in a degree of protection for the public which did not formerly exist. The activities involved in the development of land are more expensive than required for mere subdividing. Often the costs of grading and street paving, installation of curbs, storm drainage systems, water and sewer systems, etc. will exceed the cost of the raw land.

Combining the subdividing and development phases has, in addition to protecting the public, resulted in higher quality subdivisions. One individual or corporation can plan the entire project from the raw land stage to a populated subdivision. Engineers and architects can work from start to completion of the overall site plan under the supervision of one developer whose goal is quality.

C. Construction. The construction phase of land development is not restricted to the large builder or developer. The small builder often will buy a few lots in a developed subdivision for the purpose of building speculative ("spec") houses. Builders customarily receive a discount on the price of lots purchased, and construction financing is provided by local banks or savings and loan associations.

A second practice is custom building. When a developer has produced lots ready for building, the lots are frequently sold to buyers who then arrange with a contractor to build a custom-designed house. The developer will use deed restrictions to ensure that no houses will be built which might harm the value of neighbors' properties.

A third practice is tract building, or speculative building, by the subdivision developer. This type of construction often involves building five or six models of homes which may be built on the developer's lots. Each model home floor plan will usually be available in two or three different exterior treatments to appeal to as many different tastes as possible and to provide the subdivision with a more pleasing appearance.

D. Marketing. The last phase of the development and construction division of real estate is the marketing phase. For large-scale developments, the use of model homes is a very important part of the marketing function. Most developers will employ a small sales force to show their model homes, but the developing trend is for developers to rely on assistance from real estate brokers in marketing their houses and lots. Normally, developers pay for all advertising, and the brokers agree to accept a reduction in their customary sales commission to help offset this expense. This arrangement seems to work to the mutual advantage of both parties.

As mentioned previously, only two of the major divisions of the real estate business and their respective activities would be treated in this chapter. Returning to the chart on page 2 will serve as an additional overview of this important perspective before moving on to the final subject of this chapter.

Professional Organizations

No discussion of the real estate industry should ignore the important role played by various professional associations. The real estate industry as a whole is characterized by organized professional groups related to the specialized areas of the business.

The National Association of REALTORS has probably done more to 16.01
promote ethics, standardized practices, and education in the real estate industry than any other organization in either the public or private sector. Many of the state laws designed to promote professionalism and improve ethical standards have their genesis in the National Association of REALTORS' Code of Ethics. (See 16.02
Chapter III, Interpretative Memoranda, FLORIDA REAL ESTATE COMMISSION HANDBOOK for the Preamble to and the Articles of the Code of Ethics.)

The National Association of REALTORS is composed of three organizational levels. The first level, and the fundamental strength of the overall association, is the local Board of REALTORS. These local boards are organized in communities of all sizes from small towns to large cities across the entire nation. Membership in a local board is not automatic upon becoming a broker. A broker desiring membership must make an application and be approved by a membership committee acting for the board. Full membership requires that an individual be a licensed broker and have a reputation for honesty and fair dealing. When accepted, a broker then is entitled to use the term "REALTOR."

The local Board of REALTORS belongs to the second level of organization, the state association of REALTORS. In Florida, the Florida Association of REALTORS (FAR) has its headquarters in Orlando. The state association serves many purposes on behalf of its member local boards including that of a lobbyist for the statewide industry.

Each of the state associations belongs to the third level of organization, the National Association of REALTORS. Among the many purposes it serves, the national association also acts as a lobbyist, but at the national level for the industry.

As the scope of real estate has expanded, so have the affiliated organizations of the National Association of REALTORS. The following partial list of organizations indicates the various institutes, societies, and councils created by the National Association of REALTORS to serve the different specialized areas of the real estate industry.

ORGANIZATION	INDIVIDUAL DESIGNATION
American Institute of Real Estate Appraisers (AIREA)	RM - Residential Member MAI - Member, Appraisal Institute
American Society of Real Estate Counselors (ASREC)	CRE - Counselor, Real Estate
Institute of Real Estate Management (IREM)	CPM - Certified Property Manager
Real Estate Securities and Syndication Institute (RESSI)	CRSM - Certified Real Estate Securities Member CRSS - Certified Real Estate Securities Sponsor
REALTORS National Marketing Institute (RNMI)	CRB - Certified Residential Broker CCIM - Certified Commercial Investment Member
Society of Industrial REALTORS (SIR)	SIR - Specialist in Industrial Realty

Some of the other widely recognized and respected professional organizations which have no official connection with the National Association of REALTORS are:

ORGANIZATION	SPECIALIZED AREA(S)
American Land Title Association (ALTA)	Title Search and Insurance
American Real Estate and Urban Economics Association (AREUEA)	Education
American Society of Appraisers (ASA)	Appraising
Farm and Land Institute (FLI)	Farm Brokerage
International Association of Assessing Officers (IAAO)	Property Assessment
International Real Estate Federation (IREF)	International Brokerage
Mortgage Bankers of America (MBA)	Financing
National Apartment Owners Association	Property Management
National Association of Building Owners and Managers	Property Management
National Association of Home Builders (NAHB)	Construction
National Association of Real Estate License Law Officials (NARELLO)	Regulation
Society of Real Estate Appraisers (SREA)	Appraising
Urban Land Institute (ULI)	Subdividing and Developing

All of the above organizations seek to serve their members by keeping them informed of developments in their individual areas of special interest. In addition, practically all professional organizations sponsor comprehensive educational programs for members, publish trade papers, and advertise the special services which their members are qualified to provide. These and other resources help to mark the true professional -- someone who is constantly seeking to improve himself in his chosen field of endeavor.

THE REAL ESTATE BUSINESS

1. In what major division of the real estate business is the subdivision "counseling"?
   a. Investment
   b. Agency
   c. Operations
   d. Government service

2. The intangible commodity that a real estate professional has for sale is:
   a. Real property
   b. Salesmanship
   c. Beneficial investment
   d. Expertise

3. Most licensed people in the real estate business are involved in:
   a. The agency division
   b. Residential sales
   c. Commercial sales
   d. Both "a" and "b"
   e. Neither "a" nor "c"

4. The most important factor in the growth of property management is usually considered to be:
   a. Absentee ownership
   b. Acceptance of apartment living
   c. Engineering improvements
   d. Decentralization of retail business to suburbs

5. The specialized field of appraising is considered to be:
   a. An art
   b. A science
   c. Neither "a" nor "b"
   d. Both "a" and "b"

6. Appraisers are paid a:
   a. Commission
   b. Percent of property value
   c. Fee
   d. Negotiated commission

7. Licensed real estate salesmen are permitted to collect a mortgage loan "finder's fee" under which of the following conditions:
   a. Obtaining approval of a properly filled-in loan application
   b. Obtaining a loan application which is approved and closed
   c. Not legally possible without separate license
   d. When employing broker is also a licensed mortgage broker

8. The combination of subdividing and developing into one activity has resulted in:
   a. Decreased expenses for subdividers
   b. Better protection of the public
   c. Reduction in land costs
   d. Reduction of protection of the public

9. Which type of home construction involves building model homes for potential buyers to select?
   a. Custom building
   b. Speculative building
   c. Tract building
   d. Both "b" and "c"

10. Evidence indicates that a comparison between property sold by an owner and property sold by use of a real estate broker will result in:
    a. No appreciable difference in sale price
    b. Owner usually selling quicker
    c. Broker selling nearer desired sale price
    d. Owner selling nearer desired sale price

11. The average real estate brokerage firm will consist of how many licensed people?
    a. 1 to 3
    b. 3 to 5
    c. 5 to 7
    d. 6 to 8

12. Most licensed individuals are involved in (select the <u>wrong</u> answer):
    a. Residential sales
    b. The agency division of real estate
    c. Appraising
    d. Selling

13. An example of an income-producing property is (select the <u>wrong</u> answer):
    a. An apartment building
    b. An office building
    c. A retail store
    d. A single-family dwelling

14. The most noteworthy recent development in the industrial property area has been:
    a. Development of industrial subdivisions
    b. Development of non-polluting industries
    c. Development of light industry areas
    d. None of the above

15. The field of real estate that requires the most training and experience, except for counseling, is:
    a. Commercial sales
    b. Appraising
    c. Industrial sales
    d. Property management

P.S. While you are not yet expected to know the answers to the two questions posed at the beginning of this chapter, the answers should be something like:

Dear Peb:

No, it is a violation of the fiduciary relationship between broker and principal to refuse to deliver any bona fide offer to a principal (employer of the broker). Further, it is a direct violation of FREC Interpretative Memoranda 10.07 and 10.08 to conceal any offer. The Florida Real Estate Commission would like to stop this sort of unethical practice, so drop them a note citing all particulars.

Dear Cid:

Yes, your acceptance of a second mortgage would appear advisable under the conditions you describe. The $7,000 down payment represents more than 15% equity in the house, which is more than adequate for security. Secondly, use a redemption clause in your second mortgage to allow you to make any defaulted payments on the first mortgage to preclude possibility of foreclosure by the first mortgagee. Thirdly, the $7,000 down payment, plus all principal paid to you on the second mortgage during the year of sale, will still be less than 30% of the sale price, thus qualifying as an installment sale. In case you decide not to buy another house, you will only be taxed on the money received from the sale each year until the second mortgage is paid. If you insist on a down payment of more than 30%, you will be required to pay tax on the entire capital gain, at one time. Lastly, the second mortgage is often necessary to obtain a sale at any price short of an outright give-away. It is recommended that you listen to your REALTOR friend.

CHAPTER 2

FLORIDA REAL ESTATE LICENSE LAW: HISTORY, ADMINISTRATION, and ENFORCEMENT

At the beginning of the twentieth century, the real estate business was unorganized and extremely competitive. The cutthroat policy of "Caveat emptor" ("Let the buyer beware") prevailed. 7.02

During the latter part of the nineteenth century, the leading and more reputable real estate brokers of the time had formed trade organizations known as "real estate boards." These real estate boards were formed to establish trade ethics, maximum commission charges, and real estate brokerage practices. Publicity given the first real estate boards began to develop public confidence which resulted in growth of the idea. c

In 1908, the National Association of Real Estate Boards (NAREB) was formed with headquarters in Chicago. It was called "NAREB" until 1972, when the official designation was changed from NAREB to National Association of REALTORS.

In 1913, NAREB created a comprehensive Code of Ethics which has been a primary factor in moving real estate from an unorganized and somewhat suspect business to the current status of a semi-profession.

Despite the existence of the Code of Ethics, no state license laws were enacted until 1919 when California produced the first legislation in the field of real estate licensing. Since 1919, all states and the District of Columbia have enacted legislation more or less identical to the California statute. 2.03

History of Florida Real Estate License Law

In 1923, Florida passed an act patterned after the California act but provided no means of policing or enforcing the legislation.

In 1925, the Legislature of Florida created a real estate commission to keep records, conduct investigations, and prosecute proceedings to suspend or revoke registrations of brokers and salesmen. The power to grant, deny, suspend, and revoke registration was given to the county judges.

Later in 1925 at an extraordinary session of the Legislature, the Florida Real Estate Commission ("FREC") was given the power to grant, deny, suspend, and revoke registration. County judges no longer exercise jurisdiction in this area.

The Florida act was changed or amended in 1927, 1941, 1945, 1947, 1956, 1957, 1959, 1967, 1969, 1972, 1973, 1974, 1975, 1976, and 1977.

The real estate license law, as it presently exists, taken from the Florida Statutes (Chapter 475, F.S.), is contained in Chapter 1 of the FLORIDA REAL ESTATE COMMISSION HANDBOOK, published under the direction and by the authority of the Florida Real Estate Commission. 2.04

The original HANDBOOK was written in 1930 by W. H. Poe. At that time, Poe was general counsel for the Florida Real Estate Commission. The present edition of the HANDBOOK is based on the works of Poe's successors. Along with major revisions to the HANDBOOK format, changes in Florida Statutes through the 1976 legislative session were incorporated into the 1976 Edition.

In its present form, the major segments of the FLORIDA REAL ESTATE COMMISSION HANDBOOK are as follows:

CHAPTER	SECTION	SUBJECT
I	475, F.S.	Florida Real Estate License Law
II	21V-1.01 - 20.39	Rules of the Florida Real Estate Commission
III	2.01 - 17.07	Interpretative Memoranda of FREC
IV	Federal and State Laws	Other laws applicable to real estate activities
V	Procedures	Becoming registered, filing a complaint, etc.
INDEX	-	Alphabetical index of terms with Section number references
APPENDIX I	-	Civil Rights Acts of 1968 and 1866

Florida Real Estate Commission

Every state in the nation requires that those who practice real estate for another for compensation must be licensed. Each state has appointed a regulatory body to administer and enforce state laws regulating real estate practices and licensing of applicants. Different titles are used to identify real estate regulatory bodies in the various states. In Florida, the official title is The Florida Real Estate Commission. C

Purpose and Composition. The Florida Real Estate Commission (FREC) was established by Chapter 475, F.S. in 1925. FREC was created for the purpose of administering and enforcing the Florida real estate law and amendments to that law. FREC is composed of three members, each of whom must have been an active Florida real estate broker during the ten years immediately preceding his appointment to the Commission. The Governor of Florida appoints the commissioners for a term of three years, and their terms of office are arranged in such a manner that one new commissioner is appointed each year. No approvals by the Secretary of State, Attorney General, or Legislature are required after appointment by the Governor. 475.02

In the event of resignation, death, or removal from office, a new commissioner is appointed as a successor for the unexpired portion of the former commissioner's term of office. The law permits a commissioner to be reappointed to another term if desired by the Governor in office.

Officers. The commissioners elect a chairman and vice-chairman each year. The most junior commissioner is given the title 21V-20.01

"Member," and normally the junior commissioner will become the vice-chairman during his second year of office, then chairman during his third year of office since he will have become the senior commissioner at that time. This succession of office is a custom and is not an operation of the law.

FREC meets monthly, and two commissioners constitute a quorum 21V-20.02
for conducting official business. 21V-20.03

Compensation. The commissioners do not receive an annual or monthly salary. However, in lieu of salary they are paid $10 per day, or part thereof, for each day, or part of a day, they meet. In addition, they receive per diem and a mileage allowance for expenses connected with their activities in carrying out official duties as commissioners. 475.08

Annual Reorganization Meeting. At the annual reorganization meeting each year when the chairman and vice-chairman are selected by the commissioners themselves, they also appoint the Commission Executive Director and the General Counsel. The Executive Director is responsible for the day-to-day administration of FREC business subject to the direction of the commissioners. This full-time position provides continuity since new commissioners come and go. The Executive Director is normally reappointed by the commissioners year after year and therefore becomes a repository of information and experience on which newly appointed commissioners may rely. In the course of supervising the work of the Commission, the Executive Director receives assistance from staff attorneys, investigators, and administrative and clerical personnel employed by the Commission. 475.02

Location. The location of the FREC executive office is designated by the commissioners and may be changed at the discretion of the commissioners. Such a change, however, would not be directed without considerable thought and planning since the many employees of the Commission would either be uprooted or be forced to terminate their employment. 475.07

Employees. All employees of FREC, including the Executive 475.03
Director, are subject to the direction of the Commission. The 475.09
chairman's duties and powers may be extended to the other two 21V-20.11
members of the Commission, except for the actual determination of an "administrative complaint," and the passage and promulgation of rules and regulations. These activities must be conducted by the Commission meeting in session. FREC has been delegated the authority to employ and terminate the personnel deemed necessary to discharge the duties and responsibilities of the Commission. The commissioners may also prescribe the duties of employees and set the amount of compensation to be paid.

Powers and Duties. The powers and duties of FREC are adminis- 475.04
trative in nature. From the general or overall administrative 475.05
powers, four specific areas of responsibility are derived: (1) 3.03
executive: enforcement of the real estate law, investigation of 3.04
complaints, determination of violations, conduct of hearings; (2) quasi-legislative: create and pass rules and regulations; (3) quasi-judicial: revocation of registration, suspension of registration, denial of registration or granting of registration;

and, (4) ministerial: administration of office records, examination of applicants, maintenance of registration files, and issuance of registration certificates.

The chairman of the Commission may exercise and/or delegate any 475.03
of the powers in the executive or ministerial areas of responsibility. A resolution vote by FREC is sufficient to delegate any of its powers or responsibilities to an individual member. However, the responsibilities and powers lying in the quasi-legislative and quasi-judicial areas cannot be delegated to a single member nor can the chairman alone exercise these powers. These two latter powers can only be effected by a majority or quorum vote of the Commission.

In addition to the broad, general powers cited above, FREC is charged with certain specific responsibilities associated with its official functions. For example:

1. The Commission is required to have a seal, which, when 475.10
   affixed to certificates, rules, regulations, or other 3.04
   official documents, indicates that subject instruments are official, true, and correct.
2. The Commission is required to keep minutes of all 475.04
   meetings. 21V-20.04
3. The Commission is required to keep records of registrations and the issuance of certificates. All records
   pertaining to these activities are required to be made 475.04
   and kept in books or in files as may be deemed expedient 3.04
   by the Commission.
4. When requested, the chairman is required to give cer- 3.04
   tificates under his hand and the seal of the Commission stating what the records show or fail to show about any official matter.
5. The law requires the Commission to foster the education 475.04
   of real estate brokers and salesmen concerning the 3.08
   ethical, legal, and business principles which govern their conduct. The publication of the FLORIDA REAL ESTATE COMMISSION HANDBOOK and "Florida Real Estate Commission News & Report," a quarterly publication, is
   in furtherance of this duty. 475.18
6. The Commission is charged with the responsibility to 475.04
   grant or deny registration for all applicants.
7. The Commission is required to conduct investigations 9.01
   regarding complaints and/or allegations concerning registrants and applicants for registration.
8. The Commission is charged with suspending or revoking 475.29
   licenses of registrants after proper investigation and a quorum decision.
9. The Commission is required to hold hearings, as necessary. 475.27
   All findings of fact shall have the same authority and effect as those of a General Master in Chancery.

In the discharge of official functions, FREC is authorized to 475.04
subpoena witnesses and administer oaths. It should be noted that the powers of the Florida Real Estate Commission are limited to civil matters and do not extend to criminal actions. Therefore, FREC cannot levy fines or impose imprisonment as penalties. FREC

civil action jurisdiction relates to individual rights between the various parties to a suit. The purpose of such action is to enforce obligations and duties.

The members of the Commission are entitled to the same protection 475.06
and immunities as are other judicial officers in the state. In addition, the acts of the agents and employees of the Commission, when acting within the scope of their authority and employment, shall not be called in question except by the Commission. Also, its papers, documents, reports, or evidence shall not be subject to subpoena without the consent of the Commission until after the same shall have been published at a hearing. An exception to this may be made if, after notice to the Commission, and a hearing, the court shall determine that the Commission or the accused will not be unreasonably hindered or embarrassed.

Decisions made by FREC may be appealed. When an appeal is made, 475.35
the District Court of Appeals will review the decision of the Commission. This procedure has been adopted in an effort to reduce the delay of calling into effect disciplinary orders issued by the Commission. Normally, a decision reached by the District Court of Appeals may be subject to review by The Supreme Court of Florida.

Funding

All monies received by the Commission, including registration 475.11
fees collected, are paid to the State. Specifically, funds collected are paid to the Chief of the Bureau of Records Administration, which is in the Division of General Services, a part of the Department of Professional and Occupational Regulation, State of Florida. Such funds are held in a "trust fund" and are not intermingled with other State general revenue funds.

Bills and expenses the Commission incurs in the administration of 475.12
the law and official activities under the law are paid by the State from the FREC "trust fund." This is accomplished by presentation of vouchers which have been approved by the chairman and the Executive Director of the Commission. Checks are then issued in the amount approved on vouchers submitted.

Procedures for Investigations and Hearings

The administrative powers of the Florida Real Estate Commission 3.03
were mentioned earlier. These powers are generally divided into four main categories: executive powers, quasi-judicial powers, quasi-legislative powers, and ministerial powers.

Under its executive powers, FREC is authorized to conduct hearings similar to grand jury hearings and to conduct investigations in general enforcement of the real estate license law, such as complaints against brokers and salesmen.

Under its quasi-judicial powers, FREC is authorized to deny 3.04
registrations to applicants and to suspend or revoke registration of registrants who are found to be in violation of the law or rules and regulations published by FREC.

Under its quasi-legislative powers, FREC is authorized to pass rules and regulations consistent with the laws and constitutions.

Under its ministerial powers or duties, FREC maintains records and offices and conducts matters arising in the normal course of business.

While its authority generally extends to applicants and regis- 3.06
trants, the Commission is also authorized to investigate non-registrants, or the general public, for the purpose of determining whether a non-registrant is operating as a real estate broker or salesman.

FREC must also investigate applicants for registration in order to determine if they meet all the requirements and qualifications for registration. A portion of its effort must also be directed to investigation of registered brokers and salesmen to determine if they are guilty of violating the real estate law. The Commission may act as a result of a complaint or of its own volition.

In order to ensure that FREC has adequate power and authority in 475.27
these matters, the Commission has been empowered to administer 475.32
oaths and to examine defendants, witnesses, and plaintiffs. It can issue subpoenas to anyone the Commission believes to be in possession of records, documents, or information material to the question at hand. The Commission can also require that applicants and registrants provide information they may possess regarding matters pertinent to any proceedings conducted by FREC.

From what has been said earlier, it is clear that denial, revocation, or suspension of registration must be a result of two separate administrative powers of FREC: investigations conducted under the executive power and then a decision to deny, revoke, or suspend made under the quasi-judicial power. Certain procedures are required to be observed from origin to conclusion in order to protect the rights of all concerned.

Investigations. At such time as the Commission decides that a 475.04
reason may exist to deny, suspend, or revoke a registration, the 475.18
Commission will request an investigation. If the investigation 475.26
reveals a possible violation, the Commission will ordinarily ask that a formal complaint, called an "administrative complaint" (formerly called an "information"), be filed. The person who files the administrative complaint is usually the person whom FREC requested to investigate the charge and is called the "plaintiff." The person against whom the administrative complaint is directed is called the "defendant." The administrative complaint is required by law to state the facts briefly, yet completely enough that a person of ordinary intelligence may understand the charge against him and state a defense against the charge, if he has a defense. When submitting an administrative complaint, it is not necessary to point out a particular statute which is alleged to have been violated.

Administrative Complaint and Answer. Upon receipt of an adminis- 475.26
trative complaint by FREC, a notice is forwarded by registered 475.40
mail to the defendant along with a copy of the administrative 9.21
complaint. The defendant is required to file an answer to the allegations contained in the administrative complaint by a date

given in the notice, and the date designated must be at least twenty days (20 days) from the date the notice was mailed. The notice is mailed to the last address of record, or the address on an application, whichever is appropriate.

The defendant must answer the notice by the date given or show 475.30
cause why he was unable to do so. Along with his answer, the defendant may file a motion to quash if he believes that the law, as applied to the facts in the administrative complaint, entitles him to have the administrative complaint dismissed. A motion to quash may not be filed except with an answer, and FREC will not permit a motion to quash if an answer is not filed.

Failure to Answer. The defendant's defense begins with his 475.30
answer which must be either an admission to the charges or a 9.10
denial of the charges by the defendant personally and not by an attorney or designated agent. Should the defendant fail to answer, his failure is considered a default and the Commission will consider the allegations contained in the administrative complaint as true. FREC will then enter a final order against him. A final order in such a case would deny, revoke, or suspend the registration of the defendant. If the defendant's answer makes it apparent that no issue of material fact actually exists, FREC will dismiss the administrative complaint.

Motion to Quash. When a motion to quash is filed, the plaintiff 475.30(2)
may concede the validity of the motion. The plaintiff may then file an amended administrative complaint, and the defendant may file a new answer within twenty days after receipt of notice, or within such additional time as may be allowed. The defendant may also elect to let his original answer stand.

When a motion to quash is denied, the defendant then has a period of thirty days (30 days) after denial to petition for a writ of certiorari to the District Court of Appeals in his county. Because of the highly technical rules of Appellate procedure, an attorney is almost a necessity, although not required. A writ of certiorari actually orders FREC, or a lower court, to forward the case for review by the District Court. If the District Court rules in favor of the defendant, then the motion to quash prevails and the defendant's answer to the administrative complaint is immaterial since the administrative complaint will be dismissed. If the District Court rules against the defendant, then the case is returned to FREC which then proceeds to address the defendant's answer.

Examiner's Hearing. FREC now is in a position to consider the 475.27
administrative complaint containing the alleged charges and the 9.11
defendant's answer to it. If an issue of material fact or importance is discovered, FREC, or the chairman, requests the Division of Administrative Hearings, Department of Administration, to appoint a hearing officer called an examiner, who is a quasi-judicial officer, to hold hearings designed to examine both sides of the case and arrive at the facts bearing on the case.

The examiner will be an attorney employed by the State who may 475.32
subpoena witnesses, administer oaths, and cross-examine. The 475.33
examiner will record the testimony of the plaintiff, the

defendant, and all witnesses in addition to any objections to such testimony. All parties are given a reasonable opportunity to present any pertinent evidence and to cross-examine witnesses. The defendant is entitled to have FREC subpoena witnesses in his behalf, but at his own expense. When all testimony and evidence has been heard, the examiner will prepare a transcript of the entire proceedings and file a report with FREC. The report will also contain his recommendations as to what final action the Commission should take regarding that particular matter.

Exceptions to Examiner's Hearing. When the examiner's report and 475.31
recommendations have been filed, a notice of the filing is provided to all parties: the defendant, the plaintiff, and the FREC legal section. Both the plaintiff and the defendant have a period of fifteen days (15 days) to file exceptions, usually in the form of a "brief" or request for oral argument. FREC then sets a date for a last formal hearing prior to entering a final order. The defendant is notified at least five days (5 days) before the date set for the last formal hearing. He is informed of the date and place the hearing will be conducted. Ordinarily, the hearing will be held at the executive offices of the Commission; however, the Commission may designate any place of its choice in Florida. Regardless of the place selected for the hearing, the final order must always be entered at the executive offices of the Commission. Upon receipt of the five-day notice, the defendant may appear at the formal hearing in person, be represented by attorney, or both, and normally will be given an opportunity to present an oral argument before a final order is entered.

Decision of Commission. At this point, the Commission will have 475.31
the hearing officer's recommendation and report and any filed exceptions to the report, and will have heard the defendant's final arguments. The Commission now makes a determination after considering all the evidence and facts presented. FREC's final order will either dismiss the administrative complaint or will deny, suspend, or revoke registration as the the case may require.

Appeal of Final Decision. When the Commission has entered its 475.31
final order, a period of thirty days (30 days) exists during 475.35
which both parties may again petition the District Court of Appeals to issue a writ of certiorari requiring the case to be bound over to the District Court. The District Court of Appeals will not usually grant a writ of certiorari to a petitioner unless he is able to present evidence that he has been denied a constitutional or statutory right. When such an appeal is made, the final order of the Commission is stayed from taking effect until the case has been reviewed. If no appeal is made within thirty days, the final order is automatically in effect and all right of appeal is forfeited.

In the event the District Court of Appeals should reverse or 475.37
annul the final order of FREC, a writ of mandamus is issued which orders the Commission either to restore the registrant's rights or to allow an applicant to continue with his application process. In addition, the matters examined and the things decided may not be reexamined by the Commission at any future

date. In the event the District Court of Appeals should uphold the final order of FREC, the defendant can either accept the court's ruling or appeal to have the court's ruling reviewed by the State Supreme Court.

Effect of Suspension or Revocation. If a real estate broker's c 9.15
registration is suspended or revoked, it causes an automatic cancellation of all certificates issued to salesmen who work for the broker (defendant), or the certificates of all partners in a partnership, or officers and directors of a corporation. Affected salesmen, partners, officers, and directors may request new certificates under a new employer or in the same partnership or corporation if it reorganizes its personnel to requalify with the Florida Real Estate Commission and obtains certificates for its remaining or new personnel.

Witnesses at Proceedings. Witnesses and other people who are 475.32
subpoenaed to appear in FREC proceedings may be legally sub- 9.17
poenaed by the Commission, its chairman, any circuit court, the FREC examiner, or county judges. If they fail to appear, or do not answer questions directed to them at the hearing, or are guilty of disorderly conduct at the hearing, or are guilty of perjury, they can be held in contempt of court before the circuit court. However, witnesses may not be compelled to appear at hearings outside the county in which they reside without their consent. The law authorizes the use of depositions in those cases where material witnesses cannot be subpoenaed to appear. A deposition is verbal testimony taken under affidavit and reduced to writing for use in a court or legal hearing. The witness giving the deposition is sworn to tell the truth as if at the hearing.

Limits of FREC Jurisdiction. The law describes a number of civil 9.18
and criminal offenses over which the Commission has no authority since it has no criminal jurisdiction. When one of these criminal offenses is committed, such as operating without a current registration certificate, or a broker employing unregistered salesmen, or salesmen collecting money or bringing suit under certain circumstances and other offenses as set forth in 475.42 F.S., the Commission can act to suspend or revoke registration. The Commission does have the authority to investigate such cases and report violations to the officers who do have jurisdiction over such offenses.

Injunctions and Legal Writs. FREC is empowered to apply for an 475.39
injunction, a mandatory injunction, or a writ of mandamus if the 9.19
Commission has reason to believe that a person, partnership, or corporation is acting as a broker or salesman without holding a proper registration certificate, or if it believes a violation has occurred against the law or rules and regulations of the Commission itself.

While the Commission has never yet sought a writ of mandamus, it is begun by issuance of what is called an "alternate writ" which directs the doing of something or a showing of why something should not be done. The court then hears evidence and argument from both sides and peremptorily commands that the thing be done, or it quashes the alternative writ. 26

If the Commission petitions the court for an injunction or a writ of injunction, it is usually to order someone to discontinue doing something which is illegal or unlawful. If the Commission petitions the court for a mandatory injunction, it is ordinarily for the purpose of ordering someone to stop refusing to do that which he is supposed to do. 475.39(2)

CHAPTER 2

FLORIDA REAL ESTATE LICENSE LAW:
HISTORY, ADMINISTRATION, and ENFORCEMENT

1. New York State enacted the first legislation providing for license and control of real estate brokers and salesmen. T F

2. The first Florida statute designed to control and license real estate brokers was enacted in 1919. T F

3. The Florida Real Estate Commission was created in 1925. T F

4. The purpose for which FREC was created was to administer and enforce the Florida real estate license law. T F

5. The Governor of Florida appoints three Commissioners each year to fill the vacancies created by expiring appointments. T F

6. A commissioner may not be reappointed to another term immediately following his original appointment. T F

7. Florida statutes require the senior commissioner, from the standpoint of service on the Commission, to be chairman of FREC. T F

8. The chairman of FREC may delegate any of the duties and powers of the Commission to one of the other commissioners. T F

9. The general, overall powers of FREC are administrative in nature. T F

10. The administrative powers of FREC are separated into four specific areas of responsibility. T F

11. In the exercise of its quasi-judicial function, FREC is empowered to levy fines or imprisonment as penalties for certain crimes. T F

12. All license fees and other monies collected by FREC are turned over to the Department of Professional and Occupational Regulation. T F

13. The commissioners appointed to FREC receive no compensation for their services during the tenure of their appointment. T F

14. Decisions made by FREC may be appealed through the Circuit Court of Appeals. T F

15. FREC is empowered to apply for an injunction, a mandatory injunction, or a writ of mandamus if the Commission has reason to believe a violation of the law has occurred. T F

16. The Florida real estate law describes a number of civil and criminal offenses which are beyond the jurisdiction of FREC. T F

17. If a broker's registration is suspended, it automatically results in the cancellation of certificates of salesmen who work for that broker. T F

18. The authority of FREC permits the Commission to investigate members of the general public. T F

19. When a registrant receives a notice of an administrative complaint, he is required to file an answer before twenty days from the date the notice was mailed. T F

20. If the defendant named in an administrative complaint feels the law entitles him to have the allegation dismissed, he may file a motion to quash instead of an answer. T F

21. If a defendant's motion to quash is denied by FREC, the defendant has a period of thirty days after denial to file a writ petitioning the District Court of Appeals to review his case. T F

22. FREC normally schedules a formal hearing before entering a final order pertaining to an administrative complaint. Such hearings may be anywhere in Florida the Commission chooses. T F

23. A defendant is entitled to have witnesses subpoenaed by FREC to testify in his behalf at his expense. T F

24. If a defendant appeals the final order of the Commission, the order of the Commission will not be effective until the case is reviewed or the appeal rejected. T F

CHAPTER 3

REGISTRATION, VIOLATIONS, and PENALTIES

The average citizen speaks of "getting a real estate license." 475.01(4)
FREC speaks of "registration" and "registration certificates." 21V-1.01
Technically, registration consists of creating and maintaining 4.01
files in the offices of the Commission on all brokers and salesmen, to include their names and business addresses. This means all brokers, salesmen, and employers of salesmen who are not brokers (owner-developers). Registration does not entitle any registrant to operate as a broker or salesman, by itself.

Registration and Registration Certificate

Legally, registration is a status. It is a status which is 475.01(10)
gained from placing the name and business address of the regis- 21V-1.02
trant, or the home address if non-active, on the official records 4.02
of FREC. Having done this, an individual becomes a registrant who has the status of registration. The proof that an individual has acquired this status is the registration certificate, commonly referred to as a "real estate license." In order to maintain the status of registration, a registrant must renew his registration certificate within 12 months after expiration date (grace period) or he ceases to have registration status.

It is important to understand that a registrant is not permitted 475.21
to operate during the 12 months following expiration of his 4.03
certificate. When a broker or salesman actively engages in his work after the expiration date on his certificate, he is committing an unlawful act until he renews his certificate within the period prescribed by law. A registrant has 12 months to renew his registration only if he does not operate as a salesman or broker during that period. The Commission will honor a request for renewal as long as it is received within the 12-month period following expiration of the last valid certificate. It is not necessary for the registrant to receive the certificate, but only that the Commission receive his request for the certificate in proper form with the proper fee. (Schedule of all fees appears later in this chapter.)

The registration certificate is a wallet-size, written instrument 4.04
which is considered prima facie evidence that the holder is a registrant, or licensed to operate. The certificate authorizes the holder to act as a broker or salesman until the date of expiration, or until the registration is revoked, suspended, or placed on inactive status. The registration certificate (license) format is prescribed by FREC and bears: the seal of the State of Florida, the name of the Governor, and a facsimile of the signatures of the chairman and vice-chairman of the Commission plus the name and address of the registrant. If issued to a salesman, it will also bear the name and address of the employer. If the party is registered as an officer or director of a corporation, or is a partner, the name and business address of the corporation or partnership is included. The date of issuance and date of expiration are shown, and the certificate number assigned that individual registrant is noted. The certificate will be plainly

marked as "active" or "non-active."

Registration certificates are issued to every broker or salesman 4.07
after registration has been granted and a proper request filed. They are renewed every two years according to a predetermined schedule. Prior to the expiration date, which is shown on the certificate, the certificate remains valid as long as the information on the face of the instrument is correct. When any of the information on the face of the certificate is changed, the certificate must be returned to FREC for reissue to reflect the changed information.

Qualifications

The qualification standards established for individuals desiring to enter the real estate field are becoming more and more demanding. This trend is expected to continue for the foreseeable future as one method of improving the caliber of real estate practitioners. As mentioned above, the document for which new- 21V-1.04
comers to real estate must qualify is called a "registration 5.01
certificate" by the Commission. It is commonly called a "real estate license" by laymen. Before receiving a registration certificate, the newcomer must become a registrant and request that a certificate be issued. Once registered with FREC as a person who has met all qualification standards, then a registration certificate (or license) is issued as tangible evidence that the holder has, in fact, met all qualifying criteria. However, it must be understood that an individual obtains the right to request and receive a registration certificate only after first acquiring registration status as a result of meeting all established standards.

Salesman

Consider the qualifications required to become a real estate 475.17
salesman. First, the applicant must either be a United States 21V-2.01
citizen or include a sworn statement with his application that 5.02
he intends to become a citizen. Prior to July, 1972, naturalized citizens were required to have their final papers before they could qualify for registration.

Second, an applicant must show that he is honest, that he is of good character, and that he has earned a reputation for fair dealing. These requirements are normally satisfied by the references each applicant is required to list on his application form. Four references are required: two references who have known the applicant at least five years, and two references who know the applicant and currently reside and do business in Florida.

Third, the applicant must have been a bona fide resident of 21V-2.20 - 22
Florida for six months prior to making application. This particular qualification is waived for those individuals who can prove they were registered real estate brokers or salesmen in some other state during the two years immediately preceding their arrival in Florida. They must also have been exclusively engaged in the real estate business during those preceding two years and not have combined it with some other occupation. In addition, as salesman applicants, they must show that they have abandoned all

residencies outside of the state of Florida and intend to be
permanent residents in this state. Once registration has been
granted, the residency requirement applies only to active 475.14
brokers and salesmen.

Fourth, the candidate for registration must be an "adult" or have had the "disability of a minor" set aside. A candidate can be relieved of this disability through marriage or court action. As of July 1, 1973, the legal age to attain adult status in Florida became eighteen years (18 years).

Fifth, an applicant for an active salesman's or broker's regis- 5.02
tration must show that he is competent and qualified to engage in real estate transactions with safety to investors and to those with whom he may enter into a relationship of trust and confidence. He is required to disclose: if he has ever been convicted of or charged with an offense against the laws of any municipal, state, or federal governing body; if any criminal proceeding is pending against him; if any judgment or decree has been rendered against him in a case wherein the pleadings charged him with fraudulent or dishonest dealings; if he is now, or ever has been, an inmate of a mental or similar institution for the treatment of mental disabilities; or if he has ever gone under, been generally called by, or done business under any name or alias other than the name signed on his application, with sufficient information supplied to enable the Commission to investigate the circumstances.

Sixth, a salesman applicant must attend and successfully pass 21V-3.01
"FREC Course I," which includes material from real estate 21V-3.02
principles and practices and the HANDBOOK or an equivalent course 21V-3.06
as prescribed by the Commission. A written course report, provided to all successfully passing the course, must be forwarded to FREC with the application for registration.

Seventh, an application for registration as a real estate sales- 21V-2.01
man must be filed with FREC. Three passport-type photographs not more than one year old (2" by 2" in size), a fingerprint card properly filled out, and the proper application fee must be forwarded with the application.

The application for registration must be completely filled out. If any question is left unanswered, FREC can deny the entire application. If all questions have been answered but some administrative error is noted, the Commission will return the application and the applicant has a period of twenty days (20 days) to correct the error and have the application back in the hands of FREC (it is anticipated that the 20-day time period will be changed or eliminated in the near future).

If, upon receipt of the application, FREC determines the application to be in order, the applicant will be notified of receipt and tentative approval after a thorough investigation by FREC. The applicant will at the same time be given a date for taking his state licensing examination. This information is indicated on a green card approximately 3 x 5 inches in size. The card is the applicant's admission authority and in addition to name and

address will bear one photograph previously submitted by the
applicant as a means of positive identification. Each applicant
is granted a period of three months from the date of the notice
to appear for examination. Should the applicant be unable to
appear on the scheduled examination date, he should contact FREC
and request an alternate date. The date selected for examination 21V-2.11
must occur within three months from the date of the notice of
tentative approval.

The applicant must successfully pass a written examination based 21V-2.09
on the principles and practices of real estate and Florida's real 21V-2.10
estate license law with not less than a seventy-five percent 21V-2.14
(75%) passing grade. If the applicant fails the examination, he 5.06
may submit a new application anytime after notice from the Commission that he has failed. Applicants are legally entitled to review their examination at the FREC executive offices. The applicant may use the same references and other pertinent data as appeared on the first application if a second application is submitted. When the applicant is notified that he has passed the examination, he has a period of thirty days (30 days) to decide for whom he will work and to apply, on a designated request form, for his active or non-active registration certificate.

Relatively recent changes in the real estate law permit an active 475.14
salesman registrant to request and obtain <u>non-active registration</u> just as a broker is permitted to do. The active salesman must submit a renewal request form with the renewal fee. The employer's signature must appear on the renewal request form. When his non-active registration certificate is issued, FREC will forward the certificate to the non-active salesman at his home address for his retention. The certificate must be renewed by the inactive salesman before it expires just as if it were an active certificate. In those cases where a salesman registrant wants his initial certificate issued as non-active, the salesman merely returns the form received from FREC indicating thereon a request for a non-active certificate.

<u>Broker</u>

The qualifications for a broker applicant include the criteria 475.17(3)
cited previously for a salesman applicant. Also, some of the 21V-2.01
salesman's qualifications have been made more stringent and 5.02
demanding for the broker applicant.

In addition to the academic course required prior to registration 21V-3.01
as a salesman, a broker applicant must successfully complete
"FREC Course II," or an equivalent course approved by the Com-
mission, before he will be permitted to file an application for
registration as a broker. A salesman may enroll in FREC Course 475.17(3)
II anytime after completing six months as an active real estate
salesman.

A broker applicant must have completed a period of twelve months 5.02
as an active real estate salesman under one or more registered Florida brokers before becoming qualified to request registration as a real estate broker. The applicant must have served the twelve months as an active real estate salesman during the preceding five years before applying for a broker's registration.

Credit or standing as an active real estate salesman cannot be established by a real estate salesman working for an owner-developer. It can only be served while working for a registered real estate broker.

The applicant for broker must submit to FREC an application for registration as a broker, just as he did prior to becoming registered as a salesman. The proper fee for a broker application must, of course, accompany the application.

The broker applicant must then successfully pass a written 21V-2.09
examination on the Florida real estate license law, principles 5.06
and practices of real estate, and closing statements. The material covered in the examination is similar in content to the examination given salesman applicants. However, the difficulty is increased considerably for broker applicants especially with regard to preparation of closing statements.

The license law examinations for both real estate broker and 21V-20.02
salesman applicants are ordinarily given in the Orlando and Miami areas on the second Monday of each month. FREC has announced plans to conduct quarterly examinations in the Ft. Walton Beach area beginning in August, 1977. When the second Monday of a month is declared a holiday, the examinations are given on the following day.

The broker applicant is given thirty days (30 days) after 21V-2.14
receiving notice that he successfully passed the written examina- 4.03
tion to request the form of new registration desired. He is entitled to choose registration as either an active broker, a non-active broker, or a broker-salesman. Whichever he chooses, he must request that particular registration and, most importantly, he must file his request with the proper fee at FREC before beginning work in the status requested. This restriction is applicable only to the initial registration certificate and applies to both salesmen and brokers. After the initial registration certificate has been received, certificates are considered renewed when the request for renewal form has been received by the Commission accompanied by the required fee and proof that the registrant has satisfactorily completed 14 classroom hours of post-licensing educational courses as prescribed by the FREC during the preceding four-year period.

Renewal of Certificates

The 1977 session of the Florida Legislature passed a law affecting the renewal of real estate registration certificates. As amended, F.S. 475.20 now requires that renewal certificates for the next succeeding license period after normal expiration date will only be issued after each applicant proves to FREC that the applicant has completed 14 classroom hours of post-licensing educational courses. The 14 hours of educational courses must have been completed during the preceding four-year period at an accredited community college, college, university, or a private real estate school approved by FREC. No examination will be required, but proof of satisfactory completion such as a form of satisfactory completion, properly signed, will be necessary.

Two Types of Non-active Registration

At this point, it should be noted that two totally different
types of non-active registration exist. First, there is the non- 21V-1.01
active status of a qualified broker who simply does not desire to 21V-1.04
be active in the business at that particular time. This type of 21V-5.05
non-active registration might more appropriately be called 21V-5.06
"inactive." Secondly, there is the non-active status which is granted to unqualified individuals, due solely to their position as either a partner in a partnership or an officer in a corporation. Although they will never be issued a registration certificate, the law requires that such people be registered with FREC if the business with which they are affiliated engages in real estate activities. The non-active broker status of a partner or officer in a corporation can never be converted to active broker status, whereas the non-active status of a qualified broker is easily converted to an active status when he desires to do so. Partners or corporation officers never receive a registration certificate because the purpose of the law has been served when they are duly registered and identified on the records of FREC. Even though such individuals appear on FREC records, they may not assume any active role in any of the real estate services performed by their firm. Considerably more information about partnerships, corporations, and other business structures appears later in this chapter.

Registration of Private Schools

In 1957, the Florida Legislature changed the real estate license 475.451
law to provide for the regulation and licensing of persons, 21V-16 - 19
schools, and institutions offering courses in real estate. The purposes of the legislation were and are to regulate those persons who introduce new applicants to the real estate license law and the high standards of conduct required of all real estate practitioners. Regulation of the people conveying early educational impressions should result in better educated registrants over a period of time.

All schools, institutions, and persons offering courses or training programs designed to aid and assist applicants in becoming registered real estate salesmen or brokers must be registered with FREC. While accredited colleges and universities are exempt from the act, in some instances instructors in an exempt school may not be exempt. The deciding factor as to whether an instructor in an exempt institution is also exempt is the manner in which the instructor is paid. If he or she is a regularly salaried instructor of the school, that individual is exempt. If paid directly, or indirectly, from charges made for the course, the instructor is not exempt.

The personal qualifications of instructors must be the same as the qualifications of a real estate broker, except that one year of experience as an active real estate salesman is not required. Therefore, all instructors must be "broker qualified" even though they may not be brokers. In fact, a permit to teach real estate courses does not confer any right to operate as a salesman or broker. Qualification for a permit to teach is not qualification for a registration certificate. Many instructors are, however, active real estate brokers in addition to being qualified to teach.

Any individual who desires to open a real estate school, or to become a real estate instructor, must make application to the Commission for a permit. This includes individual tutors and people offering correspondence courses. The application form is provided by FREC, and all applications with fees are processed in the same manner as applications for registration as a salesman or broker.

In order to receive a permit from the Commission, an applicant must not only be personally qualified but must also show that the course to be offered conforms to minimum standards required by FREC. Three important criteria must be clearly met:

1. The course must substantially cover the material contained in the FLORIDA REAL ESTATE COMMISSION HANDBOOK;
2. The course must consist of the number of classroom hours specified by FREC for the course conducted; and,
3. The course may not be comprised solely of questions and answers.

When issued, a permit is valid until September 30 following the date of issue, or until suspended or revoked. The permit year is from October 1 until September 30, and fees for portions of a year are not prorated. Permits to operate schools, or to teach, are denied, suspended, or revoked for the same reasons, and in the same manner, as denial, suspension, or revocation of registration for a salesman or broker is invoked (treated later in this chapter). But in addition to the penalties associated with registration of salesmen and brokers, a few additional grounds for penalties exist as far as schools and instructors are concerned. For example, schools may be suspended for:

1. Guarantying that students will pass a FREC examination;
2. Offering a refund to students who fail;
3. Representing that FREC endorses the school;
4. Obtaining in any manner a list of questions which appear on any examination given by the Commission for licensing salesmen or brokers;
5. Representing that the school or an instructor has obtained a list of questions from a FREC examination; or,
6. Furnishing anyone, student or not, a list of questions purporting to be from a FREC examination.

A permit to operate a real estate school for profit is good only at the address shown on the permit. In the event a school is moved to a new address, a new permit may be obtained for a fee. Instructors pay the same fee for change of address. Any holder of a permit is required to have the permit in his or her immediate possession at all times while conducting or supervising any course of study.

Certificates and Fees 475.13

The tremendous increase in real estate activities and the number 475.23
of registered brokers and salesmen in the past few years has 9.07

underlined the wisdom of the FREC requirement regarding changes of address, name, or employer. Without such a regulation, the Commission would quickly lose contact with and thereby control of its numerous registrants.

The Commission requires all registrants to keep FREC informed of 475.23
their correct and current name and address. In addition, all 6.05
salesmen must keep FREC informed of the address and name of their employer. When any change occurs regarding any one of these important items, a new registration certificate is issued after receipt of a request and payment of the required fee.

The initial application fee for a real estate broker, salesman, etc. is an administrative charge for establishing registration status. A separate fee, called the registration fee, is a charge
for the issuance of a registration certificate. In addition, 475.481-6
a recovery fund fee is assessed all active and non-active registrants. The Schedule of Fees appears on the opposite page.

Normally, registered brokers and salesmen will be required to 10.01
obtain a local occupational license from the city, county, or municipality in which they operate. Requirements vary throughout the state insofar as cost and requirements for licenses are concerned. Brokers and salesmen should ensure that they are not in violation by inquiring locally.

Real Estate Recovery Fund

On July 1, 1976, a Real Estate Recovery Fund was established in 475.25
the Florida State Treasury for the purpose of reimbursing any 475.482-6
person or corporation that has suffered monetary damages as a result of certain acts committed by licensed registrants involving the sale of real estate in Florida. In order to receive reimbursement from the Recovery Fund, a claimant must meet all of the criteria and standards specified in Florida Statute 475.482.

Any person or corporation claiming damages and that meets all of the conditions required by law may recover up to $10,000 or the unsatisfied portion of an executed judgment claim, whichever is less. Regardless of the number of claimants or tracts involved, the maximum amount to be paid from the Recovery Fund as a result of any one real estate transaction cannot collectively exceed $10,000. A legislated maximum of $20,000 has been imposed in the event that several judgments against one licensed broker or salesman result in multiple claims for reimbursement.

If the Real Estate Recovery Fund should become depleted, FREC will satisfy unpaid claims in the order in which they are received as soon as additional money is available in the Recovery Fund. Actual payments from the Recovery Fund will be made by the State Treasurer upon receipt of an official voucher signed by the chairman of the Commission. When a claim is paid from the Recovery Fund to satisfy a judgment against a registrant, the license of that registrant is automatically revoked. The law further specifies that a discharge of bankruptcy will not relieve a person from the penalties and disabilities of this statute. It should be noted that any person, regardless of registration

SCHEDULE OF FEES

Registrant	Initial Application Fee	Registration* and Renewal Fees	Recovery Fund Fee***
ACTIVE BROKER	$ 50	$ 40	$ 7
BROKER-SALESMAN	--	40	7
NON-ACTIVE BROKER	50	10	7
BROKER BRANCH OFFICE	40	40	
SALESMAN	25	20	3
NON-ACTIVE SALESMAN	25	10	3
CORPORATION****	50	40	-
PARTNERSHIP****	50	40	-
PRIVATE REAL ESTATE SCHOOLS	100	100**	-
PRIVATE REAL ESTATE SCHOOLS - INSTRUCTOR	25	25**	-

Reissue	Fee
Broker Change of Business Address	$10 each
Broker-Salesman or Salesman Change of Employer	$10 each
Lost Certificate (all registrants)	none

A late fee penalty of $15 is authorized. Requests for renewal of expired certificates submitted more than 30 days after expiration date must be accompanied by a renewal fee of $55 for brokers and broker-salesmen and $35 for salesmen (plus applicable recovery fund fee).

* Registration fees initially prorated on an annual basis.

** Annual renewal required. All others renewed for two-year period.

*** As listed, cover a two-year period.

**** Fee structures for corporations (directors and officers) and for partnerships are determined on an individual case basis depending upon their status as active or non-active registrants and on the number of registrants involved.

status, who files a false notice or document with the Commission or who makes a material misstatement of fact or otherwise violates this act, is guilty of a misdemeanor of the second degree and liable under F.S. 775.082 or 775.083.

Initial funds to establish the Real Estate Recovery Fund were transferred from the Real Estate Trust Fund in the State Treasury. The amount transferred was $250,000. The total authorized amount of $450,000 will be accumulated by charging each registrant a fee, called a recovery fund fee, when a new license is issued or an existing license renewed.

The recovery fund fee has been established at $3.50 per year for registered brokers, active and non-active, and $1.50 per year for salespeople. When the total amount in the fund reaches $450,000, the collection of these special fees will be stopped until the amount in the Recovery Fund is reduced below $250,000.

The State Treasurer has the authority to invest the money of the Real Estate Recovery Fund in the same manner and under the same restrictions applied to other State funds. All earned interest is deposited into the Recovery Fund and becomes available for the same uses as other monies in the fund. FREC has been given the authority to adopt rules and regulations which might be required to administer this law.

Seven Services of Real Estate

Real estate practitioners commonly refer to the "seven services of real estate." These services are: Buy, Appraise, Rent, Sell, Auction, Lease, and Exchange. They are usually listed in the above order because, as a useful way of remembering them, the first letter of each service forms the memory crutch "BAR SALE."

It cannot be emphasized too often that anyone and everyone who performs any of the seven services of real estate for another person in return for compensation of any type must be registered with FREC and hold a valid registration certificate, unless specifically exempt by the provisions of Chapter 475, F.S. As an addendum to the preceding statement, it should be noted that compensation is construed to be anything of value, or any service paid, received, or expected to be paid or received. 475.01(2) 475.01(3) 475.28 475.43

Exempt Individuals

Of course, any individual owner may buy and sell his own property without being registered. Also, owners belonging to a partnership are exempt from registration when dealing with their own property if each partner is paid a share of the profits in proportion to his share of ownership. In the case of property owners who are members of a corporation not normally engaged in the real estate business, only one officer of the corporation may be designated to act for the corporation without being registered with the Commission. 475.01(2)

Several other categories have been specifically exempted from registration by Chapter 475, F.S.: 475.01(13)

1. People dealing only in cemetery lots.
2. Radio and television announcers, people in public relations,

and advertising media only if the service performed is incidental to their employment.

3. Attorneys, when acting within the scope of their legal duties as attorneys at law. 475.01(2)
4. Attorneys in fact when signing legal documents, conveyances, or contracts for someone else as that person's attorney in fact. Attorneys in fact may not negotiate and sell property for compensation unless registered with FREC.
5. People acting within the limitations of their duties as designated by proper court, legal, or statutory authorities to serve as:
   a. Personal Representatives (Executors, Administrators, and Guardians)
   b. Trustees
   c. Receivers
   d. Masters in Chancery
   e. Special Masters C
6. People dealing in personal property only, such as business opportunity brokers or mortgage brokers. If individuals in this category should attempt to negotiate a lease as a part of their employment, they would be required to be registered. 2.04
7. Individuals acting as hotel clerks or apartment managers who work for one owner only.
8. Individuals managing a condominium or cooperative apartment building who rent or lease units within that building for periods not to exceed one year, provided that the manager is acting for a client who owns or has an interest in no more than one unit within the building. 475.131
9. Employees of a public utility, rural electric cooperative, railroad, or the Department of Transportation who act within the scope of their employment, providing no compensation is received in addition to the employee's normal salary and the act is performed for the employee's employer.

Certificate Expiration Date

The schedule below has been established on an alphabetical basis, using the last names of registrants to determine when their registration certificates (licenses) expire: 21V-1.08

- For registrants whose last names begin with the letters A through F, certificates expire on March 31 of all even-numbered years (1976 - 1978 - 1980).
- For registrants whose last names begin with G through M, certificates expire on September 30 of even-numbered years.
- For registrants whose last names begin with the letters N through S, certificates expire on March 31 of odd-numbered years (1977 - 1979 - 1981).
- For registrants whose last names begin with T through Z, certificates expire on September 30 of odd-numbered years.

Void and Ineffective Certificates

In the event registration certificates are not renewed within 12 months after expiration date, FREC will consider the registration abandoned and void. If an individual would thereafter decide to renew his registration, he would be required to file a new application for registration and to complete the entire processing cycle just as one attempting to obtain registration for the first time would. 21V-1.03

Several conditions can render a certificate "void." Other conditions may cause a certificate to be "ineffectual" even though it appears to be in full force. Thus, a certificate is 4.05
void after registration has been revoked; it would be ineffective while registration was suspended. If a broker moves his office to a new address, the certificate is void.

FREC tries to give this provision a reasonable interpretation so that mere removal from one room to another in the same office building does not invalidate a certificate. The Commission interprets the law to refer to a street or building address in 21V-9.01
cities and towns that employ such designation. In small, rural towns or villages where addresses are not commonly given, the town or village is the address and moving from one business location to another in the same village does not amount to a "change of address."

If a salesman ceases to be employed by his registered employer, or the employer changes his business address, the salesman's certificate becomes void. When a registration certificate ceases 4.05
to be in force, as in the case of a broker changing his address or a salesman changing his employer, the old certificate must be surrendered or accounted for and a new certificate will be issued when properly requested with fee. The old certificate should always accompany a request for a new certificate.

If a registrant ceases to be an officer or a director of a 21V-5.08
corporation, the certificate issued him in that capacity becomes 21V-5.10
void and the certificate of the entire corporation or partnership 4.12
is automatically suspended until all necessary members, officers, or directors have proper certificates in force. The same rule applies to partners in a partnership.

A salesman's registration certificate is automatically cancelled 475.31(3)
when the registration of his employer is revoked or suspended. 9.15
The salesman, however, is entitled to receive another certificate as soon as he acquires a new employer.

Branch Offices

FREC has made provisions for brokers to conduct business at 475.24
several different locations, should they desire to do so. When- 21V-10.08
ever a registrant desires to operate at a location other than his 6.03
principal office, he may open a branch office. The branch office location may be in the same or a different city, town, or county. In fact, it may be located any place within the state. A registrant could very well have his registered, principal office in Pensacola and operate a branch office in Miami. Regardless of location, each and every place of business must be registered with FREC. Those locations other than the principal place of business must be registered as "branch offices" and the proper registration fee paid for each branch office.

The Commission may insist that a registrant open and register a branch office under certain conditions. Whenever, in the judgment of the Commission, the business conducted at a place other than the principal office is of such a nature that public interest requires registration of a branch office, then it shall be necessary for the party concerned to maintain a branch office. Further, any office shall be deemed to be a branch office if the advertising of a broker with principal offices elsewhere is such as to reasonably lead the public to believe that that office is owned or operated by said broker. (475.24) Branch offices must be registered with certificates issued for each branch office. (c) This enables the Commission to contact its many registrants more expeditiously.

FREC has ruled that a mere temporary shelter on a subdivision being sold by a broker is not a branch office if the shelter is only for the protection of customers and salesmen. However, if sales transactions are concluded there with necessary sales supplies on hand and salesmen assigned there, then the temporary structure would have to be registered as a branch office. Therefore, it becomes clear that the permanence, use, and character of activities customarily conducted at the office or shelter shall determine if it must be registered. (21V-8.01)

The student should know that certificates issued to branch offices are not transferable. (21V-8.02) To illustrate, suppose a broker has decided to close a branch office in one location and open a new branch office at another location. Even though these actions may take place at the same time, the registration and certificate of the closed office may not be transferred. The new location must be registered and the fee paid just as though the old branch office had not been closed. The broker can, however, reopen the old branch office anytime during the licensed period without reregistering it or paying an additional fee.

Types of Business Structures

In addition to the registration requirements already discussed, it is well to understand the various legal relationships that a registrant may assume with other people. (4.08) It is important for the protection of the broker (and for those entitled to his protection) that he know the legal status of those for and with whom he deals.

When two or more persons are associated in business, the law recognizes:

1. Corporations for profit * (c)
2. Corporations not for profit
3. Corporations sole
4. Cooperative associations
5. Partnerships *
6. Limited partnerships *
7. Joint ventures
8. Syndicates and trusts
9. Unincorporated associations.

*Only these three plus sole proprietorships may be registered as a real estate broker.

Corporations may consist of one or more persons. When none of these relationships exists, each party is dealing as an individual (sole proprietorship). The relationships cited above carry with them certain legal aspects and registration requirements.

1. A corporation for profit is an artificial or fictitious person which has been created by the law upon compliance with certain (475.01(3); 21V-5.01 - 11)

requirements of the statutes. The corporation may be formed for any lawful business and should be carefully described in the application for charter. 4.09
Ordinarily, corporations for profit are managed by a board of directors, acting through the officers, such as president, vice-president, secretary, and treasurer. In Florida, a corporation may be formed for the purpose of operating as a real estate broker. However, it should be noted that the power to buy and sell real estate is not, of itself, sufficient to permit a corporation to be registered or to act lawfully as a broker. In order to be registered as a real estate broker, one of the officers or directors must personally be qualified and registered with FREC as an active broker. All other officers and brokers in the corporation must be registered as either active or non-active brokers. A person registered as a real estate salesman cannot be an officer or director in a corporation registered as a real estate broker. The corporation itself holds registration and the registration certificate is issued in the name of the corporation. A corporation for profit is the only one of the several kinds of corporations permitted under the statutes to be registered as a broker under the Florida real estate license law.

2. Corporations not for profit are organized in substantially the 4.10
same manner as corporations for profit. However, they are not organized for carrying on commercial ventures, and therefore are not empowered to be real estate brokers. They, of course, may buy and sell their own real estate. Brokers should be extremely cautious, however, when dealing with corporations not for profit since such legal entities have limited powers and are often governed by principles entirely different from those normally encountered in regular commerce. If a broker is to protect the public adequately and properly, he should never permit a prospect or principal to buy property from such a corporation, or property which in the past has been held by such a corporation, without seeking the advice of a lawyer experienced in such titles.

3. A corporation sole is an ecclesiastic or church organization 4.11
which is recognized in Florida. It normally consists of a bishop or other appropriate clerical persons who have been empowered by the church to hold title to the church property. However, the title descends to his successors in office and not to his heirs. A broker should exercise the same care and caution in dealing with a corporation sole as in dealing with a corporation not for profit. Before dealing with a corporation sole, a broker should always obtain a written opinion from an attorney who has experience in such titles. A corporation sole cannot be registered as a real estate broker.

4. The laws of Florida permit the organization and operation of a 4.10
body similar to a corporation not for profit called a cooperative association. A cooperative association may permit the conduct of commercial business but cannot be registered as a real estate broker.

5. Another business structure recognized in Florida is the 475.15
partnership. A partnership exists when two or more persons en- 21V-4.01
gage in business together, each agreeing to share the profits 21V-4.03

and losses of the business. The agreement may be either expressed or implied. In a partnership, the shares of each partner need not be identical with the shares of the other(s). A partner 4.12
is not required to invest money in the business to be a legitimate partner. One partner may invest skill, knowledge, and experience, another may invest property, and yet another partner may invest money. A written contract between two or more parties setting forth their several rights and liabilities is the best method of determining whether a partnership exists or not. If the parties have undivided interests in the assets of the business or if each is to be liable for debts incurred, then ordinarily a partnership exists. However, an individual is not necessarily a partner just because he is to share in the profits of the business since that could be one means of merely paying for his services. Like the rule prohibiting salesmen from being officers or directors in a corporation, a salesman may not be a partner in a partnership registered as a real estate broker.

Partnerships may be registered with FREC as real estate brokers. 475.15
When partnerships are registered, they obtain registration in the 21V-4.02
name of the partnership. As in the case of the corporation for profit, the partnership itself holds registration and the registration certificate. At least one of the partners must be personally qualified and registered with the Commission as an active broker for the partnership. All of the partners may be registered as active brokers if they are personally qualified, otherwise all partners not qualified must be classed as non-active brokers.

Brokers sometimes share office space but conduct their business 21V-4.02(c)
separately, which is permissible. In such a case, they should not use joint names or operate under a trade name. They should have their telephones listed separately, use separate letterheads, and clearly indicate their completely separate status by maintaining individual signs as required by the license laws and rules of FREC. If they do not take care to do these things, they may, either wittingly or unwittingly, create an ostensible partnership. Under the law, such parties are held to be what they seem to be, at the option of the person deceived. If they operate so as to give a false impression, they not only may violate the real estate license law but also may be liable for the debts and torts of each other. An ostensible partnership, with all the disadvantages but none of the advantages of a true partnership, may be created by "estoppel" when a person deals with one or all of the ostensible partners while supposing that a partnership actually exists.

Normally, a partnership may not sue or be sued in the name of the partnership. It may, however, acquire or convey title to real estate in the name of the partnership. In Florida, a married woman may become a partner with her husband. A corporation, however, is not permitted to go into a partnership with an individual or with another corporation. Partnerships may be dissolved by agreement, death, or withdrawal of one party. Also, one partner may force a dissolution by court proceedings if an agreement to dissolve cannot otherwise be obtained.

The student should know that under the general law, the death or withdrawal of a partner works a dissolution of the partnership,
but under the rules and regulations of FREC, this works no ad- 475.15
ministrative change. However, FREC must be notified so as to 21V-4.05
drop the affected party from the registration record and add any new partner which may be admitted. FREC also wants to ensure that the new partner obtains active or non-active registration as appropriate, and if previously registered, ensure surrender of his certificate for a new one showing his membership in the partnership. This last requirement is important because if any member does not hold the proper certificate, the certificates of the partnership and all members are automatically suspended until all members hold proper certificates and are in force.

6. Limited partnerships may be formed by: filing a certificate 21V-4.01(b)
with the Secretary of State containing information required by 4.13
Chapter 620, F.S.; recording a copy of the certificate with the Clerk of the Circuit Court; paying fees based on invested capital; and by filing required periodic reports with the Secretary of State. There must be one or more general partners and one or more limited partners in order to qualify under the law. The limited partners must make an investment of cash or property, but not services. Also, the surname of a limited partner cannot appear in the name of the partnership unless it happens to be identical with the surname of a general partner. Of course, if the business had been conducted under the same name as that of a limited partner before the limited partnership was created, it may remain. However, if the regulation is violated, or if a limited partner takes part in the control of the business, he loses his protection as a limited partner and becomes liable as a general partner. As a limited partner, he is liable only for any unpaid part of his contribution pledged, plus any assets of the partnership in his hands, and any distribution made to him while the partnership is insolvent.

A limited partnership may be registered as a real estate broker. In fact, if the business activities of the limited partnership include any of the real estate services, it must be registered as a broker. Requirements for registration are the same as for an ordinary partnership in that all partners must be registered as active or non-active brokers. At least one of the general partners must be personally qualified as an active broker. A limited partner cannot register as an active broker and therefore must be a non-active broker.

7. A temporary form of business structure often encountered in 21V-4.01(a)
the real estate business is the joint adventure, or joint venture. 4.14
The joint adventure structure is normally utilized when two or more parties combine their efforts to complete a single business transaction or a fixed number of business transactions. No written agreements are required for the formulation of a joint adventure. The rights, duties, and obligations of joint adventurers are similiar to those of partners in a partnership except that they are restricted to the transaction for which the joint adventure was formed. Joint adventurers cannot bind each other for any new business venture. Joint adventures may, however,

bind other joint adventurers where the obligation may reasonably be implied as an obligation of all in relation to the business transaction for which the joint adventure was formed.

Real estate brokers often combine their efforts in real estate transactions to create a joint venture. The joint venture can act as a real estate broker when composed of separate real estate brokers. In such a case, the joint venture would not be required to register with FREC because the several adventurers would already be registered as brokers.

8. A syndicate or business trust is a form of business structure which may be formed to engage in transactions involving its own real estate. This form of doing business is sometimes called a "Massachusetts Trust," or a "Common Law Trust." A business trust is formed by any number of persons who make an investment at a stipulated amount per unit. The monies collected by this manner are then used to buy, develop, and/or sell real estate. Title to real estate acquired by a business trust is taken in the name of a trustee or group of trustees. The trustees of a syndicate or business trust are elected by the shareholders who purchased the units, or shares, in the venture. A declaration of trust must be filed with the Department of State, and a fee is required in order to form a business trust. In addition, the Department of Banking and Finance must approve the sale of the shares (or units) in order for the venture to be lawful. When properly registered with the Secretary of State, the business trust shareholders enjoy a limited liability in that only assets of the trust itself may be taken for payment of debts. This relieves the individual shareholders from personal liability. If not properly registered, the individual members of the trust are exposed to unlimited liability. Profits of the trust are distributed by the board of trustees to the shareholders in direct proportion to the number of shares each investor has purchased. A business trust cannot be registered with FREC as a real estate broker. However, any employee who buys or sells real property for a trust or syndicate for compensation must be registered with FREC. 4.15 609, F.S.

9. Unincorporated associations are generally recognized as groups of people associated together for some common purpose which is not commercial in nature. They are not regarded as partners and are not incorporated. An example would be a group of property owners in a subdivision who organized for such purposes as beautification, planning, maintenance, or even the performance of services, such as garbage removal. Such associations can incur liabilities, and members are liable for debts in the same manner as a partner, that is, as to creditors (each member is liable for all the debts, but as to each other, each member is liable only for his proportionate share). Some unincorporated associations, such as church congregations, sometimes buy or sell their own real estate through a trustee or board of trustees. A real estate broker or salesman should always exercise the same caution in dealing with such associations as in dealing with a corporation sole. Unincorporated associations cannot be registered with FREC as real estate brokers. 4.16

Trade and Fictitious Names

Many business structures use a trade name, or a fictitious name.
An individual broker may use a trade name. If he chooses to do 475.42
so, he must indicate the trade name on his request for a certifi- 21V-4.06
cate. It is important to remember, however, that a trade name 4.09
must be advertised in a local news publication and registered 4.17
with the Clerk of the Circuit Court regardless of whether an 8.15
individual or a firm is making use of one. This law not only 865.09
applies to real estate brokers but also to anyone doing business under a trade or fictitious name. In addition, the trade name cannot be the name of a corporation or of another registrant. Nor can an individual broker use the name of any partnership or corporation on stationery or in advertising in such a manner as to indicate that he is operating a partnership or corporation type of enterprise when he is actually an individual broker. Names of individuals are not considered trade names unless words are added, such as "and Sons" or "& Co." Trade names including the words "& Co." may be treated as corporations for tax purposes unless followed by "Not Inc."

Of the several different forms of business structures discussed previously, only four may be registered as real estate brokers: corporation for profit, partnership, limited partnership, and an individual broker acting as a sole proprietor.

Violations and Penalties

Ordinarily, the word "penalty" carries a connotation of either a 475.42(2)
fine or imprisonment inflicted as a result of criminal proceedings. It will be used not only in that sense but also to describe any quasi-judicial imposition of a forfeiture or an administrative sanction. These uses should also be distinguished from an award of damages based on compensation for a breach of duty toward an individual. The real estate license law imposes penalties of all three types for various violations of the law (criminal penalties, civil court action, and administrative suspension or revocation by the Florida Real Estate Commission).

Criminal Penalties

A violation of the real estate license law, or any lawful FREC 775.082, F.S.
order, rule, or regulation is punishable by a fine of not more 6.11
than $500 and by imprisonment for not more than 60 days. A corporation may only be fined not more than $500 since a corporation may not be imprisoned. All fines or imprisonment penalties must be obtained in a court of law since FREC lacks the authority to assess such penalties.

Civil Penalties

Civil penalties may be enforced by the courts if a broker or salesman has accomplished any of the seven services of real estate ("BAR SALE") without complying with the statute respecting registration. The courts may deny recovery of a commission, which could be a much greater fine than the one imposed by the criminal section previously cited.

Administrative Penalties

An administrative penalty may be imposed by FREC for violations
of the law or rules and regulations. This may be a denial of 475.25
registration, refusal to reissue a certificate after suspension, 475.29
or a revocation or suspension of registration.

Exceptions to Maximum Penalties. Two exceptions exist to the 475.44
maximum fine and imprisonment penalties of $500 and 60 days im- 475.47
prisonment for individuals and the $500 fine for corporations.
The penalties just cited are maximum for ordinary violations.
However, if a person makes a false affidavit for the purpose of
attempting to disqualify a member of FREC, then upon conviction
that person may be punished by revocation of registration plus
fine and/or imprisonment for a felony of the third degree as
provided in 775.082, 775.083, and 775.084, F.S. The other ex-
ception involves publishing false or misleading information. If
any person publishes, or is the cause of the publication of any
false or misleading information, in any media, for the purpose of
selling or inducing another person to buy real estate or an 475.48
interest in the title to real estate, then that person, upon
conviction, may be punished as provided for a misdemeanor of the
first degree under 775.082 or 775.083, Florida Statutes.

Although the two exceptions to normal penalties do exist, it is 6.11
generally well-accepted that as a matter of customary application,
the individual maximum of $500 fine and imprisonment for 60 days
or the corporation maximum of a $500 fine are the penalties
regarded as normal ceilings.

Grounds for Denial, Suspension, or Revocation

In addition to the fines and imprisonment penalties discussed, 475.29
FREC is authorized to deny, suspend, or revoke registration. The 475.31
grounds for these actions are numerous and are listed below for
ready reference. Each of the grounds listed is defined, and the
reader is encouraged to study them until completely familiar with
their meaning. For the purpose of organizing an approach to the 475.25
penalties associated with the various violations, the grounds for 475.42
denial of an applicant's request for registration, and the
grounds for revocation of registration will be treated separately.

Denial

Denial of an applicant's registration request precludes his 475.18
becoming licensed, or registered, to practice real estate in 475.26
Florida. Therefore, FREC has created two different types of 475.29
denials to ensure fair and equal opportunity for each applicant
to become registered, if deserving.

The first type of denial is termed "denial without prejudice." 21V-2.12
This type of denial is usually associated with errors of omission,
and not with errors of commission. Denial without prejudice
allows the applicant to file a new application anytime errors or
omissions are corrected. Grounds for denial without prejudice
are:

1. Neglecting to answer completely all questions on the
   application form

2. Neglecting to forward the proper fee with application request
3. Neglecting to correct omissions or errors on applications returned by FREC
4. Neglecting to appear for examination within ninety days after approval to do so
5. Failure to complete successfully the required written examination 475.18
6. Neglecting to request a registration certificate within thirty days after notification of successful completion of examination.

The second, and more severe type of denial is termed "denial with prejudice." This type of denial is normally based on cause, and the applicant may not again apply for registration until he has first petitioned FREC for permission to refile and has received the Commission's authorization to do so. Grounds for denial with prejudice are: 475.17 475.18

1. Lack of proof regarding residency or qualifications to register
2. Applicant does not possess the character required by the real estate license law
3. Applicant does not possess the general competence to deal with the public, or complaints against him are received by FREC
4. Applicant is guilty of acts which would have resulted in revocation or suspension of registration had he already been registered
5. Applicant acted or attempted to act as a real estate broker or salesman during the year prior to application
6. Applicant received assistance or cheated while taking the state examination.

Suspension

Suspension of an individual's registration status is a temporary penalty. The maximum period of time FREC may suspend a registrant is two years, or until the suspended party shall have complied with all of the order of suspension and other legal orders of the Commission. Sometimes the necessity to comply with all of the FREC order(s) will extend the two-year period of suspension. 475.25 475.26 475.31

The real estate license law refers to many acts which are either illegal or unethical, any one of which may result in suspension. The acts or omissions listed below are all explained within the body of this text or in the Glossary/Index. Each one constitutes grounds for suspension of registration: 475.25 475.42

1. Active broker failing to maintain an office
2. Breach of trust or bad faith (violation of fiduciary relationship or the legal duties inherent therein)
3. Broker employing unregistered salesman
4. Collecting an illegal commission
5. Collecting an overage
6. Concealment
7. Conspiracy to defraud
8. Conversion

9. Conviction of crimes involving moral turpitude
10. Culpable negligence
11. Dishonest dealing or breach of trust in a business of any type
12. Failure to account for deposits or to safeguard properly any property entrusted to a registrant
13. Failure to advise a buyer to consult an attorney or obtain title insurance regarding questions of title to property
14. Failure to appear in response to a subpoena issued by FREC
15. Failure to make available records, documents, or other data requested by FREC
16. False promises and pretenses
17. Filing false affidavits with or committing perjury before FREC or its authorized representatives
18. Filing false instruments such as liens, mortgages, or other encumbrances for public record thereby creating a "cloud on title" to real estate
19. Fraud: All embracing term (see Glossary/Index)
20. Misrepresentation
21. Offering an incorrect opinion as to the validity and marketability of title to real estate
22. Registered broker or salesman operating without a current and valid certificate
23. Salesman operating as a broker
24. Salesman operating for anyone other than his registered employer
25. Salesman suing anyone other than his registered employer for a real estate commission
26. Sharing a real estate commission with an unregistered individual, or expecting to share commissions, or paying for referral of customers
27. Temporary incapacitation due to mental illness or excessive use of alcohol or narcotics
28. Use of a trade name or fictitious name without registering same with FREC
29. Use of blind ads
30. Use of false advertising
31. Use of devices, lotteries, schemes, or tricks
32. Violation of Florida real estate law (Chapter 475, F.S.) or any lawful rule, regulation, or order of FREC
33. Violation of the law of any state in the United States, or a violation of the law of a local government if the crime involves moral turpitude or dishonest dealings
34. Violation of the Civil Rights Acts of 1968 and 1866 by allowing consideration of race, color, religion, sex, or national origin to affect residential real estate activities. HANDBOOK, Appendix I

Revocation

The last and most severe type of administrative penalty which FREC is authorized to impose is revocation of registration. This automatically terminates a registrant's certificate (or license). Therefore, when FREC revokes a registrant's certificate, that registrant is put out of the real estate business unless the revocation is "without prejudice." A revocation without prejudice 475.25

is granted in cases where registration, or a certificate, has been granted through a mistake made by the Commission.

Revocation of a registrant's certificate and registration is mandatory in certain specified instances:

1. If a registrant obtained registration by misrepresentation, fraud, or concealment; or
2. If he is confined in an insane asylum; or
3. If he is confined in any state or federal prison; or
4. If a registrant has demonstrated a lack of competency to deal with the public in a safe and confidential manner; or
5. If he has filed a false affidavit for the purpose of disqualifying a commissioner. 475.44

Becoming a resident of another state is no longer cause for mandatory revocation.

In addition to the grounds for mandatory revocation of registration, other grounds exist which would authorize the Commission to revoke a certificate holder's registration. Remember, revocation is a permanent type of administrative penalty. The only way an individual can ever again practice real estate in the state of Florida is to wait a reasonable period of time, then petition the Commission for permission to apply for registration once again. The Commission may, or may not, grant the request to reenter the field of real estate.

The discretionary reasons or grounds for registration revocation, besides the grounds cited above for mandatory revocation, are as follows: 475.25(2) 475.25(3)

1. Where registration and/or a certificate was granted or issued due to a mistake made by the Commission (revocation without prejudice)
2. Failure of a registrant to renew a registration certificate prior to expiration of the twelve-month grace period following lapse of a valid certificate (revocation without prejudice) 475.01(5)
3. Failure of a registrant to petition the Commission for reissue of a registration certificate prior to expiration of six months immediately following the end of the license year during which an imposed period of suspension expires (revocation without prejudice) 475.31(5)
4. Registrant found guilty for a second time of any violation or offense which would normally be punishable by suspension (This does not mean committing the same offense is required; committing a second violation which is punishable by suspension will result in revocation instead of suspension, if found guilty) 475.25(3)
5. Permanent incapacitation due to the use of alcohol or narcotics, or any physical or mental disability which would render an individual unable to transact business with the public in a safe manner. The emphasis in this instance is on the word "permanent" as opposed to a "temporary" condition. 475.25(2)

In connection with denials, suspensions, and revocations, there is another area which should be mentioned because it concerns denial of compensation and recovery of compensation.

Denial of Compensation

There are two different methods of denying compensation or recovering compensation already paid. One is an administrative penalty wherein FREC will act to deny, suspend, or revoke registration. Actually, FREC does not have the authority to deny payment of compensation, nor can the Commission legally direct repayment of compensation already paid. However, the Commission can issue an order to deny, suspend, or revoke registration and include in the order a stipulation that the compensation already received must be repaid before the order will be vacated (set aside), thereby indirectly influencing a registrant's decision. 475.25(1)

The second and more direct method of denying or recovering compensation is through the civil courts. Anyone acting as plaintiff may seek a civil action wherein the court is asked to impose a denial of compensation or judicial forfeiture of monies already collected, plus damages if appropriate.

Normally, the grounds for denial or recovery of compensation involve fraudulent acts by a salesman or broker, or noncompliance with Chapter 475, Florida Statutes, regarding registration.

- - - - -

In this the longest chapter of the book, a number of important topics were covered. Before proceeding, it is recommended that the student reexamine these major sections to determine personal "comfort level" with the material:

- Registration and Qualifications
- Certificates and Fees
- Seven Services of Real Estate
- Types of Business Structures
- Violations and Penalties.

CHAPTER 3

REGISTRATION, VIOLATIONS, and PENALTIES

1. Obtaining registration and obtaining a registration certificate do not mean the same thing. T F
2. An applicant who fails the FREC examination on Florida's real estate license law must wait four months to submit a new application. T F
3. A registered real estate salesman must serve as an active salesman for one year under a registered broker or an owner-developer in order to submit an application for a real estate broker's certificate. T F
4. An applicant who successfully passes the FREC examination may request a non-active registration certificate. T F
5. Anyone who performs any of the seven services of real estate for others, for compensation, must be registered with FREC or be in violation of the law. T F
6. A broker applicant must have been a resident of Florida one year and six months to apply for broker registration. T F
7. A registration certificate is regarded as proof that an individual has acquired registration status. T F
8. If the certificate issued to an officer of a corporation becomes void for any reason, the certificate issued to the corporation is automatically suspended. T F
9. The permanence, use, and type of activities customarily conducted at a temporary shelter may require it to be registered with the Commission as a branch office. T F
10. Registration certificates issued to a branch office at one location may be transferred to another location, provided the original branch office is closed and no further business is transacted at that location. T F
11. A corporation for profit is normally managed by the members of the corporation acting through the directors of the corporation. managed by directors thro officers T F
12. Corporations not for profit are organized in substantially the same manner as a corporation for profit and may be registered with FREC as real estate brokers. T F
13. A corporation sole is a commercial enterprise organized and managed by one individual. T F
14. In order to form a general partnership, two or more persons must agree in writing to engage in business together. T F

15. In a true or general partnership, the share of each partner need not be identical with the shares of the other partners. T F

16. When partnerships are registered as real estate brokers with FREC, they obtain registration in the name of the partnership and not in the name of the partners. T F

17. In order to form a limited partnership in Florida, there must be two or more limited partners and two or more general partners. T F

18. A limited partnership may register as a real estate broker. T F

19. A Common Law Trust, a Massachusetts Trust, a business trust, and a syndicate are all the same form of business structure. T F

20. A business trust is not registered with FREC; however, employees who sell real property or mineral leases for a trust must be registered with FREC. T F

21. As a matter of normal application, the individual maximum of $500 and imprisonment for 60 days or the corporation maximum of $500 fine are the penalties usually regarded as maximum. T F

22. Neglecting to correct omissions or errors on applications returned by the Commission is considered grounds for denial without prejudice. T F

23. If a registrant becomes a resident of another state, his registration is automatically suspended. T F

24. It is mandatory that FREC revoke registration in certain, specified instances. One of these instances is if a registrant has demonstrated a lack of competency to deal with the public in a safe and confidential manner. T F

25. If a registrant's registration is revoked, he may wait a reasonable period of time, then petition the Commission for permission to apply for registration again. T F

26. Only one direct method of denying compensation to a registrant, or recovering compensation already paid, is available to the Commission. going to court T F

27. Failure of a registrant to apply for reissue of a registration certificate before the twelve-month grace period expires following the lapse of a valid certificate will provide grounds for revocation of registration. T F

28. Instructors in schools which are exempt from the State law pertaining to licensing of persons, schools, and institutions offering courses in real estate may not, under certain circumstances, be exempt themselves. have to have permit T F

29. Accredited colleges and universities are exempt from the real estate license law. T F

pg 34

CHAPTER 4

OPERATING THE REAL ESTATE OFFICE

All active real estate brokers are required to open and maintain 21V-10.07
an office. The primary purpose behind this requirement is to 21V-12.06
eliminate "curbstone" operations in the real estate business. A 6.02
broker's office must consist of at least one room in a building of stationary construction which will provide the privacy necessary to conduct negotiations and closings of real estate transactions. The broker's books, records, and files pertaining to the real estate transactions of others are to be kept in the required office. FREC requires that each and every active broker must register the address of his office, or offices, with the Commission. Actually, if local zoning permits, the broker's office may be in his residence. One general prohibition should be kept in mind, however. No broker is permitted to maintain his office in or in proximity to a law office, or the office of any member of a profession which prohibits advertising or prohibits using another business from acting as a source of clients. For example, if the A.M.A. prohibits doctors from advertising or prohibits them from sending business to another profession, then a broker may not share office space with or have his office in close proximity to a member of the A.M.A.

Salesmen are not permitted to open an office of their own until achieving the status of a broker. They must be registered from and work out of an office maintained and registered in the name of their employer. Salesmen are permitted to manage or work in branch offices which are properly registered in the name of their employer.

Branch Offices

In Florida, a broker is permitted to open and operate as many 475.24
branch offices as he feels necessary. Each additional office 21V-10.08
(branch office) must be registered with the Commission as a 6.03
branch office and a registration fee paid for each branch office opened. If FREC should determine that a broker's activities in a designated area require that broker to open a branch office to protect the public's interest, then the broker in question must open a branch office as requested by the Commission, or cease whatever activity caused the Commission to decide a branch office should be opened and registered. Salesmen who regularly work out of an office other than a broker's principal office should register from that branch office. If salesmen work out of a branch office only now and then, or if their work at a branch office is temporary, they should be registered from the principal office.

Once a branch office has been registered and a certificate issued, the certificate cannot be transferred to another branch office. To illustrate, suppose a broker-developer opened a branch office in a subdivision he was developing. Then suppose sales were so fantastic that the subdivision sold out and the broker started developing another subdivision before half the life of his branch office certificate had expired. Now if the broker wants to open a new branch office in his new subdivision, he may do so. However, he cannot transfer the registration certificate from the branch office at the old subdivision to the new branch office. He must go through the entire registration process, pay the registration fee, and obtain a certificate for the new branch office. He is permitted to reopen any closed branch office without reregistering with FREC as long as the registration certificate for that particular branch office has not expired.

Signs

FREC has determined that the public interest is better served if certain signs are displayed on or about the entrance to registered real estate offices. Therefore, a registered broker holding an active certificate must erect a sign with all letters on the sign at least one inch in height. Such signs are required at the broker's principal office and at all of his branch offices and must be placed in such a manner that they are easily observed by persons about to enter any one of the offices. Each sign must contain the name of the broker, also his trade name if he has one, exactly as registered with FREC, and if a partnership or corporation, the sign must show the name of the firm or corporation. In the case of a partnership or corporation, the names of all active real estate brokers who are members of the partnership or officers of the corporation may be shown. Beneath these names shall be the words "Registered Real Estate Broker(s)" or "Reg. Real Estate Broker(s)." Samples of acceptable signs are contained in the HANDBOOK, 6.04. The only active brokers exempt from the requirement to display the signs described above are those who have temporarily retired from active business and those registered as officers or directors of a corporation, in which case the regulation pertaining to corporations would govern. 21V-10.09 6.04

If a broker desires, he may place the names of salespersons on his signs. The names of salespersons may be placed anywhere on the sign except between the name of the broker(s) and the description as registered broker(s). In all cases, a line or observable space must separate the names of the brokers from the salespersons.

Advertising

A registered real estate broker or salesman is deemed to possess expert knowledge regarding real property. For this reason, and other reasons as well, a broker or salesman is not permitted to advertise in such a manner as to convey an impression that the ad is being made by a private party not engaged in the real estate business. Letterhead stationery and personalized business cards are a form of advertising and are included in this requirement (see approved business card formats, HANDBOOK, 6.06). An advertisement which provides only a post office box number, a telephone number, or a street address is termed a "blind ad" and is prohibited. 21V-10.10 6.06

Similarly, a broker or salesman shall not advertise to sell, buy, exchange, rent, lease, or mortgage property in a manner which indicates that the offer to do so is being made by a private individual not in the real estate business. Every broker must, when advertising real estate as a business opportunity, advertise in such a way that the ad clearly reveals the registered name of the broker and the term "Broker" or "REALTOR" as the case may be. However, if the broker is the owner of a property which he is advertising, then he has all of the rights of any property owner who is not a broker.

Salesmen cannot advertise to perform any real estate service in 10.20
their own names. Their ads must represent their employer al- 10.22
though this does not prevent salesmen's names from appearing in advertisements in addition to their employer's name. However, if a salesman is the owner of property which he is advertising, then he has all of the rights of any other property owner not connected with the real estate field.

Escrow or Trust Accounts

Following the opening of a real estate brokerage office, a broker 475.25
will have occasion, from time to time, to receive funds which are 475.452
given as earnest money, binder deposits, or advance fees. The 21V-14.01(c)
real estate license law is very explicit in regulations per- 21V-14.03
taining to the manner in which such monies shall be treated. Any 21V-14.06
money, fund, deposit, check, or draft entrusted to a broker or one of his salesmen must immediately be placed in escrow. Such funds may be placed in escrow with a title company or banking institution located in Florida or they may be deposited in the broker's escrow account maintained by him in a bank located in Florida. Any and all funds deposited in an escrow account must be kept in subject escrow account until the transaction is closed or until the deposit is forfeited. Forfeiture may occur due to the buyer failing to complete the transaction after the offer has been accepted by the seller, or it may occur due to the seller defaulting by failure to perform.

Once a deposit is placed in escrow (trust), the broker concerned 21V-14.04
should ensure that the monies involved are never released until 6.09
one of the following conditions applies:

1. The transaction is successfully closed and disbursement authorized at the time of closing;
2. The seller never accepts the offer thereby requiring the deposit to be returned to the buyer;
3. The buyer authorizes the release of his deposit; or,
4. The seller accepts the offer, then subsequently he is unable to produce a good and marketable title, or refuses to sign a deed, in which case the buyer has grounds for a suit in a court of equity.

Most registered real estate brokers prefer to maintain their own 21V-14.05
escrow accounts. Despite the increased workloads and liabilities involved, most brokers feel that they can more efficiently operate to represent their principals with complete control of their own escrow accounts. However, emphasis should be placed on carefully abiding by FREC regulations for handling such accounts.

In the first place, the Commission establishes rules and regulations providing for maintenance of adequate records by the broker and the manner in which deposits are to be made. The broker is prohibited from depositing any personal monies into

his escrow account. To do so would result in co-mingling of funds and subject the broker to severe penalties. Also, time-
liness is important. It is imperative that all deposits be 21V-14.02
placed in the escrow account in an expedient manner. In the case of a salesman, he is responsible for immediately turning over to his employer all deposits entrusted to him by any person dealing with him as an agent of his registered employer. If a draft or check is made out to the salesman personally, he should immediately endorse the draft or check and turn it over to his employer who in turn must immediately deposit it into his escrow account.

The broker is required to maintain accurate and complete records 21V-14.05
of all deposits and disbursements associated with his escrow account. FREC is empowered with the right to check the records of all registered brokers, and all brokers maintaining escrow accounts must make their books and records available to the Commission for inspection at all reasonable times during normal business hours. Spot checks are conducted by representatives of the Commission to ensure that this requirement is fulfilled.

Disposition of Escrow Deposits

Although the broker keeps deposits in his escrow account, the 475.25(1i)
broker has no right to any of the deposit monies until they have 21V-14.04
become the property of the seller. This condition prevails even 6.09
though the broker may have fulfilled his obligation and earned 15.15
his commission. When a buyer makes an offer to buy and accompanies the offer with an earnest money deposit, the deposit is under the control of the buyer until the offer is accepted. When the offer is accepted, the deposit is under the control of both the buyer and the seller.

A broker is required to protect and account for a customer's 6.10
funds or property deposited with him. All earnest money deposits must be immediately placed in an escrow account and cannot be intermingled or co-mingled with the broker's funds. To do so would expose the broker to charges of conversion which could result in suspension. Earnest money deposits are ordinarily forfeited as liquidated damages if the buyer defaults after the seller accepts the offer. If the seller refuses the offer of the purchaser (buyer), the earnest money is returned.

In case both the buyer and seller make a claim on the deposit 6.09
which the broker is holding in escrow, the broker should notify FREC of the situation and attempt to arbitrate the disagreement between the parties. In the event that the two contesting parties cannot reach an arbitrated agreement, the broker has three additional courses of action open to him.

First, if the broker does not claim a part of the deposit, he can file a bill of interpleader in court against the two contestants. This action would request the court to rule as to the disposition of the deposit. In cases of this nature, the court will ordinarily permit withdrawal of the broker as escrow agent and permit him to receive reasonable court costs and attorney's fees.

Secondly, if the broker does feel that he has a legitimate claim on a part of the deposit in escrow, he can file for a declaratory decree from the court. By doing so, the broker is expected to pay his own court costs and attorney's fees as one of the claimants thereby requesting the court to decide disposition of the deposit among himself, the buyer, and the seller.

Or thirdly, the broker may request an "Advisory Opinion" from FREC regarding the disputed deposit. If one of the three above courses of action is elected and he follows the advice of FREC, no charges for failure to account for or deliver a deposit will be permitted to be maintained against the broker by one of the contracting parties.

Collection of Advance Fees

In the past, some brokers have deemed it advisable to collect fees for listing real property in advance of a transaction actually closing or prior to acceptance of a listing. In 1976, the Real Estate License Law was changed to require the establishment of special escrow or trust accounts called "advance fee trust accounts" wherein 75 percent of all advance fees collected must be deposited. Such accounts may be established in a bank or any recognized depository as long as it is located in Florida. The advance fee escrow account may not be co-mingled with any other escrow accounts or personal accounts of a broker. Separate and distinct accounting records are required for all advance fees collected for listing real property. In addition, monthly reports must be submitted to FREC on or before the 15th of the month following the period covered in the report. The format required for such reports has been specified in 21V-10.14 of the HANDBOOK. The reports submitted must include, but are not limited to, all fees collected in advance for listings, all funds expended or withdrawn from the advance fee escrow account, and all funds returned to the principal during the period of the report. Reports are to be for a calendar-month period ending at the close of business on the last day of the month.

C 475.452
21V-10.14

A broker may withdraw funds from an advance fee account if the money is to be expended in a real estate transaction for the benefit of the principal only. A broker's expenses such as office supplies, telephone, rent, automobile, commissions, or controlled publications are regarded as broker overhead and may not be paid from the advance fee account.

If an advance fee has been paid in connection with a listing and the property is not sold during the term of the listing contract or within a period of 18 months from the contract date, whichever is shorter, all funds held by the broker must be returned to the principal with a complete final accounting which will include any and all funds expended.

Violation of any portion of this section is a misdemeanor of the first degree and is punishable as stated in F.S. 775.082, 775.083, or 775.084. In addition, violation of this section of the law allows a principal triple damages for any funds misapplied plus reasonable attorney's fees.

Membership in Organizations

Most brokers find it expedient to belong to local community and
professional organizations. The brokerage business thrives on 21V-10.12
social contact, and membership in various clubs and organizations 10.15
is rewarding in many ways. However, it is important to know that no broker or salesman is allowed to use or display insignia, emblems, or names of any association, club, or organization in a manner which would cause people to think that he is actually a member unless he does, in fact, belong to the organization in question.

By the same token, only brokers who belong to the national, state, 16.01
and local Boards of REALTORS may use the copyrighted name of REALTOR. The National Association of Real Estate Boards (now the National Association of REALTORS) copyrighted the name REALTOR and that copyright has been sustained in court. Salesmen who are employed by REALTORS are called REALTOR-ASSOCIATES after they have been accepted as members of the local Board of REALTORS.

Ethical Standards

Principal - Employer

Every broker and salesman legally entitled to practice real 475.01
estate in the state of Florida is governed by the real estate 21V-6.01
license law (Chapter 475, F.S.). This law is part of that por- 2.01
tion of the law referred to as the "law of agency." When real estate practitioners represent a principal in any of the seven services of real estate, they do so as an agent of their principal. They are engaged as their principal's agent to deal with a third party or parties. Therefore, the principal who engages a broker to act as his agent becomes the employer of that broker. Note that two different terms can be used to designate the same individual for whom the broker is acting. He is correctly referred to as the "principal" or "employer." Regardless of his designation, the real estate license law and the general law of agency are very clear and explicit in stating the legal relationship which must exist between the broker and his employer.

Fiduciary Relationship

At the time a broker accepts employment from a principal, he is 7.02
obligated to recognize and adhere to a fiduciary relationship 7.04
between himself and the principal. This is not a matter of 7.05
choice or custom or applicable in some instances and not applica- 10.02
ble in others. The fiduciary relationship is a matter of legis- 10.07
lation in that the law imposes a fiduciary relationship between
the broker and principal even though the two individuals may not
personally trust each other. The law states that, whenever an 7.03
employer secures the services of another in the capacity of a broker, a fiduciary or confidential relationship is established. Whenever confidence is given, then betrayed, a remedy will be found and relief will be granted to the injured party.

Fiduciary relationships are those confidential relationships which are established and recognized between attorney and client, husband and wife, guardian and ward, broker and principal, and salesman and employer. A fiduciary relationship is the opposite of the common public relationship which exists in normal trading transactions where people with adverse interests are said to be dealing "at arm's length" with each other. In such cases, the legal doctrine of "Caveat emptor" ("Let the buyer beware") applies.

The fiduciary relationship between broker and principal is im- 10.02
posed by law because of the sequence of events which usually follows an employment agreement between the two. During the course of handling a transaction, the broker almost always learns a great deal about the property, the mental attitude of the principal toward the property, and often, about the financial condition and prospects of the principal. Much of the information gained as a result of his employment is thus of a confidential nature. Some of the information which a broker will obtain may be used at some later date by the broker for his own advantage, provided it does not work to the disadvantage of the principal. However, the broker cannot use such information for his own advantage nor can he use it for the advantage of another if its use can reasonably be to the disadvantage of the principal. This is one of the rules and regulations which continues to apply to the conduct of the broker after he has severed his relationship with the principal and is binding on the broker for the rest of his life. He is not free to use confidential information to the disadvantage of a former principal after the transaction is completed. Also, any harmful or derogatory information a broker may acquire about a principal during a fiduciary relationship cannot later be revealed after the relationship has ended.

The principal, or employer, of a broker should not have to sus- 7.04
pect the broker of unethical or unfair practices in his dealings. 10.14
Nor should he need to conduct a long and searching investigation of the broker prior to employing him, as he might reasonably do when dealing at arm's length in general commerce. A real estate broker is required to deal fairly and in good faith with his employer. He is supposed to earn and enjoy the same trust and confidence as a lawyer or banker. Therefore, the employer of a broker must be able to rely on any and all material statements made by the broker regarding the transaction for which he is employed.

In addition to the clear requirements mentioned, a broker is re- 10.09
quired to inform his principal of all facts known to the broker regarding the property in question. Any facts, reports, or rumors which might reasonably influence the principal in making a decision must be promptly reported to the principal when they come to the attention of the broker. In some instances, so-called "facts" may be nothing more than "rumors," yet the broker is duty bound to give the principal the benefit of rumors he may hear, always qualifying them as rumors and giving their source.

Adverse Interests

As a result of the relationship described above, it becomes in- 10.10
creasingly obvious that a broker is unable to represent adverse interests in the same transaction. In other words, he cannot act for both the seller and the buyer without betraying one of them.

The one exception to this rule would be in the case of a buyer wanting a certain type property and the seller wanting to sell the same type property and each asked the broker to represent him as a middleman only, that is, each wanted the broker merely to find someone interested in selling or buying such a property. The broker would be required to leave all negotiating to the 10.06 parties involved once he had introduced them to each other. Such instances do not occur often.

The overriding rule is that a broker may not adopt an attitude 10.10 which is adverse to the interests of his principal and act for 12.13 himself or some other person whose interests are adverse to those of the principal. However, if a broker's duties to his principal do not conflict with his duties to the other party, a broker may legally represent both parties in a transaction. This area of operation could prove extremely hazardous. A more practical approach to the question might be to assume that some degree of conflict will always exist between principal and prospect, or seller and buyer. However, if the broker fully discloses to each party the fact that he is attempting to represent both sides of the transaction and will be compensated by both parties, he is allowing each party to determine the degree of trust and reliance each may place in him. This could prove costly at a later date because both parties may be considered to be principals and one might decide his fiduciary relationship had been violated.

While acting as broker for a principal, a broker cannot allow his 10.12 principal to accept an offer without providing all information he may possess regarding opportunities to buy or sell at a more favorable price, or on better terms. This would also mean that a broker could not attempt to list property for sale from the purchaser with the knowledge that he can sell the property at an advanced price, and at the same time purport to represent his principal, the seller. However, after a contract for sale between principal and buyer is consummated and the sale has been arranged, the broker can then list the property from the buyer for resale.

Legal Obligations to the Principal

The moment a broker accepts a listing of property, he is ac- 10.02 cepting the seller of that property as a principal, and certain duties become legislated obligations on the part of the broker and salesmen employed by him. Failure to perform these obligations faithfully will usually be construed as fraudulent or dishonest dealing if the principal suffers any loss or damage as a result. The following eight obligations or duties of the broker will be explained:

1. Duty of obedience
2. Duty to obtain best price and terms
3. Duty to inform principal
4. Duty to avoid adverse interests
5. Duty to avoid personal interest
6. Duty to protect principal's interest
7. Duty not to bind principal
8. Duty to act in good faith.

1. Duty of obedience. The first of these obligations is the duty
of obedience to legal instructions of the principal. The broker is c
not justified in acting against his principal's instructions even 10.07
if carrying them out will result in loss to his principal. If the broker feels that carrying out his instructions will result in harm to the principal, he must promptly inform the principal of the facts and his opinions affecting the transaction. However, if the principal will not change the instructions, the broker must either carry them out or withdraw from the relationship.

2. Duty to obtain best price and terms. A second obligation of 10.08
the broker is to obtain the most favorable price and terms for his principal. If his principal is a buyer, he should attempt to acquire property at the lowest price; if a seller, he should attempt to get the highest price. In order to accomplish his obligation to get the most favorable price and terms, the broker must discuss with the principal any tax problems which might be anticipated as a result of the profit or loss involved. The broker may advise his principal to consult a tax expert before deciding on an offer. Also, a broker might produce a buyer willing and able to pay a higher price but desiring different terms than those specified by the principal. In such a case, the broker has not earned his commission if the offer is rejected. However, if the broker produces a buyer willing and able to pay a higher price on substantially the same terms, then the broker can be expected to have earned his commission. It should be remembered that the obligation to obtain the most favorable price and terms requires a broker to prevent his principal from becoming bound to accept one offer until, or unless he has informed the principal of other offers, or even the possibility of other more advantageous offers if he has any knowledge regarding such a possibility. However, after advising the principal, the broker is obligated to carry out the instructions of the principal. In any case, the broker must always immediately communicate to the principal any and all offers regardless of the degree of approval the broker may attach to them. Of course, the broker is obligated to give his employer the benefit of his knowledge and advice regarding each offer, but the final decision must rest with the principal.

3. Duty to inform principal. A third obligation of the broker is 7.10
to inform his principal promptly of all material facts, rumors, 10.09
or reports regarding the property. This was discussed in preceding paragraphs.

4. Duty to avoid adverse interests. A fourth obligation of the 10.04
broker is to refrain from acting in behalf of adverse interests 10.10
against the interests of his principal. This was also discussed in preceding paragraphs.

5. Duty to avoid personal interest. A fifth obligation of the 10.11
broker is to refrain from becoming financially interested in property his principal is attempting to sell or buy. Of course, the broker may clearly divest himself of his status as a broker, ending the broker-principal relationship, and act as an individual to buy or sell the property. But it is not sufficient for the principal to know of and approve the action of a broker to

buy the property in question. In addition to informing the principal that he wants to buy the property, the broker must also advise the principal of every fact that he has knowledge of regarding the subject property which might reasonably be expected to influence the principal's decision to buy or sell. If this were not the case, a broker would be able to locate a prospective purchaser for a property, then buy from the principal at a lower price and pocket the profit. If a broker violates this rule, his license may be suspended and the commission paid to him must be returned. Also, if the principal lost money, the broker can be made to reimburse the principal. This rule ensures that the public may reasonably expect a broker displaying a registered broker sign to conduct his business as a broker with fiduciary relations, or clearly state that he is entering into a transaction at arm's length. It should be clearly understood that a broker may inform his principal of his desire to buy a property which he was originally employed to sell and after making full disclosure of everything he knows regarding the property, the principal may decide to sell to the broker. Then, and in that event, the broker may purchase the property with the full knowledge and consent of the principal.

6. Duty to protect principal's interest. A sixth obligation of 10.04
the broker is to avoid, at all costs, advancing his own interests 10.12
or the interests of someone else to the detriment of his principal. A broker may not make a profit, collect a secret commission, or manipulate a transaction to deprive his principal in favor of anyone else. It does not suffice to explain breaking this rule by declaring that the principal received the price he asked for his property and the buyer was happy with his purchase price. If a secret commission, or overage, was manipulated so as to sell the property for more than the principal was asking and divert the surplus monies to someone other than the principal, then the broker is guilty of fraud.

7. Duty not to bind principal. A seventh obligation of the 10.13
broker is to refrain from unauthorized acts or promises on behalf of the principal. As would be expected, the unauthorized acts of a broker are not normally binding on a principal. However, if the principal gives the broker greater authority than is normally given him, the principal has bound himself. It is the duty of a broker to avoid actions or statements which might embarrass his principal or jeopardize the transaction. Unless a broker has been specifically authorized by his principal, he should not make promises or representations regarding the quality and value of lands, or the state of the title to lands, he has listed. When properly authorized to do so, a broker may conclude binding contracts for his principal and may also make decisions regarding price and terms.

8. Duty to act in good faith. The last and eighth obligation of 10.14
a broker is the obligation which requires him to act in good faith with his principal. This obligation automatically rules out any statement, act, or conduct which is not open and above board. It also requires the broker to place the interests of his principal above the interests of the broker or anyone else. This

would include the duty to preserve and maintain the property or funds of his principal to the best of his ability. All brokers are absolutely prohibited from co-mingling or intermingling their own funds or property with those of a principal's. To do so might expose the principal's funds or property to seizure by the broker's creditors.

Pretending to be a Broker

In the past, brokers have been exposed for falsely pretending to 10.15
be employed as a broker when actually selling or buying for themselves. This false pretense of acting as a principal's broker is fraudulent if done for the purpose of inviting a confidence in order to make a profit for himself.

Legal Obligations to Customers

Thus far, the discussion of the broker's obligations and duties 10.16
has related primarily to his principal or employer. FREC rules and regulations as well as the real estate license law have also specified certain obligations and duties the broker may have to prospects (customers).

A broker is required to pay heed to and uphold his obligations to his principal. At the same time, he must also act in good faith with the prospect whom he solicits. The customer has the right to expect any broker to abide by the high standards of honesty, integrity, and expertise which the law has established.

Role as an Expert

Real estate brokers, by the very nature of their business, are 10.17
supposed to possess expert knowledge regarding the field of real estate. The average layman is inclined to believe that all licensed brokers are experts in all areas of the real estate business. Most brokers, however, tend to specialize in one or a few areas of real estate and subordinate their activities in other areas. The general public is not always aware of the special fields of expertise a broker may be interested in, and therefore the public will tend to accept as fact most statements made by a broker which indicate knowledge and expertise involving special areas of real estate or real estate values. Normally, an opinion would not be a representation of fact on which anyone would have the right to rely. When an opinion is given by a so-called expert, however, then the public should be able to rely on it. Therefore, unless a broker is quoting a qualified expert, or is himself qualified, he may be guilty of fraud if he gives his own opinion which is not well-founded in fact.

Responsibility to Prospect

A broker's prospects, or customers, are entitled to rely on 7.02
material statements made by a broker regarding a transaction: 7.09
when the statements are made through the mail; when they concern 10.16
past or present income or expenses; when they are made about construction features not visible to the eye; when the broker knows he is making a wrong statement, or is simply carelessly incorrect; or, when the prospect does not have access to the property. The broker or salesman is thus accountable for any of

the above material statements made.

Many brokers have forgotten, or never knew, that a prospect 7.08
(principal) can prove a charge of fraud by merely showing that a 7.12
statement made by a broker was: (1) material to the transaction; and, (2) relied upon. The courts have ruled that simple intent to defraud is a fraudulent act with restitution not a sufficient defense against a complaint of fraud.

Anyone who employs a registered real estate broker as a c 7.03
principal has a legal right to rely on the truthfulness of the 10.14
broker. Therefore, any misrepresentation made by the broker to the prospect is fraudulent unless the prospect knows the statement is false. The customer is never expected to be placed in a position of verifying each and every statement made by a broker. However, the customer cannot rely on a broker to the extent of believing what he knows is false.

Opinions of Title

Statements regarding title to property are an especially hazard- 475.25(1h)
ous subject for brokers. A broker must first obtain a current 21V-10.01
opinion from a lawyer before he may properly give an opinion that 8.08
title to a property is good, or marketable. When questions of title arise, all brokers are required to advise their prospects to have a competent attorney examine the abstract or to obtain a title insurance policy. In the event a broker knows that the title to a property is not marketable or that encumbrances against the property exist, the broker is required to inform his customer of all such conditions.

Elaborate, not Exaggerate

The law allows the broker to elaborate or "puff" the value of 475.47
real estate, and/or the possibilities of the property when the 6.07
purchaser is available to investigate the property and inspect it 7.08
for himself. A broker may not, however, elaborate to the point 7.09
of misrepresentation.

Any representation made by a broker may later become the basis 7.02
for charges of fraud, breach of contract, or breach of trust. 7.03
In general, a purchaser ordinarily has only a limited right to 7.04
rely upon the statements of a broker. However, if a broker in- 7.07
vites another to place his trust and then betrays that trust, he, the broker, is guilty of fraud. This legal concept brings to light an important ethical principle relating to those engaged in the sale of real estate. At any time the trust or confidence of a prospect is invited, by actions or words, that trust or confidence, once given, must not be betrayed.

Compensation depends on Employment

In order for a broker to have a right to compensation, it is 10.02
first necessary that a condition of employment exists. Normally, 10.04
employment is evidenced by a written listing contract. However, 10.05
employment may be implied by actions of the parties. In Florida, verbal listing contracts are recognized as valid. In any event, a broker must have either an expressed or implied contract of employment, and he must perform according to the terms of employ-

ment in order to claim compensation.

In Florida, two general categories of broker's employment contracts are usually recognized: employment to effect a sale of the property and employment to find a purchaser.

Employment to effect a Sale. Employment to effect a sale of 6.09
property requires the broker not only to find a ready, willing, 10.03
and able buyer on the terms required by the seller, but he must 10.06
also ensure that the buyer pays all the money required and executes all notes and mortgages. If the signed offer of the buyer is materially different from the terms required by the principal, then the principal is justified in rejecting the offer and the broker has not earned his commission. Ordinarily a broker has tentatively earned his commission in this category of employment when he brings a signed offer to buy from a ready, willing, and able prospect, at the price and terms specified in the listing contract, or with terms which are considered acceptable to the seller. A successful closing will complete the required performance of the broker.

Employment to find a Purchaser. Employment to find a purchaser 6.09
requires a broker to produce a prospect who is ready, willing, 10.03
and able to buy on the terms specified by the seller, or take from a ready, willing, and able prospect an offer which can be enforced as a contract when accepted by the seller. At this point, the broker has earned his commission even though the sale may not be consummated, or perhaps the sale will be concluded on terms other than those in the listing contract. The important criterion here is that the broker did in fact find a purchaser who was ready, willing, and able to buy on the terms and at the price required by the broker's employment agreement.

Ready, Willing, and Able

An explanation of "ready, willing, and able" is helpful in under- 10.03
standing the frequent use of that term in real estate matters.

The word "ready" signifies that the customer is of a mind to complete the transaction at the time and place designated or implied. The word "willing" signifies that the customer is willing to accept the terms and price required to complete the transaction. The word "able" signifies that the customer has the financial ability to produce the amount of money required at the time necessary.

When the broker has produced a buyer who fits the requirements of a "ready, willing, and able buyer" and has delivered a written offer accompanied by an adequate earnest money deposit, he can be said to have earned his commission, even though custom may decree that the commission will not be paid until the time of closing.

No Broker's Liens

In those rare instances when an owner refuses to pay a broker's 8.14
commission after the commission has been earned, the broker may take action to collect by filing a suit against the owner for the amount due. However, the broker is prohibited from placing

a lien against the property of the owner he accepted as his principal.

Procuring Cause

Sometimes two or more brokers will claim to be entitled to compensation as a result of a sale. 10.03
Whenever this occurs, the broker who is determined to be the procuring cause of the sale is 12.14
the broker who is entitled to compensation, regardless of whether he was the broker who actually submitted the binding offer. By "procuring cause" is meant the individual who induced the customer to buy or was the first and original cause for the buyer's interest in acquiring the property.

Broker's Commission

The amount of commission to be paid is ordinarily arrived at by 15.08
agreement between the broker and his principal. In the event no agreement has been concluded, the customary commission prevailing in that locality can be said to apply. FREC does not function as a collection agency. Neither does FREC establish or regulate the amounts of commission paid, nor does Florida law.

Overage - Secret Profit

A broker cannot remain ethical, nor can he operate legally, if he 10.12
attempts to collect two types of commissions. One type of commission a broker is not allowed to collect is called an "overage." This results when a broker attempts to collect a secret profit by making more commission than agreed between the broker and the principal. For example, suppose a broker lists a property at $10,000, agrees to a 10% commission, then learns he may sell the property for $20,000. If the broker, or his agent, buys the property from the broker's principal for $10,000, collects 10%, or $1,000 commission, then turns around and sells the property for $20,000, the broker is liable to his employer for the $1,000 commission plus the $10,000 overage. He is also liable to the purchaser for the $10,000 excess charged and liable for suspension.

Delegation of Responsibilities

As an agent for his principal, a broker has no legal right to 10.19
delegate to others those tasks and responsibilities which require discretion or judgment. Nor can he authorize any act which might bind his principal without the principal's consent. A broker can utilize salesmen or other brokers to locate prospects and consummate sales. These acts do not normally require discretionary powers. However, any salesmen or cooperating brokers whom the employed broker has engaged to assist him must look to the broker of record, or employed broker, for their compensation. They may not receive a commission from the principal in the transaction.

Salesman as Subagent

In the day-to-day world of real estate, almost all brokers have 10.19
salesmen working for them. The salesman is a subagent of the broker and therefore is bound by all the laws, rules, and regulations which apply to the broker.

In order for a salesman to be active in real estate, he must be
employed by an active broker or a registered owner. A salesman
can only work for one registered employer at a time. All monies 475.42(1b)
earned by the salesman as a result of any real estate service 10.20
must be paid by his registered employer and not directly from a 10.22
principal. Salesmen are ordinarily compensated by sharing commissions paid to their broker. The share retained by the broker and the share received by the salesman is usually agreed upon before an employment agreement is reached.

When a salesman accepts employment with a broker, he automati- 10.21
cally enters into a fiduciary relationship with the broker just as the broker has a fiduciary relationship with his principal. In addition to the fiduciary relationship with his broker, a salesman must honor and observe the fiduciary relationship with the broker's principals just as if he were the broker.

Under Florida law, a salesman cannot operate as a broker nor can 475.42(1d)
he operate for himself. Therefore, all commissions he earns and 10.20
all listings he may obtain are legally the property of his broker. All salesmen are prohibited from initiating any suit or action for compensation in connection with a real estate transaction against any person except the person registered as their employer. If a salesman accepts listings, deposits, or commissions from any source, he must accept them in the name of his employer and with the express consent of his employer.

When a salesman works for an employer who operates more than one 21V-10.08
office, he must be registered with the Florida Real Estate Commission as working at the office or branch office address where he generally works.

Change of Employer

Real estate salesmen have a reputation for changing employers 475.23
somewhat more often than people engaged in most other vocations. 21V-9.04
When a salesman decides to change employers, he is required by FREC to accomplish certain specified actions before he may legally practice his vocation with the new employer.

First and foremost, he must surrender his registration certifi- 4.05
cate (license) to FREC. Next, he must request, on a form pro- 6.05
vided by the Commission, a reissue of his certificate showing the name and address of his new employer. His request for reissue also serves to notify the Commission of the termination of employment with his former employer. His former employer is also required to notify FREC of his termination of employment. Further, the salesman is required to make known his new employment to anyone with whom he intends to do business.

After leaving a former employer, a salesman may not divert a customer of his former employer from completion of a transaction.
In fact, the salesman must wait a "reasonable length of time" 10.23
before actively soliciting any customers of his former employer.

Because of the fiduciary relationship between the salesman and 10.21
his employer, the obligations of the salesman do not end when he terminates employment. The salesman is prohibited from disclosing facts learned as a result of his employment with his

former employer which might convince others to discontinue dealing with the former employer. A real estate salesman is further prohibited from doing anything which might discredit his former employer or damage the goodwill of his employer's business. 69

If a salesman is guilty of duplicating records, listings, or confidential information from the office of a former employer, he is guilty of breach of trust even though the salesman may have placed those items in his employer's records. 10.23

If a salesman should take the original records from an employer's office, as opposed to duplicating them, then the salesman is guilty of larceny and is exposed to administrative penalties by FREC, civil action in court, and criminal penalties.

CHAPTER 4

OPERATING THE REAL ESTATE OFFICE

1. The purpose behind the requirement for brokers to open and maintain an office is to eliminate curbstone operations. T F

2. Salesmen may not manage a broker's branch office until they have completed twelve months' active experience under a registered real estate broker. T F

3. A salesman may sue only his employer for compensation in connection with a real estate transaction. T F

4. All active registered real estate brokers must display a sign with all letters on the sign at least two inches in height. T F

5. When a corporation is registered as a real estate broker, the names of all officers and directors of the corporation who are active brokers may be shown on a sign at or near the entrance to the office. T F

6. A blind ad is an advertisement which provides a post office box number, telephone number, or street address without identifying the party who placed the ad. T F

7. If a broker or salesman practices real estate, he should obtain an occupational license from the city, county, or municipality where he operates. T F

8. If a broker maintains an escrow account, it must be in a Florida bank, or he may deposit valuables with a title company located in Florida. T F

9. A broker may deposit personal funds in his own escrow account if he keeps accurate records for audit by FREC. T F

10. The Commission places considerable emphasis on the timeliness with which customer's deposits are placed in a broker's escrow account. T F

11. If a salesman receives a check made out to him as a deposit on the purchase of real estate, he can either endorse the check and give it to his employer or he can deposit the check and give his employer cash. T F

12. The Florida Real Estate Commission conducts spot checks of registered brokers' escrow account records. T F

13. The fiduciary relationship between a broker and his principal does not exist if they distrust each other. T F

14. A fiduciary is the opposite of the doctrine of caveat emptor. T F

15. In order for a broker to have a right to compensation, it is first necessary that some condition of employment exists. T F

16. The law does not permit a broker or salesman to elaborate or puff up a property which he is attempting to sell. T F

17. In answering questions pertaining to quality of title, brokers are required to advise their prospects to have a competent attorney examine the abstract or obtain title insurance. T F

18. When a broker learns of derogatory or harmful information regarding a principal, he cannot reveal that information after the fiduciary relationship has ended. T F

19. A broker is required to report to his principal all rumors which might pertain to a property the broker has listed. T F

20. It is possible that a broker might legally represent adverse parties in a property transaction. T F

21. While acting as a broker for his principal, a broker should not allow his employer to accept an offer without disclosing all information he may have regarding chances to sell at a more favorable price. T F

22. Failure to perform fiduciary obligations faithfully will usually be considered fraudulent or dishonest dealing. T F

23. If a principal gives a broker instructions which will result in loss or harm to the principal, the broker is justified in not carrying out such instructions. T F

24. A broker must communicate to the principal all offers received regardless of how worthy they may be in his opinion. T F

25. When a salesman leaves the employ of his broker, he may make copies of all listings which he has personally placed in the files of his broker. T F

26. If a broker decides to buy the property of his principal, he must advise the principal of every fact which he has knowledge of pertaining to that property if it might reasonably be expected to influence the principal's decision to buy or sell. T F

27. A broker is prohibited from advancing his interests or the interests of anyone else over the interests of his principal. T F

28. A broker has a duty to avoid making statements which might embarrass his principal. T F

29. A broker may be guilty of fraud if he gives an opinion without knowledge of the subject. T F

30. If a principal refuses to pay a broker his commission after a sale has been concluded, the broker may either sue for his commission or place a lien on the principal's property. T F

31. A broker may be entitled to the sales commission even when some other broker actually submitted the written, binding offer. T F

32. The word "willing" as used in the term "ready, willing, and able" signifies that the customer is willing to accept the terms and price required to purchase the property. T F

33. FREC regulates and establishes the commission rates applicable to the various types of real property sold in Florida. T F

34. A broker has no right to delegate to his salesmen any task which requires discretion or judgment. T F

35. Any commissions which a salesman may earn in Florida and all listings he may obtain are legally the property of his broker. T F

CHAPTER 5

PROPERTY RIGHTS:

ESTATES, TENANCIES, and TITLE

This chapter includes the following major segments:

- property defined; rights included
- types of estates
- special tenancies
- title to real property
- restrictions to ownership

When you purchase a new home, and have the deed legally recorded, and move in, what prevents a stranger with a gun from dispossessing you and taking your home for himself? You have property rights of ownership guaranteed by law which will protect you or any other legal owner of real property. But what the law protects is not the property but your ownership rights. So it is obvious that ownership is a product of laws. Ownership can only be established if a government recognizes and enforces laws creating rights to own property. The individual or corporation owning such rights is considered to be the owner of real property and is said to have title to it.

The important point to be made is that there is a difference between "property" and "real property." The collection of rights which is referred to as ownership rights is technically "property." Webster defines property as, "the right to possess, use, and dispose of something; ownership: as, property in land." Most people have always regarded property as land and buildings, but that is wrong from a legal viewpoint. Property is a bundle of legal rights recognized and enforced by a sovereign power. When you sell your property, you do not deliver real estate to the purchaser, you deliver your ownership rights. The new owner can then take possession of his land and the improvements on it.

What then is "real property"? The two words together mean land, with all the permanent structures and improvements to the land. Real property, therefore, is physical in nature, whereas "property" is a legal concept.

Physical Components of Real Property

Any tract of real property is composed of three physical components:

1. That portion of the earth's surface contained within the boundaries of the tract (Surface)
2. Land below the surface in the shape of an inverted triangle with the apex located at the center of the earth (Subsurface)
3. The airspace above the tract up to heights established by law (Air)

The land surface of this country is divided into ranches, farms, and lots which are the real property of private owners. Legal descriptions identify each of the individual tracts. Most transactions involving real property include all three physical components in the exchange of ownership rights. However, it is entirely possible to retain one, or even two, of the components if mutually agreed between buyer and seller. For example, the Pan Am Building over Grand Central Station in New York City is built on air (aerial) rights. The surface and subsurface components of that parcel of real property continue to perform the same function for the same owners as existed prior to the construction of the Pan Am Building. The value of air rights in such instances can amount to millions of dollars.

Another example of the separation of component parts of real property can be found on several farms around Jay, Florida, where significant oil discoveries have been made. The owner of a farm in that locality may either sell or lease the subsurface component of his real property while retaining the surface and air ownership rights. The air rights around Jay have no appreciable value; however, the subsurface component, including mineral and oil rights, has considerable value. While the subsurface component of real property theoretically extends to the center of the earth, limits have been placed on the vertical distance into the air that air rights apply. In order to leave the skies open to navigation, the same public domain theory applies to the air rights as applies to navigable waters. In congested areas such as towns or cities, air rights extend up to 1,000 feet in the air. In uncongested areas like farm or ranch lands, air rights extend only to 500 feet to conform with air rules of navigation.

Personal Property

Real property was defined as land, together with all permanent structures and improvements to the land. There are only two basic types of assets in the world: real property and personal property. Therefore, the definition of "personal property" is made simple. Any asset which is not real property is personal property. A savings account, a car, jewelry, or cash are all personal property. Just as the term "realty" is sometimes used to denote real property, the term "personalty" is frequently used to indicate personal property. It is important to distinguish between real property and personal property in a real estate transaction. All personal property included in the sale of real property should be identified and included in the contract of sale or the seller is entitled to remove the articles.

Fixtures

Some items tend to defy categorization as either real or personal property without close scrutiny. These items are called "fixtures." Fixtures are objects which once were personal property which have been permanently attached to or made part of real property and thus are now real property. 13.27 A bathtub, for example, was personal property as it rested in its container in the plumbing supply warehouse. But once permanently attached to a house, it became real property. Some items are more difficult to classify, however, such as drapes, rugs, or a chandelier, for example. In those cases where contracting parties have not had the foresight to include such items in a sales contract, mortgage, or some instrument of conveyance, the courts generally use the following tests to decide if an item is a fixture, which would mean it is real property:

1. Intent of the parties
2. Method of annexation
3. Relationship between parties
4. Adaptation of the article

Intent of the parties. As in most points of law, intent of the party placing an article on, to, or in real property is of primary importance. A room air conditioner purchased with an installment sales contract may specifically require the item to remain personal property until paid for; or, statements made by an owner to witnesses may indicate his intent to make an item a fixture, like including a washer and dryer in a sales contract as part of the real property to be conveyed would remove any doubt of the owner's intention.

Method of annexation. The manner in which an article is attached to real property will usually indicate whether it is a fixture or personal property. Normally, if removing the item results in damage to real property, the article will be classified as a fixture. If, for example, a set of storage cabinets was built into the wall of a utility room and removal would leave a hole in the wall, the cabinets would normally be considered fixtures.

Relationship between the parties. In this test, the courts seek to determine the exact nature of the relationship between the parties. Is it buyer and seller, or landlord and tenant? Ordinarily, a tenant is required to leave any item he has attached to the landlord's real property. However, if a building is leased as a retail store and display racks are attached to the walls and counters attached to the floor, the courts will generally rule that such items are personal property and may be removed. The tenant may, of course, be required to return the walls and floors to the condition which existed prior to installation of the racks and counters. In disputes between buyer and seller, the terms and conditions of the sales contract will usually be strictly enforced unless there is some indication that the buyer was misled.

Adaptation of the article. This test seeks to determine if an article was designed for, or necessary to, the normal use of a specific tract of real property. If an item is necessary to the use for which a structure is intended, it will be classified as a fixture. For example, the owner of a service station could not reasonably expect to remove gas pumps from the service islands prior to delivery of the property to a new owner. Such items are necessary to the use for which the real property was intended. The same would be true for animal sheds on a stock farm.

The various tests for determining if personal property has become a fixture may well be time-consuming and expensive to apply. At best, such tests are remedial in nature and should not be necessary if care is taken to include all personal property to be delivered in the sales contract. This eliminates misunderstanding and possible litigation. Frequently, a potential buyer will ask a question of an owner anxious to sell, "Do the washer and dryer go with the house or are you taking them with you?" To which the owner might reply, "Oh, yes!" (yes, what?), or the owner might even make a forthright statement like, "They go with the house." In either case, the buyer would be well-advised to include the washer and dryer in the sales contract in order to remove any doubt.

General Property Rights

The evolution of property rights for private individuals has for centuries been closely related to social development. Our concept of real property ownership rights began when our early ancestors first practiced agriculture. Those primitive people wanted to keep the land they had worked hard to clear. This attitude could well have been the predecessor of our present-day allodial system of land ownership. The allodial system is based on the theory that private individuals may own land absolutely free of any duty to pay rent or perform a service for a king, lord, or sovereign power. The allodial system evolved out of the feudal system which had held that the king, or sovereign, owned all lands and allowed his subjects to use them at his pleasure. We did not completely escape the feudal system when it was replaced by the allodial system. Some of the last vestiges of the feudal system include the right of a government: to impose taxes, to have property escheat (revert) to the state, and to exercise eminent domain powers. Still, these residual characteristics of the feudal system have contributed to the creation of a society and way of life few other nations enjoy.

The beginning of our current system of ownership rights can be found in the Land Ordinance of 1785, which came into being as a result of a report written by a committee headed by Thomas Jefferson. The Land Ordinance of 1785 had two results of lasting benefit to this nation: (1) it directed the completion of the first national public land survey which led directly to creation of the government survey system of legal description; and, (2) it officially established for the first time in the struggling new nation a system of allodial land titles -- private rights to land titles not subject to feudal dues. This system of free and clear title to land became a major socio-economic factor in the growth of this nation.

The practical result of the allodial system has been government recognition and protection of private rights of ownership. Real property ownership rights include:

1. The right of use
2. The right of exclusion
3. The right of disposition

1. The right of use. This right is recognition of the owner's entitlement to completely control and utilize his land in any manner he chooses, consistent with local laws. In colonial days and throughout part of the 19th century, this right was almost absolute. As the density of population increased, it became necessary to enact legislation to ensure that one owner's use of land did not and would not result in damage to his neighbors.

2. The right of exclusion. This right is formal recognition that, "A man's home is his castle." An owner is considered to have the right to control entry onto his land and collect damages for certain forms of trespass. Other parties must have permission to enter the land of an owner with this right. This right has also been modified by judicial decisions and legislation. While an owner is still regarded as holding the right of exclusion, no owner is permitted to discriminate against any race in the sale, lease, or rental of land.

3. The right of disposition. This right acknowledges the prerogative of an owner to transfer all, or any portion, of his land during his life or by will at the time of death. This right is also subject to some modification in that statutes prohibiting discrimination must be observed. Only by operation of the law can an owner lose the right of disposition; for example, if he does not pay property taxes, or if the property is held in joint tenancy.

Estates and Tenancies

Title to real property is a legal concept. Section 13 of the 13.01
FREC HANDBOOK defines title as "the evidence of right which a 13.03
person has to the possession of property." The "right" referred to in the above definition may be a limited right or an apparently absolute right, depending on the type of estate which is conveyed with the title. Title may be conveyed or acquired by: (1) will; (2) adverse possession; (3) deed; (4) estoppel or some other court decree; or, (5) descent. Each of these methods will be discussed later in this chapter.

The various "bundles of rights" which constitute the different types of estates normally transferred by title from one party to another will first be examined. The word "estate" simply means a right or interest in property. The term, as used herein, is interchangeable with "tenancy."

Fee Simple Estate

The "fee simple estate" is the most comprehensive and the sim- 13.03
plest title. The fee simple estate is the same as absolute and complete ownership, subject only to the rights of the state regarding taxes and constitutional police powers. The name "fee simple" is sometimes shortened to "fee" and sometimes extended to "fee simple absolute." Regardless of the choice of names, they all mean the same thing and refer to the largest collection of real property ownership rights which is available. A fee simple estate is a title which denotes that the property is owned without any division of interest whatsoever, with complete power to dispose of it as the owner sees fit, or to allow it to descend to his heirs if he does not dispose of it.

Estates Carved from Fee Simple

Many different types of estates may be carved out of a fee simple 13.04
estate by dividing or grouping the various rights of ownership into different bundles.

1. Life Estate. The owner of a life estate has considerably fewer rights than in a fee simple estate. He owns the property only for the period of his lifetime. When he dies, the property reverts to an individual who is called the "remainderman." Normally, the instrument which establishes the life estate will also designate the remainderman, or remaindermen. If the remainderman is known and named, he is called a "vested remainderman"; if the exact identity of the remainderman is not known, he is referred to as a "contingent remainderman." For example, an unborn child would be a contingent remainderman. It should be remembered, however, that a remainderman must be either living or be born within 21 years after the death of someone who was living when the estate was created. Also, the estate which the remainderman acquires may be either a fee simple estate or another life estate with a remainderman or remaindermen. During the period of time an owner enjoys a life estate, he must maintain the property and do nothing to reduce its value. He must also pay the taxes and keep current any existing mortgages or liens so as to preserve the property for the remainderman. A life estate is considered a freehold estate because the duration of ownership is measured by the life of some person.

2. Estate for Years. An estate for years is not measurable by 13.01(2)
the lifetime of any person or persons. It exists for a desig- 13.05
nated period which may be any length of time from less than a 14.06
year to a period longer than the possible lifetime of any living 14.08
person. The estate for years is the lowest quality estate known
since it does not convey actual title to real property but simply
conveys for a temporary period some of the owner's rights and
interests. Rights pertaining to use, enjoyment, possession, and c
exclusion may be transferred, but the owner normally retains disposition rights. It does create an "estate in reversion" since the temporary estate will revert back to the original grantor or his heirs when the estate for years has expired. An example of an estate for years would be a leasehold created by a properly executed lease agreement.

Tenancies with More than One Owner. When real property is owned 13.06
by only one person, the owner's rights are said to be "sole." When two or more people own an interest in real property, their rights are as "joint tenants," "tenants in common," or "tenants by the entireties." Each of these forms of joint ownership have distinguishing characteristics which should be noted.

3. Joint Tenancy. A joint tenancy is created when two or more 689.15, F.S.
people take title to real property at the same time and through 13.06
the same instrument of conveyance. All owners enjoy the same and equal rights of possession and enjoyment. Formerly, a joint tenancy automatically included the right of survivorship, which meant that surviving owners divided equally the share owned by a deceased owner. The law now states that the right of survivorship no longer applies unless specific wording in the deed conveying the property provides for survivorship. This stipulation requires that in addition to designation of the type of estate or title being conveyed, in the case of joint tenancy, some wording similar to "as joint tenants with right of survivorship and not

as tenants in common" must appear on the deed to ensure survivorship. This would naturally continue that feature of joint tenancy which prevents disposition of the property by will or descent to heirs. As joint tenants expire, their shares are divided among the surviving tenants until only one owner is left. The sole survivor then has a fee simple estate. If a joint tenant desires to sell his share of a property, he may do so. However, the person who buys that share cannot be a joint tenant with the other original owners, but would instead be a tenant in common without the right to receive any property upon the death of one of the original joint tenants. Nor would the property of the tenant in common be divided among the joint tenants. It would be disposed of by will, descent, or as he wished to arrange it.

4. Tenancy in Common. The most frequently used form of joint 13.01(8)
ownership, except for husband and wife ownership, is the tenancy 13.07
in common. Any number of people may own property together as tenants in common. Each of the owners may have obtained title from the same or from different grantors. They may have acquired title at different times or at the same time, and they may own equal or unequal shares. Each may dispose of his share as he sees fit, which proves that no right of survivorship exists in a tenancy in common. Tenants in common may partition the property into units of value proportionate to their individual interest if they desire to do so, unless the property is the subject of a joint adventure which has not been completed. When division into proportionate units is not practical, the property may be sold and the proceeds divided proportionately among the tenants in common. In the event of a death, the property of a tenant in common descends to the heirs, or by action of a will if one exists.

5. Tenancy by the Entireties. This form of joint ownership is 689.11, F.S.
peculiar in that it only arises when property is owned by a 13.01(5)
husband and wife. The estate has its origin in the common law 13.08
attitude that a husband and wife are one person and their joint ownership can only be divided by the death of one or the other. Part of the "entirety" will continue to exist in the form of the survivor who emerges as the sole owner of the property. In the event of a divorce, the tenancy by the entireties is ended, and a tenancy in common results. Another advantage to this type of ownership is, if the property is a homestead, the property owned is not subject to seizure for payment of personal debts which are incurred by the owners. Of course, the usual provisions apply as far as taxes, special assessments, and mortgages are concerned.

If a husband is the sole owner of property at the time of marriage, or if the wife is a sole owner at the time of a marriage, either may create a tenancy be the entireties by merely stipulating an intent to create such an estate. However, if the property is a homestead and a widow or widower has living descendants at the time of an attempt to create an estate by the entireties, the attempt will not be successful because the prior claim of the living descendants existed before the estate by the entireties was created.

Neither the husband nor the wife may will any portion of his or her interest in an estate by the entireties. Also, the deed or other instrument of conveyance does not have to state expressly that a tenancy by the entireties exists. If the parties are truly husband and wife, the estate is implied. While not mandatory, the instrument of conveyance should reflect the tenancy by the entireties in order to serve notice to others that such an estate does exist.

Special Tenancies

1. Tenancy at Will. When a written lease expires but the tenant 13.01(8)
remains in possession of the property and pays rent by agreement 13.05
with the landlord, a "tenancy at will" is created with no defi- 14.03
nite time as to when the tenant's rights will terminate. Under 14.05
this type of tenancy, the agreement may be terminated by either party, upon proper notice, by sale of the property or death of either party. In Florida, proper notice for termination of tenancies at will is required to be a fixed period of time, depending on the time interval between rent payments. For example, if the rent is paid annually, the unwritten agreement would be regarded as a year-to-year tenancy. The notice required to terminate would be greater than if the rent intervals were on a
quarter-to-quarter basis. The notice required for tenancies at 14.03
will is as follows:

		Nonresidential	Residential
Year-to-year Tenancy-------	not less than:	90 days	60 days
Quarter-to-quarter Tenancy-	not less than:	45 days	30 days
Month-to-month Tenancy-----	not less than:	15 days	15 days
Week-to-week Tenancy-------	not less than:	7 days	7 days

2. Tenancy at Sufferance. A "tenancy at sufferance" is often 14.04
associated with leases and leaseholds. A tenancy at sufferance is usually created as an aftermath of a lawfully written lease. When the written lease expires and the tenant continues to pay rent, use, and occupy the landlord's property without any agreement, a tenancy at sufferance is said to exist. This type of tenancy may be terminated by either party without notice.

3. Homestead. Another estate in real property is the constitu- 13.09
tional homestead. This estate is much misunderstood because it is often confused with one of its several benefits called "homestead exemption." Once one understands that the homestead tax exemption is only a part of the rights provided a constitutional homestead estate, part of the confusion is dispelled. Constitutional homestead rights are granted to the head of a family for the protection of the family's home and property. To qualify as a homestead, the head of a family must own the property and must also reside on it. The courts have held that a married woman may, under some circumstances, be the head of a family if she owns the home even though she has a husband living with her. In such instances, the property could qualify as a homestead and realize all of the benefits involved.

The amount of property protected by homestead rights is restricted to 160 acres of land if outside an incorporated city or town or one-half acre if located within an incorporated area. The basic intent of homestead rights is to ensure a home for dependent children in the event of death of the breadwinner. To achieve this purpose, the property qualifying as a constitutional homestead cannot be seized by creditors to satisfy personal debts of either husband or wife.

The only valid justifications for seizure or foreclosure of a homestead are: (1) for taxes or assessments; (2) to satisfy a purchase money mortgage; and, (3) for payment of debts relating to labor and/or materials used to erect or repair improvements or work done on the lands.

A homestead cannot be sold or mortgaged except by consent of both 13.15
the husband and the wife, and one spouse may not will the property away from the other spouse and children. When the breadwinner dies and leaves a surviving spouse and/or child or children, the surviving spouse takes a life estate with a vested remainder going to the children.

Homestead status allows the head of the family who is less than 65 years of age to apply for and obtain a $5,000 tax exemption on the property each year. If 65 years of age or older and a resident of the state for five or more years, the homestead tax exemption allowed each year is $10,000. In order to obtain the exemption, one must apply for it between January 1 and March 1 of each year. After March 1, the right to exemption is forfeited for that year. The $5,000 or $10,000 property tax exemption applying to a homestead is deducted from the assessed value of the property before property taxes are computed. Filing is with the county property appraiser's office.

Homestead rights are lost through abandonment or by acquiring another homestead. However, homestead rights are not lost by divorce if there are minor children whom the head of the household is required by law to support.

4. Elective Share. Formerly there existed estates in real prop- 13.12
erty which had as their origin the relationship between a wife 13.13
and husband. These estates were called "dower" and "curtesy." 13.14
Dower rights were the rights allocated to a widow, and curtesy 13.15
rights were the rights a husband acquired in his wife's property 13.16
by legislation. Both estates were only vested in a surviving F.S. 74-106
spouse and were a result of marriage. Originally, the right of F.S. 732
dower was created first in order to ensure the right of a widow to inherit some part of her husband's property after his death even though the husband's improvidence might have otherwise lost the property to creditors.

Under the current Florida probate code, which became effective January 1, 1976, both dower and curtesy rights were abolished. In 1975, Florida Statute 732 was amended to provide that a surviving spouse (either widow or widower) shall be given an option of choosing an "elective share" of the estate of a deceased spouse. Such elective share has been defined as consisting of 30 percent of the decedent's personal property and Florida real estate, except homestead-exempt property and claims. Homestead-exempt property is not included in the elective share because a surviving spouse is already legally entitled to constitutional homestead property and a statutory family allowance regardless of whether the survivor chooses an elective share.

In order for the widow or widower to be legally qualified to take an elective share, the deceased spouse must: (1) have owned property in Florida at the time of death; (2) have been domiciled in Florida at the time of his or her death; and (3) legally file within four months of the date when the first Notice of Administration was published announcing the death of the decedent. The formal election is required to be filed in the same court in which the estate of the deceased spouse is to be administered. The clerk of the appropriate court receives and records all such elections.

If some controversy over the decedent's estate should result in litigation (for example, a challenge to the will or some other question), the surviving spouse is allowed 40 days after all legal proceedings have completely terminated to file a claim of an elective share. In the event that a guardian has been appointed to look after the affairs of a surviving spouse, the guardian may file an elective share on behalf of the surviving spouse at any time during the same time periods available to the surviving spouse.

Selection of an elective share is not mandatory. In those instances (1) where the property in question is not homestead property, (2) where the deceased spouse leaves no will (intestate), and (3) where there are no lineal descendants, the surviving spouse is entitled to the entire estate under the provisions of Florida Statute 732.102. In the event that the decedent's property was a constitutional homestead, the surviving spouse receives a life estate and the lineal descendants are all vested remaindermen.

5. Exempt Property. Associated with the elective share rights of 13.16
a surviving spouse, but completely separate and apart from such rights, is a right to property which has been legislated to be "exempt property." This is a category of property defined as "... household furniture, furnishings, and appliances in the decedent's usual place of abode, and automobiles up to a net value of $5,000." Entitlement to this exempt property is limited by and subject to any unpaid chattel mortgages or other perfected security interests. In addition to the above-named property, the surviving spouse is entitled to the personal effects of the decedent up to a net value of $1,000 unless such effects were legally disposed of by a will. Rights to exempt property have priority over all other claims against an estate and these rights are in addition to any other benefit given or passing to the surviving spouse unless a will of the decedent proves otherwise. Exempt property rights are also in addition to the benefits defined as elective share rights. In the event that no spouse survives the decedent, minor children of the decedent are jointly entitled to the same rights as would have been available to a surviving spouse.

6. Community Property. A type of estate not recognized in Florida but recognized in some other states (primarily in the western part of the nation) is called "community property." This

estate is a heritage from the Spanish laws which governed large portions of the U.S. during the early days of discovery and settlement. In those states where community property is recognized, married couples are considered to own two separate types of property:

a. Separate property
b. Community property

a. Separate property. This category includes any real property which the husband or wife owned prior to the marriage, or property acquired by inheritance, will, or gift. Separate property is considered owned independently from the other spouse.

b. Community property. Any real property acquired by either spouse during a marriage, except by inheritance, will, or gift, becomes community property and automatically belongs to both parties as co-owners. The law assigns each spouse an undivided one-half interest of all that is earned or acquired by either party, regardless of the share contributed by either spouse. Even if a deed should contain the name of one spouse only, if acquired during the marriage, ownership rights will be vested in both parties. Community property rights are not terminated in the event of divorce or death. In the case of a divorce, all real and personal property is divided equally. In case of either spouse's death, the surviving spouse takes his or her one-half interest and the other half is shared by all heirs of the deceased.

Title to Real Property

With an idea of what is involved in creation of the various estates affecting ownership of real property, it is also important to realize that title to real property is nothing more than ownership of the estate. Title represents ownership of that collection of rights called an "estate." When a person sells property, he cannot pick up the earth, rocks, trees, and streams which make up the property and deliver them to the new owner. Instead, he delivers to the new owner the estate, or all of the rights, whatever they may be. In this manner, title is delivered. 13.01 13.40

There are five ordinary methods of acquiring title to property. Use of the word "WADED" will serve as a crutch for remembering the five methods: (1) by Will; (2) by Adverse possession; (3) by Deed; (4) by Estoppel or some form of court decree; or, (5) by Descent. Although title may be obtained by court decree, it is not regarded as an ordinary method. 13.03

1. Will. (Legally called the "last will and testament.") A property owner making a will is called the "testator." When an owner dies after having made a will, he is said to have died testate. If a person dies without leaving a will, he is said to have died intestate. In his will, a property owner usually disposes of his property as he would have it arranged after his death. The person named as "executor" of his estate is then charged with carrying out the provisions of the will. A gift of real property in a will is known as a "devise," and the recipient of the gift is the "devisee."

2. Adverse Possession. This condition arises when the true owner of record has failed to maintain possession and the property has
been seized by another. If the true owner "sleeps on his rights" 13.33
and does not use the legal means available to remove a hostile trespasser, the owner will lose his rights to the property after a period of time. In Florida, title to property may be acquired by adverse possession if a person can meet the following conditions:

a. Possession by the person trying to acquire title must be "open and notorious"
b. Possession must be hostile to, and to the exclusion of, the true owner
c. Possession must be under a claim, even an imperfect claim of title
d. Possession must continue for seven or more consecutive years without the consent of the owner.

It is extremely important that competent legal advice be obtained before acquiring property from one whose sole claim to title is based on adverse possession.

3. Deed. The normal real estate transaction involves the sale of 13.17
property under a contract and is usually consummated by delivery of a deed. Also, a gift of real property is consummated by delivery of a deed. In Florida, title to property is transferred at the time of voluntary delivery and acceptance of a deed.

4. Estoppel. This is a principle of law which enables an indi- 13.35
vidual to acquire title to property over an owner because of some 13.37
act the owner did, or failed to do. If these actions, or lack of actions, result in an erroneous belief, and subsequent action is taken in good faith on the part of the individual who was misled, grounds for estoppel are created. For example, an unscrupulous owner sells property to "A." The unscrupulous owner then sells the same property to "B" a few days later. "B" then proceeds to record his deed in the public records, which "A" has neglected to do. When "A" finally gets around to recording his deed, he is "estopped" from doing so because one legal owner has already proved his title and ownership of the property. "A" will have grounds for a suit against the unscrupulous seller, but he is estopped from acquiring the property.

5. Descent. This is the oldest method of acquiring title to property. When a person dies without leaving a will (intestate), all the property he owned at the time of his death will pass to his legal descendants by operation of law. His legal descendants are known as "heirs," and their priorities as to their entitlement to share in the estate are fixed by law.

Notice to Title

Anyone who is about to acquire title to or an interest in real 13.35
property is always required to take notice of the rights of those 13.36
who are in possession of the actual property. However, it is impractical for an owner to be always physically present on his property so as to provide the world notice of his ownership. Therefore, the law recognizes two types of notice with exactly

the same validity and effect: actual and constructive. Rumors of ownership which cannot be traced do not constitute notice.

1. Actual Notice. Physical possession of property gives the 13.35
world notice of interest in a property. Actual notice may only be given to the world by physical possession.

2. Constructive Notice. Recording in the public records a prop- 13.36
erly executed and acknowledged instrument of conveyance puts the world on notice regarding the interests of an owner in real property. All states have enacted recording acts which provide that all instruments affecting real property may be recorded in the public records of the county in which the property is located. When properly recorded, these instruments are considered notice to the world, with precisely the same effect and authority as if the owner were physically in possession of the property. All people dealing with real property are bound by all recorded documents; therefore, constructive notice is just as good as actual notice. Neither actual notice nor constructive notice is superior to the other. They both have exactly the same legal effect. Recording of an acknowledged conveyance, or constructive notice, protects both the holder of the title and the public from fraud since the true ownership of property is open to inspection by the public.

Abstract of title. When a buyer is in the process of obtaining title to, or interest in, real property, one of the most important obligations is to determine the condition of the seller's title. This is normally done by an attorney, an abstract company, or a title company conducting a thorough examination of the abstract of title. Such an examination is called a "title search."

The abstract of title is a condensed history from recorded documents pertaining to evidences of ownership of a tract or parcel. Each legal document appears in the order it was recorded in public records. No instrument is allowed to be recorded unless acknowledged as required by law. Therefore, a searching examination of those recorded instruments pertaining to a title should reveal the true extent of ownership and the condition of title. The entire history of ownership of title from the first entry of record to the present time will be contained in the public records. Instruments such as land grants, deeds, divorce decrees, wills, or any other document by which title has been transferred will be included. Also appearing in an abstract will be leases, mortgages, deed restrictions, and any other instrument which places a lien or encumbrance on the title. The person preparing an abstract will duplicate or abstract from public records only those instruments pertaining to the title of present concern. When complete, the abstract is a summary of all instruments of record and provides a good indication of title condition for those skilled in title research.

Certificate of title opinion. Laws related to real property titles and the manner in which they may be transferred are complex. The average person is not qualified to examine an abstract of title and declare its condition. Many people seek an opinion of title from a competent attorney; others prefer to purchase title insurance. First, a look at what is involved in an opinion of title.

An opinion of title, also called a "certificate of title opinion," is executed by an attorney after he has studied the abstract of title. The certificate will state: that the attorney has the knowledge and training to examine the abstract; that he will be honest and diligent in his efforts; any defects or clouds on the title such as liens, easement, or other encumbrances; and, the attorney's opinion of whether the seller has a marketable title. Most attorneys do not guarantee the opinion of title. It is an opinion only, backed by legal training and experience. If the opinion should prove to be in error, negligence must usually be proved in order for the attorney's client to receive reimbursement.

Title insurance. The limited protection afforded buyers of real property by an opinion of title led to creation of title insurance companies. Abstracting companies first developed what has come to be termed a "title plant." A title plant is a system of reproduced documents from the public records, filed by legal description, not by names of owners. With a complete set of records available, abstracting companies found that they could work with greater speed and accuracy in conducting title searches. When the system was proved, abstract companies became willing to guarantee the marketability of titles which they had examined. This led to the formation of title insurance companies with a staff of lawyers, abstractors, and administrative personnel.

There are two different types of title insurance: the owner's title insurance, and the lender's title insurance. The owner's title insurance policy is issued for an amount equal to the total value of the real property, including land and improvements, if any. The title insurance company will pay damages for any defect in the title not listed as an exception in the policy. The list of excepted conditions is sometimes subject to negotiation and should be examined carefully by a purchaser of title insurance. The title insurance purchased by one owner cannot be transferred to another owner. Each owner must acquire new title insurance.

Most mortgage lenders will not make a mortgage loan unless the borrower agrees to provide title insurance for the lender. This is a policy separate from the owner's policy. The lender's title insurance is generally issued for an amount equal to the unpaid balance of the mortgage loan. Unlike the owner's title insurance, the lender's title insurance is transferable. If the mortgage lender should sell the mortgage to another investor, the title insurance would protect the new owner of the mortgage.

Premiums for title insurance are paid one time only, at the time of issue. Cost schedules vary, with premium rates graduated according to the value of the real property.

Ownership Limitations and Restrictions

Ownership of anything, including real property, is either abso- 13.01(4)
lute or limited. When referring specifically to real property, 16.08
there is no such thing as absolute ownership in the traditional

and classical sense. However, the term "absolute ownership" is sometimes used to distinguish between property owned in fee simple (free and clear) and property ownership in less than fee simple (limited ownership).

Types of Ownership Restrictions. Limitations and restrictions on the ownership of property exist in many different forms. Most authorities agree that they fall into two general categories: governmental and private. Governmental restrictions to ownership will be dealt with in this chapter. Private restrictions (deed restrictions, easements, leases, and liens) will be treated in the "Deeds and Restrictions" chapter. Both general categories have several sub-categories of restrictions and limitations.

Government Restrictions on Ownership

In the category of governmental limitations are four important sub-categories: (1) police power; (2) eminent domain; (3) right of taxation; and, (4) escheat to the state.

1. Police Power. The constitutions of the United States and each of the fifty states provide for the government to apply any restrictions deemed necessary in the interest of the general health, welfare, or safety of its citizens. Under police power, the use and occupation of real property may be regulated. From these powers come the many ordinances and regulations governing zoning, building codes, health standards, city planning, rent controls, and subdivision controls. The state governments have delegated the exercise of police powers to county, city, and village governments. Police power represents the broadest power of the government to limit or regulate the rights of property owners. Under police power, the government may not actually separate the owner and his property, or take the property from him, but the owner's use and occupation of the property can be restricted, and without any compensation to the owner whatsoever. Zoning, for example, can prevent the owner from utilizing the property in the most profitable manner, and the loss of revenue caused by the zoning will not be returned to the owner by the government.

2. Eminent Domain. The constitutions of the federal government and each of the state governments also grant the power of eminent domain. As in the case of police power, the power of eminent domain has been delegated to counties, cities, and a few special agencies. Eminent domain gives the government the power to take land from an owner, if it is done for a public purpose. A fair price must be paid for any land taken under eminent domain. This power may be exercised by the government regardless of whether the owner wants to part with the property. In Florida, if an owner believes he is not receiving a fair price for the property being taken from him, he may go to court and ask a jury to settle the question of what constitutes a fair price. If he decides to go to court, the state is required to pay his legal costs and the costs of any appraiser hired to testify in his behalf.

3. Right of Taxation. Again, this power has its source in the various constitutions. It is only fair that citizens pay for the benefits and protection provided by the various levels of government. Because of its permanence and inability to be hidden,

property is a most convenient item to tax. Therefore, property is usually the primary basis for local taxation. This gives local governments the power not only to take property by taxation, but also to destroy the economic value of property if taxes are not carefully and judiciously levied. If taxes on real property are not paid, the local taxing authority can actually take the property away from the owner. When the owner does pay his taxes, the local taxing authority is taking personal property in the form of money. The power to tax is the power to destroy if not used intelligently and moderately.

4. Escheat to the State. The power of escheat is not actually a limitation or restriction on ownership. Escheat simply provides for a government, normally a state government, to take the property of an owner who dies without any known heirs and without leaving a will to dispose of his property. Like many U.S. laws, this power has its origin in England. Under the feudal system of ownership during the Middle Ages, a serf, or tenant, held his land in what could be compared to a life estate today. When the tenant died without heirs, the land reverted back to the feudal lord or his heirs. In today's world, it is impractical to regard any property as not owned by someone; therefore, the power of escheat is a logical solution to ensure that property is always owned by someone. In many states, this power extends to personal property as well as to real property.

CHAPTER 5

PROPERTY RIGHTS:

ESTATES, TENANCIES, and TITLE

1. The word "property" means:
   a. The physical articles one owns
   b. Land only
   c. Land plus all improvements on it
   d. A bundle of legal rights
2. A tract of real property is composed of:
   a. One physical component
   b. Two physical components
   c. Three physical components
   d. Four physical components
3. Fixtures are items which:
   a. Are fixed, or attached to real property
   b. Were once personal property but are now real property
   c. Have been incorporated as a part of real property
   d. All of the above
4. The Land Ordinance of 1785 resulted in:
   a. The 13 colonies acquiring land formerly claimed by England
   b. Establishment of a system of private rights to free and clear title to land
   c. Establishment of a system of planning ordinances
   d. All of the above
5. The general rights of ownership included in real property ownership include the rights to:
   a. Buy, sell, and use
   b. Use, dispose, and improve
   c. Acquire, use, and dispose
   d. Use, exclude, and dispose
6. Community property is divided into two types called:
   a. Community property and joint property
   b. Separate property and joint property
   c. Community property and separate property
   d. Separate property and entirety property
7. A title search is:
   a. An examination of the abstract of title
   b. A thorough search for misplaced title papers
   c. A search for a former holder of title
   d. Only required when a deed is misplaced
8. An opinion of title given by a competent attorney:
   a. Provides the same degree of protection as title insurance
   b. Provides more protection than title insurance
   c. Provides less protection than title insurance
   d. Has no relation to problems related to title

9. A "title plant" is:
   a. Where deeds are printed
   b. A system of records, collected and filed by names of real property owners
   c. A system of records, collected and filed according to names of title insurance holders
   d. A system of records, collected and filed by legal descriptions

10. The mortgagor's title insurance policy is:
    a. Not transferable
    b. Transferable
    c. Transferable if the mortgage is sold to an investor
    d. None of the above

11. At the expiration of the lease period, a tenant continued to pay rent on a quarterly basis as he had during the period of the lease. He has a:
    a. Tenancy at will
    b. Tenancy at sufferance
    c. Leasehold
    d. None of the above

12. A tenant at will has been paying his rent on a month-to-month basis. He is entitled to how much notice to legally terminate his tenancy?
    a. Not less than 7 days
    b. Not less than 30 days
    c. Not less than 15 days
    d. Not less than 45 days

13. The law recognizes both actual and constructive notice. To which does the law assign greatest validity and effect?
    a. Constructive notice
    b. Actual notice
    c. Both the same
    d. None of the above

14. Which of the constitutional provisions delegated to various levels of government regulates use and occupancy?
    a. Police power
    b. Eminent domain
    c. Escheat
    d. Taxation

15. Which power of government allows the owner to be separated from ownership of real property at a fair price whether the owner is willing or not?
    a. Police power
    b. Eminent domain
    c. Escheat
    d. Taxation

16. Which power of government represents the broadest power of government to limit or regulate the rights of property owners?
    a. Police power
    b. Eminent domain
    c. Escheat
    d. Taxation

17. In order for a husband to change his wife's ownership rights, he must: c 91
    a. Have her sign a deed or conveyance
    b. Have her sign a pre-marriage agreement
    c. Divorce her
    d. Any of the above

18. A husband and wife own a home with title in both names. The husband owns two other small farms in his name only, acquired prior to the marriage. They have one minor child and one adult son. The husband dies. Which is most correct?
    a. The widow owns a life estate in all property.
    b. The property is split equally among the widow and the children.
    c. The widow owns all of the home and may claim 30% of the other two farms.
    d. The widow owns 30% of all of the real estate.

19. The amount of property protected by homestead rights is:
    a. 640 acres outside a city or town and one acre in town
    b. 160 acres outside a city or town and one-half acre in town
    c. 40 acres outside a city or town and one-half acre in town
    d. 160 acres outside a city or town or one-half acre in town

20. A constitutional homestead is owned by "X" who is head of a family consisting of himself, his wife, and their three children. "X" dies. After his death:
    a. The widow owns the homestead
    b. The widow owns a life estate in the homestead, and the children are vested remaindermen
    c. The widow may claim elective share rights of 30% of the homestead and the children divide the remainder
    d. Any of the above

21. The homestead tax exemption is deducted from:
    a. The market value of a property
    b. The assessed value of a property
    c. The sales price of a property
    d. None of the above

CHAPTER 6

DEEDS and PRIVATE RESTRICTIONS

Shortly after Thomas Jefferson became President in 1801, he successfully concluded the purchase of the Louisiana Territory (1803) from Napoleon of France for only $15 million. With this new territory nearly doubling the size of the United States, the sale of public lands began in earnest. Responsibility for public domain lands had been placed in the Central Land Office. The phrase "doing a land office business" soon became a permanent part of our jargon. The General Land Office held public land sales which ranked in importance with births and marriages to settlers moving south and west. In 1820, public land values were set at $1.25 per acre. In those days, the President personally signed the government patent conveying title to the new owners.

In 1821, Florida was purchased from King Ferdinand of Spain. This action placed all of the acquired land in the public domain, except for the few Spanish private land grants scattered over the area. Title to most of the land in Florida can be traced back to patents signed by various Presidents transferring the land to private ownership. Once in the hands of private owners, title has been and continues to be customarily conveyed by a legal instrument, normally a deed. Property may also be conveyed by a will when the landowner dies. While a will is legally an effective conveyance of title, an executor's deed will usually be used to formalize and record the transfer of ownership rights.

Many authorities refer to a voluntary transfer of title from one private party to another private party as a "private grant," whether by deed, will, or any other legal instrument. A transfer of title from any level of government to a private party is called a "public grant," whether by patent, deed, or other conveyance.

Deeds

The FREC HANDBOOK defines a deed as a "written instrument, under 13.01
seal and witnessed, which conveys title to land and which de- 13.17
clares or creates legal rights or obligations." While true, this definition is much like the iceberg -- a great deal remains unseen when first encountered.

Actually, a deed is a type of conveyance which transfers title to real property. In fact, title to real property does not usually pass from seller to buyer until a properly executed deed is delivered to, and accepted by, the new owner.

There are two parties to a deed: the grantor (owner giving 13.22
title) and the grantee (new owner receiving title). The deed must be signed by the grantor and witnessed by two people in order to be valid. The grantee does not sign the deed.

Essential Elements of a Deed

The format of a deed may differ since the wording is immaterial, as long as the intent to convey title is clearly expressed. Certain elements must be present in a deed in order to spell out clearly the necessary intent and the property to which it applies. The essential elements of a deed are:

1. Names of grantor and grantee
2. Consideration
3. Granting and other appropriate clauses
4. Interest or estate being conveyed
5. Description of property
6. Execution and two witnesses
7. Delivery and acceptance

In order to remember the seven essentials, use of the word "CEDDING" (a corruption of "ceding") is helpful as a memory device by rearranging the essentials of a deed as follows:

Consideration
Execution and two witnesses
Description of property
Delivery and acceptance
Interest or estate being conveyed
Names of grantor and grantee
Granting and other appropriate clauses

Statutory Deeds

Research reveals that more than a dozen different types of deeds are used under different circumstances and conditions. Eight different types may be listed under the general category called "non-statutory deeds." However, the first concern is with four types of statutory deeds: (1) bargain-and-sale deed; (2) general warranty deed; (3) special warranty deed; and, (4) the quit-claim deed. These deeds are called "statutory deeds" because the law sets forth a short form of deed in which the covenants or warranties mentioned in the short form are implied to exist just as if each were written out in complete and detailed form. Later in this chapter, deeds for specific purposes will be discussed.

Before detailing the various types of deeds, it is well to exam- 13.18
ine six clauses usually contained in deeds which add to, or detract from, the estate being transferred by the deed. Then it will be easier to understand the differences between the four types of deeds most commonly used.

Clauses in Deeds

1. The granting or premises clause is really the only necessary clause in a deed. It names the parties to the deed, legally describes the property being conveyed, and contains the necessary words used to convey the property, "grants, bargains, and sells." Usually, this clause will also show that some consideration was given, but the entire amount of consideration is not required to be shown.

2. The tenendum clause may be found in a deed, though it is not required. This clause is used to specify those improvements or other rights which are being transferred in addition to the land itself. The tenendum clause usually begins with the words "together with" and then follows with a recitation of rights or improvements.

3. The habendum clause is one of the most important clauses in a deed because it specifies the type of estate or interest being transferred (fee simple, life estate, etc.). The habendum clause starts with the words "to have and to hold," then usually the word "forever" will follow if the estate is fee simple.

4. The reddendum clause, also called the "reserving clause," is used to reserve some right or restriction for the grantor. It is not used to reserve land, however, since the legal description will restrict the land to be conveyed. Deed restrictions, if appropriate, usually are found in this clause.

5. The seizen clause is usually expressed as, "that the said grantor is seized of the said premises and has good right to convey same." By this covenant, a promise is given that the grantor owns the property, is in possession of it, and has a complete right to dispose of it.

6. The encumbrance clause may be used and if it is included, is used primarily to provide a covenant that the grantor has not encumbered the title in any manner, except as stipulated in the deed. This covenant makes the grantor responsible for any encumbrances not stipulated in the deed. It is required in fiduciary deeds such as administrator's deed, guardian's deed, or committee's deed.

It must be remembered that any or all of the covenants discussed above cannot, and do not, guarantee a marketable title. The covenants are only as good as the grantor. If the grantor is insolvent or unreliable, the covenants are of little or no value.

Types of Deeds

Knowing the roles of the various covenant clauses will now assist in seeing how they increase or decrease the rights conveyed by a deed.

1. Bargain-and-Sale Deed. Perhaps the most commonly used deed 13.18
for routine title transfers is some form of the bargain-and-sale deed. If a bargain-and-sale deed should be written to include all possible covenants and warranties, the name would be changed to a "full covenant and warranty deed." With less than the full number of covenants, it is referred to as a "bargain-and-sale deed." This is the deed familiar to most people in which the grantor "grants, bargains, and sells the property to the grantee, to have and to hold the same, and to his heirs, in fee simple forever." Normally, this form of deed will consist of three covenant clauses: the granting clause, the habendum clause, and the seizen clause. Sometimes, it will include the reddendum clause, or some other clause, to spell out completely the exact estate and title being transferred. However, in the bargain-and-sale deed, the grantor does not covenant or warrant to defend the title against any future claims or attacks on the title. The bargain-and-sale deed is sufficient to convey all the title which the grantor may have, which is what a deed is designed to do.

2. General Warranty Deed. Sometimes the general warranty deed is 13.19
called the "full covenant and warranty deed." Regardless of the name applied, the general warranty deed contains all the

covenants and warranties available to give the grantee every possible future guarantee to title protection. In addition to the covenants and warranties expressed in the bargain-and-sale deed, the general warranty deed contains: a covenant assuring the grantee of "quiet enjoyment" of the property; a covenant of "further assurance," which guarantees that the grantor will obtain and deliver any legal instrument which might be required to make the title good in the future; and, a covenant of "warranty forever," which guarantees that the grantor will forever be responsible for warranting the title to the property. This covenant is an absolute guarantee, insofar as the grantor is able to guarantee, that the grantor will defend the title and possession of said property for the grantee.

The additional warranties cited above are the reason for changing the designation of this conveyance from a bargain-and-sale deed to a general warranty deed.

3. Special Warranty Deed. Another type of bargain-and-sale deed 13.20
with a different name is the "special warranty deed." This designation is intended to denote a deed in which the grantor does not warrant the title in any way or manner except against acts by himself or others claiming by, through, or under him. In other words, the grantor assumes no responsibility for the title to a property except to warrant that he or his representatives have done nothing to encumber or cloud the title. This is the type of deed normally used for conveying a tax title and is, therefore, often called a "tax deed."

4. Quit-Claim Deed. This form of deed is useful for clearing 13.21
existing or potential "clouds on the title," i.e., some vague, though possibly legitimate, claim(s) upon the property. In order to clear the title of these possible trouble spots, it is desirable to have the individuals concerned release any claim or interest they may have in the property. In such cases, it would be improper for them to sign a bargain-and-sale or warranty deed because they cannot warrant that they have any positive title or possession. In cases of this nature, a "quit-claim deed" is used. Instead of the usual wording "grants, bargains, and sells," the quit-claim deed uses the words "remise, release, and quit claim." This allows the grantor to sign a deed transferring any and all interests he may have, without claiming that he does actually own any right of title whatsoever. The grantor does not warrant that he will defend the title or interest conveyed by him, nor does he claim to be transferring a valid interest. If the grantor later obtains a good title to the property, he will retain the good title because it was obtained after the quit-claim deed.

Special Purpose Deeds

Frequently, a situation will arise which creates a legal problem in conveying property from one owner to another. For example, the prior discussions have assumed that an owner was able, or willing, to sign a deed. But suppose ownership must be transferred to a grantee and the grantor will not sign the deed -- for example, after a mortgage foreclosure, or sale of property due to nonpayment of taxes. Several different types of deeds have evolved over time in order to provide solutions for these and other problems. For those instances where the legal owner, or grantor, cannot sign a deed, one of the following deeds may be used:

Personal Representative's (Executor's) Deed. An executor is appointed in a will to dispose of an estate after an owner (testator) has died. The executor operates under the direction of the court where the will was probated. As a person in temporary control of the estate of a decedent, an executor is in a fiduciary capacity. For this reason, the deed should show the full consideration paid for the property and contain an encumbrance clause which is a covenant against the grantor's acts. c

Personal Representative's (Administrator's) Deed. If an owner of an estate should die without leaving a will, he has died "intestate," and there cannot be an executor or executrix. In such a situation, the court having jurisdiction will appoint an administrator as a representative of the court to settle the decedent's affairs. An administrator is also a fiduciary, and the requirements for full disclosure of consideration and covenant against grantor's acts apply. c

Personal Representative's (Guardian's) Deed. A guardian is the personal representative of a ward and is also a fiduciary who must observe the requirements for fiduciary disclosure. Normally, the permission of a court is required for a guardian to sell or convey property belonging to his ward. When authorized by the courts, a guardian's deed will legally convey the ward's property. c

Committee's Deed. One of the essentials of a valid deed is a competent grantor. In case an owner is declared legally incompetent, or is committed to an asylum, a committee is often appointed by the court to administer the affairs of the incompetent. The committee will function under the direction of the court in conveying or disposing of the incompetent's estate. All members of a committee are required to sign the deed. A committee also must adhere to fiduciary disclosure requirements.

In those cases where the grantor refuses to sign a deed, the following deeds are frequently used:

Referee's Deed in Foreclosure. All foreclosures on real property in Florida must follow prescribed legal procedures which eventually lead to a public auction of the property. The judgment given to the lender which authorizes sale of the property will usually require that the sale be under the direction of a referee who acts as a representative of the court. It is not uncommon, however, for the court to direct that the county sheriff conduct the auction sale, and deeds given as a result are called sheriff's deeds. Where a court-appointed referee conducts the sale, the deed is a referee's deed. Although neither the sheriff nor the referee are fiduciaries, the deed given as a result of foreclosure must show the full purchase price bid by the grantee and the liens or encumbrances against the property. No covenants are given, and the buyer assumes all risks for title defects.

Referee's Deed in Partition. This deed is used to divide the real property and assets of a business or partnership. From time to time, partners will decide they do not want to continue in business as a partnership, but they cannot agree on the manner in which the assets of the firm should be divided. When this happens, the most common solution is to petition the courts to "partition" the real property and assets equitably. The assets of the firm are then sold and the proceeds divided according to the judgment of the court. Real property transferred as a result of this action is conveyed by a referee's deed in partition. It follows the same form as other referee deeds and contains no covenants, but it will show all known encumbrances and liens on the property.

Legal Requirements

If a sales contract does not specify the type of deed to be given by the seller, Florida law requires that the property be conveyed by a general warranty deed. The deed must be signed in the presence of two witnesses, and the witnesses must place their signatures on the deed as testimony that they did witness the grantor's signature.

As mentioned earlier, a deed is one form of conveyance. Technically, a conveyance is any written instrument legally sufficient to transfer some estate or interest in real property. All conveyances must be signed by the seller (grantor) and witnessed by two people. No conveyance will be effective in transferring title to property until delivered to, and accepted by, the purchaser (grantee). 13.01

While one is not legally required to record a deed in the public records, a very good case might be made for such a requirement. Placing a deed on record with the Clerk of the Circuit Court gives the world notice of true and current ownership of the property. In order to be recorded in public records, the deed, like all other instruments, must be acknowledged. 13.22

Tax Stamps on Deeds

The law requires that the seller deliver a deed which can be recorded, and no deed may be recorded until the proper State tax stamps have been physically placed on the deed. Therefore, unless the buyer agrees to pay for the taxes on a deed, tax stamps remain the seller's responsibility. In Florida, all deeds to real property are subject to two State taxes: 15.03 15.04

1. State documentary stamp tax on deeds
2. State documentary surtax on deeds

State Documentary Stamp Tax on Deeds. This tax is levied against the entire purchase price paid for real property. It is calculated at the rate of 30 cents tax due for each $100 in the purchase price. If a tract should sell for $1,000, the first step in determining the State documentary stamp tax due would be to find the number of $100 increments contained in the $1,000 purchase price ($1,000 ÷ $100 = 10 increments). To learn the amount of tax due the State for this tax only, multiply $.30 x 10 to find the tax due: $3.00. If any portion or fraction of $100 should remain after dividing $100 into the purchase price, a full $.30 tax is charged for the fractional part regardless of amount. For example, if the purchase price in the illustration above had been $1,050, the State documentary stamp tax would be increased by $.30 ($3.30) because of the $50 more than an even increment of $100.

State Documentary Surtax on Deeds. This tax is levied only against that portion of the purchase price which is "new money," meaning all of the purchase price minus the amount of existing mortgages. For example, if a house sells for $43,500 and has a $20,000 existing first mortgage which is to be assumed as part of the transaction, the taxable new money is $23,500 ($43,500 - $20,000 = $23,500). The State surtax is calculated on the basis of $.55 for each $500, or fractional portion, of new money. In the example, find the number of $500 increments in the new money ($23,500 ÷ 500 = 47 increments). Multiply $.55 x 47 increments to find the amount of State surtax ($.55 x 47 = $25.85). So the State surtax due before the deed may be recorded is $25.85.

To determine the total amount of State taxes due on this particular sale, also calculate the State documentary stamp tax:

$43,500 ÷ $100 = 435 increments

$.30 x 435 = $130.50 State documentary stamp tax on deed
+ 25.85 State documentary stamp surtax on deed
$156.35 Total tax stamps on deed

Note: The two taxes discussed above must be paid for every real estate transaction when a valuable consideration is involved. Since all licensed practitioners of real estate must explain to owners of properties they sell how the above taxes are determined, students should practice calculating each of these taxes until they cause no concern, regardless of amounts involved. Where property owned by two or more persons is to be divided with no difference in value involved, or where the only consideration is love and affection, the minimum tax allowable is $.30 for State documentary stamp tax and $.55 for State documentary surtax.

Private Restrictions on Ownership

In the category of private limitations on ownership of property are usually included: (1) deed restrictions; (2) easements; (3) leases; and (4) liens.

1. Deed Restrictions. Probably the most common and the broadest restrictions to ownership in the private category are deed restrictions. Deed restrictions are a part of the deed or are attached to the deed and limit, by covenant, the use of the property which is described in the deed. The limitation may be either perpetual or for a specified period of time. While the covenant is in effect, it restricts the use of the property not only for the first owner but also for all subsequent owners. Any restriction may be included in a deed which does not discriminate against race, color, religion, sex, national origin, or against public policy.

2. Easements. An easement is a right given or belonging to
another for some specific use of an owner's property. Easements
are considered an interest in real property. They may be created
by contract, by mention in a deed, by express or implied grant,
by prescription, or by necessity. When an easement is to "run
with the land," that is, continue indefinitely through owner
after owner, it should be in writing and recorded in the public
records. When the use of property for certain purposes, such as
pathways or roadways, has continued openly and without interrup-
tion for more than twenty years, an easement by prescription is c
considered to have been created and must be recognized. On the
other hand, if an easement right is not used, the right will be
considered to have been abandoned and extinguished.

3. Leases. A lease constitutes an interest in real property, but 14.01
does not convey ownership. A lease is an agreement between the 14.02
landlord (lessor) and another (lessee) which grants the right of 14.06
possession and use of the property for a specified time and for 14.09
an agreed amount of compensation. Therefore, a lease creates a 14.10
"tenancy for years" because its duration does not depend on
measurement by a natural life period. A tenancy for years may be
for a few days or for more years than a normal lifetime. Florida
law requires that a lease for a period of more than one year be
in writing in order to be enforceable. Any verbal contract or
agreement between the lessor and lessee for a period of more than
one year is legally nothing more than a "tenancy at will." In
fact, all verbal leases and all written leases which do not fix a
definite date for termination are tenancies at will. Leases are
not measured by the lifetime of the parties involved, but rather
by the period of time between the starting date and the ending
date of the contract. If the owner of the property should die 14.03
during the lease period, his heirs are required to honor the
lease. The same is true of a new owner who might buy or other-
wise acquire the property, that is, existing leases must be
recognized and honored. If a lease is given on mortgaged prop-
erty, then the mortgage is superior to the lease. However, if a
mortgage is given after the lease has been signed, the lease
would have to be honored if the lease had been recorded.

Assignment and Sublease. The rights of a tenant (lessee) are 14.01
assignable unless a specific prohibition is contained in the text 14.07
of the lease to the contrary. If a lessee assigns to another all
of the leased property for the full remaining portion of the
lease, such action is called "assignment" of lease. If the
lessee assigns less than the entire property, or assigns all the
property for less than the full remaining period of time, such
action is called a "sublease." Both the assignment and the sub-
lease are considered a personal interest in real property just as
the lease is. Any leasehold, by definition, is a personal
interest in real property held under a lease arrangement for a
definite number of years.

The estate created by a lease expires at the end of the lease 14.03
period. The estate then reverts back to the landlord or his 14.09
representatives. As a result of the requirement for leases of
more than one year's duration to be in writing, should the

landlord attempt to conclude an oral lease for a period of more 100
than a year, the law will only recognize a tenancy at will in such a case.

With only a limited discussion of leases and leaseholds herein, it 14.06
should be kept in mind that leases are often complicated and involved agreements. For this reason, leases should always be prepared by an attorney experienced in their preparation. Two witnesses should sign the lease as verification of its proper execution. While a lease does not convey title to property, it does convey an interest representing specific rights to the property. To show the tenant's rights to the property, the tenant could give constructive notice to the world by first having the lease acknowledged and then recording the instrument in the public records.

4. Liens. A lien is a right given by law to a creditor, or a 13.23
unit of government, to have a debt or charge satisfied out of 14.14
some specific property belonging to a debtor. Lien laws have been enacted by every state in the nation and are enforceable in some form even when possession, control, or title remains with the debtor. Liens can entitle the holder of the lien (lienor) to have property sold, regardless of the desires of the owner (lienee). A lien creates a relationship between the creditor and debtor, and even though the relationship may have been voluntary, the satisfaction of a lien is completely outside the realm of the debtor's willingness. As a debtor, the property owner has no choice but to pay the lienor or have his property disposed of by the courts in order to satisfy the lien. All liens are, therefore, encumbrances on a property; however, not all encumbrances on property are liens. Encumbrances can also be easements, covenants, deed restrictions, and governmental regulations.

Major Classifications of Liens

Legally, liens may be considered to be divided into two major 13.23
classifications: "general liens" and "specific liens." Each of these classifications includes several different types of liens: general liens consist of four types and specific liens consist of seven different types. Representative types from both classifications are also regarded as "superior liens," i.e., they have precedence and priority over all other types of liens. An examination of each classification and type follows in order to clarify purpose.

General Liens. A general lien is not restricted to one property but may affect all the properties of a debtor. The four types of liens which are included in this classification are:

1. Judgment Liens. A decree of a court awarded as a result of a suit may be a judgment lien. It usually stipulates that one party owes another party for money or labor and when properly placed in the judgment docket register becomes a general lien on all property of the debtor not specifically exempt by law. It is important to examine the county clerk's judgment docket when searching to determine if any liens exist against a property. A judgment takes effect when filed with the Clerk of the Circuit Court and may result in the sale of any non-exempt property of

the debtor which is found.

2. Decedent's Debts. Title to the real property of a decedent is subject to any liens which existed at the time of the decedent's death. In addition, most just debts against the estate are considered a lien on the property. All liens and just debts are first paid from the personal property in a decedent's estate. If there is not enough personal property to satisfy the liens and debts, then the decedent's real property may be sold to liquidate all debts (unless specifically protected by law). Therefore, it is important to obtain proof that all claims against a decedent's estate have been paid before buying or acquiring title to property owned by a recently deceased individual.

3. Inheritance Tax Liens. Although Florida does not have an 13.23
inheritance tax, the federal inheritance tax (also called "estate 15.13
tax") becomes a lien on both real and personal property at the time of death of the owner. The tax is applied upon the entire net estate of the decedent and not against individual shares. The tax rate is progressive as the worth of the estate increases, and the lien created by the tax applies to all property for a period of ten years or until satisfied.

4. Corporation Franchise Tax Liens. A corporation franchise tax is levied on corporations in return for their right to do business in a state. When applied, the tax becomes a general lien on all property of a corporation and may be enforced by seizure and sale.

Specific Liens. Liens in the specific classification do not affect all property of a debtor but apply only to a certain specified property. Seven liens included in this classification are:

1. Mortgage Lien: This is a lien voluntarily placed on real 13.24
property by a borrower (mortgagor) who pledges his property as 13.26
security to the party he borrows from (mortgagee). The date 15.09
the mortgage is filed and recorded with the Clerk of the Circuit 15.11
Court establishes the priority of the lien against other claims on the property. In the event of default by the mortgagor, the mortgagee can proceed to force sale of the property in order to satisfy the debt.

2. Property Tax, Special Assessment, and Municipal Utility Liens. 13.23
Municipal governments have been delegated the authority to levy real estate taxes, special tax assessments, and where utilities are owned by the municipality, the authority to determine and levy charges. Unlike other debts and liens, taxes and special assessments become liens as soon as the assessment is complete. In Florida, property tax liens are filed against all taxable real property each year. For tax purposes, real property is assessed on January 1 each year, and the property taxes become a lien on the property on that same date although the property owner will not receive his tax bill for some months after January 1. All real estate taxes are due and payable on November 1 following the January assessment each year. Taxes become delinquent if not paid by April 1 of the year following. Therefore, real estate taxes are paid "in arrears" because they are assessed in January and normally not paid until the end of the year or the first

portion of the following year.

Special assessments are levied against property to pay for all, or part of, an improvement which will benefit the property being assessed. The courts have ruled that special assessments may be levied only against properties which are benefited by increased value to the properties. Special assessment liens on properties for improvements which are not entirely completed are called "pending special assessment liens." Where an improvement has been completed they are called "certified special assessment liens." All assessments become liens as soon as they are definitely known and fixed. Special assessment liens are ahead of private liens in priority and second only to real property tax liens.

Where utilities such as electricity or water are provided by municipalities with taxing authority, the charges for such utilities become liens when they are entered in the accounts of the municipal agency. If not paid after a specified period, the municipality may proceed to enforce the lien just as if it were a special assessment lien.

3. Mechanic's Lien. This lien is based on that principle of law 13.24
called "unjust enrichment." This theory holds that a property owner may not use the labor or material of another party to add value to the owner's own property without reimbursement to the other party. A mechanic's lien (or materialman's, or laborer's lien) is a statutory right of a laborer or a material supplier to place a lien on property which has been improved by their labor and/or supplies. A mechanic's lien must be filed with the Clerk of the Circuit Court not later than 90 days after the last labor is performed or last supplies are delivered in order to assume priority over any mortgage liens created after the first work/material appeared on the property affected. This, in effect, allows a mechanic's lien filed after work is completed to become retroactive to the first day of work or first delivery of material. If a mortgage is placed on the property during the period when construction is in progress, the mechanic's lien filed after construction is completed will go back and precede the mortgage in priority. Once filed, a mechanic's lien is effective for one year. The party which places the lien on the property must foreclose during the year's lifetime of the mechanic's lien or forfeit his privilege. A mechanic's lien may be discharged or cancelled by: (1) expiration of time as mentioned above; (2) payment of the debt; or, (3) by court action through a suit.

4. Vendee's Lien. The buyer of a property is called the "vendee" and the seller is referred to as the "vendor." If a vendor defaults on a contract for sale, the earnest money deposit made by the vendee creates a lien on the property. Such a lien also includes any money spent by the vendee to improve the property. A vendee's lien is enforceable by foreclosure.

5. Vendor's Lien. If a buyer of property (vendee) is unable to 13.25
make the full down payment required, a seller (vendor) will frequently allow a purchase money mortgage to make up the amount

of money the buyer is unable to produce. The purchase money mortgage creates what is commonly called a "vendor's lien." Actually, any portion of the sales price remaining unpaid to the vendor creates a vendor's lien for the amount of the unpaid balance on the property, even in those instances where a formal, written agreement has not been concluded between the buyer and the seller. A vendor's lien is only enforceable against the party obtaining title from the vendor and will not apply against later purchasers unless a written mortgage has been executed and placed in the public records. Since a vendor's lien is a type of mortgage, it is enforceable by foreclosure.

6. Income Tax and State Intangible Tax Liens. Florida does not 13.23
presently have a state income tax; however, failure to pay 15.05
federal income taxes can result in a lien on property anywhere in 15.06
the nation. An income tax lien is effective from the date filed 15.13
and recorded with the Clerk of the Circuit Court. Both income tax liens and State intangible tax liens are created by legislation and are, therefore, involuntary liens, that is, involuntary as far as the owner is concerned, and they both can apply to any property owned.

7. Attachment. An attachment is a statutory privilege given by the courts to a party in a suit for money damages. When awarded, it can become a lien on real property pending a judgment by the court. By filing an attachment, the plaintiff in the suit can assure that the property owner will not dispose of the property until a judgment is obtained, and he thereby ensures that there will be some property which can be converted to cash if his suit is successful. In order to prevent indiscriminate use of this privilege and to protect the rights of a defendant, anyone attempting to obtain a "writ of attachment" must first file a written bond that if the defendant wins, the plaintiff will pay all costs plus any damages the defendant suffers as a result of the attachment.

- - - - -

One final note on deeds, conveyances, and private restrictions is 13.39
in order. Remember that a broker, or salesman, is allowed by Florida statutes to draw listing, sales, and option contracts, but not deeds, unless conveying property in which he owns an interest. The drawing of a deed may be construed as practicing law.

DEEDS and PRIVATE RESTRICTIONS

1. A "private grant" is a:
   a. Transfer of title from one person to another
   b. Confidential transfer of title to land
   c. Transfer of land from the government to a private person
   d. Transfer of land from a private person to the government

2. Following a legal foreclosure auction sale of a farm, the foreclosed owner refused to sign a deed. The property can legally be conveyed by:
   a. An administrator's deed
   b. An executor's deed
   c. A referee's deed
   d. A committee's deed

3. You sold your house for $44,550. The buyer paid $14,550 cash and assumed your mortgage of $30,000. What will the cost be of your State documentary c
   stamps for the deed ("doc stamps")?
   a. $133.80
   b. $133.50
   c. $90.00
   d. $33.00

4. Title to real property legally transfers from grantor to grantee when:
   a. The deed is signed
   b. The deed is recorded
   c. The deed is delivered and accepted
   d. The proper amount of stamps are placed on the deed

5. Courts at various levels have ruled that:
   a. Constructive notice is superior to actual notice
   b. Actual notice is superior to constructive notice
   c. Neither constructive notice nor actual notice is required
   d. Constructive notice and actual notice have equal legal priority

6. In order for a deed to be valid, the:
   a. Grantor, grantee and two witnesses must sign the instrument
   b. Grantor and two witnesses must sign the instrument
   c. Grantee and two witnesses must sign the instrument
   d. Grantee only must sign the instrument

7. The type or form of deed used to clear clouds on the title of real property is the:
   a. General warranty deed
   b. Special warranty deed
   c. Bargain-and-sale deed
   d. Quit-claim deed

8. If the sales contract does not specify the type of deed to be delivered, the seller is required to provide a:
   a. General warranty deed
   b. Special warranty deed
   c. Bargain-and-sale deed
   d. Quit-claim deed

9. The type of deed in which the grantor does not warrant the title in any manner, except against his acts or the acts of his representatives, is called a:
   a. General warranty deed
   b. Special warranty deed
   c. Bargain-and-sale deed
   d. Quit-claim deed

10. The encumbrance clause in a deed is designed to show:
   a. The grantor has not encumbered the property in any manner except as noted on the deed
   b. The grantee is responsible for any unpaid encumbrances
   c. The grantee has not encumbered the property
   d. The grantor will not encumber the property

11. The habendum clause in a deed specifies:
   a. The type of estate being conveyed have & to hold
   b. The improvements being transferred with the land
   c. The rights reserved by the grantor
   d. That the grantor actually owns the property and has the right to sell it

12. The tenendum clause in a deed specifies:
   a. The type of estate being conveyed
   b. The improvements being transferred with the land
   c. The rights reserved by the grantor
   d. That the grantor actually owns the property and has the right to sell it

13. The seizen clause in a deed specifies:
   a. The type of estate being conveyed
   b. The improvements being transferred with the land
   c. The rights reserved by the grantor
   d. That the grantor actually owns the property and has the right to sell it

14. The covenant in a general warranty deed, which is considered an absolute guarantee that the grantor will defend the title to property, is the:
   a. Covenant of quiet enjoyment
   b. Covenant of further assurance
   c. Covenant of seizen
   d. Covenant of warranty forever

15. The clause in a deed which names the parties and describes the land to be conveyed is the:
   a. Granting clause
   b. Tenendum clause
   c. Habendum clause
   d. Seizen clause

16. What private restrictions are probably the most common and the broadest restrictions to ownership of real property?
   a. Liens
   b. Deed restrictions
   c. Easements
   d. Mortgages

17. An easement by prescription is created by:
    a. Mention in a deed
    b. Express or implied grant
    c. Contractual agreement
    d. Open and uninterrupted use

18. Any verbal contract or agreement between a lessor and lessee for a period of 18 months is a:
    a. Lease
    b. Tenancy at sufferance
    c. Tenancy at will
    d. Tenancy for years

19. An example of an encumbrance on title to real property would be:
    a. An easement
    b. A covenant
    c. A lien
    d. All of the above

20. In Florida, real property is assessed on January 1 of each year and becomes a lien on the property on:
    a. November 1, the same year
    b. April 1, the next year
    c. January 1, the same year
    d. December 31, the same year

21. Special assessment liens are ranked in priority:
    a. Ahead of mortgage liens
    b. Behind property tax liens
    c. Both of the above
    d. Neither of the above

22. A vendor's lien:
    a. Is automatically created by a purchase money mortgage
    b. Must be in writing to be enforceable
    c. Is a general lien
    d. All of the above

CHAPTER 7

CONTRACTS

A contract is an agreement. However, all agreements are not 11.02
contracts. A simple, practical, and technically correct defi- 11.09
nition of a contract is: "A deliberate agreement between two or more competent parties to do, or abstain from doing, some legal act for an adequate consideration."

Preparation of Contracts

The preparation of legal documents or instruments for other 5.05
people is regarded as practicing law. Since only a few real 13.39
estate brokers or salesmen are qualified attorneys, it is extremely important that brokers and salesmen do not prepare deeds, mortgages, promissory notes, or other legal documents. While contracts are also legal documents, three types of contracts are not included in the category of prohibited actions because the broker or salesman is a party to the document. Those three types of contracts are the listing, option, and sales contracts. While each will be explained in detail later in this chapter, a brief sentence about each one is appropriate.

The listing contract is a broker's employment contract and, indirectly, the salesman's authorization to operate. An option
contract is usually prepared when the broker is one of the con- c
tracting parties. The sales contract, or deposit receipt contract, is normally concluded with the broker or salesperson acting as agent for one of the parties. All real estate practitioners would do well to remember that preparation of additional legal instruments for others, such as leases, deeds, notes, or mortgages, may jeopardize their registration, regardless of whether they are to receive compensation.

Statute of Frauds

The absence of a written contract is only significant in special 11.17
cases where the law requires the agreement to be in writing. 14.09
Contracts pertaining to real estate are among the special cases which are required to be in writing. This requirement stems from the statute of frauds, the substance of which has been enacted into the laws of each state in the United States. The original statute of frauds was adopted to prevent disputes and injustices by requiring that transfer of real property could not be enforced unless an agreement for such transfer was in writing and signed. Prior to the adoption of the statute of frauds, the title to real property was transferred by delivery of possession. Since no written records were kept, it was not uncommon to discover that false statements and bought witnesses had permitted gross frauds. As a result, laws now usually specify that contracts involving the transfer of real property must be in writing to be valid, except for two specific instances. The first exception is when an oral contract has been concluded and the buyer has not only paid a part of the purchase price but has also entered into possession of the property. The second exception is similar in that an oral contract is valid and enforceable when the buyer has paid part of the purchase price and has also made substantial

improvements to the property.

Essentials of a Contract

Contracts in general must contain four essential elements of an 11.03
agreement to be "valid" (legally enforceable in court). Contracts involving the transfer of real property must, in addition to the four essentials, be in writing and signed. Therefore, most authorities agree that a valid real estate contract has five
essentials. If the real property is homestead property, the 12.27
Florida Constitution requires two parties to witness the seller's signature. However, the normal essential elements of a real estate contract are:

1. Competent parties
2. Offer and acceptance
3. Legality of object
4. In writing and signed
5. Consideration

The five essentials have been listed in the above order in an effort to provide a "memory crutch" (mnemonic device) designed to help in retaining the essentials of a valid contract. Note that the first letter of each essential element when combined forms the vertical word "COLIC." Each of these essentials will be discussed briefly.

1. Competent Parties. What is meant by this term is two or more 11.03
parties having the capacity to contract. Competence is related 11.14
to all parties meeting on the same mental plane (no mental defects or insanity in either instance), and also meeting on the same legal plane (both of legal age to contract). A sane man contracting with an insane person would clearly produce an invalid contract, just as an adult contracting with a minor would produce the same result.

2. Offer and Acceptance. This essential is sometimes referred to 11.03
as "arriving at a meeting of the minds." This implies that one 11.10
party offers to give possession and title, and the other party 11.12
accepts that offer and in turn offers to pay a specified price 11.15
in accordance with designated terms. A complete and mutual understanding must exist in order to produce a meeting of the minds.

3. Legality of Object. To be enforceable, a contract must have a 11.03
purpose which is not prohibited by law or contrary to public 11.16
policy.

4. In Writing and Signed. This is intended to prevent fraudulent 11.17
proof of a fictitious oral agreement which could strip an owner 12.27
of his property. A contract for sale of real property is required by law to be in writing and signed by all parties who are to be bound by the agreement. It can be written on any substance and may be in any language which can be translated into English.

5. Consideration. Each party to the contract must obligate him- 11.03
self by placing some consideration in the agreement. An action 11.13
by one party to the contract must be supported by an undertaking 12.30
of the other party. In real property contracts, the seller normally obligates himself to sell and convey, and the purchaser

obligates himself to pay a certain amount for the property. Most people commonly think of "consideration" as money; however, technically there are three types of consideration: valuable, good, and illegal. "Valuable consideration" is money or something which can be converted into money. "Good consideration" may be love and affection. "Illegal consideration" is, of course, anything which the law prohibits and which would serve to invalidate the contract. Only valuable consideration is regarded as sufficient to enforce a contract, although good consideration is sufficient for a deed or an executed contract.

A contract does not have to be in any particular format in order 11.09
to be valid. As long as the agreement contains the essential elements of a contract, it is enforceable under the law. A contract is an instrument designed to spell out clearly the meeting of the minds between parties on a particular subject, and it thereby creates certain enforceable rights. It is also designed to provide a remedy for the affected parties if the contract should be breached.

Contract Categories

Contracts can, and do, cover the entire spectrum of complexity 11.09
ranging from a simple purchase in an automatic vending machine to the negotiation of an international treaty. Only the two major categories of contracts will be examined here: the formal contract and the parol contract. The various classifications of contracts in the two major categories will also be studied.

1. Formal contract. A formal contract is one which is in writing 11.04
and under "seal." Frequently, the formal contract is referred to as a "special" or "specialty" contract. The "seal," as used today, has evolved from the old wax impression on a document to the word "seal" or the letters "L.S." (Locus Sigille) which appear after the signature of parties signing the contract. The seal is not necessary to make the instrument valid or legal. It does have some legal effect, however, in that use of the seal extends the statute of limitations (or period of enforcement) to twenty years (20 years), and it implies that a consideration has been given.

2. Parol contract. A parol contract is a contract which is not c 11.05
in writing. A parol contract was formerly any oral or written contract which was not under seal (often previously referred to as a "simple contract"). A parol contract may be entirely oral or it may be partially oral and partially implied by the actions of the parties involved. Remember that some oral contracts dealing with subject matter other than real property are recognized by law as enforceable.

Contract Classifications

With an idea of the two major categories of contracts in mind, it is appropriate to examine the various reasons for classifying contracts. The very name of the classification into which a contract falls is often indicative of the state of performance or the way in which the contract was arranged, or even the parties bound by the contract. It is not unusual for a contract to change from one classification to another as the degree or state of performance progresses. Concern here will be with the following six classifications of contracts:

1. Bilateral contract: any contract which obligates both parties to perform in accordance with the terms of the contract. A sales contract is an example of a bilateral contract in that both the seller and the buyer are bound to perform. 11.08

2. Executed contract: when all parties to a contract have completely performed all obligations and promises contained in the contract. For instance, a sales contract for transfer of property becomes an executed contract after the closing and all promises of both buyer and seller have been fulfilled. 11.07

3. Executory contract: when a contract has been concluded between parties, but something remains to be done by one or both parties in order to fulfill the conditions of the contract. It is not yet a performed contract. A real estate sales contract, between the time of signing the contract and the time of closing the transaction, is an executory contract. 11.07

4. Expressed contract: when all the terms and conditions have been expressed and a meeting of the minds is reached in words of agreement and understanding. An expressed contract may be either formal or parol, that is, it may be in writing or verbal or a combination of the two. The primary requirement is mutual understanding and agreement. 11.06

5. Implied contract: (This classification is sometimes called a "quasi-contract.") Some of the obligations or conditions of a contract are not expressly stated but may be reasonably implied by the acts of the parties or by the nature of the transaction. For example, if a broker identified himself as a real estate broker to an owner of a property and stated that he had a buyer for the property at a good price with the usual commission rate, the law would require the owner to pay a commission even if he had remained silent but accepts the sale of the property by the broker. 11.06 12.04 12.12 c

6. Unilateral contract: obligates only one party to an agreement without any obligation on the other party involved. An example of a unilateral contract is the ordinary option. If the man asking for an option (the optionee) pays a consideration to the person granting the option (the optionor), then the optionor is obligated not to sell to anyone but the optionee during the life of the option, while the optionee is not bound to perform anything whatsoever. If the optionee chooses to exercise the option, then he may do so because the optionor is bound to honor his desires. The contract is therefore unilateral unless the optionee decides to exercise his option and so notifies the optionor. At that point, the unilateral contract becomes a bilateral contract because the optionee has promised to exercise the option. A listing contract which obligates a seller to pay a broker a commission could also be a unilateral contract because the broker is not obligated, nor has he promised, to sell the property. 11.08 12.02

Offer and Counteroffer

In the normal course of concluding a contract, one party must
begin the sequence of events by making an offer. The person who 11.10
makes an offer is called the "offeror." The person (or parties) 11.12
who receives the offer is referred to as the "offeree." Frequently, the offeree will make what is called a "counteroffer" by altering the terms of the original offer made by the offeror. When a counteroffer is made, it actually kills the original offer and substitutes in its place a modified offer. In this manner, the offeree who received the original offer has become the offeror by creating a different set of terms or conditions and offering them back to the original offeror who now becomes the offeree. It is not uncommon for a series of offers and counteroffers to take place before a meeting of the minds is accomplished. However, when a meeting of the minds is reached by one party accepting the offer of the other party, a contract has been concluded and both parties are obligated to perform according to the contract.

It is important for real estate practitioners to remember that an 11.11
offeror is allowed to withdraw his offer at any point in time until acceptance by the offeree is communicated back to the offeror. However, this is not true in those cases where the offeree or his representative has given some type of consideration to the offeror to keep the offer open for a specified period of time.

Ordinarily, when an offer is made, a time limit for acceptance of 11.11
the offer is specified and the offer is terminated after expiration of that time. In the event no time limit for acceptance is specified, the offeree is considered to have a "reasonable length of time" based on such considerations as the method of communication used, location of the parties involved, the terminology and nature of the offer, etc. When time of acceptance and/or time of performance are important, the term "time is of the essence" is included in the contract. When these words are used, and agreed to, the parties to the contract will be held to exactly the times expressed in the contract. Any period of time beyond the specified time can be considered a breach of contract.

Remedies for Breach

FREC ordinarily has no authority or jurisdiction over breach of 11.23
contract actions. Satisfaction is obtained through civil courts. 11.24
There are three common remedies for breach of contract available to all parties who consider themselves wronged:

1. Suit for specific performance. In those instances where 11.24
awards of money damages do not afford sufficient relief, the wronged party may sue to have the courts force the other party to perform as the contract specifically states. This action is technically termed a "relief in equity," referring to the fact that such judgments are enforced in a court of equity. This means that, should the plaintiff prevail, the court will issue a decree ordering the defendant to convey the property or suffer a fine or imprisonment. Where the buyer defaults, property may be sold and the buyer ordered to pay the seller any difference

between the sale price and the contracted amount.

2. A wronged party may also sue for "cancellation." This type of suit is also considered a "relief in equity" and is primarily based on the fact that no real meeting of the minds was accomplished. In this type of action, each party to the contract is to be returned to the same condition and position occupied prior to making the contract. 11.24

3. A third and perhaps more common remedy for breach of contract is a "suit for damages." Usually the party bringing suit will seek an amount of money equal to the extent of loss suffered. A wronged party may find that a certain property was misrepresented to him but decide to accept the property, and in addition, sue for damages. On the other hand, he may decide to refuse the property misrepresented to him and still sue for damages. Damages are classified into two major categories: liquidated damages and unliquidated damages. Liquidated damages are those specified in the contract in case the contract should be breached. Unliquidated damages are those not specified in the contract but requested as a result of the contract having been breached. 11.23 11.24

A new and additional remedy has begun to appear more frequently in recent years, the declaratory judgment. The suit brought to obtain a declaratory judgment is, essentially, asking a court of equity to interpret the words used in a contract for the purpose of establishing the correct meaning. Strangely enough, the two parties to a contract usually seek this remedy when they can agree to the words used in making the contract but disagree as to the meaning of those words. Often a suit of declaratory judgment is a friendly suit, though this is not always the case. 11.25

Termination of Contracts

Six recognized methods for terminating contracts exist. Each can be and has been applied to contracts associated with real estate, specifically listing contracts and sales contracts. Therefore, the discussion will be directed toward termination of contracts between a broker and others. The six ways to terminate a contract are listed in alphabetical order. 11.21

1. Abandonment
2. Breach
3. Lapse of time
4. Performance
5. Renunciation
6. Revocation

1. Abandonment. A contract may be abandoned by either party or by both parties. In a real estate situation, if a broker simply forgets a listing and makes no attempt to sell a listed property, he can be considered to have abandoned the listing contract. Or if a broker refuses to show a listed property to a prospect when he has contracted to effect a sale, the contract will be considered abandoned. 11.21 12.18

2. Breach of Contract. A breach of contract can be caused by either party. A breach on the part of one party gives the other party an election to terminate the contract and file suit for damages. It is important to understand the difference between the "power to breach" and the "right to breach." Either party has the power to breach a contract, as is proved when a breach 11.23 12.21

occurs. However, neither party has the right to breach because if either party has the right to revoke, withdraw, or terminate a contract, then no breach can occur when the right is exercised.

3. Lapse of Time. A contract may be terminated by lapse of time 11.21
whether a definite time limit is specified in the terms of the 12.16
contract. If the contract includes a definite time limit, the promised performance must occur during the specified period, otherwise the parties have not complied with the terms of the contract. If no definite time limit is fixed, the contract expires, in any event, by the passage of a reasonable time. The circumstances of each case dictate what may be considered a "reasonable time." Fluctuation of values in an area due to improvement of other nearby property, discovery of mineral deposits, the known wishes and requirements of an owner, all can materially affect the time period which could be considered reasonable. In the case of a listing contract between an owner and a broker, the contract will be considered to have been extended beyond a specified time limit if the broker continues to sell the property after expiration of the fixed time limit with the knowledge and consent of the owner. However, if the broker continues to try to sell without the consent of the owner and produces a prospect, the owner is under no obligation to deal with the prospect.

4. Performance. When both parties have fully performed the terms 11.07
and conditions of a contract, the purpose of the contract has been accomplished and the contract is terminated. The emphasis in this instance is on full performance of each and every term or condition.

5. Renunciation. Contracts may be renounced, which is an action 11.21
closely akin to abandonment, but held to be a separate method of 12.19
termination. Renunciation is accomplished by the mutual agreement of both parties to abandon the contract. A broker may also renounce a contract by simply notifying the owner of a property that he will no longer continue his efforts to sell a property. Renunciation can be effected by one or both parties but is usually a mutual agreement between both parties.

6. Revocation. Contracts may be revoked by any party legally en- 12.17
titled to revoke. In real estate transactions, an owner may terminate a listing contract by revocation. This is accomplished by notice to the broker of the owner's intentions, or by acts inconsistent with the listing contract (for example, the owner selling to someone not produced by the broker). In the case of an exclusive listing, the owner may revoke the listing contract by giving notice to the broker and withdrawing the property from the market or selling it himself. The right of the broker to a commission is lost unless he has already earned it by actual performance before he was informed of the revocation, or unless the broker promised a valuable consideration in the listing contract which has been delivered (advertising the property, for example).

Statute of Limitations

The statute of limitations has a definite bearing on the period 11.19
of time the terms of a contract may be enforced. The statute of limitations allows a person to defend himself against being

compelled to perform after a period of time has expired.

1. In the case of a contract in writing and under seal, the time is twenty years (20 years). 95.11, F.S.
2. If the contract is in writing and not under seal, the time is five years (5 years).
3. If a contract is entirely oral, the time is three years (3 years).
4. If a contract is partly in writing and partly oral, the time is dependent on which portion of the contract is to be enforced: if the written portion, five years (5 years); if the oral portion, three years (3 years).

Assignment of Contracts

Except where the terms and conditions of the contract provide otherwise, or where specifically prohibited by law, a contract is assignable (transferable). Even in cases where the terms of a contract specifically forbid an assignment without consent of the other party, a principal to a contract may assign his right to receive any compensation due him by reason of his performance. A person who assigns or transfers his legal rights in a contract to another party or person is called an "assignor." The person to whom legal rights in a contract are transferred or assigned is called the "assignee." 11.20

An assignor does not free himself of his obligation to perform the terms and conditions of the contract, or to see that the terms and conditions of the contract are performed, by assignment of the contract to another without the consent of the other party. In the event that an assignor either accidentally or intentionally assigns the same thing or things to two or more assignees, the first assignee to notify the other party to the contract of the assignment prevails over all other assignees, regardless of the actual dates of the various assignments.

Types of Contracts

As mentioned at the beginning of this chapter, three types of contracts are of special significance to real estate brokers and salespersons because they are a party to the contracts. An explanation of listing, option, and sales contracts follows.

A. Listing Contracts

In Florida, a listing contract may be written, oral, or implied by knowledge and consent of the property owner. Florida law recognizes oral listing contracts with the exception of an "exclusive right of sale" listing, which must be in writing. However, it cannot be overly emphasized that all listings should be in writing whenever possible. This is true because, as was stated earlier, the listing contract is a broker's employment contract. If litigation should result from some misunderstanding, default, or breach, it is much easier to find a rememdy if written terms and conditions are available than if a mass of credible testimony must be obtained to prove the terms or conditions of an oral listing. Still, listing contracts are not covered in the statute of frauds, and therefore, oral listing contracts are enforceable with the proper amount of evidence and 12.02 12.03 12.05

testimony. Leases of less than one year are in this same category and are therefore valid and enforceable though oral.

Power to Bind a Principal

Listing contracts will refer to the property owner as the "principal" of the broker, the latter being the one who acts as the principal's agent in handling some interest in real property. Although the broker does operate, to a limited degree, as his principal's agent, he does not have the authority or power to sign a contract for his principal or to bind his principal to a contract. In order for a real estate broker to sign a contract for his principal or to bind his principal to a contract, it would be necessary for him to have a power of attorney from his principal, or an option with the principal. 10.02 10.13

Power of attorney is a written legal document signed by one or more persons and designating some other person as the attorney in fact. The attorney in fact can then bargain and sign for the person who granted the power of attorney. In the real estate business, one may be exposed to both the "general power of attorney" and the "special power of attorney." The general power of attorney authorizes the attorney in fact to act generally for the principal in all matters. The special power of attorney limits the attorney in fact to one specified area of activity or one special act, such as signing a contract for sale or purchasing a designated property. When power of attorney is granted for acts which may have an effect on title to real property, the instrument must be witnessed, acknowledged, and recorded in the public records in the county in which the property is located. The word "acknowledged" or "acknowledgment" simply refers to the act of a notary public certifying (notarizing) the authenticity of signatures before a document may be included in public records. For the purposes herein, assume that the principal has not given power of attorney to his broker, which is normally the case. The signatures of both parties on the listing contract have created some special situations.

Conditions Created by Listing Contract

First, a unilateral contract has been concluded because the principal may normally revoke the contract at any time before the broker performs. In other words, the principal does not have to do anything until and unless the broker fully performs the terms of the contract. 11.08 12.02

Next, a fiduciary relationship has been created between the broker and his principal. 7.07 10.02

Further, the task of the broker has been expressed so that no misunderstanding should result. The broker will be required to "find a purchaser" or to "effect a sale." 11.06 12.03

If required "to find a purchaser," the broker must produce a customer who is ready, willing, and able to buy at the terms specified by the principal, or take from the customer to the principal an offer to buy at the prescribed price and terms. The offer must be in such a form as to be enforceable as a contract if accepted by the principal. When the broker has done either of 6.09 10.03

the above actions, he is entitled to a commission, even though the buyer and seller finally negotiate a sale on different terms.

If required "to effect a sale" by the terms of his listing con- 6.09
tract, the broker must not only find a buyer ready, willing, and 10.03
able to buy on the terms specified, but he must also ensure that 15.09
that the buyer signs all necessary notes, mortgages, and other instruments and pays all monies required, <u>or</u> at least obtain from the buyer a signed contract for purchase of the property at the terms required by the principal. If the buyer's offer is materially different from the terms prescribed by the principal, then the offer may be rejected and the broker is not entitled to a commission.

<u>Types of Listings</u>

Usually listing contracts will fall into one of four basic classifications: (1) the open listing; (2) the net listing; (3) the exclusive agency listing; and (4) the exclusive right-of-sale listing.

1. <u>Open listing</u>. The open listing exists when the owner gives the 10.06
listing to a number of brokers and reserves the right to sell the 12.06
property himself. The owner, or principal, is not obligated to pay a commission to any broker except the broker who first sells the property. If the owner sells the property himself, no broker is entitled to a commission. In the active real estate markets
of today, very few brokers will accept open residential listings. c

2. <u>Net listing</u>. The net listing is created by a principal 12.10
specifying the net amount of money he requires from the sale of of his property after all commissions and/or expenses have been paid. The broker must then calculate his commission and closing costs to arrive at a total sales price, or asking price. The broker is not permitted to establish a sales price which would result in a greater amount of commission than normal, nor may he raise the sales price so as to benefit himself and work a disadvantage to his principal. The normal commission customary in that locality for the type of property listed must be his criterion, unless the principal specifically agrees to a higher commission. Any other type of listing may become a net listing when the principal quotes a minimum price he will accept.

3. <u>Exclusive agency</u>. The exclusive agency listing is given when 10.06
a principal has selected one specific broker to handle his prop- 12.07
erty but reserves the right to sell the property himself without paying a commission to the broker. If the broker performs by selling the property before the principal is able to do so, the broker is entitled to a commission. The broker who has the listing may normally cooperate with other brokers in selling the property.

4. <u>Exclusive right of sale</u>. The exclusive right-of-sale listing 10.06
is the most advantageous from the broker's viewpoint. This type 12.08
of listing is given to a selected broker who then becomes the exclusive agent for sale of the property during the time the listing contract is effective. The broker, therefore, is assured of a commission regardless of who sells the property. Even if the owner himself sells the property during the contract period,

the broker is entitled to a commission. This particular type of listing contract must be in writing and must be supported by valuable consideration in order to preclude misunderstanding.

Option as a Listing

An option given by a principal to a broker may actually function 12.11
as an exclusive right-of-sale listing. This happens when a principal gives a broker an option on property with no consideration, or only token consideration. Usually the principal and broker both understand that the broker has no intention to buy. The option simply gives the broker temporary control of the property, and the purchase price cited in the option represents the amount which the principal will accept for the property. The broker's asking price for the property is arrived at in the same manner as in a net listing. The option may be exercised by the broker any time he finds a buyer during the period the option is in effect.

A listing not often encountered but which does arise from time to 12.12
time is the "implied listing." An implied listing is dependent upon an owner having knowledge of a broker's actions to sell the owner's property without specific authorization, and giving consent or tacit approval to the broker's actions. In this instance, the implied listing is created by the actions of both parties, with the broker negotiating a sale without an actual listing but with the knowledge and consent of the principal.

Obligation for Two Commissions

It is entirely possible that the actions of a principal may 12.15
obligate him to pay a commission to more than one broker. For example, if the principal had previously given an exclusive right-of-sale listing to Broker X and then learned of Broker Y's negotiations with an interested buyer and consented to the actions of Broker Y who then concluded a sale, the principal would be obligated to pay a commission not only to Broker X because of the terms of his exclusive right-of-sale listing contract, but also to Broker Y because of an implied listing and sale. This is true because performance is the essence of a broker's contract with a principal. A broker's legal claims to compensation are based on performance.

Procuring Cause

Conflicts between two or more brokers sometimes arise as to who 10.03
actually is entitled to the commission resulting from a property 12.14
transaction. The courts will rule that a broker is considered to have substantially performed his contract of employment if his efforts are the procuring cause of a transaction. The circumstances in each case involving conflicts between brokers will determine who, or which one, was actually the procuring cause. It is not enough that one broker may have shown the property first. To be declared the procuring cause, it must be definitely established that a broker's efforts were directly or indirectly responsible for the consummation of the transaction. For example, a broker may show a property to a prospect who thereafter leaves the broker and begins to negotiate directly with the principal.

If a sale results, the broker is entitled to a commission as the procuring cause.

In those instances involving open listings where several brokers 12.06
have buyers for the same property, the owner, or principal, must 12.15
take care to ensure that he does not become liable for two commissions. In some cases, competition between buyers will cause the "would-be" purchasers to offer higher prices than the owner has asked. In this event, the first broker who produces a buyer ready, willing, and able to meet the terms of the open listing is entitled to a commission, regardless of whether the owner accepts or rejects the offer. If the owner refuses the first offer to accept a second broker's contract for a higher price, then the owner is obligated for a commission to each of the two brokers.

B. Option Contracts

In real-life situations arising in the field of real estate, 12.26
option contracts are often written with considerably less care 12.30
and attention than sales contracts. This is unfortunate and somewhat shortsighted because option contracts are easily converted into sales contracts by the simple act of notifying the optionor that the option is exercised. For this reason, if for no other, care should be given to the creation of an option contract.

Option contracts are required to be in writing by the statute of 11.17
frauds. If the entire contract is not written, some memorandum of the main facts must be made and signed by the party bound to perform.

Unilateral Contract

Options are merely agreements, as are sales contracts. Options c 11.08
are also based on a consideration, just as sales contracts are. One major difference exists between option and sales contracts: in an option, the owner (optionor) is required to perform the terms of the option if requested to do so by the optionee. The optionee, however, may elect to perform or to walk away from the deal. This makes the option a unilateral contract. In the normal bilateral sales contract, if either party does not perform all of the terms of the contract, the other party may sue for breach of contract.

Information Required

The content of an option contract is important and, as earlier 12.11
stated, should be given careful attention. The complete terms of 12.26
the transaction and the exact length of time the option is effective must be clearly specified. The price of the property, a complete legal description, and a definite consideration must also be included.

Consideration

The consideration given to create an option deserves some ex- 475.43
amination. An option contract may provide for any monies paid as 11.13
a consideration to be applied as a part of the purchase price in 12.30
the event the option is exercised. However, if the option allows the consideration to be returned in full to the optionee in the

event the option is not exercised, the option is not a valid contract because there would be no consideration of any substance.

Paragraph 475.43 of Florida Statute 475 stipulates that, "All contracts, options or other devices not based upon a substantial consideration...are hereby declared void and ineffective in all cases, suit or proceedings had or taken under this chapter..." Therefore, it is important that more than a fleeting thought be given to the type and amount of consideration given to create an option contract.

Options Assignable

Unless prohibited in the terms of the contract, an option con- 11.20
tract is assignable. In actual fact, options are often sold or assigned before the optionee ever takes possession of a property.

It was earlier stated that a broker may use an option contract as 12.11
an exclusive right-of-sale listing contract. However, if a broker or salesman is really interested in obtaining an option on a property as a true optionee, then he must first divest himself of his identity as a broker or salesman and give a valuable consideration for the option contract, just as any non-registrant would be required to do. This means he must inform the property owner that he is not functioning in the capacity of a real estate broker or salesman but is personally interested in acquiring an option on the property.

Before leaving the subject of contracts, some special mention is in order for that instrument which is most commonly used by brokers and salesmen, the real estate sales contract.

C. Sales Contracts

Unlike the option contract, the real estate sales contract is a bilateral contract since it contains promises to perform by both parties.

While the courts have required oral sales contracts to be honored 11.17
in some instances, the Florida statute of frauds requires that 12.27
sales contracts transferring an interest in real property must be in writing in almost all cases. In addition, a real estate sales contract must include certain information to comply with the statute of frauds.

Information Contained in Sales Contracts

All sales contracts must identify the property affected; there- 12.27
fore, a complete legal description must be included in the con- 12.28
tract. The names of the parties to the contract (the vendor and 12.32
the vendee) must be shown; a valuable consideration must be indicated; the total purchase price must appear; any terms which have been agreed to must be in writing; any arrangements for financing the purchase must be included; the closing date must be shown; remedies for breach by either party indicated; and, all agreements reached between the two parties should be included in the sales contract.

If the sales contract makes no mention of any mortgages or other 12.28
encumbrances, then the buyer (vendee) may assume that the

property will be conveyed free and clear. Unless otherwise stated in the sales contract, a good and merchantable title is to be conveyed, and the buyer can legally refuse to perform unless, or until, such a title is delivered.

One of the agreements usually found in most real estate sales contracts is a promise by the buyer that the seller may regard the earnest money deposit as liquidated damages to the seller in the event of breach by the buyer. Usually any deposit which is forfeited by a buyer is divided between the seller and the broker in accordance with a previous listing agreement or an agreement included in the sales contract. The broker's portion of the forfeited deposit cannot exceed the amount of his normal commission for a completed sale, unless the seller has been informed and has specifically consented to the broker receiving a larger amount.

Most sales contracts will require the seller to provide the buyer 12.28
an up-to-date abstract or a title insurance policy. In the event no such requirement is included in the sales contract, the seller is under no obligation to deliver either document.

In today's real estate market, most properties transferred have 12.29
existing mortgages which must be taken into account. There are at least three different methods of dealing with existing mortgages. First, an existing mortgage can be paid off by the seller thereby removing the mortgage as a factor in the transaction. Second, the buyer may purchase the property "subject to the mortgage." And third, the buyer may buy the property and "assume the mortgage." In any event, the method used to recognize and dispose of the existing mortgage should be indicated in the sales contract. Each of these three methods will be discussed in more detail in the chapter entitled "Financing Real Estate."

It is important that the wife of a married man always joins her husband in executing a real estate sales contract. If the seller's wife signs the sales contract, she indicates a willingness to convey her ownership rights when the time comes to sign the deed which transfers title. If the buyer's wife joins her husband in signing the sales contract, she indicates her agreement to the price and terms which may avoid difficulties at the time of closing.

Terminology

Reference has been made to the owner of a property as a "principal," as an "optionor" (when giving an option), as a "seller," and now in sales contracts as a "vendor." The person buying from a vendor is referred to as a "vendee." The term "vendor" has caused the use of a catchy little phrase used to define a vendor's lien: when the "vendor is the lender." In other words, the vendor loans the vendee (purchaser) part of the sales price by taking a second mortgage which is sometimes called a "purchase money mortgage."

CHAPTER 7

CONTRACTS

1. A valid contract is legally enforceable in court. T F

2. In addition to the requirement to be in writing and signed, real estate contracts must contain four essential elements to be valid. T F

3. Where the terms of a contract specifically forbid assignment of the contract without the consent of the other party, a principal to the contract may assign his right to any compensation due him by his performance. T F

4. The statute of limitations allows a contract, in writing and under seal, to be enforced for a period of twenty years and a written contract not under seal to be enforced for a period of ten years. T F

5. When a broker has contracted to effect a sale of a property and refuses to show that property, he is considered to have abandoned the contract. T F

6. All of the six methods of terminating contracts in general will apply to contracts associated with real estate. T F

7. When two parties initiate a suit in a court of equity to have the court establish the correct meaning of words used in a contract, they will have asked for a "declaratory judgment." T F

8. In a "suit for damages" as a remedy for breach of contract, a wronged party may decide to keep the property and, in addition, sue for damages. T F

9. When an offeree makes a counteroffer, the original offer is terminated, or killed, by the counteroffer. T F

10. A sales contract for transfer of real property becomes an executory contract after closing when all promises have been fulfilled. T F

11. In order to be enforceable, an option must be signed by the optionee. T F

12. A parol contract is a contract which is not in writing. T T

13. Although the law recognizes both good and valuable consideration, only valuable consideration is regarded as adequate to enforce a contract. T F

14. A registered real estate broker may prepare any legal instrument required to transfer, or convey, title to real property. T F

Listing Contracts

15. Listing contracts come under the jurisdiction of the statute of frauds. T (F)

16. A listing contract is regarded as an employment contract. (T) F

17. If an owner refuses the offer of the listing broker's prospect who has agreed to the terms of a listing contract and the owner accepts a higher price from another broker's prospect, the owner is obligated to pay two commissions. (T) F

18. An option given to a broker by an owner may be used as an exclusive right-to-sell listing. (T) F

19. The most advantageous type of listing from the broker's point of view is the exclusive agency listing. T (F)

20. Any type of listing may become a net listing when the property owner quotes a minimum price he will accept. (T) F

21. A general power of attorney authorizes an attorney in fact to act for the principal in all matters. (T) F

22. If a power of attorney is used for acts which affect title to real estate, the instrument must be witnessed, acknowledged, and recorded in the public records in the county in which the property is located. (T) F

23. A listing contract is an executory, bilateral contract until completely performed. T (F)

24. If a buyer and seller negotiate a sale on different terms than those the broker relayed to the seller from the buyer, the broker will not be entitled to a commission. T (F)

Option Contracts

25. All that is needed to convert a unilateral option contract into a bilateral sales contract is a notification to the optionor that the option is exercised. (T) F

26. Like the listing contract, an option contract may be in writing, oral, or implied and be enforceable. T (F)

27. In order to obtain a true option, a broker or salesman must divest himself of his identity as a registrant and give a valuable consideration for the option contract. (T) F

28. An option may be sold before the optionee has acquired possession of the property. (T) F

29. When an option contract allows the consideration paid to be returned in full to the optionee if the option is not exercised, the option is not a valid contract. (T) F

30. In addition to the essential elements of all contracts, a real estate sales contract must contain:
    a. Names of the parties and a legal description
    b. Purchase price and consideration
    c. Terms and financing arrangements
    d. Closing date and remedies for breach
    e. All of the above
    f. "a" and "b" only

31. If the sales contract makes no mention of mortgages or encumbrances:
    a. The seller can be held responsible for all encumbrances of record
    b. The buyer may assume the property will be delivered free and clear
    c. The buyer can be held responsible for all encumbrances of record which he could check by a search of records
    d. "a" and "b" above
    e. All of the above

32. It is important that a buyer's wife joins her husband in executing a sales contract because:
    a. This indicates a willingness to convey her ownership rights
    b. It will help to avoid difficulties at closing
    c. It indicates her agreement to the price and terms
    d. "a" and "b" above
    e. "b" and "c" above

33. When a property is sold with an existing mortgage:
    a. The seller may remove the mortgage by paying in full
    b. The buyer may buy the property subject to the mortgage
    c. The buyer may buy the property and assume the mortgage
    d. All of the above
    e. "b" and "c" above

34. Normally, a sales contract involving real property will contain a provision that in case of breach by the buyer, the earnest money deposit will be regarded as:
    a. Unliquidated damages to the seller
    b. Liquidated damages to the seller
    c. Unliquidated damages to the broker
    d. None of the above

35. In the event the real estate sales contract makes no mention of an abstract or title insurance:
    a. The seller is required to provide an abstract only
    b. The seller must provide both abstract and title insurance
    c. The seller is not required to provide either an abstract or title insurance
    d. None of the above

CHAPTER 8

LEGAL DESCRIPTIONS

Prior to 1513 when it was discovered, named, and claimed by the Spanish explorer Juan Ponce de Leon, Florida was occupied from time immemorial by various Indian tribes. Then came settlers from Spain, France, and England seeking land and wealth. Following this long and turbulent history, Florida was purchased by the United States from Spain by treaty (the Adams-Onis Treaty, signed in 1819, ratified in 1821). The acquisition price was $5,000,000! Admitted to the Union in 1845 as the 27th state, Florida's size, 58,560 square miles, is comparable to that of England and Wales.

Excluded from the above Treaty were large tracts of land conveyed previously by the rulers of Spain to private individuals and companies. Since that time, those particular large, private land grants have been divided and subdivided using the metes and bounds method of legal land description. The rectangular method (government land survey system) has not been commonly used to describe them because they were not included in the Treaty.

In addition to those parcels of land, Florida has many fractional portions of townships and sections called "government lots." Each government lot has an assigned number for ease in identification. The origin of these government lots is due to several factors including surveying errors, wildness of the land, and land irregularities caused by vast amounts of water forming interior and coastline boundaries. Usually, these fractional sections were divided into tracts not exceeding 80 acres.

Basic to the real estate business is a working knowledge of 12.33
"legal land descriptions" (often shortened by practitioners to 12.34
"legals"). Unless property can be located accurately, the best of contracts and the combined efforts of the most knowledgeable brokers in the world would be defeated. In addition, once a property has been accurately located, that particular spot on earth must then be described in order to have deeds, mortgages, and other instruments affecting transfer of ownership prepared.

Various systems and methods have been devised and utilized down through the ages. Four different types of legal land descriptions may be encountered in working with real estate in Florida:

1. metes and bounds
2. government land survey
3. lot and block numbers
4. monuments.

Only the first three methods are recommended in Paragraphs 12.33 and 12.34, Section 12, of the <u>FLORIDA REAL ESTATE COMMISSION HANDBOOK</u>. Selected measures associated with legal land descriptions may be found at the end of this chapter.

Purposes of Legal Descriptions

While the chief purpose of land description is to identify a particular parcel of property, four additional purposes are served and benefits derived from the process of surveying and writing descriptions:

1. Current and accurate boundary information required to write a legal description is obtained.
2. The exact quantity of area within a described tract, whether it be described in square miles, in acres, or square feet, is established.
3. Boundaries which may have become lost or obliterated are reestablished.
4. Data required to divide a large tract into smaller units for development and sale are obtained.

An examination of the different types of land descriptions mentioned earlier will reveal varying degrees of accuracy. The most exact and accurate method of describing land is the metes and bounds system, while the least accurate is the monuments system. It is only natural, therefore, that the metes and bounds system is used where property is more valuable, while the monuments system is utilized only to describe relatively less valuable property. For example, a tract in the desert located in Arizona or New Mexico might be adequately described by the monuments method, while a tract in the middle of Times Square in New York City would have to be accurate down to a fraction of a foot.

Types of Legal Descriptions

Since the accurate description of land is of major importance, an analysis of each of the four methods commonly used follows:

1. Description by Metes and Bounds. "Metes" refers to measurements and "bounds" refers to direction. This method of describing property is normally used in cities and wherever land is of considerable value. The critical feature in this method of land description is the "point of beginning" (POB). If this exact point is in error, the entire description is worthless. For this reason, neither an ordinary lawyer nor an ordinary broker should ever attempt to write his idea of a metes and bounds description. This is a job for a land surveyor. If done by a competent surveyor, the metes and bounds system can be used to describe either regular or irregular shaped tracts of any size or location. This method is especially adapted to describing tracts of land which are carved out of former land grants because of the flexibility provided by utilizing compass directions and exact measurements along the compass bearing angles.

Despite the fact that the writing of metes and bounds descriptions should be left to qualified land surveyors, all registered real estate brokers and salesmen should be capable of reading a properly written description and closely approximating the described tract's size, shape, and dimensions. A description of a triangular-shaped tract could be as follows:

> Beginning at a point (POB) on the north side of Page Avenue 100 feet east from the corner formed by the intersection of the east boundary of Gore Street and the north boundary of Page Avenue; running thence North 01 degrees East 210.04 feet; thence North 90 degrees East 124.5 feet; thence South 59 degrees 20 minutes 34 seconds West 244.17 feet to POB.

Plotting the above metes and bounds description is not as difficult as it might first appear to be. The first thing to remember is that the point of beginning, and <u>all</u> turning points, should be regarded as being the exact center of a circle. All circles, regardless of size, are divided into 360 degrees. The point called "North" is the beginning and the end of the circle, so start at North and move clockwise around the edge of the circle numbering the degrees 01 through 360. North is 0 degrees <u>and</u> 360 degrees on a compass.

Every compass has four cardinal directions: North, South, East, and West. By drawing a straight line connecting North and South, then drawing a second line connecting East and West, the result is a circle divided into four quarters or "quadrants." The straight line connecting North and South is regarded as the "primary reference line." In land descriptions, all directions begin by designating either North or South as the primary reference direction, then move a stated number of degrees either East or West up to a maximum of 90 degrees. The reason one cannot use more than 90 degrees in moving away from the primary reference direction is because one would pass the point midway between North and South and begin to move toward the other primary reference direction. For example: "South 45 degrees East" means to start in the center of a circle looking due South, then to move toward East 45 degrees which would be halfway between South and East. On reaching South 90 degrees East, however, one is just as near North as South, so from that point on begin one's direction by referring to North and indicate a specified number of degrees East of North instead of South. Thus, it is not, for example, "South 95 degrees East," but rather, "North 85 degrees East," which brings one to the exact same spot. In effect, both North and South are 0 degrees, and one can then move up to 90 degrees toward the East or West before starting toward the other 0.

The following diagram is offered as a further aid in understanding compass directions for legal land descriptions.

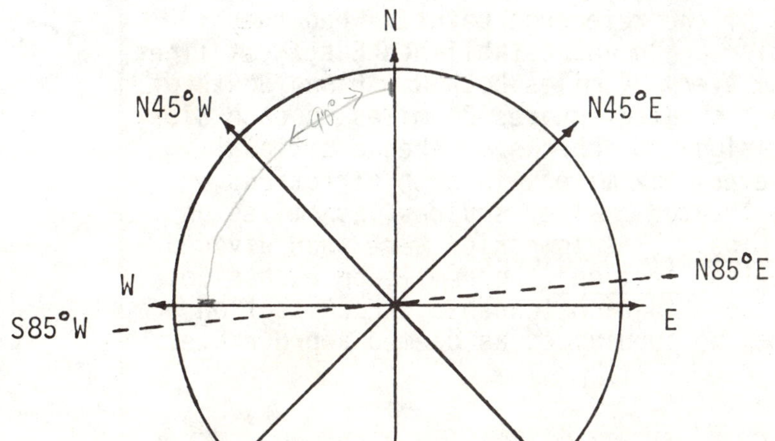

Directions are given in degrees, minutes, and seconds. One degree has 60 minutes of measurement separating the degree mark from its neighbor on either side. Each minute is then divided into 60 seconds. The symbols for degrees, minutes, and seconds always follow the number in the same place that symbols for feet and inches are placed when used. Ten degrees is written 10°; ten minutes as 10'; ten seconds as 10".

2. Description by Government Land Survey. (Sometimes called the 12.34
"rectangular method.") In April, 1785, the federal government adopted the rectangular land survey system for the purpose of dividing vast undescribed areas west of the original 13 colonies. It has come to be called the "government land survey system" and is used in Florida and all states except: the original 13 colonies, the states later created from their original territories, and Tennessee, Kentucky, West Virginia, and Texas. The merit of this system is that, once understood, it is simple and accurate and permits land to be described in concise symbols and words, resulting in a kind of land description shorthand.

This system is based upon government survey lines which were drawn in a North/South direction and in an East/West direction. These survey lines created large squares which were divided into smaller squares by additional survey lines. Therefore, one needs only to understand the names and relationships of various squares to be able to use the government land survey system for the purpose of locating or describing real property.

The federal government has designated geographical locations all over the U.S., where principal meridians running North-South and their base lines running East-West intersect, for the purpose of forming the basic reference point for a pattern of squares which constitutes the government survey system. In Florida, the principal meridian and the base line cross at a point in the city of Tallahassee. The principal meridian runs North and South; the base line runs East and West. Beginning at the intersection of the principal meridian and the base line, surveyors established North/South lines parallel to the principal meridian every 24 miles both East and West of the reference point. Then they started at the intersection again and established East/West lines parallel to the base line every 24 miles both North and South of the reference point. This created squares 24 miles on each side, and these squares were designated "checks." Then additional survey lines were added every six miles, in both directions, within the checks. This created smaller squares, six miles on each side, called "townships." The townships were then divided into smaller squares, called "sections," one mile on each side, making a total of 36 sections in each township. Each section contains 640 acres and may be subdivided as deemed appropriate.

Illustration of
GOVERNMENT LAND SURVEY SYSTEM
(not to scale)

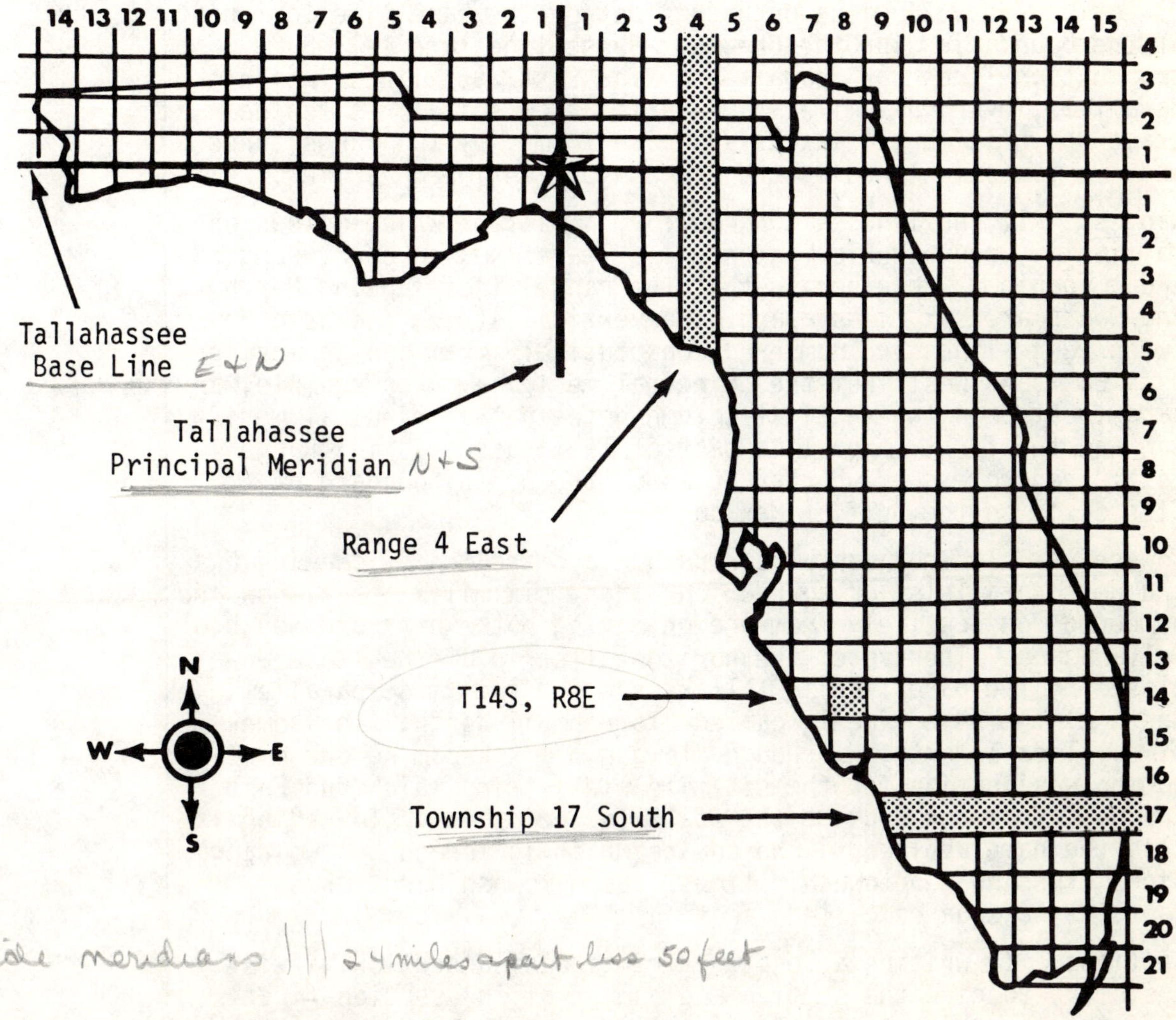

Reviewing what has been done to create the government survey system in Florida, the principal meridian and base line cross in Tallahassee. There are lines parallel to the principal meridian every 24 miles called "guide meridians" on both sides of the principal meridian. The guide meridians are so named because they terminate every 24 miles and are offset approximately 50 feet toward the principal meridian to correct for converging of North/South lines at the two poles. In between the guide meridians are North/South lines every six miles and paralleling the meridians. These lines, located every six miles and running North/South, are called "range lines."

Referring back to Tallahassee, the lines running in an East/West direction every 24 miles on both sides of the base line form part of the boundaries for the checks. These lines are called "correction lines" or "parallels." The East/West lines inside the parallels, every six miles, are called "township lines." The tract which is formed inside a square formed by two range lines and two township lines is the "township" mentioned earlier.

Ranges. All the lines drawn now form a pattern which allows one to find any spot in Florida once one learns how to count ranges and townships. Remembering that the range lines running North and South are six miles apart, the vertical strips enclosed between range lines are numbered consecutively from one on moving both East and West from the principal meridian. For example, any land located in the vertical column between the principal meridian and the first range line east of Tallahassee is in "Range 1 East," regardless of whether it is on the north boundary of Florida or on the Gulf of Mexico.

Townships. The horizontal strips of land created by drawing East and West parallels, or correction lines, six miles apart, now are numbered consecutively from one on moving both North and South of Tallahassee. Therefore, the horizontal strip of the state enclosed by the base line in Tallahassee and the first parallel North of the base line is called "Township 1 North, " or sometimes "Tier 1 North," although "township" is becoming the more common designation for the six-mile wide strips which run East and West from one side of the state to the other. "Township" is also the name applied to the square which is formed by two range lines crossing two township lines. Each township so formed contains 36 squares called "sections."

Sections. In writing a legal description of a section, it is customary to give the section and number of the section first, then the township number and direction, and last the range number and direction. For example, "Section 24, Township 1 North, Range 1 East of the Tallahassee Principal Meridian and Base Line" would identify a section immediately northeast of the intersection of the principal meridian and base line. It would normally be abbreviated to "Sec 24, T1N, R1E, etc."

Sections are an important subdivision of land description and merit more than casual attention. Each township contains 36 sections, and the sections are numbered in a somewhat unique manner. In all townships, section number one is located in the extreme northeast corner of the township. The numbers progress consecutively as one moves left (west) from the upper right corner of the township across the top row of sections to number six. The second horizontal row begins directly under number six and progresses from seven to twelve moving to the right (east). Section thirteen is directly under number twelve, and one moves to the left (west) with section eighteen last in that row. This method of numbering is repeated until section number thirty-six is reached, which is always in the southeast, or lower right, corner of every township.

Locating Sections. Suppose you want to locate a section of land in Florida, and the legal description given you is, "All of Section 36, Township 1 South, Range 1 West, Tallahassee Principal Meridian and Base Line." The numbers assigned to the township and range tell you immediately that you are dealing with property very near Tallahassee since the range (1 West) is the first six-mile segment immediately West of the principal meridian. The township (1 South) must be the first six-mile segment immediately South of the horizontal base line. Knowing how sections are numbered, Section 36 cannot be anywhere except in the lower right corner of the township. Therefore, the section you seek is six miles South of the intersection of the Tallahassee Principal Meridian and Base Line.

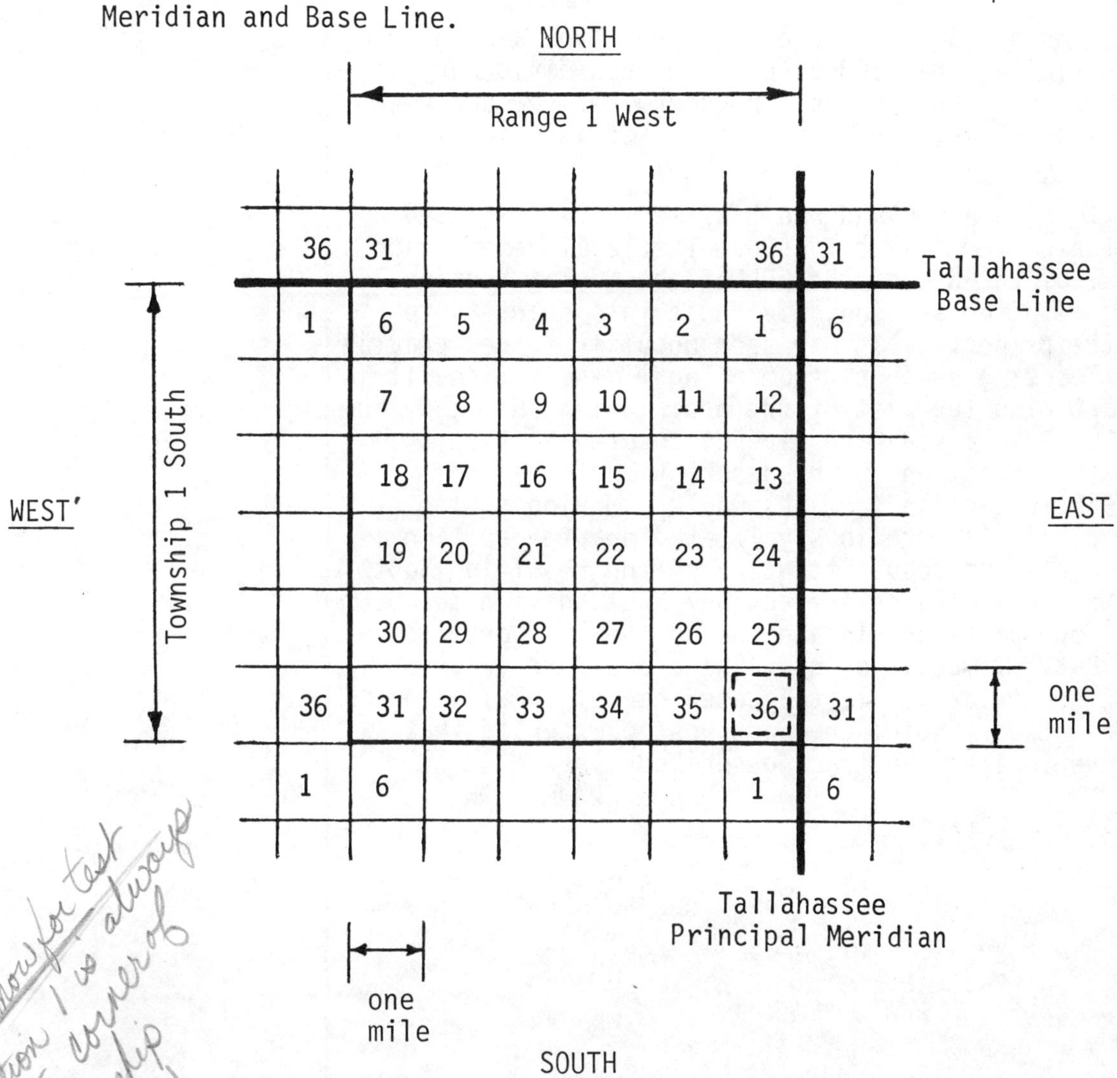

<u>Subdividing Sections</u>. Each section, theoretically a square with all sides measuring one mile, contains within its boundaries 640 acres. It is important to remember the exact number of acres in a section because the 640 figure is used for so many purposes. One of the reasons is that the section is the basic reference when writing a legal description of land. It is also the reference when calculating acreage in subdivided tracts. Each section can easily be divided into halves, then into quarters, and so on down into smaller divisions until the particular property one wants to locate or describe has been pinpointed.

Suppose you are only interested in a quarter section, 160 acres, of Section 36. First, divide the entire section (Section 36) into fourths by drawing a straight vertical line through the center of the section and a straight horizontal line through the center of the section. The two lines are perpendicular and cross in the exact center of the section. The quarter section now situated in the upper right corner of the section is called the "Northeast Quarter"; the one in the lower right corner is the "Southeast Quarter"; and so on around the section. Directions are always given in terms of the direction from the center of the section where the two dividing lines intersect.

All quarter sections contain 160 acres. Suppose you are interested in a tract smaller than 160 acres. You can divide any quarter just as you did the section. Furthermore, you can keep on dividing the results until you find the tract in which you are interested.

Assume you need to find a two and one-half acre tract located somewhere near the center of Section 36. The legal description given you is "SW¼ of the NE¼ of the SE¼ of the NW¼ of Section 36, etc." Beginning with the section, divide it into quarters to start locating the property. It may seem peculiar to new practitioners, but in locating property from a legal description, it is necessary to start with the last of the description and read from right to left. So, since you have already located Section 36, now move to the last fraction in the description (NW¼) and separate that quarter section from the whole. Moving to the next fraction (SE¼), divide the previously located quarter section (NW¼) into four parts and focus attention on the resulting Southeast quarter. Moving to the next fraction (NE¼), divide the SE¼ of the NW¼ into four parts and locate the Northeast quarter of that division. But remember, you still have one more fraction (SW¼) remaining, so divide the last located parcel (NE¼) into fourths once more, then finding the Southwest quarter of that division, you have located the tract described.

1 chain = 66 feet = 100 links
1 rod = 16½ feet
1 link = 7.92 inches
4 rods = 1 chain

Section 36

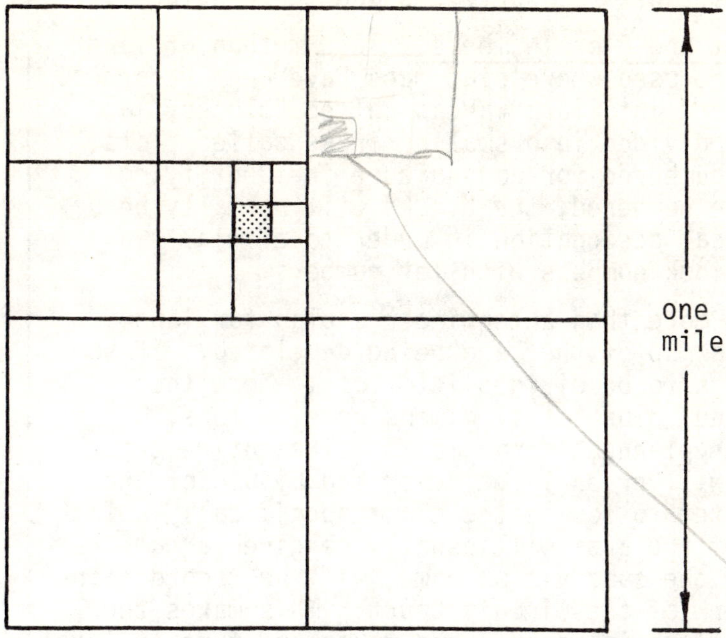

SW¼, NE¼, SE¼, NW¼ of Section 36 (partial legal description)

4 3 2 1 (sequence to locate property)

In order to find the number of acres in the tract, several approaches are possible. One way is to work backwards from the 640-acre section, calculating the number of acres resulting from each division. Another method, and more precise since it is simple arithmetic, is to multiply each denominator (the bottom portion of a fraction) times its neighboring denominator and then divide the result into 640 acres. For example, in "SW¼, NE¼, SE¼, NW¼" multiply the first "4" times its neighbor the next "4" getting 16; next, multiply the 16 by the next "4" giving 64; then, multiply the 64 times the last "4" arriving at 256. Divide the 256 into 640 acres and the answer is 2.5, which means that the tract in question contains 2½ acres.

The above exercise to determine the size of a given tract demonstrates among other things that the longer a legal description, the smaller the number of acres contained in the parcel described. With practice, one becomes familiar with the fact that a description containing four 4's will always result in a 2½-acre tract, a description with only three 4's will result in a 10-acre parcel, etc. When fractions other than fourths are used, the method for calculating acreage is still the same.

It should be noted that, although the government land survey system of legal description is used as if it were absolutely accurate, in reality the township measurements and distances are nothing more than close approximations. This is due to four contributing factors: the curvature of the earth, inaccuracy of surveyors' instruments, wildness and inaccessability of some of the country, and carelessness of surveyors and their helpers.

3. Description by Lot and Block Numbers. This method of land description can only be used where plat maps have been recorded. The plat will be divided into large areas called "blocks," and each block will be subdivided into smaller areas called "lots." The lots are usually numbered for convenience in identifying them. If the lots are numbered, the blocks will normally be assigned an alphabetical designation in order to eliminate a chance of confusing block numbers with lot numbers.

Plat maps are nothing more than an engineer's plan for land utilization shown on a map of the land being developed. It shows how the mapped tract is to be divided into lots, where the streets will be located, plus actual dimensions for lots, streets, and any other planned improvements. The entire tract appearing on the map will probably be described by use of the government survey system to locate the tract specifically. The planned subdivision of the area will usually be given a name. The plat map, bearing the subdivision name, will be recorded in the office of the Clerk of the Circuit Court. This makes the plat map a part of the public records and makes any further legal description of the lots a simple matter.

It is important to note that descriptions by lot and block numbers are of no great importance unless they refer to a plat which has been properly recorded. Most municipalities and counties in Florida prohibit the sale of lots of any appreciable size unless the plat thereof has been duly recorded after approval by appropriate authorities.

4. Description by Monuments. This type of legal description is written with the use of physical features called "monuments" as points of reference to describe the boundaries enclosing a property. The monuments may be either man-made or natural features. This type of land description is normally used only where land is not so valuable. The disadvantages of the monuments description are that some of the monuments may be moved or may disappear since such things as river banks, trees, and fences are sometimes used as monuments. Also, the monuments system is not precise as to directions or distances. About the only favorable features are that it is simple and it saves the expense of a survey. A monuments description could be written as follows:

> "All of that property belonging to Davy Crockett at Bowie, Texas, bounded and described as follows: Beginning at the Stone Bridge over Little Knife Creek on the Pecos-Bowie Road; thence Westerly along the Pecos-Bowie Road approximately two and one-half miles to the two oak trees at the foot of Granite Mountain; thence Southerly about three miles to the stone outcropping known as Indian Mound; thence Easterly approximately two miles to the West bank of Little Knife Creek where the Jones Boat Dock is situated; thence meandering Northerly along the West bank of Little Knife Creek to the Stone Bridge on the Pecos-Bowie Road, the point of beginning."

To reiterate, the monuments method of land description is not used where land is valuable or where better land description methods are available.

- - - - -

Selected Measures Associated with Legal Land Descriptions

Township:	A square which is 6 miles on each side (6 miles square) containing 36 square miles.
Section:	A square which is 1 mile on each side containing 1 square mile.
Section:	One square mile containing 640 acres.
Acre:	43,560 square feet (approximately 208.71 ft. x 208.71 ft.).
Mile:	5,280 feet in length.

CHAPTER 8

LEGAL DESCRIPTIONS

1. The process of surveying and writing legal descriptions of real property will also establish the exact amount of area within a described tract. T F

2. The <u>FLORIDA REAL ESTATE COMMISSION HANDBOOK</u> recommends the use of metes and bounds, government survey system, description by monuments, and description by lot and block numbers for describing real property. T F

3. The most exact and accurate method of describing land is the government survey system. T F

4. In the metes and bounds method of description, "metes" refers to direction and "bounds" refers to distance or measurements. T F

5. The government survey system is especially adaptable to describing odd-shaped tracts of land carved out of former land grants. T F

6. An ordinary broker or lawyer should not attempt to write a metes and bounds description. T F

7. Guide meridians are located every 24 miles on both sides of the principal meridian. T F

8. Correction lines or parallels are located every six miles parallel to and on both sides of the principal meridian. T F

9. The tract of land located inside a square formed by two range lines and two township lines is called a "township." T F

10. The vertical strip of land six miles wide beginning at the principal meridian and extending six miles east along the length of the principal meridian is called Range 1 East. T F

11. If you have located a township numbered T1N, R1E, the township due North of that township is:
    a. T1N, R2E
    b. T1S, R1E
    c. T2N, R1E
    d. T2N, R2E

12. Each township contains:
    a. 36 sections
    b. 36 square miles
    c. Both "a" and "b" above
    d. None of the above

13. The number of acres in a section is:
    a. 360
    b. 640
    c. 320
    d. 660

14. The north boundary of Section 36, Township 1 South, Range 1 West is located:
    a. 35 miles south of Tallahassee
    b. 35 miles west of Tallahassee
    c. 25 miles west of Tallahassee
    d. 5 miles south of Tallahassee

15. Township measurements and distances are only close approximations due to : (select the incorrect answer)
    a. Wildness and inaccessibility of the country
    b. Surveyors' lack of sobriety
    c. Inaccuracy of surveyors' instruments
    d. Curvature of the earth

16. A legal description which reads in part, "N½, NE¼, NW¼, Section 12, Township 42 South, Range 12 East" would describe a tract of:
    a. 10 acres
    b. 20 acres
    c. 5 acres
    d. 2½ acres

17. The physical features used in the monuments type of land description are:
    a. Natural features
    b. Made by man
    c. Both "a" and "b" above
    d. None of the above

18. Plat maps used in the lot and block number method of legal description will show:
    a. How the tract will be divided into lots
    b. Dimensions of streets and improvements
    c. Both "a" and "b" above
    d. None of the above

19. In writing the legal description of a section, it is customary to give first:
    a. Range number, township number, section number
    b. Section number, township number, range number
    c. Township number, range number, section number
    d. Section number, range number, township number

20. In the government survey method of legal description, the squares which are 24 miles on each side are called:
    a. Tiers
    b. Townships
    c. Government lots
    d. Checks

CHAPTER 9

APPRAISING REAL PROPERTY

All real estate activity has some relation to value. Whether one is a buyer or a seller, a renter or a landlord, value lies at the heart of the transaction. A new real estate salesperson will not be long in the business before encountering some situation which will emphasize the necessity for having the ability to place a value on real property.

Suppose your neighbors ask you what their house is worth. Or suppose you own a developed residential lot which you decide to sell. How will you decide on a price for each? You could guess at a price for each; or, you could auction either property hoping competition among bidders would bring a fair price; or, you might ask a broker for help. Still another solution could be for you to master enough of the fundamentals of property appraising to use as a reliable guide. The best solution would be to retain a real estate appraiser with experience in the community and knowledge about the type of properties concerned.

It seems appropriate at this point to emphasize that the same law which permits applicants to receive a real estate license certif- 10.17
icate also cautions holders of such a certificate about engaging 21V-1.06
in appraising real property for others without proper training and experience. The real estate certificate, which authorizes a registrant to be paid for selling, buying, auctioning, leasing, exchanging, or renting for others, also authorizes a legally licensed person to appraise for a fee. But the law recognizes that years of training and experience are necessary in order to become a qualified appraiser. For this reason, it warns all those who might be tempted to collect a fee for appraising before they are adequately trained that they will be held responsible for any damages which might result.

For many, this chapter may be their only exposure to appraising. 16.10
For others, this may be the first in a sequence of formal exposures to appraisal. Regardless, this chapter will not prepare a student to undertake professional appraisals. It should, however, help students to communicate better with others in the field of real estate appraisal, and the authors hope that it will bring students to the door of a most interesting future by explaining the basics of a very comprehensive art. While appraising employs many scientific techniques and methods, it remains an art, not a science.

Market Value

The subject of value has occupied the thoughts of philosophers and economists since long before Aristotle's time. What is value? Is it beauty and truth as claimed by Aristotle, or is it the cost of production plus profit as Adam Smith contended? Both are correct when considered from each individual's viewpoint. This serves to illustrate that value has many faces. If an alphabetical list of the different types of value was drawn up beginning with appraised value, then assessed value, and on through warranted value, no doubt 20 or 30 different types of values would be listed. But the appraiser of real property is primarily concerned with only one type of value -- market value.

In order to ensure uniform use of the term market value, the major organizations of professional appraisers have published definitions of the term. One of the most widely accepted definitions is:

> "The highest price in terms of money which a property will bring in a competitive and open market under all conditions requisite to a fair sale, the buyer and seller, each acting prudently, knowledgeably, and assuming the price is not affected by undue stimulus."

However, for the newcomer to appraisal, the authors provide the following definition of the term "market value":

> That price which a property would likely bring if it is exposed for sale on the open market by a willing seller to a willing buyer.

Inherent in the above definitions are the assumptions that:

1. Market value applies to a certain date and may change with the passage of time.
2. The terms of sale are all cash or its equivalent.
3. The property is exposed for sale on the open market for a reasonable length of time.
4. The buyer and seller are both fully informed.
5. Neither buyer nor seller are under any compulsion or pressure to conclude a sale.
6. The seller is able to convey a marketable title.

It is important to understand that true market value does not indicate that one party in a transaction is supposed to benefit at the expense of the other party. Like any other economic decision, determining market value involves an estimation of the relationship between what is given up and what is received. The seller wants the benefits received in terms of dollars to equal at a minimum the property given up. The buyer wants the benefits received in terms of property to equal the sacrifice made in terms of money. Thus, each real estate transaction involves an exchange of benefits and sacrifices by both parties. What the buyer and seller are actually doing is exchanging items of value.

The concept of market value is based on a theory that, in any open market, there will be a number of buyers and sellers. If hundreds of transactions are concluded over a period of time, some parties will pay too much and some will sell for too little, but the vast majority of value decisions by both buyers and sellers will tend to converge into a fairly small area. That small area represents a range of market value, whether the market is dealing in houses, oranges, shoes, or whatever. This type of market value is the result of interaction between many buyers and sellers.

Adam Smith, a gifted economist, called this type of value "exchange value" to indicate that true market value is determined by the ability of any item to command other goods or services in exchange. It is not price, and it is not cost. If a seller attaches a price of $100,000 to a vacant lot where neighboring lots are selling for $8,000, his lot does not have the ability to command that number of dollars in exchange. So price and exchange value are different. Remember that one definition of "market value" began with the words, "The highest price in terms of money . . ." We could set a price in terms of gold, silver, steak, or bread. Money is merely a medium of exchange and has little value if not regarded in that light.

Ten $1,000 bills do not require much ink or much paper to manufacture; the total cost of ink and paper alone would probably not exceed fifty cents. But their power to command goods and services far exceeds their cost to produce. This illustrates that exchange value and cost are not the same.

The reason that it is important to understand the concept of exchange value is that time and other influences will cause changes in price, cost, and value. The problem is that price, cost, and value do not always change at the same time or to the same degree. Professionals in the business of real estate need to be capable of calculating the effects of inflation and time on real property values. The fact that one paid $25,000 for a house in 1967 and sold it for $35,000 in 1977 does not mean that the exchange value of the property has increased. Will the $35,000 in 1977 still buy the same amount of gold, bread, steak that $25,000 would buy in 1967? Fortunately, the Bureau of Labor Statistics in the U.S. Department of Labor provides a method for measuring fluctuations in real or exchange value: the Consumer Price Index.

Consumer Price Index

Also called the "cost-of-living index and the "CPI," the Consumer Price Index measures average price changes of goods and services which are usually bought by urban wage earners and clerical workers. The index is based on about 400 items which are selected to reflect the price trends of all goods and services in the marketplace. Prices are collected from roughly 18,000 establishments in 56 urban locations across the nation. Prices of food, fuels, and a few other items are collected each month. Prices of other commodities and services are collected every month in the five largest areas, and every three months in the other fifty-one areas. Prices are obtained by personal visits of trained personnel. A few prices such as local transit fares, public utility rates, and newspaper prices are obtained through questionnaires.

The current CPI is based on the year 1967. This means that the 1967 dollar is regarded as 100 percent of exchange value or purchasing power. A new base year is expected to be designated in the near future, but in mid-1977 the cost-of-living index (CPI) was using 1967 as the base year. As the cost of living increases, it will be reflected by the CPI moving upward from 100 to 109.8, 116.3, and so on. If the cost of living should decrease, the CPI would reflect the decrease by a downward movement indicating the percent of decrease as measured across the nation and in regional areas. The CPI for April, 1977, was 179.6, which indicated a

79.6 percent increase in the cost of living since 1967. Knowing the April, 1977 index, determine if that same house, bought in 1967 for $25,000, has increased or decreased in real or exchange value if it sold in April, 1977 for $35,000. Remember that, when dividing the 1977 price by the 1977 CPI, the index number (179.6) is really a percentage.

Solution:	1977 sales price	$35,000
	1977 CPI	÷ 1.796
	Real value in 1967 dollars	$19,487.75

What has happened to the exchange value (purchasing power)?

1967 price	$25,000.00
1967 dollars	-19,487.75
Loss in exchange value due to inflation	$ 5,512.25

The value of knowing how to use the CPI to calculate gains or losses in exchange value is obvious. Anyone might be inclined to accept less than the real value of a property because the number of dollars involved had increased. The CPI is a tool to prevent such a loss.

In order to ensure an ability to use the CPI, several details should be emphasized. First, the CPI will normally be quoted as a large number with one digit after the decimal (179.6 for example). But remember that the CPI is an expression of percentages (179.6 indicates a 79.6 percent increase in cost of living). Second, always use the CPI and number of dollars related to the same year. For example, never divide a 1977 CPI into a 1967 or a 1974 dollar amount. Many have erred with respect to the CPI by dividing the CPI for the year of sale into the dollar amount paid at time of purchase.

The illustration used above which indicated a loss of $5,512.25 in purchasing power is not actually a true-to-life example. Historically, real estate prices have increased faster than the overall cost of living. If a parcel of real property is acquired at market value or less, an owner will normally find that the sale price will increase faster than the cost of living. This ability to maintain or increase purchasing power is one reason real estate is regarded as one of the best protections against inflation. It is possible, however, to pour more money into a property than good judgment would indicate might be recaptured. For example, if the owner of a $25,000 house in a neighborhood of similar homes added a $6,000 swimming pool, or a $10,000 addition to the house, it is doubtful that the total cost would be recaptured when the property was sold. The two additions cited in the previous sentence are illustrations of "overimprovement." An overimprovement occurs when an owner invests more money in a structure than may be reasonably expected to be recaptured.

An entire building might be an overimprovement. If someone should build a $50,000 home in a neighborhood of $25,000 homes, the entire house would be an overimprovement. If a buyer could afford to pay $50,000 for such a home, it is normal to prefer that the house be located in a $50,000 neighborhood. So when the owner of the overimprovement is ready to sell, he will find few buyers willing to pay a price approaching his investment. This is another example of the point that cost and value are not the same thing. Value, then, is a concept. It is the price which should be paid for something, but not necessarily the price asked or the price actually paid.

Characteristics of Value

In any economic transaction, a good or service must possess certain traits or characteristics in order to have value. The mandatory characteristics are:

1. Demand. Economically, demand is more than a desire or need. Demand also implies the available means to obtain what is desired. Herdsmen and farmers who live in the desert lands of the world desire more fertile land, but they do not have the means to obtain other, more expensive land. Consequently, their desires alone do not have any economic impact on the supply of fertile land or on the price of such lands. In contrast, look at Miami Beach where people desire to live and have the means to acquire the use of part of the available supply. The need or desire combined with the economic means serve to create value.

2. Utility. To be valuable, a good or service must be able to fill a need. It must be useful. In real estate, this means the ability to provide useful services and benefits to an owner or tenant.

3. Scarcity. The supply of a good or service in relation to present or anticipated demand determines scarcity. If the supply exceeds demand, there is no scarcity and the value falls. If demand exceeds supply, a scarcity is created and value increases. When the number of available apartment units in an area exceeds the demand for apartments, the element of scarcity is missing and landlords must reduce rents or lose tenants. When the reverse is true, landlords can increase rents and the excess demand will fill any resulting vacancies.

4. Transferability. The legal ability to convey title and possession of a good is transferability. This is an unusually important factor in real estate. If a smooth-talking salesman sells an unsuspecting buyer the Brooklyn Bridge, the buyer can realize no value from his purchase because the seller cannot transfer legal title and possession. Where rights in land and the use of property cannot be transferred, all of the other characteristics of value may be present but there is no value created.

The above characteristics have been listed in a particular order to serve as a memory device. The first letter of each characteristic as listed above forms the word "DUST."

Three Approaches to Value

The commonly accepted techniques for estimating market value can all be grouped into three standard approaches. These main approaches to appraising are the:

1. Market or Sales Comparison Approach
2. Cost Approach
3. Income Approach

A thorough and complete narrative type appraisal report will utilize all three approaches in estimating the market value of a property. If all of the information utilized to prepare the appraisal were perfectly accurate, and if the real estate appraiser were perfect in his/her use of the information, the results from each of the three approaches would theoretically be the same. However, in this imperfect world, most appraisers must reconcile the varying results from each of the three different approaches. Each one of the three approaches is reviewed for possible errors in calculation or a possible misapplication by the appraiser. Any detected errors are corrected and a degree of priority (importance) based upon the type of property is assigned to each approach used. For example, if the property being appraised is a vacant lot in an established neighborhood, the market approach would be given top priority. If the property is an income-producing property, the income approach would be raised to top priority. The cost approach will almost always be used to cross-check the other two approaches and will be the top priority approach when appraising special purpose properties like hospitals, schools, or government buildings.

Each of the three approaches to market value is intended to provide an answer to a basic question:

Market Approach:	What is the current sales price for comparable properties?
Cost Approach:	What is the reproduction cost, less the "used-up value," as of today?
Income Approach:	What is the present worth of the future income?

1. Market or Sales Comparison Approach

The most widely used approach to value, largely because it is also the simplest approach, is the market or sales comparison technique. The market approach is actually an appraisal by comparison. It is based on the premise that the value of a property can be accurately estimated by reviewing recent sales of similar properties and comparing those properties with the property being appraised. Since time can affect property values, the sales used for comparison purposes must meet two qualifications: (1) they must have occurred recently in the same market area; and, (2) the properties must have been similar to the subject property (the property being appraised).

In recognition of the fact that no two properties are exactly alike, adjustments must be made for any differences between the subject property and each of the comparable sale properties.

Several types of special forms are available to assist appraisers in making adjustments for property differences as well as for differences in time, location, size, etc. All adjustments necessary to achieve the maximum degree of similarity must be made to the comparable properties, not to the subject property. A simplified Comparable Sales Adjustment Chart follows which illustrates one method of adjusting similar and recent property sales to arrive at a market value for a subject property.

Comparable Sales Adjustment Chart

Adjustment Factor*	Sale 1	Sale 2	Sale 3	Sale 4
Location		- $200	- $300	
Lot	- $200	- 200	- 300	
Carport				+ $500
Quality			-1,000	
Age, Condition, Appeal	- 300	+ 750	-1,012	+1,000
Size		-4,500		- 500
Net Adjustment	- $500	-$4,150	-$2,612	+$1,000
Sales Price	$28,500	$32,900	$31,112	$28,000
Adjusted Sales Price	$28,000	$28,750	$28,500	$29,000

Reconciliation: Sale 1: $28,000 x 40% = $11,200 c

Sale 2: $28,750 x 20% = $ 5,750

Sale 3: $28,500 x 10% = $ 2,850

Sale 4: $29,000 x 30% = $ 8,700

100%

Reconciled value = $28,500

*Adjustment factors may be added, deleted, or combined at the discretion of the appraiser to ensure appropriate consideration of value factors.

Note the method of reconciling four different adjusted sales prices. This is entirely a matter of judgment on the part of the appraiser. Whatever the market value is determined to be, it will represent 100% of the property's worth in the open market. In this instance, Sale 1 was considered most similar to the property being appraised, so it received a reconciliation weight of 40%. This means that 40% of whatever the appraised value is going to be should be based on the sales price of that property. Sale 4 was next in similarity and therefore was awarded a reconciliation weight of 30%. In each case, the adjusted sales price is multiplied by the reconciliation weight assigned, producing a part of the eventual reconciled value, which will be the estimated market value. c

The market approach gives a result which is the real estate market speaking instead of one person's opinion. By using only sales already transacted, the market tells us about that particular type of property. Regardless of what someone might wish for a sales price, the market indicates what value buyers and sellers have already established for properties similar to the subject property. The principle of substitution applies from that point: If a similar property of similar quality can be bought at a price lower than the subject property price, a buyer will substitute the lower-priced property. This economic concept thus sets an upper limit of value for any particular property by establishing the cost of acquiring an equally desirable substitute property on the open market, provided no additional problems are encountered. The substitution principle is the basis for the market, cost, and income approaches to value.

Where vacant lots are the subject of appraisals, the same technique is employed. Select 8 to 10 recent sales, and from those pick the 4 to 6 lots most similar to the subject lot. Differences in size or shape are neutralized by the use of a common unit of comparison like front feet or square feet. Using the recent 4 to 6 sales selected as market indicators, one can find the price paid per square foot or front foot for each lot. The reconciled average of all comparable sales will give the approximate value per square foot or front foot of the subject lot. c
One caution to observe in calculating the average cost per square foot of any property is, always divide square feet into dollars.

What is the estimated market value of a subject lot which is 110' x 120' (13,200 sq. ft.) if no reconciliation is required? c

Comparable Sales:

Sale 1. A lot 100' x 120' located across the street from subject property, sold three months ago for $6,800.
Sale 2. A lot 110' x 120' in the same neighborhood as subject lot, sold one month ago for $7,000.
Sale 3. A lot 100' x 100' in a separate but similar quality neighborhood, sold four months ago for $6,000.
Sale 4. A lot 130' x 150' located in a similar neighborhood but near a railroad, sold nine months ago for $9,800.

Solution:

Sale 1:	$6,800 ÷ 12,000 sq. ft. = .5666 or	$ .57	per sq. ft.
Sale 2:	$7,000 ÷ 13,200 sq. ft. = .5303 or	.53	per sq. ft.
Sale 3:	$6,000 ÷ 10,000 sq. ft. = .6000 or	.60	per sq. ft.
Sale 4:	$9,800 ÷ 19,500 sq. ft. = .5025 or	+ .50	per sq. ft.
		$2.20	
	Number of comparable sales	÷ 4	
	Average price per square foot	$ .55	

Total square footage of subject lot	13,200
Average price per sq. ft. (comparables)	x $.55
Estimated market value of subject lot	$7,260

2. Cost Approach

The cost approach to finding value is based on the premise that the value of a property can be estimated by the total investment required to replace or reproduce the building, less the accumulated depreciation and obsolescence, plus the value of the land. As the last sentence suggests, land value and building value are obtained separately and then added to get total value. The basic steps in the cost approach are:

1. Estimate the value of the land as if it were vacant.
2. Estimate the cost to reproduce the building in new condition.
3. Estimate the total depreciation and obsolescence of the building.
4. Subtract the depreciation and obsolescence from the cost to reproduce the building.
5. Add the depreciated reproduction cost to the value of the land.

An appraiser has several methods available to help in estimating building reproduction costs. The three cost estimating methods below are offered with the most technical and precise method first and with succeeding methods less precise but more convenient to use.

Quantity Survey Method. This involves a detailed inventory of all labor, materials, products, and indirect costs, plus profit required to reproduce a building. The number of items are then multiplied by the cost per item. For example, in a single-family dwelling with three baths, multiply the cost of one commode by 3, the cost of one bathtub by 3, etc. Or, if 1,000 lineal feet of 2x6's are required at a cost of $.50 per foot, the cost would be $500. The man-hours for each type of labor involved are estimated and multiplied by the cost per hour. All costs are totaled then added to overhead and indirect costs. The builder's profit is then added. The aggregate of all costs would be the reproduction cost of a new building.

Unit-In-Place Method. This method requires less technical ability than the quantity survey method and is almost as accurate. The cost of materials plus the cost of labor to install them is calculated for each component part of a structure, such as the driveway, parking area, the roof, foundation, walls, and floors. For example, a supplier of concrete will quote the cost per yard. The cost of putting the concrete in place and finishing will be added to the materials cost. Then the cost of one yard of concrete in place will be known. By multiplying the total number of yards needed by the unit-in-place cost per yard, the cost of all concrete needed to complete the structure is found. Each separate component is treated in the same manner. When the costs of equipment, fixtures, and builder's profit are added, the total cost of the structure is known.

Comparative Square Foot or Cubic Foot Method. This method is by far the most commonly used by appraisers because it is so much simpler to apply. It is sometimes called the "comparative market method" and sometimes the "unit comparison method." One reason why this method has so many names may be that so many people use it. The cost to reproduce a recently built property similar in size and function is often used as a basis for estimating the reproduction cost. Several cost calculation publications are also available to appraisers for determining standard square foot costs in different geographic regions. (Two of the most widely used commercial cost information services are the DODGE BUILDING COST CALCULATOR AND VALUATION GUIDE by McGraw-Hill Information Systems Co., and the BOECKH BUILDING VALUATION MANUAL by the American Appraisal Company.) In order to reduce errors in this method, square foot or cubic foot costs are obtained for a standard (or base) house of average size for the area involved. Adjustments are then made for quality, shape, and extra features. An abbreviated version of the comparative square foot method is provided to illustrate its use.

Comparative Square Foot Method

Estimated replacement cost new:			
Main dwelling			
1,241 sq. ft. @ $17 per	=	$21,097	
Utility room			
117 sq. ft. @ 8 per	=	936	
Loggia			
75 sq. ft. @ 4 per	=	300	
Carport			
412 sq. ft. @ 5 per	=	+ 2,060	
Total estimated replacement cost new			$24,393
Value of landscaping and driveway:			
Landscaping	=	$450	
Driveway - 300 sq. ft. @ $.75 per	=	+225	
Total value			+ 675
Total replacement cost with all improvements			$25,068
Less accrued depreciation			- 4,115
Total depreciated replacement cost			$20,953
Add value of land (by comparison)			+ 7,000
Total value of property via cost approach			$27,953
Total value of property via cost approach (rounded)			$28,000

Depreciation - Loss of value for any reason at all - usually physical

Depreciation is a very critical part of the cost approach to determine value. If five appraisers estimate the value of a subject property, the single item which will characteristically cause the greatest discrepancy in value will be the amount of depreciation each appraiser deems appropriate. For this reason (i.e., difficulty in accurately determining the exact amount of depreciation a building has accrued), the cost approach is

land is never depreciated only the building + other improvements.

considered the least accurate approach in measuring market value because it is only as accurate as an appraiser's judgment of accrued depreciation. Depreciation can be defined as any loss in value for any reason. The three main classifications of depreciation are:

1. Physical deterioration: ordinary wear and tear due to use, lack of maintenance, exposure to the elements, and physical damage.
2. Functional obsolescence: anything that is operationally inferior to a new structure of the same type (for example, an inefficient traffic pattern, an outmoded design, too few bathrooms, lack of modern facilities).
3. Economic obsolescence: any loss of value due to influences originating outside the boundaries of the property (for example, an expressway across the street, an industrial area next door, deterioration of the neighborhood). Normally economic obsolescence is beyond the control of the property owner.

Land is not depreciated, only the building or other improvements to land are subject to the three types of depreciation. This is the reason that the cost approach to measuring value begins by estimating the value of the land separate from the building. When the cost to reproduce the building is determined, depreciation is only applied to that portion of the property.

Depreciation is most frequently calculated by the "straight-line method." This means that an equal amount of building value is lost each year until the economic life of the building is exhausted. How does one know the amount of depreciation to deduct each year? The number of years of economic life are estimated and assigned to the building. Economic life is the total estimated time in years that a property can be profitably useful. Suppose you are appraising a five-year old building with a reproduction cost of $100,000 and an estimated economic life of 25 years (when new). This means that 25 years is equal to 100% of the life of the building. To find the amount of depreciation to deduct each year, divide 25 years into 100% and continue the calculations.

Solution: $\frac{\text{100\% of economic life}}{\text{25 years of economic life}} = $ 4% loss of economic life per year

Reproduction cost new	$100,000
Depreciation per year	x .04
Depreciation in dollars per year	$4,000.00
Annual depreciation	$4,000
Age of building in years	x 5
Total accumulated depreciation	$20,000
Reproduction cost new	$100,000
Total accumulated depreciation	- 20,000
Depreciated reproduction cost	$ 80,000

The cost of labor and materials today is undoubtedly different and would result in an investment of $100,000 to construct the same building new. This cost is the amount to be depreciated; it makes no difference what the original cost of the building might have been. Therefore, as the preceding calculations show, the five-year old building being appraised has a value of $80,000 today.

(Occasionally, other methods of depreciating real property are used by appraisers. Unless students of real estate are going to specialize in appraising, there is little or no reason to explore the more involved methods of depreciation.)

To find the total estimated value of the above subject property, all that is necessary is to add the value of the land to the depreciated reproduction cost. The value of land is normally determined by the market comparison approach explained earlier. Thus, if neighboring comparable properties are selling for $2.00 per square foot and the lot on which this building stands has an area of 11,000 square feet, the lot value must be $22,000. Adding the land value of $22,000 to the depreciated reproduction value of $80,000 gives a total property value of $102,000.

To summarize, the cost approach to determine market value is used on all types of improved properties, usually as a cross-check on other approaches which might be considered primary. However, as mentioned earlier, it is the only feasible approach to measure the value of special purpose properties.

3. Income Approach

The income approach is a complete departure from the other two methods of estimating market value. The objective of this approach is to measure the value of a flow of income projected into the future. It is not concerned with the cost of the lot or the reproduction cost of the building. The income approach develops an estimated market value based on the present worth of future income from the property. It is the primary approach for appraising income-producing property.

To determine the value of a property using the income approach, the appraiser must know the net income which the property produces. He may have access to the accounts, or be provided that information, or in some cases he may project the net income from available information and experience. Net income is then divided by an acceptable rate of interest (called the "capitalization rate") to obtain present market value.

There are many ways to arrive at a capitalization rate, but for the purposes herein, a rate of interest on the money invested which is acceptable to the investor will be used. A formula utilized by nearly all investors to express the method of determining present market value is as follows:

$$\text{Present Market Value} = \frac{\text{Net Income}}{\text{Capitalization Rate}}$$

or,

$$PV = \frac{NI}{R}$$

what investors want

always yearly

Suppose a small business property which produces a net income of $8,000 per year is to be appraised. The client wants the appraisal to help him make a decision regarding the amount of money he should invest in the property. He requires a return of at least 10% on any money invested or he will look for some other investment. The task is to tell him how much he can pay and still receive a return of 10% on his money.

$$PV = \frac{NI}{R}$$

$$PV = \frac{\$8{,}000}{.10}$$

$$PV = \$80{,}000 \text{ present value}$$

Therefore, the client can pay $80,000 for the property and realize his goal of receiving a 10% rate of interest on his investment.

The income approach is sometimes called the "highest and best use approach." This is because the potential buyer, who will use the property for a purpose which will produce the highest net income, can pay more than a buyer who would use it for some other purpose. For example, Ms. A wants a corner property but so do Mr. B and Dr. C. Ms. A will use the property for a business which will produce $18,000 per year net income. Mr. B has in mind another type business which will produce $16,000 per year net income. Dr. C will realize only $14,000 from the use he has in mind. All three will be satisfied with a return of 10% on their investment. How much can each of these buyers afford to bid for the property?

Ms. A: $\frac{\$18{,}000}{.10} = \$180{,}000$ (present market value)

Mr. B: $\frac{\$16{,}000}{.10} = \$160{,}000$ (present market value)

Dr. C: $\frac{\$14{,}000}{.10} = \$140{,}000$ (present market value)

The question now arises, How do investors or appraisers know what the net income will be, or should be, for a property? If the property is a vacant lot, there are no accounts of an existing business to which to refer. In such a case, a "pro forma" statement can be developed using the average results of several existing properties which are being used for the same purpose.

Suppose an investor is considering building an apartment complex with 10 units. A survey of other apartment projects of similar size and quality in the community will disclose the rent per apartment and the vacancy rate which might be expected. Further, assume you are appraising the property zoned for apartments on which the potential investor wants to build the 10 apartments. Your survey reveals that each apartment should be competitive if it rents for $200 per month. The survey also discloses that most apartment projects of this type have an average vacancy rate of 10%. By using normal costs of operation, a pro forma statement can be developed to find the probable net income.

Solution:

Competitive rent per month	$200	
Number of apartment units	x 10	
Potential gross income per month	$2,000	
Number of months in a year	x 12	
Potential annual gross income	$24,000	
Vacancy and collection losses (10%)	- 2,400	
Effective annual gross income		$21,600
Expenses (per year):		
Taxes	$ 2,260	
Insurance	430	
Management	10,000	
Repairs and maintenance	2,210	
Reserve for replacements	+ 700	
Total annual expenses		$15,600
Effective annual gross income	$21,600	
Total annual expenses	-15,600	
Net annual income		$ 6,000

Capitalization rate acceptable to investor = 12%

If the improvements to be constructed are expected to represent 80% of the total property value and the land is expected to represent 20% of the total property value:

$6,000 x .20 = $1,200 (net income attributable to land only)

$$PV = \frac{NI}{R} = \frac{\$1,200}{.12}$$

PV = $10,000 (present market value of the property)

Your client now knows the maximum amount he can pay for the property to realize his goal of earning 12% on money invested. If he is able to buy the property for less, his rate of estimated return will be increased.

Reasonable and sound income and expense data are critical in the use of the income approach. Many investors have been led down the primrose path by overly optimistic income figures which had no resemblance to actual income or occupancy rates experienced by similar existing properties.

It is important to see that a definite relationship exists between present value, net income, and capitalization rate. If, for example, the capitalization rate (R) is increased and the net income (NI) remains constant, the present value (PV) will be less. Or, if the net income goes up and the capitalization rate remains constant, the present value will be greater.

The Appraiser's Data Sources (Appraisal Plant)

An appraiser is almost totally dependent upon information he must obtain from a number of different sources. In order to ensure that the information needed is available and current, appraisers maintain a library of up-to-date statistical data and business publications. Most appraisers will include the following data sources in their "appraisal plant":

1. National statistical publications from the Department of Commerce, Bureau of the Census, Department of Labor, trade publications, etc.
2. A complete set of city and county maps (including recorded subdivisions)
3. Land-use studies with zoning maps
4. Economic studies
5. Growth projections (Usually information published by city or county planning bodies will be added to and modified by the appraiser himself using his own observations and experience.)
6. Services and utilities data (existing and planned networks of water, sewer, gas, electric, telephone, etc.)
7. Sales data (day-to-day recording of property transfer information, sales prices, location of sales, etc.).

More and more appraisers are turning to computers for use with their regular sources of information. The savings in time and effort may be well worth the cost. In spite of the numerous aids and resources available to appraisers, the most accurate and reliable appraisals are generally produced by qualified individuals of character and integrity who are thoroughly familiar with the local area. However, the best appraisal possible is not intended to represent exact market value; it is an estimate of market value provided by a knowledgeable authority. Thus, an appraisal can only be accurate when it is based on sound judgment backed by factual data.

CHAPTER 9

APPRAISING REAL PROPERTY

1. An appraisal of real property is:

   I. An estimate of value
   II. An exact value

   a. I only
   b. II only
   c. Both I and II
   d. Neither I nor II

2. The ability of a commodity to command other commodities is:

   I. Exchange value
   II. Market price

   a. I only
   b. II only
   c. Both I and II
   d. Neither I nor II

3. Appraising real property is:

   I. An art
   II. A science

   a. I only
   b. II only
   c. Both I and II
   d. Neither I nor II

4. An appraiser of real property is primarily concerned with:

   I. Sales price
   II. Market value

   a. I only
   b. II only
   c. Both I and II
   d. Neither I nor II

5. Inherent in the definition of market value is the assumption that:

   I. Neither buyer nor seller is under any compulsion
   II. Both buyer and seller are fully informed

   a. I only
   b. II only
   c. Both I and II
   d. Neither I nor II

6. In appraising, the comparison of a property with other properties of established value is the:

   I. Cost approach
   II. Market data approach

   a. I only
   b. II only
   c. Both I and II
   d. Neither I nor II

7. The CPI used to measure average price changes of goods and services is:

   I. The Consumer Price Index
   II. The Cost-of-living Index

   a. I only
   b. II only
   c. Both I and II
   d. Neither I nor II

8. The capitalization process is used in the:

   I. Income approach to value
   II. Market data approach to value

   a. I only
   b. II only
   c. Both I and II
   d. Neither I nor II

9. When more money is invested in a building than can reasonably be expected to be recaptured, it is:

   I. Economic lack of utility
   II. Overimprovement

   a. I only
   b. II only
   c. Both I and II
   d. Neither I nor II

10. The highest price in terms of money which a property will bring in an open market is called:

    I. Sale price
    II. Market value

    a. I only
    b. II only
    c. Both I and II
    d. Neither I nor II

11. Loss of value for any reason is called:

    I. Depreciation
    II. Economic obsolescence

    a. I only
    b. II only
    c. Both I and II
    d. Neither I nor II

12. Characteristics required to create value include:

    I. Demand, Scarcity
    II. Utility, Transferability

    a. I only
    b. II only
    c. Both I and II
    d. Neither I nor II

13. The approach to value most appropriate for appraising a community college would be the:

    I. Cost approach
    II. Income approach

    a. I only
    b. II only
    c. Both I and II
    d. Neither I nor II

14. The approach to value most appropriate for appraising an undeveloped tract of 1,000 acres would be the:

    I. Income approach
    II. Market data approach

    a. I only
    b. II only
    c. Both I and II
    d. Neither I nor II

15. In the market data approach, all adjustments required to achieve the maximum similarity between properties are made to the:

    I. Subject property
    II. Comparable property

    a. I only
    b. II only
    c. Both I and II
    d. Neither I nor II

16. The economic concept which sets an upper limit of value for any particular property is called the:

    I. Principle of substitution
    II. Capitalization process

    a. I only
    b. II only
    c. Both I and II
    d. Neither I nor II

17. The "comparative square foot or cubic foot method" used by appraisers is part of the:

    I. Income approach
    II. Cost approach

    a. I only
    b. II only
    c. Both I and II
    d. Neither I nor II

18. A loss of value due to influences originating beyond the boundaries of a parcel is called:

    I. Depreciation
    II. Economic obsolescence

    a. I only
    b. II only
    c. Both I and II
    d. Neither I nor II

19. The first step in the cost approach to value is:

    I. Estimating the economic life of the building
    II. Estimating the cost to reproduce the building

    a. I only
    b. II only
    c. Both I and II
    d. Neither I nor II

estimate value of land

20. The economic life of a building is the total number of years the building will:

    I. Exist
    II. Be useful financially

    a. I only
    b. II only
    c. Both I and II
    d. Neither I nor II

21. Market value by the income approach is based on the:

    I. Future worth of present income
    II. Present worth of future income

    a. I only
    b. II only
    c. Both I and II
    d. Neither I nor II

p. 149

22. In computing the market value by the income approach, net income is divided by:

    I. An acceptable rate of interest
    II. The capitalization rate

    a. I only
    b. II only
    c. Both I and II
    d. Neither I nor II

Present Market Value = Net Income / Capitalization rate

$PV = \frac{NI}{CR}$

23. In the income approach, if the capitalization rate is increased and the net income is constant:

    I. The present value will be less
    II. The present value will be more

    a. I only
    b. II only
    c. Both I and II
    d. Neither I nor II

24. A four-bedroom home with one bathroom would be an example of:

    I. Depreciation
    II. Functional obsolescence

    a. I only
    b. II only
    c. Both I and II
    d. Neither I nor II

CHAPTER 10

FINANCING REAL ESTATE

Before the turn of the century, a person who wanted to become a homeowner was very often required to pay cash. No standards for appraising real property had been developed and the market value, on which mortgage loans need to be based, was generally a matter of guesswork. For these reasons, those lenders willing to make mortgage loans normally used a borrower's total financial assets as the only underwriting criterion for making a loan, and at least 50 percent cash was almost always required to purchase real property. Loan-to-value ratios of 25 percent loan to 75 percent cash were not uncommon.

While being in debt for any reason was formerly regarded as practically immoral, today going into debt to buy a home is not only moral but also absolutely necessary in most instances. The current underwriting standards used by most lenders in making mortgage loans are:

1. First and most important, the quantity and quality of the homebuyer's income
2. Other assets
3. Past credit history

In addition to the change in lender's and borrower's attitudes toward mortgage loans, the sheer growth in mortgage volume has caused some other dramatic changes in financing real estate. The recent experience with the highest interest rates in the history of mortgage lending, plus continuing inflation, has created shock waves among the institutional lenders and mortgage specialists. As a result, new practices and variations of former lending procedures are in evidence which require careful study in order to remain current in the real estate finance area.

Real Property as Security

Two primary reasons account for the popularity of real property 13.26
mortgages as investments. First, the property, which is the lender's security, is fixed as to location and cannot be transported out of the reach of the lender in case he should need to foreclose. And second, the property has a longevity or durability which cannot be matched by other securities. Of course, the constant and continued rise in property values, aided by inflation, provides an additional hedge against the decrease in value of the lender's security and serves to make a mortgage on real property more attractive as an investment. Fortunately, this is true because only a very small fraction of the real estate transactions concluded in this country would take place if 100 percent cash was the only method of transferring property. Indeed, the practice of placing mortgages on real property is referred to in the Old Testament (Nehemiah 5: 3-4), and the practice has become a necessary facet of the real estate business in today's world.

Mortgage Instruments

Although the form of mortgage instruments changes from time to time, the requirement for a mortgage and a note have remained constant. Therefore, attention to the instruments used to create a mortgage is now appropriate.

Mortgage. A mortgage is any instrument in which property is used 13.26
as security for a debt. It is a type of lien on property which is voluntarily given by a borrower in return for a sum of money, or valuable consideration. The property then becomes security for the lender, legally sufficient to ensure recovery of the amount loaned. A note or bond must accompany all mortgages in Florida.

Note or Bond. The note or bond (in Florida, a note is more common) performs a definite function in mortgage lending. The note is legal evidence of a personal debt, and as a personal obligation to pay, it can be used as a basis for seizure of any real or personal property the borrower may own. The note may be a separate instrument, or it may appear on the back of the mortgage. The note is the primary obligation of the borrower. It will recite the total amount of the debt, the interest rate, and the term or time period. In short, the note contains all of the information regarding the debt. The mortgage instrument often will not indicate the interest rate because the mortgage is the instrument recorded in public records, while the note may, or may not, be recorded. This practice is intended to prevent "raiding" by other mortgage lenders when interest rates drop.

Parties to a Mortgage. There are always two parties to a mort- 13.01
gage, the mortgagor, who is the borrower (debtor), and the mortgagee, who is the lender (creditor). The mortgagor owns the property and the mortgagee owns the mortgage. A mortgage is regarded as an investment or a chattel by the mortgagee and, like other investments (chattels), may be sold by the mortgagee to another investor if deemed desirable since mortgages are personal property.

Enforcement of Mortgage Instruments. In case of default by the mortgagor, the mortgagee may elect to bring suit on the basis of the mortgage, or the note, or both. If a suit is initiated based on the mortgage, the suit must be filed and prosecuted in the county where the mortgaged property is located. The mortgagee may decide to sue on the note instead of the mortgage, or after a suit based on the mortgage is concluded. If the suit is based on the note, the legal action can be initiated anywhere in the nation where the mortgagor may be found.

In order to enforce a mortgage, it must be foreclosed in chancery 13.30
court (court of equity). Usually, an individual designated a "Master of Chancery" will handle the foreclosure. If the sale of the property at foreclosure should fail to bring enough money to pay the expenses of the sale and completely satisfy the mortgage debt, a "judgment for deficiency" will be requested against the person who signed the note or bond which accompanied the mortgage. When granted, a "deficiency decree" can extend to include all personal property belonging to the maker of the note. The

proceeds from a foreclosure sale will first be used to pay the expenses of the sale, then the delinquent taxes, before being used for payment of the mortgage debt.

Two Legal Theories of Mortgages

Custom and past experience, if repeated a number of times, begin to develop accepted practices which later take on the status of common law. Many of the current practices in real estate finance began in just that fashion. Today, what was formerly common law has been enacted into statutory law in a number of instances. One of these areas is the legal theories of mortgages.

Like many U.S. laws, the existing statutes affecting mortgages are based on common laws imported from England. Prior to the 14th century, two different approaches to mortgage lending were practiced in England. One group of lenders did not believe in charging an unfortunate borrower interest, but they took possession of his real property and collected the harvest or rents in place of interest. The other group of lenders left the mortgagor in possession of his land and charged a stipulated rate of interest. After the 14th century, most lenders accepted the theory of charging interest on mortgage loans and leaving the mortgagor in possession of his land. The two former mortgage practices have left their mark on the legal theories existing in different states today, i.e., the lien theory and the title theory. One of the main differences between the two theories involves the question, "Does a mortgage transfer title to the lender until the debt is paid, or does it only create a lien on the title?"

Title Theory. In the 13 states where the title theory of mortgages has been adopted, the title to mortgaged real property is vested in the mortgagee. However, the written form of mortgages used in title states permits the mortgagor to remain in possession of the land as long as he abides by the terms and conditions of the mortgage. In the event of default by the mortgagor, possession of the mortgaged property as well as title to the property is passed to the mortgagee without the requirement for legal foreclosure as practiced in lien theory states. This is a definite advantage for the lender as it negates the requirement for lengthy and expensive legal foreclosure procedures. It does, however, constitute a disadvantage to the unfortunate mortgagor.

Lien Theory. The lien theory is the prevalent mortgage theory in the nation: 32 states, including Florida, have adopted the lien theory of mortgages. This concept is based on the principle that a mortgage is intended to provide security for the mortgagee by creating a lien on the title of mortgaged property. The lien, in turn, gives the mortgagee both the power and the right to seize and sell the property in the event the mortgagor defaults on his agreement to pay back the money borrowed. The lien theory does not give the lender either title or right of possession. Even after a mortgage default occurs, the mortgagor is entitled to retain possession until legal foreclosure procedures have been completed.

(Five states use a combination of the two theories.)

Mortgage Clauses

Defeasance Clause

The written form of most mortgages would at first appear to be conveying title to the property to the mortgagee. A very important part of the mortgage called the "defeasance clause" defeats the actual transfer of property to the mortgagee, as long as the mortgage payments are made as required and all the terms of the mortgage are fulfilled. The defeasance clause will also indicate that a note (or notes) has been given as evidence of the debt created, then proceeds to stipulate that the conveyance of title shall be void if the mortgagor complies with all conditions. Thereafter, the defeasance clause will usually specify the conditions to be met and the terms of the mortgage. An easy way to remember the name and purpose of the defeasance clause is to associate the name "defeasance" with its purpose, "to defeat the mortgage." The defeasance clause may be a part of the mortgage instrument or in an instrument separate from the mortgage instrument. 13.26 13.29

In addition to the defeasance clause, there are a number of other clauses usually found in mortgages with which the real estate broker and salesman should be familiar. Only nine other of the many clauses encountered in real property mortgages will be examined here. c

1. Insurance Clause. After the defeasance clause, the insurance clause, or covenant, requires the mortgagor (borrower) to acquire and keep current a hazard insurance policy or policies issued by a company approved by the mortgagee (lender). The insurance must be adequate in amount to cover 100 percent of the unpaid balance of the mortgage placed on the property and is to be maintained until the mortgage is paid in full. The mortgagee is the beneficiary of the insurance up to the unpaid balance of the mortgage. This clause is usually worded in such a manner as to allow the mortgagee to procure adequate insurance if the mortgagor fails to do so. The cost of the insurance is then charged to the mortgagor. 13.32 15.12

2. Acceleration Clause. The acceleration clause is so named because the mortgagee is authorized to accelerate or advance the the due date of the entire unpaid balance if the mortgagor should fail to perform certain conditions. This means that the lender is given the power and the right to declare all of the unpaid mortgage due and payable, and further, to foreclose on the property if the mortgagor defaults. 13.32

3. Prepayment Clause. A prepayment clause is normally a part of FHA and VA mortgages on real property. The prepayment clause provides that the mortgagor will be allowed to pay the mortgage debt ahead of schedule without penalty. Often, the prepayment clause will stipulate conditions and terms under which the mortgage may be prepaid ahead of schedule, that is, as many multiples of the regular monthly payment may be permitted as the mortgagor wants to pay. However, some prepayment clauses prohibit payment of one and one-half regular monthly payments, or any other fractional part of a payment. Most all prepayment clauses allow

prepayment in full without penalty.

4. Penalty Clause. In the event the mortgagee does not desire the mortgage to be prepaid ahead of schedule, the mortgage will normally contain a penalty clause in place of the prepayment clause. The penalty clause will then require the mortgagor to pay an extra sum of money as a penalty for making payments in advance of the normal due date, or for prepayment of the entire mortgage debt. Normally, the penalty sum will be expressed as a percentage of the unpaid balance of the mortgage existing at the time the prepayment was tendered.

5. Tax Clause. Practically all mortgagees will require a tax 13.26
clause as a part of a mortgage. The tax clause requires the 15.10
mortgagor to pay all legitimate property taxes. If he should 15.11
fail to do so, the mortgagee will normally use the tax clause as an option to pay the taxes and charge them to the mortgagor, or he may choose to foreclose due to default of this obligation. In either event, the mortgagee would pay the taxes to prevent loss of the property.

6. Receivership Clause. A clause is included in most mortgages 13.32
related to property which is income-producing. This receivership clause is designed to require that income from the property be used to make mortgage payments in the event the mortgagor defaults. If it should become necessary for the mortgagee to foreclose on the property, it is possible that the legal proceedings could take several months to conclude the action. If no provisions were made for this contingency, the income from the property would continue to go to the owner who is in default. The owner would probably not be inclined to use any of the income to maintain the property if he was in default and facing foreclosure. The receivership clause permits the mortgagee to appeal to the courts for appointment of a "receiver" to take over management of the property and collection of rents or other income. The receiver pays the bills and carrying charges until the foreclosure action is concluded by sale of the property. Any net profits at the conclusion of his receivership may be used by the mortgagee to satisfy the mortgage debt, if need be.

7. Release Clause. If the mortgage relates to property intended 13.28
for development, a very important clause is the release clause. The situation which would require a release clause in the mortgage usually occurs in what are called "blanket mortgages," which cover a number of parcels, usually building lots. The mortgagor is the owner of record and normally wishes to sell the lots, but he does not want to pay off the whole blanket mortgage covering the entire tract. Normally, the owner plans to use the money from the sale of a lot to pay off part of the whole mortgage. A release clause in the blanket mortgage will stipulate the conditions under which the mortgagee will grant a release of the lots, free and clear of the mortgage.

8. Maintenance Clause. Most mortgages will require mortgagors c
(borrowers) to maintain mortgaged property in good condition. If this requirement were not included in the mortgage agreement,

the value of some mortgaged properties might diminish to the extent that the unpaid balance of the mortgage loan would exceed the uncared-for or unmaintained property value. c

9. Redemption Clause. A right exists for the mortgagor, all later purchasers, mortgagees, lienors, and creditors which is called "equity of redemption." This right is contained in the redemption clause and allows such parties to redeem from or update the mortgage by paying whatever amount is due until they are made parties to a foreclosure suit and the property is sold. This permits the redeeming parties, except the mortgagor, to foreclose against the mortgagor. 13.31

Types of Mortgages

Mortgages were formerly classified in such general categories as "insured," "guaranteed," and "uninsured." With the increased use of private mortgage insurance (PMI), these classifications have become less distinct in definition. Today, mortgages are generally regarded as belonging to one of three more descriptive categories: FHA, VA, and conventional. Variations and combinations of the three basic categories may occur, but the basic types of mortgages are the FHA, VA, and conventional.

Before each of the three basic types is discussed in more detail, the unique characteristics of each basic type can be pointed out in order to differentiate among them. FHA does not make loans, it insures loans; VA does have a limited direct-loan program, but it is chiefly involved in guaranteeing (not insuring) loans made by private lenders; and, conventional loans are those loans which are neither FHA nor VA and receive no government insurance or guarantee (conventional lenders can elect to obtain private mortgage insurance if they choose).

Federal Housing Administration Mortgage (FHA Loan)

Organized in 1934, the FHA's original purpose was to encourage reluctant lenders to invest their money in the mortgage market thereby stimulating the depressed construction industry.

The various types of loans FHA is allowed to insure are defined in the National Housing Act of 1934, and later amendments. Title I of that act deals with the financing of home improvements and conversion of existing buildings. Title II concerns all residential mortgage insurance programs. A condensed summary of the various FHA mortgage insurance programs may be found at the conclusion of this chapter.

FHA is authorized to insure private loans made by approved lenders. Borrowers pay a monthly insurance premium (MIP) as part of their regular mortgage payment. All MIP payments go into a central fund called the "Mutual Mortgage Insurance Fund" which is used to pay private lenders when an FHA-insured loan is declared uncollectable. The MIP insurance premium is one-half of one percent of the balance of the loan. The private lender who collects the regular monthly mortgage payment also collects the MIP and periodically forwards the premiums to FHA.

FHA mortgage interest rates tend to follow the cost of mortgage money in the free money market. However, the Secretary of the Department of Housing and Urban Development (HUD) has been delegated the authority to set FHA interest rates as deemed necessary, within a range of interest rates established by Congress. The fact remains that FHA interest rates are not free to react to money market changes until the Secretary, HUD, authorizes a change. This restriction has sometimes caused a wide gap between FHA rates and conventional mortgage rates. As a result, a system of "discounting" was created which permits lenders to charge extra "discount points" for FHA (and VA) mortgage loans. The purpose of this discounting system is to make FHA (and VA) loans more competitive with conventional loans. The extra yield to lenders from the discount points charged increases the real yield to the lender, and the interest earned on FHA (and VA) loans then approximates the yield from conventional loans made at higher interest rates. (See "Mortgage Discounting" in the next chapter.)

The FHA regulates lenders, borrowers, and the real property offered as security for the mortgages. All lenders are automatically approved to make FHA mortgages if they are members of the Federal Reserve System, Federal Deposit Insurance Corporation (FDIC), or Federal Savings and Loan Insurance Corporation (FSLIC). When a lending institution is not a member of one of these organizations, it can be placed on the list of approved lenders by providing the Federal Housing Commissioner evidence of previous experience in mortgage loans, of financial capability, and of satisfactory business capacity.

All properties purchased with FHA mortgage insurance must first be appraised. When the property has been qualified as meeting FHA standards, the borrower must also qualify in the three areas listed at the beginning of this chapter and detailed as follows.

Mortgage Underwriting (Risk Analysis)

1. Quantity and Quality of Income. When a private lender takes an application for an FHA loan, the prospective borrower provides information about his present employment, past financial history, and present obligations. This information is forwarded to the FHA for their use in making a decision of approval or rejection. The FHA is primarily interested in the debt-paying ability of the borrower and the degree of risk involved. The quantity of the borrower's income is, of course, the amount earned. However, amount alone is not sufficient, because the probable duration of income is also important when the debt obligation may extend up to 30 years. So the quality of the income is also evaluated -- how long the applicant has worked in his or her present employment and what the probable continuity is. FHA will also evaluate existing demands on a prospective borrower's income, such as life insurance premiums, income taxes, installment credit accounts, proposed mortgage payments, and property taxes. All of these items will deplete the income earned by the borrower.

2. Other Assets. The second area of concern in analyzing a loan application is the total amount of other assets belonging to the applicant. Other real estate, savings accounts, stocks, bonds,

and equity in personal property are examples of assets which could act as sources of funds for mortgage payments in case the applicant's income should be interrupted.

3. Credit History. The third area of concern is the applicant's credit history. Strange as it may seem, many people with considerable annual incomes have a history of ignoring debt obligations, or being extremely slow to pay their debts. An indication of past credit history can be obtained from a credit report by a local credit bureau. The existing national network of credit bureaus permits a comparatively rapid check of new residents from other states.

The entire process of analyzing a loan application as outlined is called "loan underwriting" and is not unique to FHA but is practiced by all mortgage lenders. However, FHA has contributed a great deal toward the practices of underwriting mortgage loans.

Down Payment Consideration ("Required Investment") c

When a loan application is approved by FHA, it does not mean that FHA will lend the money. The loan approval tells a local FHA lender that he can make the loan and FHA will insure him against future loss. However, the lender is required to use FHA forms and comply with FHA policies and procedures in order to qualify for FHA mortgage insurance. One of the strictly controlled features of an FHA loan is the matter of down payments required from borrowers to finance the purchase of homes under Section 203(b). The required amount of down payment increases as the appraised value of the property increases. The new graduated scale of required down payments is divided into two separate levels of appraised value plus closing costs: c

Total Appraised Value and Closing Costs	Down Payment (Required Investment)
All or any part of first $25,000	3%
All over $25,000	5%

The maximum FHA loan amount is $60,000.

Example: Compute the required down payment for a house with an appraised value and closing costs of $61,500.

Three separate computations are required:

First computation: 3% of value up to, but not more than, $25,000	$61,500 -$25,000 x 3% =	$ 750
Remaining:	$36,500	
Second computation: 5% of all over $25,000	$36,500 x 5% =	$1,825
Third computation: add the results of the first two computations to give the Total down payment required:	+	$2,575

Thus, the loan required would be $58,925 ($61,500 - $2,575). (In actual practice, the FHA lender must always round the required investment up to the next highest even $50 increment, which, in this example, would result in a down payment of $2,600.)

The current maximum FHA loan available for a single-family dwelling is $60,000. FHA loans are permitted to be written for a period of 30 years, or 75 percent of the remaining economic life of an existing property, whichever is less. Some FHA loans not related to Section 203(b) residential properties are allowed terms of up to 40 years. These extended mortgage terms are authorized for housing for the elderly, cooperative housing, and slum clearance.

Veterans Administration Mortgage (VA or GI Loan)

In 1944, Congress enacted legislation entitled the Servicemen's Readjustment Act of 1944 to aid returning World War II veterans in the fields of education, hospitalization, employment training, and housing. That portion of the act pertaining to veteran's housing proved to be revolutionary in the world of real property mortgages. Nicknamed the "GI Bill," this original law guaranteed the repayment of $2,000 or 50 percent of the mortgage amount, whichever was less, to lenders who would make mortgage loans to veterans with no down payment required. The veteran was not charged a fee for this guarantee, and the government agreed to stand any losses that might result as a token of appreciation for military service in the war. From the lender's point of view, the government guarantee of $2,000 represented the same safety cushion for their loan as a $2,000 down payment. Subsequent amendments to the original GI Bill have gradually increased the government guarantee to the present level of $17,500 or 60 percent of the amount of the loan, whichever is less. Inflation was one of the reasons for increased guarantee amounts, but the major factor which convinced Congress to liberalize the guaranteed amount of VA loans was the unexpectedly good credit history established by military veteran homeowners. The government costs associated with the VA loan programs were much less than anticipated; in fact, foreclosures on veteran no-down-payment loans were at a lower rate than foreclosures of FHA loans.

The primary interest of the Veterans Administration has been to aid veterans. The law governing VA loans forbids a veteran to pay any discount points. Furthermore, the veteran, the lender, the property, the interest rate, the term, and the loan amount are all subject to strict VA rules covering all phases of the loan. The intent is to make certain that the veteran is undertaking an obligation within his or her capabilities.

The VA has not established a maximum on the amount of a VA loan, except that the loan cannot exceed the appraised reasonable value of the property as determined by a VA appraiser. The same underwriting criteria for FHA loans apply to VA loans. Many lenders feel a veteran can purchase a home up to a range between $65,000 and $70,000 with a $17,500 loan guarantee. The deciding factor will be the ability of the veteran to make monthly payments on the mortgage, including principal and interest plus property taxes and hazard insurance. Both VA and FHA require borrowers to pay one-twelfth of annual property taxes and hazard insurance with each month's mortgage payment. Although the GI Bill authorizes no-down-payment mortgage loans, each individual lender must make the decision about making a no-down-payment loan. Some lenders feel that every homebuyer should own some equity in his home in order to develop pride of ownership. It would be very unusual to find a lender who would lend 100 percent of the reasonable value on a $70,000 home.

The maximum period of years for a VA loan is 30 years. The veteran must be granted prepayment privileges in a VA loan, that is, he or she may elect to pay all or part of the principal balance remaining on the loan at any time without penalty.

Interest rates for VA mortgages are set by the Administrator of Veteran Affairs. The law providing this authority requires the Administrator to consult with the Secretary, HUD, before changing interest rates. Traditionally, changes in FHA and VA interest rates have changed at the same time, with simultaneous announcements by the Administrator and the Secretary.

VA loans may be used to acquire a residential property of one to four units, but the veteran must reside in one of the units. VA loans can also be used to purchase a farm, but it must be the personal residence of the veteran. Construction of a new home or alterations, repairs, and improvements to an existing home are also permitted.

Unlike the FHA, the VA has a limited direct-loan program for veterans living in areas where other mortgage funds at VA-approved rates are not available. When a direct loan is made to a veteran, it is limited to a maximum amount of $25,000, except in designated high-cost areas.

To be eligible for a VA loan, a veteran must have served a period of active duty equal to, or more than, the days of active duty indicated on the following schedule:

Period of Service	Days of Active Duty
September, 1940 to July, 1947	90
July, 1947 to June, 1950	181
June, 1950 to February, 1955	90
February, 1955 to the present	181

One of the first steps for a veteran interested in buying a house is to submit VA Form 26-1880, Request for Determination of Eligibility and Available Loan Guarantee Entitlement. Submission of this form will result in confirmed eligibility from the Veterans Administration. The veteran will then know if he or she is qualified for a loan and the amount of guarantee available. Many veterans are unaware that a 1975 law change resulted in additional eligibility for veterans who had previously used all of their entitlement. Take the case of a veteran who bought a home in 1970 and used his full mortgage eligibility of $12,500, which was the maximum in that year. Then suppose the veteran sold his house in 1977 and allowed the buyer to assume his VA loan without obtaining release from liability. The veteran now has an additional $5,000 eligibility as a result of the 1975 law which permits veterans to use any difference between the new $17,500 limit and the amount of mortgage guarantee previously used, if any.

Conventional Mortgage Loans

A conventional loan is the easiest of all three basic mortgage types to define. Any mortgage loan which is not insured by FHA or guaranteed by VA is a conventional loan. Conventional loans are made by private lenders and usually have a slightly higher interest rate and a lower loan-to-value ratio than either FHA or VA loans. This means that a lower percentage of the property value is loaned, or another way of expressing it, higher down payments are required by conventional lenders. This characteristically higher down payment has caused many people to prefer financing by FHA or VA mortgage loans, despite the fact that conventional loans could normally be processed and approved in much less time than either FHA or VA loans.

Conventional lenders are regulated by the governmental agency which issued their charter, or the FDIC or the FSLIC, if they are members. Most conventional lenders are restricted to loan-to-value ratios of 80/20 of appraised value (80 percent loan to 20 percent equity) unless additional security is provided for any increased loan amount exceeding 80 percent. If a buyer wanted to purchase a house appraised at $42,000, the restriction on lending more than 80 percent of value would require a down payment of $8,400. The same house purchased with FHA financing would require a $1,600 down payment. Obviously, the 80/20 limitation made conventional loans less competitive. In 1957, the Mortgage Guaranty Insurance Corporation introduced a system of private mortgage insurance (PMI) which permitted conventional lenders to exceed the 80 percent of appraised value restriction by insuring that portion of the mortgage loan which exceeded 80 percent. Conventional lenders could now lend up to 95 percent of appraised value if the borrower agreed to pay the insurance premium for PMI. The cost of private mortgage insurance has averaged slightly less than the one-half of one percent cost for FHA insurance. Most potential buyers are happy to pay for PMI in order to obtain more liberal financing. In the illustration used above, with PMI a prospective buyer could finance the $42,000 home by use of a 95 percent loan and 5 percent down payment ($2,100). Private mortgage insurance has resulted in conventional loans becoming more competitive and more commonly used to finance purchases of real property in spite of interest rates which usually are higher than FHA or VA rates.

The Amortized Mortgage

Prior to 1930, so-called "term mortgages" were commonly used to purchase real estate. Term mortgages were more popular with lenders than "amortized mortgages" because no part of the principal was paid back until the full term of the mortgage had expired. This allowed lenders to collect periodic interest payments on the full amount of the loan until the end of the mortgage term. The last payment would include all of the mortgage amount plus the last interest payment. The term loan was a financial burden for homebuyers and contributed to many of the foreclosures which occurred in the great depression of the 1930's.

When the federal government entered the real estate financing scene in the chaos of the depression years, one of the beneficial changes made was a conversion from term to amortized mortgages. Private lenders were later forced to convert to amortized mortgages in order to be competitive. Today, the most common and the most popular loan payment plan is the fully amortized mortgage. Webster defines the word "amortize" as meaning to extinguish or deaden. This definition indicates the theory of amortized loans. An amortized mortgage is gradually and systematically killed or extinguished by regular, periodic payments.

When the various components of a mortgage loan are known (the amount borrowed, the rate of interest, and the term or number of years), the level or constant monthly payment can be calculated by use of compound interest tables. Each monthly payment includes both interest and a partial repayment of the principal. While the same amount is paid each month, the portion of the payment used for paying interest decreases each month while the portion used for repayment of principal increases monthly. Naturally, this means the first few monthly payments are almost entirely used to pay interest, and the last few monthly payments are almost entirely principal repayment.

The type of mortgage payment plan discussed above, in which each monthly payment is the same amount throughout the life of the mortgage, is the level, or constant, payment plan. Several other payment plans are used to amortize mortgages: the straight principal reduction plan, the partially amortized mortgage, and the graduated payment plan. These plans will not be discussed here; however, the serious student of financing real property should become acquainted with these and other types of payment plans in order to broaden his or her choice of alternatives in real estate transactions.

All real estate students must learn how to compute the portion of each monthly mortgage payment allocated to interest, and the portion remaining for repayment of principal. A simple method for making these calculations is explained in the chapter entitled, Computations and Closing Statements.

Construction Loans

A cardinal rule observed by all lenders, one which is never knowingly violated, is never lend more money than the appraised value of the property which is security for the loan. This rule sometimes appears to be violated by lenders of construction loans, but be assured it is not. For example, a builder owns a lot valued at $8,000. He contacts a local commercial bank to arrange a construction loan of $30,000 in order to put a house on the lot. The builder then plans to sell the house and lot for $45,000. The existing security for the construction loan is his $8,000 lot. The lot owner and lender will sign an agreement giving the lender a first mortgage lien on the lot and any later improvements added to the lot in exchange for construction funds. This agreement is actually a loan commitment which provides for the funds to be disbursed at designated intervals during the construction period. The construction loan term may vary from six months to eighteen months.

Interest rates charged for construction loans are normally based on short-term credit rates and not on normal long-term mortgage rates. Many lenders today establish a base rate, or floor, of perhaps 9½ percent. But the actual rate to be paid will be a variable rate based on the lender's prime lending rate. A typical construction loan agreement may establish the interest rate at two points over prime with a minimum of 9½%. If the prime rate goes up to 8 percent, the borrower pays 10 percent, etc.

When the loan agreement is concluded, disbursements will be made in installments or "draws" which will only be paid after a scheduled amount of construction has been completed and inspected. This practice is utilized to ensure that the value of the lot has been increased by the construction process to the extent that the value of the improved lot will exceed the money disbursed. Disbursements will usually be made in either four or five draws as the construction process progresses. Most lenders will withhold about 10 percent of each draw until final completion of construction. The funds withheld provide a reserve to settle unexpected claims of suppliers or subcontractors. A common practice, and one which should always be observed, is to require contractors and subcontractors to sign an agreement that they have been paid for all work up to the date of the signature. This will preclude later claims or mechanic's liens.

When all construction has been completed and inspected by the lender's representative, the final disbursement is made. The 10 percent withheld funds are later paid when the lender receives the acknowledgments of contractors and subcontractors that they have been paid in full. When the builder sells the house and lot, he will pay the construction lender from the proceeds of the sale. The buyer will either pay cash or arrange for a long-term permanent mortgage. In either case, the builder receives his money and is able to pay the construction lender.

Purchase Money Mortgage

Much attention has been focused on the question of what consti- 13.25
tutes a "purchase money mortgage." Actually, the definition of a purchase money mortgage is quite simple: Any mortgage given as a part of the purchase price is a purchase money mortgage. It makes no difference whether the loan is made by the seller or some other party. The mortgage instrument should specifically state that the mortgage being created is a purchase money mortgage. This is required in order to remove any doubt concerning its status, since a purchase money mortgage is regarded as a lien which is prior to any other private lien against the purchaser. Where the seller of the property takes the mortgage as a part of the purchase price, it creates, automatically, a "vendor's lien" (where the vendor is the lender).

Package Mortgages

Just a few decades ago, the name of "residential mortgage" was applied only to a loan made to purchase land and a basic house. Any equipment or fixtures added to the house had to be purchased by the homebuyer in separate transactions. The gradual evolvement of mortgage loan practice has caused a completely new attitude toward the type and number of items that may be included in residential mortgage agreements.

The name "package mortgage" indicates a mortgage agreement that includes land and improvements to the land such as houses, fixtures, and building equipment as security for the debt. Common fixtures include wall-to-wall carpeting, chandeliers, and luxury lighting fixtures. Equipment normally acceptable to lenders includes such items as dishwashers, ranges, refrigerators, clothes washers and dryers, garbage disposals, trash compactors, and automatic garage-door openers. Any and all of these articles can be included in a package mortgage. Most residential mortgages today do include some of the items mentioned. The package mortgage is becoming so common that it is the rule rather than the exception. Consequently, the title "package mortgage" is used less and the word "mortgage" is commonly substituted.

The inclusion of fixtures or equipment in a package mortgage must be by mutual consent of the mortgagee and the mortgagor. When included as part of the security for a mortgage loan, the individual items should be enumerated in the mortgage after the legal description of the real property. Following the list of fixtures and equipment will usually appear a statement to the effect that, "These articles are and shall be considered to be fixtures and thereby are in all respects deemed to be a part of the security offered for this mortgage."

There are advantages and disadvantages to the package mortgage. Some of the advantages are:

1. The mortgage interest rate is usually less than half that a buyer of identical equipment would pay under an installment credit purchase.
2. The buyer includes payments for several items in one mortgage loan payment, thus avoiding a variety of monthly payments.
3. The down payment on the house includes the down payment for fixtures and equipment.
4. The builder who installs the fixtures and equipment can usually buy in large quantities and pass the reduced cost to homebuyers.
5. For young couples without accumulated savings, they can enjoy an improved standard of living.

But, there are also disadvantages to package mortgages, some of which are:

1. The monthly mortgage payment is increased by the number of fixtures and equipment included as part of the mortgage.
2. The term of the mortgage will usually be from 25 to 30 years, while the economic life of fixtures and equipment will normally only range from 5 to 15 years.
3. The interest rate may be lower, but the total amount of interest paid over a 25- or 30-year mortgage will be much more.
4. When the owner sells his home, he is obligated to convey all of the items listed in the mortgage agreement unless

the loan is paid in full.

Each homebuyer must make his or her individual decision regarding the type and number of fixtures and equipment to be included in a package mortgage. A glance at a mortgage rate book will reveal that the level monthly payment for an amortized, conventional mortgage of $35,000 at 8 3/4% interest for 30 years is $275.35. If $6,000 of fixtures and equipment are added, the required monthly payment becomes $322.55. Whether the use of the new items is worth $47.20 per month can only be answered by the individual considering the purchase.

Purchase of Mortgaged Property

Property which is mortgaged may be bought in three ways. First, 12.29
the mortgage may be paid and the property delivered free and clear at the time of closing. If this is to be the situation, the broker is required to ensure that all liens and mortgages are paid and to obtain proper receipts or satisfactions of mortgages before releasing any of the purchase monies. Of course, if the buyer and the seller have a clear understanding and agreement that the seller alone is responsible for such matters, the broker is relieved of this obligation.

The second method of buying mortgaged property is by buying or acquiring property "subject to the mortgage." The buyer is responsible for regular, periodic payments of the mortgage in order to remain in possession of the property. He does not become obligated for the note or the mortgage. In fact, the seller remains primarily responsible for both the note and the mortgage. In the event the buyer defaults, the mortgagee can proceed to foreclose. If the foreclosure sale does not satisfy the mortgage debt, a deficiency judgment can be sought against the original mortgagor, who remained responsible for the mortgage when he sold the property.

If the property is sold with an "assumption of the mortgage" (the third method of buying mortgaged property), the buyer assumes the primary obligation of the mortgage. The seller is moved into a position of secondary responsibility as surety for the mortgage debt. This means that in case the vendee (buyer) should default on the mortgage and a foreclosure sale should result, any deficiency sought would be against the vendee first. Only after his assets had been exhausted, and the deficiency still remained unpaid, would the vendor (seller) be called upon to make good on the note and the mortgage.

"Chattel mortgages" have not been treated because they are liens on personal property and, therefore, not a facet of the real estate business as such.

Summary of Number Synonyms for FHA Housing Programs

Most of the individual FHA housing programs are known by the numbers of the Sections of the National Housing Act. The principal numbers and the programs they identify are:

Title I	Housing renovation and modernization.
Title II	Mortgage loan insurance:
Sec. 203(b)	Homeownership, regular program
Sec. 203(i)	Low-cost homes in outlying areas and farm homes
Sec. 203(k)	Repair of homes not in urban renewal areas
Sec. 203(m)	Seasonal homes
Sec. 207	Rental housing, regular program
Sec. 213	Cooperative housing
Sec. 220	New and rehabilitated homes and rental housing in urban renewal areas
Sec. 220(h)	Repair and rehabilitation of homes and multi-family housing in urban renewal areas
Sec. 221	New or rehabilitated homes and rental housing for displaced families or low- or moderate-income families
Sec. 221(d)(3)	New or rehabilitated rental housing for displaced or low- or moderate-income families with mortgages bearing below-market interest rates (BMIR) and purchased by GNMA under its special assistance program
Sec. 221(h)	Nonprofit rehabilitation of deteriorating or substandard housing for resale to low-income home purchasers at below-market interest rates
Sec. 221(i)	Conversion of 221(d)(3) BMIR projects to condominium ownership
Sec. 221(j)	Conversion of 221(d)(3) BMIR projects to cooperative ownership
Sec. 222	Homeownership for servicemen
Sec. 231	New or rehabilitated housing for the elderly
Sec. 232	New or rehabilitated nursing homes
Sec. 233	Experimental housing, homes and rental
Sec. 234	Condominium housing
Sec. 235	Homeownership for lower-income families with aid of "mortgage assistance payments"
Sec. 235(j)	Nonprofit or public rehabilitation of deteriorating or substandard housing for resale to lower-income families
Sec. 236	Rental housing for lower-income families with the aid of "interest reduction payments"
Sec. 237	Credit assistance and counseling for low- and moderate-income home purchasers
Sec. 240	Purchases by lessees of fee simple title to property on which their homes are located
Sec. 241	Supplemental loans for multi-family projects
Sec. 242	Nonprofit hospitals
Sec. 809	Homes for civilian employees at a research or development installation of military department, NASA, AEC, or a contractor thereof.

CHAPTER 10

FINANCING REAL ESTATE

1. Current mortgage underwriting standards assign the most important priority to the home buyer's:

   I. Income
   II. Financial assets

   a. I only
   b. II only
   c. Both I and II
   d. Neither I nor II

2. The acceptability of real property mortgages as investments is attributable to the:

   I. Immobility of real property
   II. Durability of real property

   a. I only
   b. II only
   c. Both I and II
   d. Neither I nor II

3. In a mortgage transaction, the legal evidence of a personal debt is the:

   I. Note
   II. Mortgage agreement

   a. I only
   b. II only
   c. Both I and II
   d. Neither I nor II

4. The title theory of mortgages represents an advantage for the:

   I. Mortgagor
   II. Mortgagee

   a. I only
   b. II only
   c. Both I and II
   d. Neither I nor II

5. The mortgage clause which prevents transfer of the mortgaged property to the lender as long as the terms of the agreement are fulfilled is the:

   I. Release clause
   II. Defeasance clause

   a. I only
   b. II only
   c. Both I and II
   d. Neither I nor II

6. FHA makes insured loans through:

   I. Approved lenders
   II. Members of FDIC and FSLIC

   a. I only
   b. II only
   c. Both I and II
   d. Neither I nor II

7. The purpose of the mortgage discounting system is to:

   I. Make FHA and VA loans more competitive with conventional loans
   II. Reduce the long-range cost of mortgages

   a. I only
   b. II only
   c. Both I and II
   d. Neither I nor II

8. The down payment required to purchase a $44,000 home under FHA Section 203(b) would be:

   I. $4,400
   II. $1,700

   a. I only
   b. II only
   c. Both I and II
   d. Neither I nor II

c

9. The maximum FHA loan available for a single-family dwelling is:

   I. $60,000
   II. $45,000

   a. I only
   b. II only
   c. Both I and II
   d. Neither I nor II

c

10. Congress authorized an increase in the VA guaranteed amount of a VA loan to $17,500 because of:

   I. The good credit history of veterans
   II. Inflation

   a. I only
   b. II only
   c. Both I and II
   d. Neither I nor II

11. The maximum amount of a VA loan is:

   I. $49,999 don't loan
   II. $70,000 —no maximum loan— —guarantee max of 17,500

   a. I only
   b. II only
   c. Both I and II
   d. Neither I nor II

12. The cost of private mortgage insurance has averaged slightly:

   I. More than FHA insurance
   II. Less than FHA insurance

   a. I only
   b. II only
   c. Both I and II
   d. Neither I nor II

13. The word "amortize" means to:

   I. Love or increase
   II. Deaden or kill

   a. I only
   b. II only
   c. Both I and II
   d. Neither I nor II

14. A construction loan is normally disbursed in:

   I. Installments
   II. Draws

   a. I only
   b. II only
   c. Both I and II
   d. Neither I nor II

15. An FHA mortgage given as part of the price paid for a house is a:

   I. Purchase money mortgage
   II. Term mortgage

   a. I only
   b. II only
   c. Both I and II
   d. Neither I nor II

16. The person most knowledgeable about whether a package mortgage should be used is the:

   Pg. 170

   I. Lender
   II. Mortgage broker Lien mortgagor home buyer

   a. I only
   b. II only
   c. Both I and II
   d. Neither I nor II

17. In Florida, the legal concept regarding mortgages on real property is the:

   I. Title theory
   II. Lien theory

   a. I only
   b. II only
   c. Both I and II
   d. Neither I nor II

18. A mortgage is:

   I. Any instrument in which property is used for security
   II. A lien on property given in return for a loan

   a. I only
   b. II only
   c. Both I and II
   d. Neither I nor II

19. The person who borrows money to help pay for the purchase of real property is called at various times the:

 I. Mortgagor
 II. Mortgagee

 a. I only
 b. II only
 c. Both I and II
 d. Neither I nor II

20. If a lender initiates a suit based on the note accompanying a mortgage, the suit will only be productive if filed:

 I. In the county where the real property is located
 II. Wherever the borrower in default may be located

 a. I only
 b. II only
 c. Both I and II
 d. Neither I nor II

21. A mortgage and a lien are exactly the same thing. T F

22. When a vendee buys "subject to the mortgage," he moves into a position of primary responsibility for the mortgage. T F

23. The right of redemption allows the redeeming parties to foreclose against the mortgagor. T F

24. The proceeds from a foreclosure sale go first to satisfy the mortgage which was foreclosed. T F

25. When a property is sold at foreclosure and fails to produce enough money to pay off the mortgage debt, the person who signed the note accompanying the mortgage can be required to pay the deficiency. T F

26. Any mortgage given as part of the purchase price is a purchase money mortgage. T F

27. A release clause in a mortgage will stipulate the conditions required for a mortgagee to release tracts of property free and clear. T F

28. The tax clause in a mortgage is normally used as an option for the mortgagee either to pay the taxes or to foreclose due to default. T F

29. A receivership clause is usually associated with mortgages on income-producing property. T F

30. A prepayment clause and a penalty clause are designed to protect the mortgagee. T F

31. A mortgage creates a lien on the mortgaged property and gives the mortgagee the right but not the power to seize and sell the property in case of default. T F

32. A mortgage must always consist of the mortgage instrument and a note or bond. T F

CHAPTER 11

THE MORTGAGE MARKET

In July, 1976, a member of the President's National Committee on Economic Policy advised Florida's homebuilders to obtain construction mortgage money from foreign investors. The reason behind this unusual financial advice was past interaction within the mortgage market which had resulted in major losses for real estate investment trusts, banks, and other lenders.

An understanding of mortgage market operating conditions and participants is basic to advantageous borrowing and lending. Like other markets, the mortgage market is irrevocably tied to the law of supply and demand. One of the most basic principles, actually an economic fact of life, is the inverse relationship between the amount of money available in the mortgage market and mortgage interest rates: when the amount of mortgage money decreases, mortgage interest rates increase, and vice versa.

Knowledgeable real estate salespersons and brokers should make a point of knowing mortgage market conditions, trends, and indicators. They should also be well-acquainted with proper borrowing procedures and should know which financial institution to contact for the type of loan desired.

In this chapter will be discussed the need for interaction between primary lenders and secondary lenders, what constitutes a primary market and a secondary market, what institutions and agencies are active in each, and how the potential borrower is affected. The very strong thread which connects all of these individuals, institutions, and agencies is money, in the form of mortgage loans.

The supply of mortgage money available at any given time is dependent upon the continuous and orderly flow of savings into various types of financial institutions and a few non-financial institutions. Some of the financial institutions involved in the mortgage market are regulated by the states in which they operate, some are regulated by the federal government, and some are regulated by both federal and state governments. Moreover, different institutions exercise differing lending policies regarding preference for residential, commercial, or other types of mortgage loans. Some institutions do not make FHA-VA mortgage loans, while others prefer these lower-risk loans. Such differences create an obligation for the professional real estate person to be knowledgeable enough to advise and assist potential borrowers in their search for a lender who offers the type mortgage desired.

The general size of the mortgage market may not seem impressive until it is compared with a known quantity. According to a Federal Reserve bulletin, as of April 1, 1977, mortgages represented approximately 910 billion dollars. This means that, for example, the total federal debt amounted to only 70 percent of mortgages outstanding at that time. This percentage relationship has tended and is expected to remain the same.

Primary and Secondary Lenders

Primary lenders are those financial institutions which participate directly in the creation of mortgage loans along with borrowers. They consist of savings and loan associations, life insurance companies, commercial banks, and mutual savings banks. However, it is not unusual to find pension funds, individuals, and others functioning as primary lenders. Many authorities are beginning to regard mortgage bankers as primary lenders (as will be explained later in this chapter); however, they are more accurately termed "middlemen" since they often merely act as an agent lending funds belonging to some financial institution.

At this point it may be helpful to examine the different roles and functions of a mortgage banker and a mortgage broker. Both act as agents, or middlemen, between borrowers and lenders, but the scope of the mortgage banker is much greater. The role of the mortgage broker is limited to acting as an agent. He is normally paid a finder's fee or commission in the neighborhood of one percent of the loan arranged. A mortgage broker does not have the authority to approve or reject a loan on behalf of a lender. Once the loan application has been accepted and approved by a lender, the mortgage broker drops out of the transaction. Mortgage brokers do not act as servicing agents or as correspondents for life insurance companies, mutual savings banks, or other lenders.

The mortgage banker also functions as a middleman, but his role is not restricted to that activity. Frequently the mortgage banker acts as the correspondent, or local representative, for life insurance companies, mutual savings banks, or other lenders located in distant areas. The mortgage banker often has been authorized to make loans for, and on behalf of, an institutional lender located elsewhere. After making a loan for a lender, the mortgage banker frequently services the loan by maintaining contact with the borrower, sending monthly payment notices, collecting escrow funds for taxes, and in general acting as a branch office of the lender. More on mortgage bankers will be found later in this chapter under "loan correspondents."

As might be expected, secondary lenders are those institutions and agencies which buy mortgage loans previously made by primary lenders or which make loans by using a "middleman" or representative to qualify and close the loan. Some financial institutions are both primary and secondary lenders. The major secondary lenders are federal government agencies, life insurance companies, and mutual savings banks. Among the federal agencies most active as secondary lenders are:

1. Federal National Mortgage Association (FNMA)
2. Government National Mortgage Association (GNMA)
3. Federal Home Loan Mortgage Corporation (FHLMC)

FNMA

The Federal National Mortgage Association (nicknamed "Fannie Mae") was established by Congress in 1938 as an official agency of the federal government for the purpose of creating a secondary market for mortgage loans. A secondary market is any market which buys and sells commodities or securities already existing.

A primary market differs from a secondary market in that the primary market is the market where the security or good is actually created. For example, if a commercial bank lends a homebuyer the money to buy a house through the use of a mortgage loan, that would be a primary market activity. Suppose that same commercial bank desires to recover the funds loaned, perhaps with some profit if conditions permit. The commercial bank might then sell the mortgage to FNMA ("Fannie Mae"). The transaction between the bank and FNMA would be a secondary market activity because the mortgage had been created by a previous transaction. Fulfilling this secondary mortgage market role allows FNMA to provide liquidity for mortgage lenders who may be desirous of converting residential mortgage investments into cash. This is the major purpose for which FNMA was originally created. FNMA not only buys residential loans but also services and sells loans in performance of its secondary market role. In actual practice, FNMA purchases mortgages from any approved lender when the overall supply of loanable funds is short. When money becomes more plentiful, FNMA sells mortgages to financial institutions which have funds to invest. The cycle can be repeated as economic needs dictate. Although FNMA originally bought and sold only FHA and VA loans, it now deals in conventional as well as FHA and VA mortgages. Fannie Mae is no longer a governmental agency. In 1968, it became a government regulated corporation, but the corporation stock is privately owned.

GNMA

In the same year that FNMA was converted to a government sponsored private corporation, the Government National Mortgage Association (GNMA) was created by Congress as a part of the Department of Housing and Urban Development (HUD). The purpose of GNMA ("Ginnie Mae") was not to replace FNMA completely as a government agency when FNMA became a private corporation. GNMA did take over the special assistance functions formerly the responsibility of FNMA. These involve supplying funds for: (a) low-cost housing; and, (b) residential mortgages in capital deficit areas. The money required to support these activities is provided by borrowing from the federal government. The methodology employed to accomplish GNMA's special assistance goals has been called the "Tandem Plan." This name signifies the close cooperation between GNMA and FNMA to assist sponsors of low-cost housing. What actually happens is that GNMA issues a firm commitment to the sponsor of a low-cost or a nonprofit housing project. In the commitment, GNMA promises to buy mortgages at a fixed rate (say, for example, 7 3/4%) after construction of the housing is completed. With the GNMA commitment, the sponsor/developer can obtain construction loan money to build the project. GNMA meanwhile obtains an agreement from FNMA to buy the mortgage package from GNMA at current market prices. When the mortgages are delivered to FNMA, it is understood that GNMA will absorb any loss resulting from the transaction due to any difference between GNMA's fixed rate paid and the market rate allowed FNMA (for example, 8 1/2%). In this manner, GNMA avoids holding all the mortgages in its portfolio, which would tie up large blocks of money. GNMA is providing special assistance to the housing sponsor/developer by paying what amounts to a discount the sponsor normally could not afford. By paying only the discount and receiving reimbursement from Fannie Mae for the remainder of the loan, then Ginnie Mae has more money available for other projects. GNMA is also responsible for increasing the amount of funds available for residential lending and for managing an extensive mortgage portfolio.

A most significant power granted GNMA is authority to guarantee payment of principal and interest on government-backed "pass-through securities." Pass-through securities are backed by a group of mortgages which are either insured or guaranteed by the government. All mortgages selected to form a mortgage pool as collateral for pass-through securities must meet GNMA standards regarding interest rates, loan maturity periods, and type of property. No mortgage in such a pool can be more than one year old when the GNMA commitment is issued. Homeowner payments made on the mortgages in the pool are used to make interest payments on the securities sold. Proceeds from the sale of securities backed by pools are then used to create additional mortgages.

FHLMC

A third major participant in the secondary mortgage market is the Federal Home Loan Mortgage Corporation (FHLMC). Nicknamed "Freddie Mac," FHLMC was created by Congress in 1970 and placed under the supervision of the Federal Home Loan Bank Board. It functions as a secondary mortgage market through the purchase and sale of conventional, FHA, and VA mortgages. The purpose of Freddie Mac is to create the maximum liquidity for mortgages. This enables mortgages to compete for capital on an equal basis in the money market. As part of the Federal Home Loan Bank System, Freddie Mac is particularly important to federal savings and loan associations since they can use Freddie Mac to convert mortgages to cash, then use the cash to make new mortgage loans.

Actions and interactions of the primary and secondary mortgage markets are illustrated below:

PRIMARY AND SECONDARY MORTGAGE MARKETS

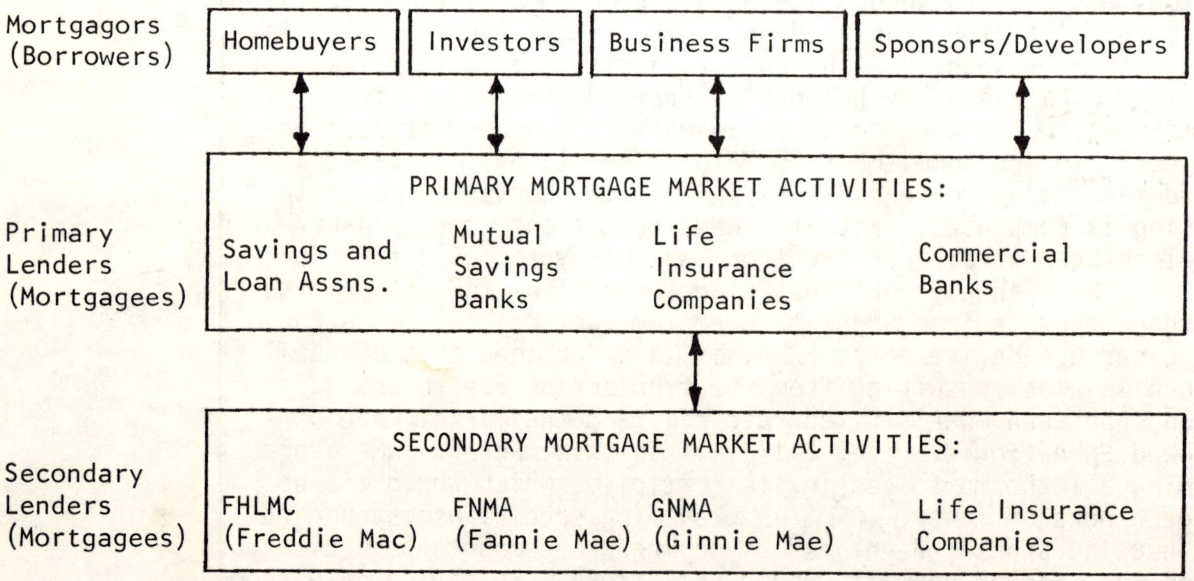

The savings and loan association idea did not originate in this country. Our modern savings and loan associations evolved from the early building societies which originated in Europe. In 1831, the first "building society" in America was formed in Pennsylvania. The early American building societies had a single objective: to enable members to purchase or build a house. The added goal of thrift came later (saving as well as borrowing).

By the late 1800's, the number of savings and loan associations was so great that government supervision was deemed necessary. At first, each state created individual statutes regulating "S & L's." By 1931, 46 of the then 48 states had statutes controlling S & L activities in their states.

FHLBS

In 1932, Congress created the Federal Home Loan Bank System (FHLBS) for the purpose of establishing a central source of credit for residential financing institutions. In 1933, the system of federally chartered savings and loan associations was authorized to operate as a part of the FHLB System. All federally chartered S & L's must belong to the FHLB System. Membership in the system is open to state chartered S & L's, mutual savings banks, and life insurance companies. As of January 1, 1977, the FHLB System included approximately 2,050 federal S & L's, 2,900 state chartered S & L's, 57 mutual savings banks, and 2 life insurance companies.

Almost all state chartered S & L's prefer to be members of the FHLB System and subject to its supervision. One of the primary reasons is that members are allowed to borrow from a Federal Home Loan district bank when necessary. Another important reason is to qualify for membership in the Federal Savings and Loan Insurance Corporation (FSLIC). The FSLIC will insure all deposits in member institutions up to $40,000 per account for privately owned accounts. All federally chartered S & L's must have their deposits insured by FSLIC and most state chartered associations voluntarily qualify for membership in order to provide their depositors this insurance protection. The resulting depositor confidence has done much to stimulate rapid growth in total assets of savings and loan associations.

It is easy to determine if an S & L is federally chartered. The word "federal" must appear in the name of the association if federally chartered. Those S & L's chartered by the state may not use the word "federal" in their business name or title. Another difference between the two types of associations may be found in their method of organization and ownership. All federally chartered S & L's must be mutually owned. This means that each depositor's account represents a proportionate share of ownership of the association and the depositor is a shareholder. The income earned by a depositor's savings account is not "interest" as many people think. The income earned by each account is a "dividend" paid according to the amount of the share owned. State chartered S & L's may be either mutually owned or privately owned by stockholders, depending on the state in which they operate. A few capital stock type S & L's were operating in

Florida in 1977 on a somewhat experimental basis. According to the U.S. League of Savings Associations, 4,964 were operating in the United States as of January 1, 1977.

Historically, savings and loan associations have been the most important source of mortgage money for single-family homes. This is still true today. Whether federally or state chartered, most S & L's have retained their local character and continue to invest over 80 percent of their assets in one- to four-unit dwellings. Rules and laws which regulate the operation of S & L's have had much to do with retention of local character and investment in residential mortgages.

The long experience of S & L's with residential mortgages has resulted in an expertise which allows for a greater degree of self-reliance in underwriting and making mortgage loans on single-family houses. Practically all S & L's prefer to make conventional mortgage loans instead of FHA or VA loans. This preference allows them freedom to employ the judgment and experience resulting from more than 100 years of residential loan activity. Although most S & L's have a few FHA and VA mortgages in their overall investment portfolios, few loans are made today that are not conventional mortgages.

Formerly, S & L's were limited to making loans up to 75 percent of the appraised value of a property. Today, with the approval of an association's members, an S & L is permitted to make loans up to 90 percent of a property's appraised value or the purchase price, whichever is less. Under certain conditions, loans up to 95 percent of loan-to-value ratio can be made. Loan-to-value ratio has resulted from the availability of private mortgage insurance (PMI). All of the mortgage representing more than 90 percent of appraised value must be insured by a private mortgage insurance company, or the association may establish a loss reserve for such loans. PMI charges compare favorably with the monthly insurance premium charged by FHA.

Residential mortgage loans made by federal S & L's are usually amortized on a monthly basis, and the maximum term allowed on installment loans is 30 years. Such loans must be secured by first mortgage liens on properties within 100 miles of the office making the loan. Rates of interest charged are regulated by usury laws of the state. In Florida on loans of less than \$500,000, the maximum interest an individual may be charged is 10 percent. Corporations may be charged 15 percent legally.

Federal savings and loan associations are authorized to make term loans up to 5 years in duration, provided that the amount loaned does not exceed 50 percent of appraised value. Term loans can be made up to 60 percent of appraised value, but approval of association members must first be obtained and then such loans are restricted to a period of 3 years.

Although federal savings and loan associations have, since their origin, invested more than 80 percent of their assets in residential mortgage loans, they are permitted to make loans on other improved properties. They also make construction loans for periods up to 3 years and are authorized to make loans on leaseholds if the lease period is at least 10 years longer than the term of the loan. As raw acreage becomes more and more expensive, it would be reasonable to expect enterprising developers and builders to make use of leasehold loans as a substitute for loans on fee simple properties. Those S & L's with general reserves, surplus, and undivided profits totaling more than 5 percent of withdrawable accounts can make land acquisition, site improvement, and housing development loans. This authority combined with a leasehold approach to land development could be a future trend as land prices increase.

Several changes in S & L lending authorizations occurred in 1972. One of the changes was designed to encourage more lending in below-average neighborhoods by permitting federal associations to make partially amortized loans on residential and commercial buildings in those areas. These loans are complete departures from normal lending procedures. They can be made for periods as short as 10 years, but monthly amortization payments are based on periods as long as 30 years. This means that a large portion of the loan will remain unpaid at the end of 10 years and therefore a "balloon payment" will be due at the end of the loan period. However, if the mortgagor has performed his obligations in a satisfactory manner during the initial 10-year period, the lender is authorized to convert the balloon payment into a new loan with more orthodox terms at prevailing interest rates.

A second innovation which occurred in 1972 was authorization by the Federal Home Loan Bank Board for member S & L's to make loans with scheduled diminishing monthly payments. This particular type of loan was designed to benefit older people approaching retirement. Amortization schedules for such loans are set up to permit large payments during the years prior to retirement while the income of the borrowers is still high. After retirement, a drop in income normally results. A corresponding drop in loan payments would also take place as a result of higher-than-normal payments made earlier.

During the more than 140 years since the first building societies came into being, savings and loan associations have become the primary source of residential mortgage assistance. When the actual lending patterns of S & L's are analyzed, one finds that the real strength of S & L's is in the well-developed knowledge of local market conditions. This enables them to develop neighborhood expertise in the proper valuation of loans on new and existing housing. They can also judge local markets more carefully and work out individual arrangements for specific individual requirements better than many other lenders. This local expertise often results in higher appraisals by S & L's than by other lenders. It should be noted that the same elements mentioned above enable S & L's to sometimes charge a slightly higher interest rate for their loans than may be available elsewhere. They are also sometimes a fraction of a percent higher in their loan origination fees.

Commercial Banks

While S & L's are acknowledged to be the dominant force in the residential mortgage field, they are not the largest financial institution. That distinction belongs to the commercial banks ("CB's"). The CB's are the largest group of financial institutions from the twin standpoints of assets and numbers. At the beginning of 1976, there were approximately 14,400 commercial banks in the country with assets estimated at more than 900 billion dollars. Despite their huge size, CB's hold only approximately 50 percent of the amount of mortgage loans held by savings and loan associations: commercial bank mortgage loans amount to approximately 140 billion dollars compared with approximately 278 billion dollars in mortgages held by S & L's. Nonetheless, the amount of dollars invested in real property mortgages by CB's has been steadily increasing over the past few years.

There is no doubt that CB's are the primary reservoirs of commercial credit in this nation. Their increased participation in the residential mortgage market promises to be beneficial to all parties. Reports published by the Federal Reserve Bank of Atlanta indicate that CB's were hurt by bad mortgage loans during the 1974-75 recession. A close analysis of the mortgage loans on real property which went bad reveals, however, that they were, in almost every case, short-term, high-interest-rate, construction or development loans. The mortgage loans made by commercial banks on residential dwellings (one- to four-family units) were the most stable, best performing loans in their mortgage loan portfolios. This fallout from that period of economic recession should cause CB's to give greater attention to long-term, residential loans.

Commercial banks, like S & L's, are chartered by either the state or federal government. The chartering agency prescribes the rules and regulations which govern the business operations of a bank. If chartered by the federal government, a CB must display the word "national" somewhere in the name of the bank. No bank, except nationally chartered banks, may use "national" as a part of its title. In general, state chartered CB's and federally chartered CB's have paralleled each other in the evolution of real property lending programs. However, due in part to less stringent regulation, state commercial banks have been the forerunner in real estate lending practices.

The growth of commercial banks is perhaps best illustrated by comparison with the growth of mutual savings banks. In 1917, the combined total savings deposits of both state and national commercial banks were approximately equal to those of all mutual savings banks. Today, the combined total savings deposits of all commercial banks is approximately four times that of all mutual savings banks. For this reason, if for no other, greater participation by commercial banks in the mortgage markets across the nation will benefit the housing and construction markets, and eventually the overall economy.

In 1970, national CB's were authorized to allow home loans up to 90 percent of appraised value with a maximum term of 30 years.

They were also permitted to make loans on leaseholds provided the lease term extends at least 10 years beyond the maturity date of the loan. They may not, however, make real property loans in excess of their surplus and unencumbered capital, or their time and savings deposits, whichever is greater.

National banks, and state banks where state laws allow, may make loans on real property secured by secondary or subordinate liens. The amount of the secondary lien must be added to any existing prior lien, and the total amount cannot exceed the appropriate or normal loan-to-value ratio for that type property. For example, suppose the appraised value of your home is $43,000 and the commercial bank you are dealing with uses the maximum authorized 90/10 loan-to-value ratio. Further, assume you have owned the property long enough to have reduced the existing first mortgage to $24,000. The 90/10 loan-to-value ratio would permit the bank to lend $38,700 on your home. The difference between the existing first mortgage ($24,000) and the appropriate loan-to-value amount ($38,700) leaves an amount of $14,700 which you might borrow from the bank and secure the loan by a second mortgage. Keep in mind, however, that just because the law authorizes a bank to use a 90/10 loan-to-value ratio it does not mean that all banks will choose to make use of this authorization. A more conservative bank may decide to restrict its loans to an 80/20 loan-to-value ratio, or even 75/25.

National CB's are permitted to classify some real estate loans as other type loans in order to keep the amount of outstanding real property loans from exceeding the maximum allowable. For example, national CB's are not required to categorize as real estate loans any FHA, VA, or any other loan insured, guaranteed, or backed by the credit of the federal or a state government. Also, construction loans of less than 5 years are classified as commercial loans if they are secured by a commitment from a financial institution to pay the amount of the construction loan when the improvement is completed.

Commercial banks make conventional, FHA, and VA mortgage loans, but they are not as active in mortgage markets as other financial institutions for several reasons. First, many CB's prefer short-term commercial loans to long-term real estate loans. Only the absence of commercial loan demand causes these CB's to become active in the mortgage market. Secondly, many CB's realize that their business expertise is in the commercial loan field. Real property mortgage lending has traditionally been the domain of the S & L's. As a result, CB's usually approach real estate loans with caution. Many commercial banks will, as a matter of policy, use smaller loan-to-value ratios in order to increase their margin for error. Thirdly, the experience of some commercial banks with real estate investment trusts ("REIT's") in the early 1970's was not a pleasant or profitable one. During this period (1969-1974), many CB's decided to sponsor REIT's in order to: (1) create additional funds to lend on real estate mortgages which would also generate new loan service fees for the sponsor; (2) extend the legally allowable lending program beyond the regulatory limits of the sponsor; and, (3) generate advisory fees for the sponsor. The failure of most of the REIT's during the economic recession of 1974-75 resulted in an increased degree of conservatism in the attitude of commercial banks toward real property loans. However, the increase in savings deposits since 1976 has encouraged many CB's to take a new look at residential mortgage loans. In addition, legislation which has been introduced in the Congress may result in a greater interest in residential mortgages. New funds resulting from an increase in mortgage lending by CB's should not only hold down interest rates but should also increase economic growth.

Mutual Savings Banks

There are no federally chartered mutual savings banks ("MSB's"). All MSB's are chartered by the states in which they operate. This is one of the existing differences between MSB's and CB's. A second difference is that MSB's do not hold demand deposits in the form of checking accounts. With few exceptions, commercial banks are the only banks with checking accounts. A third major difference is related to location. While commercial banks are located in all 50 states and Puerto Rico, mutual savings banks are located in only 17 states and Puerto Rico. They are concentrated primarily in the New England states. Massachusetts, Connecticut, and New York alone had 351 of the 476 mutual savings banks active in 1976.

Mutual savings banks are some of the oldest financial institutions in the United States. The first MSB was organized in Philadelphia in 1816, some 15 years before the first S & L was formed. The purpose of the early MSB's was to encourage thrift and frugality. Working people were encouraged to save a portion of their wages for some future time of possible need. From the very beginning, MSB's basically viewed themselves as a financial service for people of small means and humble station who might spend all that they earned if not encouraged to save. The number of MSB's grew steadily until the year 1875. Since that time, the number of MSB's has declined but total assets have continued to grow. At the beginning of 1976, total assets of MSB's were slightly more than 120 billion dollars. MSB's can apply for and obtain from the Federal Deposit Insurance Corporation (FDIC) insurance of up to $40,000 for each individual savings account.

Since each mutual savings bank is chartered by the state in which it operates, there exists a considerable variance in the state regulated mortgage loan programs. FHA and VA loans are exempt from the state laws regulating distance limitations, loan-to-value ratios, proportion of assets invested in mortgages, and maximum term. However, for conventional loans, the loan-to-value ratio varies among states from a low of 50 percent to a high of 90 percent. Maximum terms of such loans are usually either 25 or 30 years, depending on state law. Unless an MSB was lending on an FHA or VA loan, state laws formerly restricted MSB lending distances to the state in which they were chartered and adjoining states. It therefore becomes apparent why mutual savings banks became active investors in FHA and VA loans all over the nation. By using mortgage bankers or other representation in fast-growing, capital deficit areas, MSB's are able to extend their lending activities into such areas whenever they choose to do so.

Despite the latitude of operation offered by government insured or guaranteed loans, most of the real property mortgage loans held by MSB's at the beginning of 1976 were conventional loans made within their local lending areas. Recent changes in state laws where most MSB's are concentrated have removed restrictions on out-of-state lending. This could very well cause MSB's to become more competitive with S & L's and CB's for residential mortgage loans in capital deficit states such as Florida.

Disintermediation

The three financial institutions discussed previously are all considered to be "thrift institutions," although the term is more appropriately applied to S & L's and MSB's than to CB's. It is a fact that all three types of institutions are financial intermediaries (middlemen) for their individual depositors. Most individuals have neither the knowledge regarding investments nor the necessary funds to make large mortgage or business loans. As a result, thrift institutions are able to consolidate many small savings accounts belonging to individual depositors and invest those funds in large diversified projects. This serves to reduce risk and promote a higher rate of return. Individual depositors receive either "dividends," interest on their savings, or some other benefit as an inducement to continue the flow of savings into the thrift institutions. Since the funds necessary to make mortgage loans depend directly on the flow of savings into these financial intermediaries, any interruption or reduction in the savings flow has a marked effect on both availability and cost of mortgage money.

From time to time, the yield on U.S. Government bonds, state and local bonds, or corporate bonds will increase to the point that a disparity will exist between the yield available to a depositor in one of the thrift institutions and the yield available on the same amount of money invested directly in bonds, for example. When this condition occurs, many depositors will choose to withdraw savings and invest directly in bonds without need for an intermediary. Of course bonds are but one example of many securities and investments constantly competing with thrift institutions for individual savings. When a substantial amount of funds are withdrawn from thrift institutions, the process is called "disintermediation," signifying a disengagement of depositors from intermediary institutions. The result is a so-called "credit crunch" and a shortage of mortgage funds. This situation occurred in 1969 and 1973-74. In 1969, the average annual yield paid on savings deposited with S & L's around the nation was approximately 4.8%, while the same amount of money invested in Triple A corporate bonds would yield over 7%. In 1974, S & L's were yielding well over 5%, but Triple A corporate bonds were yielding more than 8½%. The result was disintermediation. People, households, and businesses moved their savings from thrift institution intermediaries and invested directly in various other assets such as stocks or bonds. As funds available for mortgages decrease and credit shortages occur, interest rates on mortgage money increase. In turn, as interest rates rise, demand for mortgages declines and economic activity in the real estate industry falls off. Fortunately, these periods of yield disparity and disintermediation have been relatively short-term in nature.

Life Insurance Companies

Life insurance companies ("LIC's") are regulated by the laws of the states in which they operate. Most of the state laws governing the operation of LIC's were enacted so long ago that many of the original restrictions on their activities are not practical restrictions today. For example, the New York law states that a life insurance company may not invest more than $30,000 or 2 percent of its total assets (whichever is greatest) in any single property or mortgage. With assets of several hundred millions of dollars, an LIC in effect has little worry about restrictions on the amount of money which can be invested in any one mortgage loan.

LIC's also enjoy a freedom of nationwide scope in their mortgage investment programs, if authorized to do business as a life insurance company in all states. In fact some states (Texas for example) require that a life insurance company domiciled outside the state but doing business in the state must invest not less than three-fourths of the reserves required to protect (Texas) policyholders in that state's mortgages or securities as the price of doing business in that state.

LIC's are not thrift institutions nor are they organized for the primary purpose of financing real estate. As insurance companies, they generate enormous amounts of funds, estimated to be accumulating at a rate of more than 15 billion dollars per year. These funds are mostly policyholders' reserves. They must be invested in order to build sufficient amounts to pay the policyholders or beneficiaries in later years. They can predict their funds available for investment with a high degree of accuracy since a major portion of income comes from premiums. Relatively accurate mortality tables help to predict required expenditures. The difference between income and expenditures represents funds available for commitment to investment of some type. LIC's evaluate all types of available investment opportunities before deciding on the type(s) for which to allocate their funds. Real property mortgages are generally selected as an investment vehicle only when the possibility of meeting investment objectives indicates mortgages to be the best choice.

A noticeable change in life insurance company lending patterns has occurred since 1964. Prior to 1964, more than 50 percent of all LIC mortgages were of one- to four-family residential types. By the beginning of 1976, emphasis had changed so that apartment and commercial properties accounted for more than 70 percent of LIC mortgage holdings, with one- to four-family mortgages representing approximately 20 percent. Many factors contributed to the change of emphasis, two of which were increased competition by local lenders for conventional residential loans and erosion of long-term yields caused by inflation.

Life insurance companies do contribute to the availability of residential mortgage funds by buying residential mortgages in bulk from secondary mortgage markets. They will very seldom compete with other lenders for individual residential mortgages, however. First, the cost of administrative overhead is increased by making fifty loans of $40,000 each, instead of one loan for $2,000,000. Secondly, there is little opportunity for participation in either profits or equity when making residential loans. If a residential loan of $40,000 was made in 1968 at 6½% for 30 years by an LIC, that loan was earning only 6½% in 1976 when residential loans were being made at 9% or above. The LIC was unable to counteract the effect of inflation because of the long-term commitment at 6½%. The same situation did not apply to loans made on income-producing property. LIC's could, and did, demand participation in income earned by developments made possible by their financing, in addition to normal interest rates. In some instances, LIC's participate in equity ownership in lieu of participation in income. Either approach permits a degree of protection against inflation. Added to the necessity for protection against inflation is the constant pressure to obtain the highest yields possible commensurate with the safety of policyholders' money. As a result, the percentage of LIC assets invested in mortgage loans since 1970 has declined from about 34 percent to approximately 30 percent. They remain a major source of mortgage market funds with a distinct preference for apartment complexes and commercial properties. The approximately 1,900 life insurance companies in the U.S. have invested approximately 90 billion dollars in mortgage loans. Much of this has been invested through "loan correspondents" in rapid growth areas all around the nation.

Loan Correspondents

The individual borrower has little or no opportunity to walk into a life insurance company and arrange a loan. One reason is that the LIC's usually deal only in large blocks of residential loans. Another reason is that the LIC lending offices are generally not located where loans are made. More and more LIC's have displayed a trend toward using loan correspondents located where growth has created a demand for mortgage funds. Generally, these loan correspondents are mortgage bankers (mortgage companies) which are well-established in their own operating territories. Mortgage bankers frequently act as loan correspondents for 30 or 40 separate lending institutions, including LIC's, MSB's, and CB's. They receive a commission for originating and processing loans in accordance with standards established by the lending institutions they represent. After the loan is closed and delivered to the lending LIC, MSB, or CB, the correspondent frequently continues to service the loan for an additional servicing fee. Mortgage bankers acting in the capacity of correspondents have enabled lenders which are located in stable and no-growth areas to invest in distant, rapidly growing areas.

Many mortgage bankers (companies) are often able to make direct loans using their own funds, or funds borrowed from a local bank. This provides the borrower a much faster, more competitive service. It also permits the mortgage company to take advantage of good loan opportunities which might go to some other lender, and it does constitute a service for the borrowing public. Most correspondents will collect these individual loans into a "mortgage package" which will then be sold to one of the lending institutions with which they commonly deal. Sometimes the package will be sold to one of the other secondary market investors or a government agency. This allows the mortgage company to recover its capital to lend all over again. Not only does the correspondent benefit from this process, but also the investor who buys the qualified and closed loans, the borrower, and the overall economy benefit.

Money Market Impact

Real estate mortgages are big business as can be seen from earlier portions of this chapter. More money is borrowed for mortgage purposes each year than for any other single type of borrowing. Although no exact count is known to exist, it is estimated that more than 20,000 separate lending institutions are engaged in the mortgage market.

Despite the large number of lenders participating in the mortgage market, there are frequently times when a potential borrower encounters considerable difficulty in borrowing even though a good credit risk. The complex nature of the mortgage market and its relation to the larger, national money market account for part of the difficulty.

While common reference is made to the "mortgage market," a close examination reveals a far different structure from that of most classical markets. The mortgage market is composed of many submarkets. There are markets for one- to four-family residential units, for multi-family residential units, for commercial properties, for hotels and motels, and many more in the non-farm category alone. As an example, look at the sub-market for commercial properties. It breaks down into smaller sub-markets for apartments, office buildings, and retail store properties. The point is that even though all sub-markets may deal in a particular type of mortgage loan, each sub-market will have an influence on the other sub-markets as well as the overall mortgage market. Money loaned to build a $9,000,000 shopping mall will affect the amount of money in the mortgage market available for single-family houses. A common thread which ties all of the lenders in the mortgage market together is the fact that each is engaged in long-term credit lending with real property as security. Also, despite their different locations and operating policies, all lenders are mutually dependent on the overall supply of money existing in the nation. For this reason, price movements of money in the separate sub-markets are related. When a corporation in San Francisco decides to borrow $50,000,000 from a mutual savings bank in Boston, the money in the mortgage market is depleted by that amount. The result could be higher interest rates for loans made in Orlando, Florida by that same MSB.

Thus, each sub-market is a component of the entire mortgage market. The entire mortgage market is in turn only one component of the vast financial system called the overall "capital market." As interrelated parts, each is responsive to changes affecting the whole system. In fact, it is the total demand for mortgage funds interacting with the total available supply of funds which determines the interest rate (cost) of mortgages.

At any given time, a number of businesses or institutions are "renting" mortgage money to other businesses or individuals. The rent paid for use of money is called "interest." When money is plentiful and available from many sources, there exists a situation in which the supply of money exceeds the demand, called an "easy money market." The rent charged for money loaned during an easy money market will be less than in a "tight money market." A tight money market exists when demand for funds exceeds the available supply. In this type of market, the rent charged for money is increased -- borrowers pay a higher interest rate. The ideal situation is to keep a reasonable equilibrium between supply and demand.

The demand for mortgage money is increased or decreased by a number of influences. Six of the major influences on demand are:

1. Changes in the number and size of households
2. Shifts in geographic preference for households
3. Existing inventory of structures
4. Changes in employment rates and income
5. Changes in costs of real property services, taxes, and maintenance
6. Changes in construction costs

Influences on the supply side of the mortgage money market are also varied. Because mortgage loans are considered long-term loans, mortgages do not compete directly with short-term demand for funds. Mortgages must compete directly with other long-term claims for money, such as corporate stocks and bonds and long-term bonds issued by the various federal, state, and local governments. As a consequence, the mortgage market, the stock market, and the bond market are all in competition for the overall supply of funds in what is called the nation's "capital market."

Federal Reserve System

The Federal Reserve System (commonly called "the Fed") is probably the most important influence on the nation's financial markets and on the money supply. This governmental agency has the responsibility of managing the nation's monetary system. Commercial banks belonging to the Federal Reserve System hold about 80 percent of the deposits in all U.S. banks. Member banks are required to keep a designated percent of their time and demand deposits on reserve in Federal Reserve System district banks. The amount which member banks are required to keep on deposit is called the "reserve requirement." Raising or lowering this reserve requirement is one of the methods used by the Federal Reserve System to control the supply of money in circulation.

The Federal Reserve System actually has three primary methods for influencing the supply of money and all financial markets. The three methods are listed in the order most often used.

1. The most commonly used method of controlling the money supply is open market operations. The Federal Reserve System maintains an inventory of U.S. Treasury securities. This inventory is

changed periodically by purchase of additional securities or sale of those on hand. The result is an increase or decrease of money in circulation. For example, when the Fed decides to sell securities on the open market, all funds received are held by the Federal Reserve System. This reduces the supply of money in circulation. This, in turn, causes a drop in loanable funds and causes interest rates to rise. Higher interest rates cause some businesses and individuals to postpone borrowing. As borrowing drops off, the economy slows down and inflation is reduced. When an increase in economic activity seems needed, the Federal Reserve System buys securities thereby releasing money back into normal circulation and increasing loanable funds.

2. Perhaps the second most commonly used method of controlling the supply of money is changing the discount rate. The discount rate is the rate of interest charged member banks for money borrowed from the Federal Reserve System. If the discount rate is increased, it means that member banks will have to pay a higher interest rate for money borrowed from the system. This higher interest rate will be passed on in the form of higher interest to customers of the member banks. The result is a reduction of loans made. Changing the discount rate is not as effective in controlling the money supply as the two other methods, but it has assumed an important role in the overall system because it usually signals a decision by the Fed to increase or decrease the money supply. If the discount rate is raised, it usually will be followed by sale of U.S. Treasury securities in the open market. Both actions will serve to decrease the supply of funds available for loan.

3. The third method of influencing the supply of money by the Fed is the change in reserve requirements previously mentioned. This is regarded as perhaps the most abrupt or drastic way to influence the supply of money. Since most member banks have large amounts of time and demand deposits, a very small change in reserve requirements has an immediate result in the amount of funds taken out of circulation. When the economy shows signs of responding in the desired direction, reserve requirements will be changed again to allow a return to normal.

The actual decisions regarding increase or decrease in the nation's money supply are made by the twelve-person Federal Open Market Committee which meets the third Tuesday of each month. Every effort is made to ensure strict secrecy of these meetings, and no announcement of the decisions are made until they are implemented. People serving on the committee are the seven Reserve Board governors and five presidents of different Federal Reserve Branch Banks. There are twelve Federal Reserve Banks operating in different geographic regions, with 24 branch banks making up the system. Obviously the decisions of the Committee are critically important to the mortgage market.

Another important influence on the mortgage market is refinancing of the national debt. The U.S. government owes the owners of short-term and long-term securities hundreds of billions of dollars. At the present time, this debt is periodically refinanced by sale of new securities on the open market. When the Treasury sells enough securities to pay interest on say 500 billion dollars, it drains a large amount of funds from the capital market. This means less funds available for the mortgage market and higher interest rates.

Mortgage Discounting

As conventional mortgage interest rates increase, the interest rates for FHA and VA mortgages remain unchanged until an increase is authorized by the Secretary, Department of Housing and Urban Development. As a result, FHA and VA mortgage interest rates usually linger behind conventional rates.

The first FHA mortgage interest rates were very competitive with prevailing market interest rates. During and after the Korean War, conventional mortgage interest rates began to rise above the fixed FHA-VA rates. A few lenders were willing to accept a slight difference in interest rates because they recognized that FHA insurance or a VA guarantee reduced the risk of loss on their mortgage loans. However, when the disparity between conventional mortgage interest rates and FHA and VA rates became too great, lenders stopped loaning on the FHA and VA mortgages because of the reduced yield or return on their loans. Local lenders could not change or increase the FHA-VA interest rates, and they could not afford to make loans at the lower FHA-VA rates when the same amount of money could earn one or two percent more as a conventional mortgage. FHA and VA mortgages simply could not compete with conventional mortgages in the open market. In order to solve this dilemma without raising FHA and VA mortgage interest rates to a par with conventional loans, FHA authorized mortgage lenders to charge "discount points," provided the buyer was not allowed to pay the discount.

The practice of discounting, or charging discount points, is designed to make FHA and VA mortgages competitive with conventional mortgages, even when FHA-VA mortgage interest rates must remain unchanged in a rising mortgage market. Discounting raises the lender's yield on an FHA or VA loan. However, the borrower can be required to pay the discount points on a conventional loan. Some builders and developers estimate the mortgage discount cost before setting a sale price on their houses. This estimated cost is frequently added to their other acquisition and development costs in arriving at a sale price. Discount points are being charged on conventional mortgages much more often today. When this is done, it is simply a method of increasing the lender's yield without showing an increase in interest rate. Nevertheless, the primary purpose of discounting is to keep FHA and VA mortgages competitive with conventional mortgages.

The term discount point is merely a unit of measurement. When calculating the cost of discount points, each point is used as if it is one percent of the loan amount. Focus, for example, on a $40,000 FHA loan for which the lender is charging 6 points. For the seller to find the dollar cost which he will be required to pay, he would multiply .06 x $40,000 and find that he must pay the lender $2,400 as a mortgage discount. When the lender receives the $2,400 from the seller, only $37,600 will be needed from the lender's funds in order to make up the total $40,000 which will be loaned to the borrower. When the loan is made, the lender will receive interest on the entire $40,000 during the full term of the loan.

The number of discount points charged by lenders is not a matter of guesswork. The real yield to a lender includes both the interest earned by the money loaned ($37,600 in the example above) plus the discount charged ($2,400 above). But in order to express accurately the discount as a part of the real yield, the lender must convert the discount to an annual percentage rate. FNMA and FHLMC have a method of determining the increase in interest earned by the one-time payment of the discount. They can determine how much the discount adds to each year's earnings by spreading the lump sum payment of the discount over a period of twelve years. Although most residential mortgages are made for a term of 30 years, the average residential loan is paid off in less than 10 years by resale or refinancing. FNMA and FHLMC have compromised and selected 12 years as the period over which they will distribute the increased yield to a lender.

In everyday situations a simpler, more practical rule of thumb is used to convert the discount to an annual percentage rate which can be added to the stated mortgage interest rate. The rule of thumb is: for each discount point charged by the lender, add one-eighth (1/8) of one percent to the stated mortgage interest rate. For example, assume a buyer wants to obtain an FHA mortgage of $40,000 and a lender agrees to make the loan at 8 percent interest plus six points. What will the real yield be to the lender? The quoted interest rate is 8 percent, but to that must be added 1/8 of one percent for each point, or 6/8, which reduces to 3/4. Add the 3/4 to the mortgage interest rate of 8 percent and the charging of a discount of 6 points increases the lender's real yield to 8 3/4 percent on the money actually loaned by the lender.

Frequently a lender will state that FHA or VA mortgages are going at 96 or 94. This is merely a different manner of quoting discount points. It means that the lender is only willing to lend 96 percent or 94 percent of the amount needed for a mortgage loan. If the seller is willing to come up with the remaining 4 percent or 6 percent, then the lender will make the loan. It means exactly the same thing as the lender saying he is charging 4 points or 6 points. Regardless of the method used, the real interest rate earned for the lender will be increased about 1/8 of one percent for each point charged.

As far as the buyer of an FHA or VA house is concerned, the number of discount points charged for the loan is immaterial except that it may be included in the sale price agreed to for the house. The seller must pay the discount related to FHA or VA loans. So the buyer usually does not know that the lender actually loaned less than 100 percent of the amount the buyer borrowed.

There is need to relate discounting to the previously discussed Federal Reserve System control of the money supply. Suppose the national economy is booming and inflation threatens to get out of hand. The Fed decides to decrease the amount of money in circulation as an inflation control effort. Securities are sold to absorb part of the money in circulation, and the discount rate at which banks are permitted to borrow is raised. The money supply drops and interest rates rise. Conventional mortgage rates go to 9½ percent, but FHA and VA interest rates are fixed at 8½ percent. To offset the one percent loss in yield, most lenders would make FHA-VA loans with an 8-point discount. This means the lender would actually be lending only 92 percent of the amount needed; the additional 8 percent of the loan would come from the seller.

To illustrate, a buyer agrees to pay $48,000 for a house contingent on obtaining FHA financing. He is to make a down payment of $1,900 which will be refunded if the loan is not approved. A lender is found who will make the $46,100 loan required. The existing interest rates are 9½ percent for conventional loans and 8½ percent for FHA loans. The lender requires a discount of 6 points. The seller agrees to pay the lender the discount in order to sell the property. The buyer will now sign a mortgage for the full amount needed ($46,100) and the mortgage will state that the buyer is paying an 8½ percent interest rate. All mortgage payments made by the buyer in the future will be calculated on the basis of $46,100 loaned at 8½ percent. But the lender only loaned $43,334. The other $2,766 portion of the mortgage was money the lender received from the seller. The real yield to the lender on the $43,334 actually loaned will be about 9¼ percent (8½ percent plus 3/4 of one percent from discount points.)

Other Sources of Income to Lenders

In addition to discount points charged for making a loan, lenders frequently levy other charges. Normally a lender will charge the borrower a loan origination fee. Different lenders may charge varying amounts as a loan origination fee. Typically, it will include a one or two percent commission plus the total of all expenses encountered by the lender in obtaining credit reports, preparing loan documents, and processing loan applications.

Another source of income to lenders takes the form of "commitment fees." Often the developer of a subdivision, shopping center, or an apartment complex will need to obtain a written commitment from a financial institution certifying that permanent financing will be provided when the project is completed. The point here is that the financial institution is willing to become the permanent lender in the future, but first the developer must find a lender of "construction money." With the written commitment of the future permanent lender, called a "take-out commitment," it is much easier to find a construction money lender. When the project is built, the permanent lender will advance the amount committed and the developer will repay the construction lender. Most lenders who issue a take-out commitment charge a non-refundable fee for making the commitment. The borrower, in this case the developer, will be required to pay the fee at the time the commitment is made.

Lenders make many kinds of commitments, in addition to the take-out commitment, but the person to whom a commitment is made will normally be charged a fee at the time. All commitments will be worded such as to limit the effectiveness to a definite period of time. Upon expiration of that period, a new commitment will be required if the proposed project is not completed or the commitment has not been used.

Many lenders are also equipped to service mortgages which they originate and then sell to large financial institutions. This is an additional source of income for such lenders. Today, "servicing fees" typically range from 3/8 to 3/4 of one percent of the unpaid balance of loans serviced. FNMA and FHLMC have traditionally paid 3/8 of one percent servicing fee and GNMA has normally paid .44 percent to lenders who continue to service mortgages sold to those agencies. Should a lender average 1/2 of one percent service fee for several blocks of mortgages totaling $100,000,000, this would mean a gross income of $500,000 per year from that source alone. As might be expected, lenders are generally anxious to retain servicing of any loans sold to institutional investors.

Summary

The mortgage market, like all other markets, is irrevocably linked to the principles of supply and demand. Mortgages, or more properly mortgage loans, are the chief source of funds for financing real property. Mortgage loans involve a borrower (mortgagor) and a lender (mortgagee).

Three basic types of mortgage loans exist: conventional, FHA insured, and VA guaranteed. Interest rates are charged for use of money loaned, and discounting comes into play in order to make FHA and VA mortgage loans competitive with conventional loans.

Primary mortgage market activity generally involves lenders that originate loans and thus supply funds directly to borrowers; secondary mortgage market activity generally involves lenders that buy mortgages as investments or that make loans by using intermediaries.

Real estate professionals need to know about and keep current with mortgage market sources, procedures, trends, and opportunities.

CHAPTER 11

THE MORTGAGE MARKET

1. The relationship between the amount of money in the mortgage market and the mortgage interest rates is:

   I. A direct or positive relationship
   II. An inverse relationship

   a. I only
   b. II only
   c. Both I and II
   d. Neither I nor II

2. The role of the mortgage broker is to act as:

   I. An agent
   II. A middleman who approves, closes, and services loans

   a. I only
   b. II only
   c. Both I and II
   d. Neither I nor II

3. Primary lenders are those lenders who:

   I. Are the primary source of money loaned by correspondents
   II. Create loans by lending directly to borrowers

   a. I only
   b. II only
   c. Both I and II
   d. Neither I nor II

4. A commercial bank sold a group of 10 mortgages directly to FNMA. This would be an example of a:

   I. Secondary market activity
   II. Primary market activity

   a. I only
   b. II only
   c. Both I and II
   d. Neither I nor II

5. FNMA currently buys and sells:

   I. FHA, VA, and conventional mortgages
   II. FHA and VA mortgages only

   a. I only
   b. II only
   c. Both I and II
   d. Neither I nor II

6. FNMA is a corporation:

   I. Which is government regulated
   II. Whose stock is privately owned

   a. I only
   b. II only
   c. Both I and II
   d. Neither I nor II

7. One of the most significant powers granted GNMA is the authority to guarantee principal and interest on:

   I. Revolving treasury notes
   II. Pass-through securities

   a. I only
   b. II only
   c. Both I and II
   d. Neither I nor II

8. As a method of converting existing mortgages to cash, "Freddie Mac" is particularly important to:

   I. Commercial banks
   II. Savings and loan associations

   a. I only
   b. II only
   c. Both I and II
   d. Neither I nor II

9. All federally chartered savings and loan associations must belong to the:

   I. Federal Home Loan Bank System
   II. Federal Reserve System

   a. I only
   b. II only
   c. Both I and II
   d. Neither I nor II

10. What word must appear in the name of a federally chartered savings and loan association?

    I. National
    II. Security

    a. I only
    b. II only
    c. Both I and II
    d. Neither I nor II

11. Income earned by a deposit in a mutual savings and loan association is:

    I. Interest
    II. A dividend

    a. I only
    b. II only
    c. Both I and II
    d. Neither I nor II

12. Most savings and loan associations prefer to make:

    I. FHA and VA loans
    II. Conventional loans

    a. I only
    b. II only
    c. Both I and II
    d. Neither I nor II

13. Rates of interest charged for mortgage loans made by a federally chartered savings and loan association are regulated by the:

    I. Federal government
    II. State governments

    a. I only
    b. II only
    c. Both I and II
    d. Neither I nor II

14. The largest group of financial institutions are the:

    I. Commercial banks
    II. Savings and loan associations

    a. I only
    b. II only
    c. Both I and II
    d. Neither I nor II

15. The primary reservoirs of commercial credit in the U.S. are the:

    I. Retail stores
    II. Commercial banks

    a. I only
    b. II only
    c. Both I and II
    d. Neither I nor II

16. Historically, the most important sources of mortgage loans for single-family dwellings have been:

    I. Savings and loan associations
    II. Commercial banks

    a. I only
    b. II only
    c. Both I and II
    d. Neither I nor II

17. If chartered by the federal government, a commercial bank must use as part of its name the word:

    I. National
    II. Federal

    a. I only
    b. II only
    c. Both I and II
    d. Neither I nor II

18. Federally chartered commercial banks are authorized to make home loans up to:

    I. 90% of appraised value
    II. 30 years

    a. I only
    b. II only
    c. Both I and II
    d. Neither I nor II

19. All mutual savings banks are:

    I. Federally chartered
    II. State chartered

    a. I only
    b. II only
    c. Both I and II
    d. Neither I nor II

20. Mutual savings banks invest in what type of mortgage loans?

    I. FHA and VA
    II. Conventional

    a. I only
    b. II only
    c. Both I and II
    d. Neither I nor II

21. When funds are withdrawn from thrift institutions by depositors for direct investment elsewhere, the process is called:

    I. Intermediary distribution
    II. Disintermediation

    a. I only
    b. II only
    c. Both I and II
    d. Neither I nor II

22. Life insurance companies have changed their lending patterns from residential to commercial mortgage loans because of:

    I. Competition from local lenders
    II. Inflation

    a. I only
    b. II only
    c. Both I and II
    d. Neither I nor II

70% are comm. loans because of 1 + 2 - inflation

23. In order to invest in mortgages created in local growth areas, more and more life insurance companies are using:

    I. New branch offices
    II. Loan correspondents

    a. I only
    b. II only
    c. Both I and II
    d. Neither I nor II

24. The activities of mortgage bankers (companies) benefit the:

    I. Mortgage investor and loan correspondent
    II. Borrower and the overall economy

    a. I only
    b. II only
    c. Both I and II
    d. Neither I nor II

25. A tight money market exists when the:

    I. Demand for funds exceeds the supply
    II. Supply of funds exceeds the demand

    a. I only
    b. II only
    c. Both I and II
    d. Neither I nor II

26. The most commonly used method of controlling the national money supply is for "the Fed" to:

    I. Engage in open market activities
    II. Change the discount rate

    a. I only
    b. II only
    c. Both I and II
    d. Neither I nor II

do use both but said most common

27. When discount points are charged for conventional loans, it is done for the purpose of:

    I. Making FHA and VA loans more competitive
    II. Increasing the lender's yield

    a. I only
    b. II only
    c. Both I and II
    d. Neither I nor II

28. The rule of thumb used to convert discount points to annual percentage rate is each discount point equals:

    I. ¼ of 1% of APR
    II. 1/8 of 1% of APR

    a. I only
    b. II only
    c. Both I and II
    d. Neither I nor II

29. FHA and VA loans require any discount charged to be paid by:

    I. The seller
    II. The buyer

    a. I only
    b. II only
    c. Both I and II
    d. Neither I nor II

30. Lenders who issue take-out commitments usually charge a:

    I. Refundable commitment fee
    II. Non-refundable commitment fee

    a. I only
    b. II only
    c. Both I and II
    d. Neither I nor II

CHAPTER 12

THE REAL ESTATE MARKET

"My house is on the market."
"They are in the market for a home."

These are statements familiar to nearly everyone. In discussing real estate, reference may be made to such terms as "market value," "market data approach," "marketable title," and other allusions to "market." What is this "real estate market"? How does it work? Is it different than any other "market"? The answers to these and other questions are the subject of this chapter.

The word "market" has many meanings depending upon usage. It can mean a place where farmers and tradesmen display their produce and products for buyers. It can mean an exchange of goods or securities such as the commodities market or the stock market. Regardless of difference in form, the basic principles of market operation hold true for all. A market can only function when producers and consumers interact. Many markets need a middleman (intermediary) to stimulate a healthy degree of activity between producer and consumer, and the real estate market is one such market.

Three Key Questions

In a totalitarian society, the state performs the role of middleman in a much more authoritative manner than in a democratic society. The state may decide the key questions of what will be produced, who will do the producing, and who will get what is produced, and even the price to be paid. The same approach to market control may be true in socialist states, to varying degrees. Regardless of political structure or controlled versus free market system, all economies must deal with the same basic questions.

Whether by design, coincidence, or divine inspiration, the fact remains that a new economic system called "capitalism" was joined with a new political system upon the birth of the United States of America. It is highly doubtful that any other political form would have allowed the free enterprise system inherent in capitalism to exist. Yet it is undoubtedly true that the free enterprise system, or capitalism, has been a major factor in the growth of the political union called the United States.

As mentioned previously, no matter what type of political system controls an economy, every economy in every land in the world has to deal with three basic questions:

1. What will be produced?
2. Who will do the producing?
3. Who will get what is produced?

In a capitalistic society, reliance is on the free market mechanism, or price system, to provide answers to these three basic questions. Under the price system, any producer can place his product or service in the marketplace where he must rely on the quality and price of his product to compete with similar products offered by other producers. Consumers will evaluate the worth, quality, and price of the competing products and services and indicate their choice by spending dollars to obtain that item considered best for the dollars spent. The products sold are a signal to producers telling them which products are preferred by consumers. Those products which do not sell can no longer be produced at a profit, and profits are necessary in order to remain in business. So the answer to basic question Number 1 above is that the consumers actually decide what will be produced. Those products not desired by consumers produce little or no profits and will have to be replaced by new products for consumers to evaluate.

The answer to question Number 1 also contributes to finding the answer to question Number 2: Who will do the producing? As an example, imagine you are a producer of canned grapefruit sections. You are competing in the marketplace against four other producers of canned grapefruit sections, all of similar quality and price. You analyze your situation and decide that you do not want to sacrifice quality or quantity but you do want to acquire a competitive advantage. A thorough analysis of your production methods and equipment reveals that a change in procedure will permit you to reduce your price slightly below that of competitors and still retain the quality and quantity of product. Gradually thereafter your product begins to be selected more and more frequently. You decide to expand your factory and increase the amount of grapefruit sections produced. In time, other producers obviously must either become more efficient, as you have, or be forced out of business due to a decrease in their sales and profits. Thus, the answer to question Number 2 is the producer who can produce a comparable quality product more efficiently will do the producing.

Note that the answers to both questions 1 and 2 are dependent on the consumer, the individual who exercises freedom of choice in the marketplace and therefore is the real decision maker. Thus, one of the characteristics of the free enterprise system is that individual consumer desires and decisions are the primary determinants in the system. In a controlled economy, the state or representatives of the state make those decisions.

Another characteristic of the price or free enterprise system is the "automatic" working of the system. No committee from the Department of Commerce or any other agency has to survey the national market to determine which goods and services are selling well and which ones should be removed from the marketplace. The same results are accomplished automatically by the millions of individual consumer choices exercised every minute of every day. Those products which sell well will be replaced with more of the same. Those products which do not sell well will be removed and replaced with other products. Computers can be more accurate than governmental committees in many instances, but the automatic adjustments made as a result of millions of individual buying decisions are the most reliable indicators for producers of all goods and services.

Questions 1 and 2 basic to the functioning of markets have been answered. What about question Number 3? Who will get the goods and services produced? Keep in mind that any economy will have to operate with a limited money supply spread throughout the entire economy. No economy can remain sound very long if the state adopts the attitude that no limits need be set for the overall money supply. Printing new money without sound financial backing does not strengthen an economy. The U.S. national money supply is controlled by the Federal Reserve Board and the Department of the Treasury. The location of each dollar within the overall money supply is constantly changing as a result of the automatic market operation. Some people have more dollars than others, but the number of dollars held by any one person is usually changing as people go in and out of the marketplace.

Earlier comments indicated the importance of individual desires for certain products. In a socialist, communist, or fascist state, the desires of individuals do not generally regulate the market. If the state decides to produce tractors instead of television sets, individual citizens will find it difficult to buy television sets regardless of the amount of money they have available. In a free enterprise system, anyone can decide to produce television sets if one has the means. If the producer has accurately estimated the demand for television sets, he will make a profit. Other producers of items not selling well may become aware of the profits realized by the television set producer and decide to switch production in their plants and factories to the more profitable television sets and thus become competitors for the buyer's dollar. Consumers willing to spend part of their available supply of dollars will get the television set of their choice.

So the answer to question Number 3 is those people who are willing to spend their dollars in the marketplace will get what is produced. If more than one person wants the same article, the one willing to spend the most dollars will usually get the item. While it may seem unfair that people with more dollars to spend can outbid those with fewer dollars, no system is perfect. It is a fact that this nation, operating under the free enterprise system, has consistently produced more items and provided its people with a wider range of choice than any other nation in history. As a result, we do not worry about whether there will be enough cars or television sets for us to be allowed the privilege of buying one. We know cars and television sets will be available. Our problem is in selecting the best product within the limits of our income. So it is with real estate. The marketplace determines the sales prices, not sellers and not real estate agents. Thus, participation in the free enterprise market is limited by income, and under this political and economic system income is basically limited only by individual effort and initiative.

The Factor (Resource) Market

Most of us tend to regard ourselves as consumers. But we are also producers. Up to this point, the discussion of market functions has revolved around the three basic questions: What will be produced; Who will do the producing; and, Who will get what is produced. These questions have assumed availability of resources, money, and people to accomplish the many tasks required to borrow the money to build a factory, hire managers, recruit workers, and market products. Analysis of the many jobs to be performed before a product appears in a retail outlet reveals that the continued operation of the general market for goods and services which we have been discussing is completely dependent upon a more basic market called the resource or factor market.

The factor market is the market where the four major elements or factors of production are bought and sold. The four major parts or factors of production are:

1. Labor
2. Capital
3. Management
4. Land

No production occurs until some or all of these factors are utilized. When the optimum proportions of labor, capital, management, and land are combined, maximum production and utility result. Each of us is a producer from the standpoint that we have labor ability to hire out, or we have money to lend at interest, or we have management ability to contract out, or we have property to lease or sell. Each of us supplies one or more of the four factors of production in the factor market, then with the proceeds from that exchange, we become consumers in the general market for goods and services.

Real Estate as a Sub-Market

The general market for goods and services is made up of many, many sub-markets. When left free to operate without private or governmental interference, each sub-market and the general market as a whole should theoretically regulate themselves by the laws of supply and demand.

One of the sub-markets is the real estate market which in turn has several sub-markets of its own. Real estate is a commodity just as wheat, gold, and sugar are, but real estate is a basic commodity none of us can do without very long. By combining the other factors of production with land, we can produce wheat, gold, sugar, or buildings.

Principle of Highest and Best Use

The use to which we put land will determine its value. Suppose three persons are anxious to acquire the same parcel of land and each makes an offer to the landowner. To whom will the owner sell? Normally, he will sell to the one who offers the most dollars. The use each of the three persons intends for the land will determine the value of that tract to each of the prospective buyers. Suppose the use the first one has in mind will produce a net income of $6,000 per annum. Another has a use in mind which will net $8,000 after expenses. The third has decided to use the property in such a way that it will provide $12,000 per annum, after expenses. Which one could afford to bid the highest price to the owner of that parcel? The third person could theoretically bid twice the amount the first one could afford and still make the same percent of profit due to the better use intended for the property.

This is perhaps an overly simplified reference to a most important real estate concept called "highest and best use." Land may have many highest and best uses over a long period of time, but it can logically have only one highest and best use at any given point in time. That use which will result in the greatest amount and longest duration of net income flow which accrues to the land itself is considered the highest and best use. Some authorities call it land's most economically effective use, some say land's most profitable use, but all are really saying the same thing: the highest and best use of land is the legal use which will produce a projected income stream resulting in greatest value of the land.

Characteristics of Real Estate Markets

From the information above, it becomes clear that if the real estate market were allowed to operate without any interference or restraint whatsoever, each person could use his or her property for whatever purpose he or she felt would produce the greatest return. This could result in one person's use of property which would cause a loss in value to another person's property. Obviously we cannot permit land to be used for whatever purpose the owner thinks best for his individual private gain. The social costs to adjacent properties may often preclude the private gain for one or a few individuals. For example, if you lived in a very nice residential subdivision and your neighbor bought two undeveloped lots adjoining your property for use as a pig farm or for a paper mill with its offensive odors, the social costs to you and the rest of the subdivision would far outweigh the private gain to your neighbor. Therefore, the real estate market cannot be permitted to operate free of all controls and restraints.

One of the characteristics which sets the real estate market apart from most other markets is the amount of control exercised by government. These controls are required because of competition between landowners to increase the profits which their land can produce. Such controls as zoning, building codes, and health ordinances form the basis for city planning and orderly growth.

Before discussing this and the other characteristics of the real estate market, it is useful to list the primary characteristics affecting ownership and sale which set real estate apart from other markets:

1. The market is local in nature
   - -- immovable product
2. It is slow to respond to change
   - -- supply of
   - -- demand for
3. Relative permanence of improvements
   - -- committed to location
   - -- durability

6. Limited # of buyers + sellers
7. lots of external influences (example: people in Canada buying)
8. R.E usually takes a lot of money

4. The market is unorganized and without central control
   - -- no standard product
   - -- no central information — no such thing as a standard market
5. Governmental controls influence the market
   - -- zoning
   - -- building codes
   - -- taxes — many govt control

RE market has sub-markets + make sub-sub market (urban residential)

1. The market for real estate is uncommonly local in nature as compared to other markets. The reason for this is, of course, the fact that land and the improvements thereon are immovable. We cannot transport a farm or a lot to some other location. If we were in the tomato market, we could haul our produce to the place where demand might be greatest. However, despite the demand for housing in the Washington, D.C. area, we cannot produce an apartment complex or a single-family subdivision on land located in Florida and take it to where greater demand exists.

2. The real estate market is also unusually slow to respond to changes in supply and demand. An illustration could be the motel situation in central Florida before and after the development of Disney World. In 1969, the number of motels (supply) began to fall behind the demand for transient accommodations created by visitors. The forecast transient population growth indicated a good future market for motels. Unfortunately, many investors and developers did not do complete market analysis studies of the number of building permits issued. Instead, each proceeded to plan for additional motel units as if their group alone would produce motels. Since the design, land acquisition, site preparation, and construction phases of real estate are so time-consuming, it was not until approximately 1972-73 that motel complexes began to mushroom and the market became flooded. The equilibrium between supply and demand was destroyed since the supply of motel units far exceeded the demand. If some different commodity had been involved, the excess supply could have been moved to wherever a greater demand existed. In the real estate market, the nature of the product forces us to live with our mistakes. Therefore, the surplus motel space will either remain empty until demand builds up to the available supply, or cut-throat competition will drive profits down for all.

3. The characteristic referred to as permanence of improvements is also closely related to the above characteristics. Take the motel example once again. Once a motel complex is built, it has a long economic life as compared to other commodities. We are stuck with a motel when we perhaps should have invested our time and money in single-family housing, or restaurants, or something else. But the permanence of the improvements created eliminates many alternatives available to other markets. If Ford Motor Company produces an Edsel one year, it can change to a Thunderbird or Mustang the next year or so. In the real estate market, constructed motel complexes will be around for many years.

4. Another characteristic of the real estate market is the lack of a single central exchange for dealing in real estate nationwide. Compare this situation with the stock market. If one wishes to buy a hundred shares of General Motors' stock in

California, the product will be the same as GM stock bought in Florida. However, if one wishes to buy a hundred acres of farmland in California, the product will be different in many respects from a hundred acres of Florida farmland. This focuses attention on the two main reasons why there is not a central exchange for real estate. First, the product cannot be standardized. No two tracts of land are the same. Even two lots side by side on a street have different geographical locations on this earth. Secondly, there is no central data bank or information source which can tell about property in Fresno, California, Walla Walla, Washington, and Micanopy, Florida, plus any point in between. If we want to know about real property in any of these locations, we would be well-advised to go to that particular place and seek local information.

5. Government controls, the fifth and last of the primary characteristics of the real estate market, play an inordinately important role when compared to other markets. Most people are familiar with direct controls such as zoning, building codes, or health ordinances which govern use of septic tanks and other health-related matters. But the government also exercises indirect controls. Indirect controls such as the monetary policies of the federal government or local government policies regarding planned future growth will have marked effects on real estate markets. If the Federal Reserve Board decides to slow the rate of inflation by reducing the overall money supply, the result will be higher interest rates for mortgage loans. This will, in turn, drive many potential buyers out of the real estate market. Also, when the U.S. Department of the Treasury must borrow to make payments on the national debt, such large amounts of money taken out of the available supply of loan funds causes the remaining funds to be loaned at higher interest rates.

Some of the more familiar indirect influences are federal, state, and local tax laws. Because real property is valuable, immobile, and durable, it is an exceptionally good subject for taxes. The federal government does not levy a tax on real property; however, the federal government does have a profound effect on property use as a result of its income tax laws, rules, and regulations. For example, the federal government encourages real property ownership by providing income tax benefits in the form of depreciation for improvements which are used to generate income. Also, owners of real property can realize significant tax savings as a result of the capital gains provisions of our tax laws.

At the state and local level, the real estate market is more directly affected by taxes. The Florida Green Belt Law creates an agricultural use exemption from property taxes. This benefit motivated speculators to acquire undeveloped tracts located in the path of forecast growth, ostensibly for agricultural purposes, but actually for future development or value appreciation. By placing a few head of livestock on the property, or preparing the ground as if to plant a crop, the preferential agricultural exemption was obtained. This resulted in such inequities and abuse of the Green Belt Law that changes were enacted. Today, a property owner must claim an agricultural exemption each year, just as a homeowner must claim homestead exemption, but the agricultural exemption must be rejustified each year. This change in the enforcement of the law was necessary because operators and speculators had abused the Green Belt Law to the extent that the law was protecting speculators as much or more than it protected the farmers. Requiring proof of agricultural use each year has helped to return the real estate market to a more natural condition.

Major Sub-markets of Real Estate

Earlier it was mentioned that the real estate market was composed of several sub-markets. Generally, these sub-markets are categorized according to the type of property traded in that sub-market. Most authorities agree that the major sub-markets of real estate are:

1. Residential
2. Commercial
3. Industrial
4. Agricultural
5. Government and Special Purpose Properties

These five categories are termed major sub-markets because each one of them is further divided into minor sub-markets. For example, "residential" as a major sub-market can itself be divided into minor sub-markets:

1. Urban
2. Suburban
3. Rural

Each of these three minor sub-markets can be further divided into single-family and multi-family, which could then each be classified as owner-occupied or rental. The point is, what appears to be one big but simple real estate market is, in reality, a complex structure of many individual sub-markets, each of which contributes to the overall market.

It should be noted that each market and sub-market is subject to the five characteristics previously listed. Also, each sub-market is controlled by its own supply and demand characteristics for that particular market, although other sub-markets may exert an influence. Whenever the supply and demand equilibrium of a market is upset by excess supply, there develops a "buyer's market." The number of excess units in that particular market allows a potential buyer to shop between anxious owner-sellers and obtain better prices and terms. When this condition exists, more intelligent builders may well stop building because of the lack of profit resulting from excess supply. On the other hand, when an excess demand exists, it is a natural result of short supply and this condition creates a "seller's market." This allows sellers to demand higher prices from buyers who are forced to compete for whatever space is available. This causes more building to result in an effort to participate in the profits being produced and eventually leads to over-supply once more.

Variable Factors Influencing Supply and Demand

A study of markets and their operation will reveal several factors which influence demand and a few factors which affect supply. The influences on supply are primarily associated with cost. This fact emphasizes the principle that the value received from increased supply must exceed the total costs of producing the unit supplied.

A. Demand

Whether looking at the real estate market, the wheat market, or the stock market, one of the most important variable factors influencing the demand in any market is price. When prices are considered too high, demand is not absent but demand builds up and is held in check just as water backs up when held in check by a dam. When prices are lowered, the pent up demand is exercised until the available supply is consumed and prices begin to rise again. This repeated cyclical occurrence proves that demand is inversely related to price. What this means is that when prices are high, demand is lowered due to inability or unwillingness to pay the high prices. When prices are low, demand is increased by greater willingness or ability to pay the lower prices.

Another important variable related to demand is population numbers and composition. Most of the transactions in the real estate market are residential property transactions. Shelter is a basic need and cannot be long ignored. However, the demand for dwelling space is dependent upon both numbers and composition of the population in every market area. For example, many experts point to a national demand of approximately 600,000 new dwellings of various types each year merely to accommodate the average growth in population numbers. Add to this number the new dwelling spaces caused by changes in size of households, increased affluence, undoubling of households, and population mobility, then the estimated demand is for 1,300,000 to 1,400,000 new dwelling spaces per year. But even this figure does not count the demand for replacement of demolished or destroyed units.

Mere numbers of people do not provide sufficient information for accurately estimating the demand for dwelling space, nor does a count of families. Modern lifestyles, changes in economic conditions, and reduced family size have caused the "household" to become the basis for most population analysis. A household is defined by the Bureau of the Census, U.S. Department of Commerce, as any person or group of persons occupying a separate housing space. Thus, a household means a single person living in a rented apartment, or a husband and wife with four children living in their own home in the suburbs, or two unmarried adults living in a condominium near the city center. Each constitutes a household.

It is only when Bureau of the Census data are analyzed that the benefits of "demand trend forecasting" are realized. Just before the turn of the century, 100 dwelling units would accommodate 490 people due to the average size of households then. The 1970 Census revealed that the decreased size of the average household (3.2 people per household) would require approximately 153 dwelling spaces to accommodate 490 people. The change in average household size alone had therefore caused an increase of 53 percent in demand. Demographers and others who study population trends state that a further reduction in average household size should be anticipated. This will again change the demand for housing, not only in numbers of units but also in size of dwellings.

An estimated demand for 1.3 to 1.4 million new dwellings per year does not mean that each of the 50 states and the District of Columbia will share this growth on a proportionate basis. Natural increase in population (that is, the number of births exceeding the number of deaths) and in-migration are two important components of the population factor. Increased longevity of our elderly contributes to the natural increase of population by increasing the number of births over deaths even if the birth rate remains static. As a result, Florida has experienced exceptional population gains along with California and Arizona. This has been reflected in increased demand for housing.

While important, natural increase in population as discussed above is not the most important component of Florida's population increase. The most important cause of population increase for the state as a whole has been in-migration -- new residents who have moved here from other places. Every reason exists to suppose that this trend will continue. The winter of 1976-77 may have been inconvienient for some in Florida, but the weather nationally plus uncertainties created by the "energy crunch" will more than likely combine to accelerate the rate of in-migration in the future.

The next variable influence on demand for dwelling space is income of consumers. Whereas price is inversely related to demand, income is positively related to demand. As income increases, so does demand for dwelling space. This does not imply that a doubling of income will result in a doubling of demand. It merely reflects a human desire for more units or a larger amount of space as income permits such desires to be gratified.

Today, most homes are bought on time payment plans through mortgage loans. The real estate market in general, and the residential market in particular, are very sensitive to fluctuations in income. Prior to making a loan, most lenders will analyze a potential borrower very carefully to determine both the quality and quantity of income. As a result, any change in local employment/unemployment rates or salary/wage levels will be reflected by a change in demand for dwelling space and attendant loan considerations.

The fourth variable influence on demand for dwelling space is mortgage credit. The availability and cost of credit has been called the barometer of the real estate market. Since the purchase of an average residential property involves between two and three times the buyer's annual income, it is easy to understand why more than 90 percent of homebuyers use credit to arrange the purchase.

During the period from 1940 to the present, general attitudes toward credit and debt have undergone profound changes. In earlier times, the general public regarded a person who deliberately incurred debt as one whose morals might be questioned. As time passed, the value of a good credit rating has been learned and only a small percentage of today's population insists on doing without until they can pay cash. Consequently, the average homebuyer today is primarily concerned with the amount of the monthly payment on a mortgage loan (principal and interest). If a potential homebuyer can afford the monthly mortgage payments, plus taxes and insurance, the total cost of the house is of secondary importance.

The monthly mortgage payment includes both amortization (principal) and interest. The amortization portion of a monthly payment can be increased or decreased by: (a) the amount of down payment made on the property; and/or, (b) the term of the loan (the period of time in which the loan is to be paid back). Both of these influences have a direct bearing on demand for housing. If substantial down payments are required, thousands of potential buyers may be driven out of the residential market due to limited equity funds. Also, if a very short period of loan time should become standard policy, it would mean that higher payments per month would be required and this would eliminate many more thousands of potential buyers.

All indicators point to trends in the opposite direction. Demand for more houses is stimulated by present credit policies which permit buyers to borrow up to 95 percent of appraised value if private mortgage insurance is obtained to protect the loan. Demand is further stimulated by increasing the term of loans for longer periods, thereby reducing the amount of each monthly payment, although the total cost of credit will be greater. However, most people today are not deeply concerned with the total amount paid for a house over a 30- or 40-year period. Since most home loans today are either assumed by a new owner, paid off, or refinanced within a period of less than seven years, the monthly payment on a mortgage is a greater influence on demand. When a tight money market develops and interest rates rise, a corresponding drop will be reflected in housing demand because the amount of money needed to make monthly mortgage payments will be increased. For example, a $30,000 mortgage loan at 7½% interest for a period of 30 years will require a monthly payment of $209.77, excluding taxes and insurance. The same amount of money for the same period of time but at 9½% interest will require a monthly payment of $252.26 -- an additional $42.49 per month. It becomes apparent why an increase in mortgage interest rates of only 1% will cause a definite drop in demand for housing.

The final variable factor relating to demand concerns consumer tastes or choice. Different architectural designs are sometimes introduced into the residential market and sometimes enjoy brief periods of popularity. Generally speaking, however, enduring changes in consumer tastes occur slowly, over extended periods. Most of the basic housing traffic patterns used to create today's dwellings are modifications of residential layouts dating back to

Colonial times.

Outside elevations or exterior appearances may be subject to change in consumer tastes. For example, today there is more and more preference for what is loosely termed "modern contemporary" exteriors. Spanish or Mediterranean style homes have been popular for some time as has the French Provincial. The ranch style and the bungalow have enjoyed their time of popularity and are not built as often today. Naturally, owners and builders are constantly attempting to increase demand (profit) by appealing to consumer tastes. Whatever style and type of house the buying public demonstrates a preference for, that is the type of dwelling which will be built more often until a new style creates a new demand.

Changes in the forms of ownership have also influenced demand. Many homeowners also own condominiums or second homes for vacation purposes, which can also be a source of income if desired. For years, "empty-nesters" (those parents whose children are grown and have moved away) continued to live in the same house where they had reared their children, although it was entirely too large for their needs as a couple. The numerous chores of the homeowner related to maintenance, repair, and grounds upkeep were often a joy but sometimes too demanding physically. The advent of condominium ownership offered a solution to these empty-nesters and other small families. Maintenance, repair, and grounds care is normally performed by the personnel hired by either the condominium association or a professional manager. While condominium ownership dates back to the days of the Roman Empire, it is relatively new in the United States and has created great demand in the residential market.

Let's summarize in list form the above variables related to <u>demand</u> before turning to supply:

1. Price of real estate
2. Population numbers and composition
3. Income of consumers
4. Mortgage credit
5. Consumer tastes

B. <u>Supply</u>

At any point in time, the existing market conditions are a result of the interaction of supply and demand. The number, or inventory, of existing dwelling units is the supply. New construction or the remodeling of existing structures can increase the supply. Conversely, the supply can be reduced by destruction or changing dwelling space to another use.

The variable factors which influence the supply side of the real estate market are all related to the costs involved in the four basic factors of production plus materials. In order to justify any addition to existing supply, all costs incurred in production of new units must be less than the resulting market value. Put another way, the reason builders are willing to build new dwelling units is that they expect to receive more than their total costs expended on labor, capital, management, land, and materials.

The cost of labor is an important influence on the supply side of the market. It will depend on such things as community growth, unemployment rates, skill levels required, and union versus non-union wage scales. When an area is growing rapidly, the growth will usually be characterized by much construction in progress with resulting high employment in construction industry skills. These conditions cause competition for labor and bidding causes the cost of labor to increase. When labor costs reach a point where the builder cannot compete in the market without over-pricing his product, it is not feasible to add more units to the existing supply. Either demand must increase to the point that consumers will pay a higher price or building will decline and the high-cost worker will be unemployed.

The costs of capital are those expenses related to financing and discount points. In order to remain in business, a builder/developer must include in the sales price the known or estimated cost to finance construction plus anticipated discount points, if appropriate. Construction loans are made to provide all or most of the funds to complete a structure. From these borrowed funds a builder can pay for labor, materials, subcontractors, and auxiliary professional services. The loan is repaid after the building is sold, or a purchaser may want to assume the loan after paying an agreed amount to the builder. In either case, the builder must pay the lender for the use of money used in the construction process.

Costs of management may be paid to a contractor, or to several subcontractors, or retained by the builder/developer himself. Management costs are justified for two reasons: (1) for responsibility and protection of the investment in the property; and, (2) for supervising and coordinating the many facets of construction to achieve optimum efficiency and economy.

Land costs have moved into a new and higher cost plateau. Although land seems physically plentiful, the type and location of land most in demand is always scarce. When the costs of improvements to the land such as streets, sewers, and utilities are included, land costs can be the determinant which will decide the feasibility of proposed construction. Historically, the highest and best use of residential lots has resulted when an improvement-to-land ratio of 4-6 to 1 was observed. Applied to actual situations, this meant that a residential lot costing $5,000 would be utilized at its highest and best use when a house was built on it costing between $20,000 and $30,000. Residential lots which formerly sold for $5,000 between 1968-1970 now sell for approximately $9,000. If the traditional ratio is utilized, the lot will require a house costing between $36,000 and $54,000, resulting in a property value of $45,000 to $63,000. The "average" citizen is thus priced out of the market and land cost will cause a supply of unsold homes to accumulate.

Costs of materials are determined by the supply and demand conditions in the materials markets. The cost of any material will depend upon the total costs of raw materials, production, transportation, and profit margin. In the northwestern part of the United States, the supply of lumber is normally plentiful and the resulting cost is less than in Florida, for example. Most builders, therefore, find it less costly to build with and seek out materials homogeneous to the area.

Interpreting Market Conditions

The discussion of real estate markets in general and the residential market in particular has demonstrated that existing market conditions are a result of past decisions which produced an interaction between supply and demand. What the average real estate salesman and broker would like to have is some sort of dependable reference or guide to help interpret market conditions. Fortunately, there are several indicators which help to clarify what the market is doing. Some of the more important indicators are:

1. Supply of existing unsold houses
2. Occupancy/vacancy ratios
3. Number, prices, location, and types of houses sold

1. The very characteristic which causes real estate to be considered prime security for mortgage loans also acts as a constant or known factor in interpreting market conditions. Due to the immobility of real estate, the supply side and the demand side of the market cannot be brought into equilibrium by relocation. Therefore, when demand drops for any reason, inability to withdraw existing supply from the market will result in an oversupply. A "buyer's market" often results until the oversupply is reduced. Since prices received by builders must exceed total costs of construction, a buyer's market will cause a drop in construction until the inventory of unsold houses is reduced.

2. Occupancy/vacancy ratios in rental properties act on the market in the same manner as unsold inventory. When vacancy ratios begin to increase, it indicates a surplus of housing space, generally in rental units and homes for sale. Apartment dwellers who have been waiting to buy a home of their own find a buyer's market in houses for sale and move out of apartments. This causes increased apartment vacancies and eventually a drop in rents as well as a halt in construction of new apartments. One of the first indications of a revived real estate market has always been an increase in rental occupancies which cannot be attributed to reduced rents or give-away programs.

3. There are many ways to collect information on the number and prices of homes sold during the recent past. Anyone can go to the public records and laboriously extract the number of houses sold the previous week and from the state documentary tax stamps calculate the approximate sales price of each. Most towns and cities have newspaper publication of sales during the past week or past month. From these published accounts, one can extract information on how many sales occurred, what the approximate sales prices were, where the properties sold were located, and sometimes the types of houses involved. Those towns and cities which have a multiple listing service (MLS) find the job a great deal easier.

None of these market indicators are of any value unless one learns how to use them. A card file system, arranged by subdivision, by streets, or alphabetically can be of great value in building a current sales data file. A large scale model of a town or those areas of a city where interest is high can become a valuable tool in pinpointing areas of greatest activity and in forecasting direction of growth. When a sale is reported in a publication, a color-coded pin can be placed on the map to indicate price range and location of property. A glance at such a map shows where most sales are occurring and the general price ranges. Direction and rate of growth can also be estimated from a sales data map.

Summary

A market permits products and services to be bought and sold. But goods and services have no value in and of themselves. It is only when they are wanted by consumers that they have value. Thus, the function of every market is to facilitate exchange between buyers and sellers.

One of the sub-markets of the general market for goods and services is the real estate market. While the real estate market differs in a number of distinctive ways from other markets, it acts much like all markets with respect to changes in supply and demand but with a slower response time. It has the appearance of being a single, simple entity when in fact the real estate market is itself composed of many, complex sub-markets.

Professionals in the real estate business have a responsibility to themselves and their principals to keep abreast of market activities through continuing study of the local real estate marketplace in particular.

CHAPTER 12

THE REAL ESTATE MARKET

1. Any economy in any land must find answers for the questions: "What will be produced?", "Who will do the producing?", and:

   I. "What will production cost?"
   II. "Who will get what is produced?"

   a. I only
   b. II only
   c. Both I and II
   d. Neither I nor II

2. One characteristic of the free enterprise system (also called the price system) is that it:

   I. Works automatically
   II. Is a regulated system

   a. I only
   b. II only
   c. Both I and II
   d. Neither I nor II

3. The answers to "What will be produced?" and "Who will do the producing?" are dependent upon decisions made by the:

   I. Producers or manufacturers
   II. Consumers or customers

   a. I only
   b. II only
   c. Both I and II
   d. Neither I nor II

4. The factor market includes which of the following?

   I. Capital and management
   II. Labor and land

   a. I only
   b. II only
   c. Both I and II
   d. Neither I nor II

5. At any given time, a parcel of land can have:

   I. One highest and best use
   II. Several highest and best uses

   a. I only
   b. II only
   c. Both I and II
   d. Neither I nor II

6. The definition of "highest and best use" is that use which will result in:

   I. The greatest amount and longest duration of net income flow
   II. The land's most economical use

   a. I only
   b. II only
   c. Both I and II
   d. Neither I nor II

7. The real estate market:

   I. Must be allowed to operate free of controls
   II. Cannot be allowed to operate free of controls

   a. I only
   b. II only
   c. Both I and II
   d. Neither I nor II

8. The real estate market is local in nature because:

   I. The demand for real estate is local
   II. Land and improvements are immobile

   a. I only
   b. II only
   c. Both I and II
   d. Neither I nor II

9. The real estate market responds to supply and demand changes:

   I. Slowly
   II. Rapidly

   a. I only
   b. II only
   c. Both I and II
   d. Neither I nor II

10. No central market exchange for real estate exists because:

   I. The product cannot be standardized
   II. There is no central source of national real estate information

   a. I only
   b. II only
   c. Both I and II
   d. Neither I nor II

11. U.S. tax statutes regulating depreciation:

   I. Encourage real estate ownership
   II. Discourage real estate ownership

   a. I only
   b. II only
   c. Both I and II
   d. Neither I nor II

12. An agricultural property owner is required to claim an agricultural exemption:

   I. One time only
   II. Every year

   a. I only
   b. II only
   c. Both I and II
   d. Neither I nor II

13. Most authorities agree that the real estate market is divided into:

   I. Four major sub-markets
   II. Five major sub-markets

   a. I only
   b. II only
   c. Both I and II
   d. Neither I nor II

14. When the equilibrium of the real estate market is upset by an excess supply:

   I. A seller's market exists
   II. A buyer's market exists

   a. I only
   b. II only
   c. Both I and II
   d. Neither I nor II

15. A person or group of persons occupying a separate housing space is technically defined as a:

   I. Household
   II. Family

   a. I only
   b. II only
   c. Both I and II
   d. Neither I nor II

16. The most important cause of population increase in Florida has been:

   I. The number of births exceeding deaths
   II. In-migration of new residents

   a. I only
   b. II only
   c. Both I and II
   d. Neither I nor II

17. The barometer of the real estate market is: how much the money costs.

   I. The cost and availability of credit
   II. The fluctuations of housing starts

   a. I only
   b. II only
   c. Both I and II
   d. Neither I nor II

18. The average homebuyer today is primarily concerned with the:

    I. Total cost of the house under consideration
    II. Amount of the monthly mortgage payment for the house under consideration

    a. I only
    b. II only
    c. Both I and II
    d. Neither I nor II

19. Condominium ownership:

    I. Is relatively new in the U.S.
    II. Dates back to the days of the Roman Empire

    a. I only
    b. II only
    c. Both I and II
    d. Neither I nor II

20. The variable factors affecting the supply side of the real estate market are related to:

    I. Costs
    II. Production

    a. I only
    b. II only
    c. Both I and II
    d. Neither I nor II

21. One of the first indicators of a revived real estate market has always been:

    I. An increase in rental property occupancy rates not attributable to reduced rents
    II. An increase in sales of single-family homes not attributable to reduced prices

    a. I only
    b. II only
    c. Both I and II
    d. Neither I nor II

CHAPTER 13

REAL ESTATE TAXES

As this nation entered the 20th century, taxes on real property contributed more than 75 percent of local and state government revenues. By 1972, property taxes contributed no more than 25 percent of state and local government revenues. This does not signify a reduction in individual property taxes; it serves to indicate that local and state governments have found additional and different sources of income. Despite the foregoing statements, property taxes across the nation have been rising at an average rate approaching 10 percent per year and continue to be the predominant source of local government revenues. This is a reflection of the increased cost of growth and government.

Each individual has a viewpoint regarding property taxes. If one is in government, property taxes are a source of the revenue needed to ensure the orderly process of administration. If one is a member of a school board, property taxes are the major source of revenue needed to operate the educational system. If one is a property owner, property taxes are a large annual drain on personal finances but are an income tax deduction. Whatever one's attitude, property taxes play an extremely important role in real estate, as this chapter will reveal.

Most property owners would not willingly accept a legal structure or local government which did not provide protection for one's legal rights of ownership. That is, in a sense, the basis for the constitutional right of the government to levy property taxes. Property taxes provide a large portion of revenue needed to enable local governments to provide law enforcement, fire protection, and protection of our legal rights. To guard against possible abuse of the power to tax, many states, including Florida, have either included provisions in state constitutions or enacted state statutes which limit the burden which may be placed on individual property owners. Without such safeguards, property taxes might be increased to the point of economic confiscation.

Florida has what is called the "ten mill cap" which applies to city and county tax districts. An "eight mill cap" applies to county school boards. These terms indicate that although a city or county may levy a tax rate of 10 mills or less, each may not legally levy a property rate of more than 10 mills. In the case of school boards, the ceiling of 8 mills may not be exceeded. If voters in a city or county have approved separate bond issues, the revenue required to secure those bond issues may be raised by adding increased millage to the ten mill cap or the eight mill cap. However, these levies are not property taxes and the voters themselves make the decision regarding such authorized increases to the tax rate ceilings.

Levels of Government Involved

General real estate taxes, commonly called real property taxes, are levied on an "ad valorem" basis, which means taxed according to value. Three major levels of government and numerous special tax districts are empowered to levy ad valorem taxes directly on real property in Florida. As mentioned above, city, county, and school board districts levy property taxes. State and federal governments do not levy direct property taxes, although both do levy taxes which affect real property transactions and values. State and federal property-related taxes are dealt with elsewhere.

School boards and city and county governments operate with powers delegated to them by the state government. State law now requires that the county property appraiser assess for all three levels of government, thus avoiding duplication and possible controversy. In addition, all real property assessments must be updated annually.

If the costs associated with operating schools, city hall, and county government were a one-time expense, it would not be necessary to pay property taxes more than once. However, these are recurring costs and therefore property taxes must be paid annually to ensure continuation of civic services. Property taxes are levied on a calendar year basis. This means that taxes are paid "in arrears" for the period January 1 through December 31 each year. Property taxes become a lien on all real estate in Florida on January 1 each year. This lien is legally superior to any other lien regardless of date. Taxes are payable to the county tax collector, not the county property appraiser, effective November 1 each year. A discount system permits property owners to realize a savings by prompt payment of taxes. If taxes are paid during November, a 4% discount is allowed on the overall tax bill. If paid in December, a 3% discount is allowed, and the discount continues to decrease 1% per month through February. All property taxes paid on or after March 1 must be the full amount of taxes levied. Property taxes become delinquent on April 1 each year.

Determining "Just Value"

Property taxes are levied against land and all permanent improvements to the land. The assessed values of the land and improvements are arrived at in separate actions and then combined to reflect a single tax statement. The State Supreme Court has interpreted Florida Statutes as requiring that all real property must be assessed at "just value" which is considered to mean "fair market value." This ruling provides a goal of uniformity in assessing all real property across the state's 67 counties. Each individual property owner may protect his interest by protest if an assessment error is detected or even suspected.

In arriving at a just valuation, county property appraisers must take into consideration the following:

1. The present cash value of the property
2. The highest and best use to which the property can be expected to be put in the immediate future, and the present use of the property
3. Location of the property
4. The quantity or size of the property
5. The cost of said property and the replacement value of any improvements thereon

6. The condition of said property
7. The income of said property
8. The net proceeds of the sale of said property, as received by the seller, after deduction of all usual and reasonable fees and costs of the sale, including costs and expenses of financing.

All three approaches to value (market, cost, and income) are represented in the above criteria. Also, if the property is sold during the year, the sale price becomes a factor for consideration in assessing the value of the property, but it is not controlling.

In order to ensure that all property owners are treated fairly, most property appraisers have turned to computers for assistance. Representatives of the property appraiser's office typically go out to assess a property with the aid of forms and recording procedures. The information obtained from the field trip is then processed through a computer by utilizing appropriate formulas. The computer will then render an objective assessment value.

It should not be inferred that a thorough and painstaking examination is made of each lot or parcel. In those subdivisions and neighborhoods where lots are generally standard in size, a thorough inspection may often be made of a single lot selected as the standard or typical lot. The assessed value assigned to that standard lot can then be applied to all other lots in the subdivision or neighborhood which correspond with the standard lot. Physical features may cause some variation but the use of standard lots simplifies the county property appraiser's job to an appreciable degree. Corner lots or lots with unusual topographic or locational features are then the only exceptions which must be dealt with on an individual lot basis.

While the majority of lots in a subdivision or neighborhood may be considered similiar, the buildings and improvements on those lots are a different matter. Almost every house will be different, at least when viewed from the outside. Each house, plus all other improvements to the lot, must therefore be assessed on an individual basis. For example, a three-bedroom, two-bath house with a swimming pool will be assessed at a higher value than the same house without a swimming pool. This merely reflects the ad valorem nature of property taxes and carries out the State Supreme Court ruling that assessed value must correspond to market value.

Once an assessment has been placed on a property, the owner must be informed. This requirement is considered to have been carried out when a value notice is mailed to the property owner at the last address of record. It is the responsibility of each property owner to see that a current address is on file in those counties where he owns property. This helps to ensure timely receipt of a notice of change in assessment or a tax statement before the time allowed for protest has expired.

Any property owner is entitled to protest a property assessment, but not every protest will be successful. For example, an owner of a home on a standard lot in a large, completely developed subdivision would have little hope of getting his assessment changed if he complained that his lot was assessed too high. If the assessed value of his lot were changed, all similar lots would also have to be changed. On the other hand, the same homeowner might have a very good chance of obtaining a lowered assessment if he could prove his house was assessed at a value greater than justified. The county property appraiser will have fairly complete details on the house: size, construction materials, date built, and amount of depreciation allowable since the date of construction. He will also have records showing the assessed values of similar structures in the neighborhood. However, if the owner can point out that other structures similar to his have been assessed at a lower value, he has a good chance of receiving a lower assessment.

Protest Procedure

Florida has what amounts to a three-step procedure for objecting to the assessed value of real property. The first step is to seek an adjustment by contacting the county property appraiser or a representative of his office. A property owner is allowed two weeks after receipt of his assessment notice to protest that assessment to the county property appraiser. If the arguments of the property owner are valid and have a basis in fact, the county property appraiser is authorized to make a change and lower the assessed value.

But suppose the property owner's request for a changed assessment is rejected. The second step in the protest procedure is to file an appeal with the Property Appraisal Adjustment Board. The Property Appraisal Adjustment Board is made up of five members: three county commissioners, appointed by the chairman of the County Commission, and two county school board members, appointed by the chairman of the County School Board. Since the purpose of the Property Appraisal Adjustment Board is to act as a review board and thereby assure that all property owners receive a fair hearing, the law purposely requires that all members be elected officials. In this way, taxpayers have an opportunity to change the composition of the board if a member or members are considered unfair or biased. In fulfilling its purpose, the Property Appraisal Adjustment Board at least provides a review process designed to be fair and objective. Each protest is conducted as an "adversary proceeding" with the county property appraiser stating his case and the property owner stating his case. If the board agrees with the taxpayer that the assessed value of his property is too high, the board has the authority to change the assessment. If the board decides the county property appraiser was right in the assessment value assigned, the board will reject the taxpayer's request for change of assessment. Such an action would mark the end of the second step in the protest procedure.

The third step available to a property owner seeking a change in assessed value is usually litigation in the courts. The unhappy taxpayer may file a petition requesting a "certiorari" proceeding. His petition must be filed within 60 days of the certification of county tax rolls, usually around October 15. If granted, a writ of certiorari will be issued by the court. A writ of certiorari merely directs a lower court or agency to forward to a higher body the record of whatever case is being contested. In this instance, the court would direct that the taxpayer's request for change of assessment be forwarded to the court for adjudication. Upon examination of all the evidence presented by both sides and a review of the procedures originally employed by the county property appraiser, the court will issue a decision. The court cannot arbitrarily assign an assessment value to a property. It can, however, specify methods and procedures for the county property appraiser to use in reassessing the subject property. If the court should agree that the original assessed value is fair and equitable, then the property owner has utilized all the steps available under the protest procedure.

Most property owners are inclined to hold the county property appraiser (formerly tax assessor) responsible for the amount of their taxes. This is a mistake because the county appraiser is involved in only one of the three important phases of the real property taxation process.

The three major phases of the taxation process are:

1. Property appraisal and assessment
2. Budget and tax rate levy
3. Tax billing and collection

The first phase related to appraisal and assessment has already been treated to some degree. It is the second phase involving budgeting and calculation of a tax rate which requires some attention at this point.

Tax Districts: Budgets and Tax Rate Levy

In Florida, a taxing authority, called a "tax district," may be a village, town, city, county, school board, or special tax district. Each fiscal year, all tax districts must prepare an operating budget for the next fiscal year. The fiscal year for all cities and counties in Florida runs from October 1 through September 30, so all city and county budgets must provide for expenditures anticipated during that period.

The operating budget prepared by each tax district is actually a summary of several departmental budgets received from lower echelons. For example, the police department will submit one budget intended to reflect the estimated cost of operating every phase of that department's activities during the coming fiscal year. If new police cars or additional police personnel are to be added during the next year, those estimated costs must be in the budget submitted. The same process is followed by public works, health, fire, and all other departments or agencies. When consolidated, all of the individual department budgets make up the city or county budget for the next fiscal year.

With the budget in hand, the tax district knows just about what to expect regarding costs for the next year. But what about revenue (income) to pay those costs? No elected official is anxious to levy higher property taxes than absolutely necessary to operate the city, county, or school board. So before a general real estate tax is calculated, an attempt will be made to estimate the revenue which can reasonably be expected from all sources except real property taxes. Each tax district may have different or unique sources of income ranging from outright federal grants to profits resulting from municipally owned utilities. Fines paid in courts, parking meter income, fees from occupational licenses, and tax funds returned by the state government are a few of the many sources of income. Estimating the amount of income from these non-property tax sources is made easier by records of preceding years which generally indicate a predictable trend.

With a reasonable estimate of the revenue expected from all non-property tax sources, the tax district is then able to predict the amount of money needed from property taxes. All of the next year's budget not financed by sources other than property taxes must be obtained from property taxes.

The total value of all taxable (non-exempt) property assessments in the tax district, whether a city or county, is called the "tax base." Put another way, the amount of property taxes paid into a tax district must come from its tax base, which is the total assessed value of all taxable property in the tax district. Assume that the city of Nofreeze, Florida has within its boundaries properties valued at $178,450,000. Government land and buildings account for $6,200,000 of that total valuation. The tax base, or total assessed value of taxable properties, would be $172,250,000.

Once the total assessed value of taxable properties in the city or county is known, determination of a tax rate is close at hand. The missing component needed to calculate a tax rate is a summary of the number and type of property tax exemptions granted.

Exemptions from Property Taxes

Exemptions from property taxes are defended by some and cursed by others. For example, not all people feel the same toward homestead tax exemption as they do toward the exemption of church property from real estate taxes.

To illustrate, assume that a small town must have a certain amount of revenue in order to operate, say $100,000. If 1,000 citizens live in the community and no one is exempt from a fair share of taxes, the job of distributing the tax burden is not too difficult. But if 200 residents are exempted from paying property taxes, does it reduce the $100,000 needed to operate the local government? No, the $100,000 is needed regardless of the number of contributors. The result of this overly simplified example is that 800 residents must contribute the $100,000 instead of the entire population. It is true that tax exemptions decrease the overall tax base of a community. It is also true that tax exemptions increase the tax rates of those properties not exempt. Fortunately, the previously mentioned tax mill caps act as a ceiling. The losers in situations of this nature are generally the renters. All landlords are forced to shift higher taxes to their tenants in the form of higher rents. Thus, the tenant bears the cost of increased property taxes but receives no income tax benefits which are available to taxpaying property owners.

Several different categories of property are not included in the taxable property tax base. Some people erroneously group all of the non-taxed properties into one overall category called "exempt properties." To be accurate, one should refer to federal, state, and school properties as "immune" from taxation. Only that property belonging to cities, counties, and special categories are exempt. The distinction may not be apparent until one thinks of the immune properties as not subject to taxation. Exempt properties are subject to taxation but exempt from the obligation. When city or county properties are rented or leased by private parties, the exemption is removed. This is often the case at municipally owned airports.

Then, too, some properties are granted partial exemption, homestead tax exemtion for example. For this reason, one cannot always regard the assessed value of a property as the taxable value of that property. It is important to remember that the real taxable value of a property is not known until existing exemptions are subtracted from the assessed value. For example, suppose you own a home assessed at $40,000 and you have qualified for regular homestead tax exemption. What is your taxable property value? The regular homestead tax exemption of $5,000 must be deducted from the assessed value of $40,000 in order to arrive at the taxable value. Incidentally, regardless of the number and type of exemptions for which an owner might be qualified in Florida, no combination of exemptions may exceed $10,000 unless the property owner is either:

1. a quadriplegic;
2. a totally disabled veteran; or,
3. a disabled veteran confined to a wheelchair.

Real estate salespeople are frequently asked questions concerning the various requirements to qualify for different types of property tax exemptions. The following summary may be of assistance.

First, no exemption is automatic. All exemptions must be applied 13.09
for between January 1 and March 1 of each year. The initial application should be made in person at the county property appraiser's office. Subsequent annual renewals of exemption status can be made by mail. When filing for the first time, applicants claiming exemption based on disability must be prepared to show a certificate from two professionally unrelated physicians who are licensed in Florida, or a certificate from the appropriate governmental agency knowledgeable about their condition (e.g., Florida Bureau of Blind Services, Veterans Administration, etc.).

$5,000 Homestead Exemption

Any person who has legal or equitable title to real property in Florida and who resides there as his or her permanent home is eligible. If title to the property is in the name of one spouse alone, the other spouse can legally file for this exemption with the consent of the husband or wife who owns title to the property.

When filing for regular homestead exemption the first time, owners must be prepared to show:

1. Owner(s) of record as of January 1
2. Address of the property
3. Length of time a legal resident of Florida (a Certificate of Domicile or voter's registration will be proof if dated prior to January 1)
4. Florida driver's license and automobile license plates
5. Actual residence in the dwelling on January 1.

(NOTE: Homestead exemption does not exempt property from taxes levied by special tax districts for fire, hospital, flood control, etc.)

$5,000 Senior's Additional Homestead Exemption

Those considered eligible for this additional exemption must first qualify for the regular homestead exemption as detailed above. In addition, eligible applicants must:

1. Have been a permanent resident of Florida for five consecutive years prior to the date of application
2. Be at least 65 years of age as of January 1 preceding application
3. Provide proof of age.

$500 Widow's Exemption

Any widow who is a bona fide resident of Florida may claim this exemption. If she remarries, the eligibility expires. If a husband and wife divorce prior to the death of the husband, the divorced wife is not eligible for this exemption.

$500 Disability Exemption

Any resident of Florida who is blind or totally and permanently disabled is eligible. Also, any veteran who is disabled at least 10 percent by service-connected misfortune is entitled to this $500 exemption. When filing for the first time, applicants should be prepared to show one of the following:

1. If totally and permanently disabled, produce a certificate of proof as mentioned above; or, not in a wheelchair
2. If claiming the veteran's ten percent disability, produce a certificate of disability; or,
3. If exemption is based on blindness, show certificate of proof issued by an appropriate agency.

$4,500 Disabled Person's Additional Homestead Exemption

To be eligible for the above exemption, an applicant must:

1. Qualify for regular $5,000 homestead exemption
2. Qualify for the $500 disability exemption as totally and permanently disabled
3. Have been a permanent resident of Florida for five consecutive years prior to the date of application.

(This exemption is not available to those granted the $5,000 Senior's Additional Homestead Exemption due to the statutory $10,000 limit on any combination of the above exemptions.)

Service-connected Total and Permanent Disability Exemption

Any honorably discharged veteran with designated service-connected disabilities which are certified as total and permanent is eligible for total exemption from property taxes. In some cases, this exemption can carry over to the veteran's widow after his death. The county property appraiser must rule on each individual case.

Exemption for Totally and Permanently Disabled Persons

Any real property owned and used as a homestead by a quadriplegic is totally exempt from property taxation. Also, any real property owned and used as a homestead by a paraplegic, hemiplegic, or other totally and permanently disabled person who must use a wheelchair is exempt from property taxation. To be eligible for this exemption, applicants must:

1. Have been a resident of Florida for five consecutive years prior to application
2. Prove that the gross income of all persons residing in the homestead does not exceed $8,200 (gross income includes social security benefits)
3. Present proof of condition as cited above.

Florida's Green Belt Law 193, F.S.

Although not an exemption from property taxation, Florida's Green Belt Law authorizes county property appraisers to assess agricultural land by a more favorable method than is used for non-agricultural properties. If a taxpayer's land is classified as agricultural for assessment purposes, the county property appraiser must base his property tax assessment solely on the land's current agricultural use. The highest and best use of such land is not a factor in arriving at the just value for agricultural purposes.

Florida's Green Belt Law is designed to protect a farmer from having his taxes increased just because his land might be well-suited for development. Without such protection, a farmer's taxes could be raised to the point of economic confiscation. When a farmer is granted an agricultural land classification, it results in a lower property assessment which in turn results in lower property taxes. Because of lower taxes levied on farm land, speculators have been attracted to such properties if located in the path of urban growth. In many instances, the law which was intended to protect the farmer was used as a tax protection by speculators. To stop this practice, the Florida Green Belt Law was changed in 1974. Florida Statute 193.461 now requires all county property appraisers to classify all lands annually within the county as either agricultural or non-agricultural. All property owners desiring their land to be classified as agricultural must request such classification on or before March 1 each year. If their request for agricultural classification is denied, property owners may appeal the denial through the same process used by non-agricultural property owners to protest an assessment: first, to the county property appraiser; second, to the Property Appraisal Adjustment Board; and third, in the courts.

How the Property Tax Rate is Established

Every city, county, and school board uses the same general procedure for establishing a general real estate tax rate. While all property owners pay taxes based on the assessed value of their real property, it is the taxable value and the tax rate which determine how much those taxes will be. In recognition of this fact, the following simple formula is recommended for determining the tax rate of school boards, cities, or counties:

$$\text{Tax Rate} = \frac{\text{Approved Budget minus Non-property Tax Revenue}}{\text{Total Assessed Valuation minus Exemptions}}$$

For example, assume the county officials of Foamcrest County have approved a budget for next year indicating expected expenditures of $12,500,000. A review of past and present experience indicates a reasonable expectation of $2,500,000 in revenue from sources other than property taxes. The county property appraiser reports a total assessed valuation of all taxable properties in the amount of $1,020,000,000. Homestead tax exemptions have been granted to 3,000 property owners below the age of 65 and to 500 taxpayers 65 years of age or older. Apply these figures to the above formula:

$$\text{Tax Rate} = \frac{\$12{,}500{,}000 - \$2{,}500{,}000}{\$1{,}020{,}000{,}000 - \$20{,}000{,}000}$$

$$\text{Tax Rate} = \frac{\$10{,}000{,}000}{\$1{,}000{,}000{,}000} = .01 \text{ or ten mills}$$

Thus the tax rate to be applied to all real property by Foamcrest County will be ten mills per dollar of taxable value.

Tax rates are stated in so many different ways that students should take time to ensure that they know how to deal with tax rates expressed in different terms. One mill is properly written in decimals as .001. This shows that a mill is one-thousandth part of a dollar. A mill is also one-tenth of a penny. When the decimal .01 is used it means one cent, or 10 mills. Always use three digits to express tax rates in order to avoid confusion. If expressing 20 mills, write .020; if a tax rate is 25.9 mills, make sure that the 5 is the third digit right of the decimal point in calculating any tax rate problem (.0259).

Using a previously described situation where your home was assessed at $40,000 and you qualify for regular homestead exemption, the calculation of your county property taxes is as follows:

Assessed value	$40,000
Homestead exemption	- 5,000
Taxable value	$35,000
County tax rate	x .010
Annual county property taxes	$350.000 = $350

Note that two separate types of value are involved in determining the actual property tax. The tax rate, in mills, is always applied to the taxable value. Where no exemptions apply, the taxable value and the assessed value are the same. However, any exemption must be applied to the assessed value. The result is taxable value. The taxable value is always multiplied by the tax rate to find the amount of tax. The tax rate will usually change each year due to differences in operating budget costs and revenues.

Not all property owners are subject to the same tax rates. A homeowner living in a city will pay city, county, and school board taxes. Perhaps additional taxes will be required as a result of bonds or other obligations approved by the voters. By contrast, a homeowner living in the county, but outside city limits would pay only county and school board taxes. Often, additional taxes are required of county residents who are located in special tax districts. In Orange County, for example, special tax districts have been established for fire, hospitals, downtown development, water control, flood control, library, etc. In almost all cases, special tax districts may not levy more than 3 mills per district maximum.

Consider the example of Mr. Pasco who owns a home in Whipsaw, Florida, in Brevard County. The city tax rate is 8.7 mills, the county tax rate is 9.2 mills, and the school board rate is 8 mills. Mr. Pasco is 66 years old and a disabled veteran. He has qualified for homestead exemption. His home has been assessed at $34,500. What must Mr. Pasco pay in property taxes?

First, begin with the assessed value: $34,500. From the assessed value, subtract all exemptions up to but not exceeding $10,000. Last, apply the total tax rate to the taxable value to find Mr. Pasco's total tax obligation:

Assessed value	$34,500
Less exemptions	-10,000
Taxable value	$24,500
Tax rate (8.7 + 9.2 + 8 mills)	x .0259
Total property taxes	$634.5500 = $634.55

If Mr. Pasco is interested in finding the amount of savings in property taxes realized by homestead exemption, he simply multiplies the $10,000 exemption by the tax rate and he will find that he saved a total of $259 in property taxes by qualifying for the senior citizen homestead tax exemption.

But what if Mr. Pasco lived outside any city limits in the same county? How much difference, if any, would there be in his property taxes? The solution is exactly the same with one exception. Subtract the city tax rate of 8.7 mills from the former total 25.9 mills, leaving a new effective tax rate of 17.2 mills (.0172):

Assessed value	$34,500
Less exemptions	-10,000
Taxable value	$24,500
Tax rate (9.2 + 8 mills)	x .0172
Property taxes	$421.4000 = $421.40

Special Assessments

The discussion has, until now, been related to those annual property taxes required to help pay the cost of government and education. At this point, notice should be taken of a one-time tax levied on property owners to help pay for some improvement which, in theory at least, adds to the value of their property. The name given to this type of one-time tax is "special assessment."

When city sewers are extended to neighborhoods previously dependent on septic tanks, or when unpaved streets are paved, it is assumed that the properties affected will receive an increase in value due to the improvement. Sometimes the municipal authority which levies the special assessment will consider affected properties to have benefited in value when the improvement may have actually caused a decrease in value. A quiet residential street which is widened into a four-lane boulevard to relieve congested access routes might be an example. The increased traffic with its resultant noise, pollution, and danger to children could cause property values to drop instead of increase. In such cases, the property owners can look for relief from the courts. Laws which permit the levying of special assessments specifically require that all improvements must benefit any property against which a special assessment is levied. Court records are replete with instances where courts at all levels, up to and including the Supreme Court, have ruled in favor of property owners when improvements did not enhance the value of affected properties.

Special assessments are not an ad valorem tax, i.e., they are not always levied according to the value of a property. Usually, special assessments will be levied on a front-foot basis for sidewalks, street paving, etc. They are often levied on a pro-rata share basis for utility and sewer hookups. For example, a 100-lot subdivision may have the utility and sewer assessment spread evenly overall so that each lot pays one-hundredth (1/100) of the total cost. The assessment for street paving is a little different.

Suppose you live on an unpaved street. The city is petitioned to pave the street and agrees to do so. The paving cost is found to be $24 per running foot, and the city is to pay 30 percent of the cost. If your lot frontage on the street is 100 feet, what will your special assessment be for street paving? Don't forget your street has two sides and the property across the street must bear its fair share.

Solution:		
	Your lot frontage	100 feet
	Cost per front foot	x $24
	Cost to pave 100 feet	$2,400
	City's percent of cost	x .30
	City's share of cost	$720.00
	Cost to pave 100 feet	$2,400.00
	City's share of cost	- 720.00
	Cost to property owners	$1,680.00
	Your half of street paving cost	$840

Non-payment of Taxes

As was mentioned earlier, property taxes constitute a lien superior to all other liens on real property. Special assessments are next in priority. When a property owner fails to pay property taxes, the taxing authority must take steps to obtain the tax money needed to help pay for the cost of government.

In Florida, unpaid property taxes are considered a debt owed to the county or city just as if the property owner had signed a promissory note for the amount of the taxes. Further, the property is security for the debt and can eventually be sold to satisfy the obligation if the taxpayer fails to pay taxes over a period exceeding more than two years.

Meanwhile, the county or city government is responsible for the cost of its day-to-day operation and to meet those costs it must collect delinquent taxes in some manner. To do this, property tax certificates are issued in the amount of taxes owed. A property tax certificate is issued for each delinquent property. A comprehensive list of all delinquent properties is made up soon after the April 1 deadline for payment of taxes has lapsed. This list is then published in a newspaper which has general circulation throughout the county. This procedure gives all delinquent owners notice that property tax certificates will be sold on their property if the tax lien is not satisfied prior to the date of sale.

The published list of properties in arrears will specify a date, time, and place for public auction of tax certificates on each property listed. At the auction, any person is entitled to bid for the tax certificate on any property. Current state law allows the successful bidder to collect interest up to a maximum annual rate of 18 percent on property tax certificates. The bidding at the auction is by rate of interest. Bidding starts at the maximum rate, and those desiring to purchase a particular certificate indicate this desire by bidding a lower rate than a previous bidder. If only one person bids on a property, that individual will usually receive the tax certificate at an 18 percent rate of annual interest. In a spirited competition for a particular tax certificate, the person bidding the lowest rate of interest becomes the owner of the certificate. The minimum interest paid on tax certificates is 5 percent per annum. Interest on property tax certificates is computed each month. Each tax certificate has a maximum life of 7 years. In order to remove the lien, the owner of property for which a tax certificate has been issued must pay the taxing authority the amount of delinquent taxes plus all accrued interest.

When a holder of a tax certificate has held that certificate for a period exceeding 2 years after April 1 when the taxes were declared delinquent, he or she can request that a tax deed be issued. This does not mean that a tax deed will be issued directly to the holder of the certificate. It sets in motion a statutory process which requires that the property be offered for sale at public auction. The highest bidder will receive title to the property. The holder of the tax certificate will be paid the amount invested plus interest if he or she is not the successful bidder for the property.

Tax Advantages of Owning Real Property

No law, whether federal, state, or local, requires a person to pay the maximum tax that person can afford. Any prudent individual is expected to arrange his affairs so as to keep his taxes as low as legally possible. No one has a duty to pay more taxes than the law requires. A person who plans ahead and conducts his affairs in an ethical manner designed to reduce tax obligations legally is nothing less than wise. Therefore, what are some of these legal provisions which enable property owners to act in a prudent manner regarding taxes?

Federal income tax laws are deliberately written to encourage homeownership. In fact, ownership of any type of real property is encouraged as evidenced by the different benefits available to all property owners. Owners of investment or commercial properties are allowed to deduct property taxes, mortgage interest paid, and of primary importance to them -- depreciation. Homeownership also has tax advantages in the form of:

1. Income tax deduction for interest paid on a mortgage;
2. Tax deduction for the full amount of property taxes; and,
3. Deferral of tax on profit from sale of personal residence.

The income tax benefits to homeowners are only available if tax deductions are itemized. However, most homeowners find it well worthwhile to itemize deductions. For example, suppose a married couple has a combined income which places them in the 32 percent income tax bracket. If their property taxes are $1,200 per year and there is a $36,000 mortgage with interest payments of $3,000 per year, they will pay $1,344 less income tax as homeowners than if they rented ($1,200 + $3,000 = $4,200 x .32 = $1,344). That equates to more than $100 per month reduction in housing costs as a result of being homeowners.

Federal tax laws classify real property as a capital asset; therefore, a property owner's home is a capital asset, and qualifies for capital gains treatment when sold or exchanged. For tax year 1977, gain (or loss) on the sale or exchange of property held more than nine months is classified as a long-term capital gain (or loss), rather than a short-term capital gain (or loss). For tax years beginning with 1978, the asset must be held longer than one year before the gain will be considered long-term. This long-term capital gain classification (when the required period of ownership is met) is advantageous to the homeowner since only one-half of any profit received is subject to taxation. (Persons age 65 or older may be eligible for even greater income tax reductions.) But the homeowner can defer or postpone indefinitely the capital gains tax if an existing home of equal or greater value is purchased during a period 18 months before sale to 18 months after sale of the old residence. The selling homeowner is not required to invest all of the capital gain in another home. The important factor is the purchase price of the new house. If he or she pays as much or more than the old residence sold for, the capital gain is deferred. Often the new residence will be bought with a very small down payment and a large mortgage. This does not affect eligibility for capital gains deferral.

Any gain on the sale of a residence is also tax deferred if the seller builds a new home within 24 months from the sale of a previous home. In order to qualify for this deferral, construction of the new home must be started within 18 months from the sale of the old residence, and the new home must be occupied within the 24-month period. For example, suppose you bought a house in March, 1972 for $34,000. In June of 1977, you sold the house for $42,000. No tax will be required on any portion of your profit if you begin construction of a new home not later than December, 1978 and occupy it not later than June, 1979. Of course, the purchase price of land, plus cost of all improvements, must equal or exceed the $42,000 sales price of your former residence.

Tax laws are constantly changing. They are also very complex. For these and other reasons, it is always well to retain professional counsel where complicated tax situations are encountered. Those individuals interested in specializing in real estate investments or sale of income-producing properties will find it necessary to become much more knowledgeable about tax laws and Internal Revenue Service interpretation of those laws than is possible by this brief exposure. Almost any professional in the field of real estate will confirm that sales productivity is directly related to knowledge of local, state, and federal tax laws affecting ownership of real estate.

CHAPTER 13

REAL ESTATE TAXES

1. In Florida, the eight mill cap applies to:

   I. County tax districts
   II. City tax districts

   a. I only
   b. II only
   c. Both I and II
   d. Neither I nor II

2. In Florida, the State and the federal government:

   I. Levy taxes which affect real property transactions
   II. Do not levy direct property taxes

   a. I only
   b. II only
   c. Both I and II
   d. Neither I nor II

3. Real property taxes are levied on a:

   I. Calendar-year basis
   II. Fiscal-year basis

   a. I only
   b. II only
   c. Both I and II
   d. Neither I nor II

4. In Florida, property taxes become delinquent after:

   I. December 31, each year
   II. March 31, each year

   a. I only
   b. II only
   c. Both I and II
   d. Neither I nor II

   DUE on APRIL 1

   c

5. In a well-established subdivision, assessed values of real property are usually arrived at by:

   I. A thorough examination of each lot in the parcel
   II. Use of a standard lot system

   a. I only
   b. II only
   c. Both I and II
   d. Neither I nor II

6. A property owner will have a better chance of getting his property assessment changed if the basis for his change request is the assessed value of his:

   I. Lot
   II. House

   a. I only
   b. II only
   c. Both I and II
   d. Neither I nor II

7. The first step in protesting the assessed value of real property is to:

   I. Contact the county property appraiser or a representative
   II. Contact the Property Appraisal Adjustment Board

   a. I only
   b. II only
   c. Both I and II
   d. Neither I nor II

8. The Property Appraisal Adjustment Board is composed of:

   I. Three school board members and two county commissioners
   II. Two school board members and three county commissioners

   a. I only
   b. II only
   c. Both I and II
   d. Neither I nor II

9. The tax base of a city or county is the:

   I. Total tax district
   II. Total value of all taxable property assessments

   a. I only
   b. II only
   c. Both I and II
   d. Neither I nor II

10. Federal, state, and school properties are all:

   I. Exempt from taxation
   II. Immune from taxation

   a. I only
   b. II only
   c. Both I and II
   d. Neither I nor II

11. What is your <u>taxable property value</u> if: the tax rate is 10 mills, your age is 66, and your assessed property value is $45,000?

   I. $40,000
   II. $45,000

   a. I only
   b. II only
   c. Both I and II
   d. Neither I nor II

12. What would be the amount of your property taxes if: the property assessment is $38,000; you qualified for homestead exemption; and, the property tax rate (total) is 28 mills?

   I. $924
   II. $1,064

   33,000 x.028

   a. I only
   b. II only
   c. Both I and II
   d. Neither I nor II

13. A disabled veteran, who is 68 years old and has been granted senior homestead exemption, is married to another disabled veteran age 32. What will be their total property tax exemption?

   I. $10,000
   II. $11,000

   a. I only
   b. II only
   c. Both I and II
   d. Neither I nor II

14. In arriving at a just value for agricultural property, the highest and best use is:

   I. Always a factor
   II. Not a factor

   b

   a. I only
   b. II only
   c. Both I and II
   d. Neither I nor II

15. Florida's Green Belt Law:

    I. Is intended to protect the farmer
    II. Has protected land speculators

    a. I only
    b. II only
    c. Both I and II
    d. Neither I nor II

16. Property owners pay taxes based on assessed value, but the amount of dollars paid as taxes is determined by the:

    I. Taxable value of the property
    II. Tax rate levied by the tax district

    a. I only
    b. II only
    c. Both I and II
    d. Neither I nor II

17. Ad valorem taxes would include:

    I. Real property taxes
    II. Special assessments

    a. I only
    b. II only
    c. Both I and II
    d. Neither I nor II

18. If: your lot frontage is 100 feet; paving costs $20 per running foot; and, the city will pay 25% of paving costs, what will your special assessment be?

    I. $1,500
    II. $750

    a. I only
    b. II only
    c. Both I and II
    d. Neither I nor II

19. Property taxes constitute a lien superior to all other liens on real property except:

    I. First mortgage liens
    II. Special assessment liens

    a. I only
    b. II only
    c. Both I and II
    d. Neither I nor II

20. Current State law allows the buyer of property tax certificates to collect interest up to a maximum of:

    I. 18 percent
    II. 12 percent

    a. I only
    b. II only
    c. Both I and II
    d. Neither I nor II

CHAPTER 14

PLANNING and ZONING

The Indians who originally inhabited this country probably were the last people able to live within a system attuned to nature and free of planning for the future. They took their food and shelter from the land. They could return their refuse to the environment and nature would absorb it for them.

Planning and land-use control has been practiced in this country to varying degrees since the first European settlers arrived. At first it was taken for security and protection, later to promote economic and social welfare, and finally to accommodate additional new settlers. The early settlers had a unique opportunity in a new and undeveloped country to build towns and cities which were improved versions of those they left behind in their homelands. A number of the early arrivals had traveled sufficiently in Europe to know the best features of several cities in different lands. Some early city planners attempted to combine the worthy features of several European cities into a single, planned city in the new world. Philadelphia, planned in 1682, Savannah, planned in 1733, and Washington, D.C., planned in 1791, are notable examples.

It is apparent that city planning in the United States is not a new development. The origins of planning for new communities and new growth go back to a time before this nation came into existence. The evolution of city planning in the U.S. since that time has not shown consistent development but rather has experienced highs and lows in popular acceptance. An attitude of on-again, off-again was probably the most discernable characteristic of city planning until the early 1900's. There were several causes for this alternating acceptance and rejection of city planning.

One of the causes was the creation of the rectangular survey system in 1785. This system of describing land boundaries and location permitted the newly born nation to convert land to money. The vast expanse of land west of the Appalachian Mountains which had formerly been claimed by England was ceded to the United States at the conclusion of the Revolutionary War. Some of the land was used to pay debts to foreign governments and to veterans of the war. Some of the land was sold to speculators who could use the rectangular method to survey new town sites and then sell the lots. Once the sites were sold, the speculators moved on. The development and growth of these new towns was left to the new settlers.

Another way the creation of the rectangular survey system helped to reduce interest in city planning was the emphasis placed on identifying and locating rural tracts for farming. By using the new method of describing real property, it was relatively simple to identify tracts of farmland from five or ten acres on up to and including whole townships of 36 square miles. Many Revolutionary War veterans as well as those who had loaned money to help finance the war were given farmland in these new territories as a substitute for money. The result was an emphasis on development of uncleared farmlands instead of planned growth of towns and cities.

A second major cause of decline in city planning was the economic and political attitudes prevailing during the 1800's. The new nation was growing rapidly due to an abundance of natural resources and the initiative of its citizens. As the industrial capacity of the country increased, the desire for planning and regulation of land-use decreased. The economic philosophy of laissez faire dominated the attitudes of business and political leaders. The philosophy of laissez faire is essentially a philosophy of noninterference by the government in private business affairs. This philosophy advocates letting the owners of land and business fix the rules of competition. The government is expected to function only as an arbiter or judge when a dispute arises or the rules are broken. During the period when this attitude prevailed, planning and regulation of growth was largely ignored. Property owners utilized their land in whatever manner produced the greatest private gain regardless of social costs to the community. The seeds for many present-day ghettos and urban problems were planted during this period. As industrial output of cities increased, more people left the farm for city jobs. Unplanned growth was the result. As isolated instances of unplanned growth became more frequent, further damage to private property values resulted until it became apparent that control of growth had to be reestablished.

In 1905, the University of Pennsylvania established the first course in the nation designed to teach real estate and urban development. Other colleges and universities followed and began to offer courses in city planning and urban development. Today, there are professional planners in practically all cities who are graduates of urban development planning programs. They are the support personnel who carry out the policies of planning boards or commissions.

By the end of the 19th century, it was already obvious that city planning would have to go beyond simple land-use maps if social and economic growth were desired. As a consequence, more attention was devoted to the quality of sanitation, water purification, paved roads, and city beautification. Although some cities established planning commissions, their task was not to control or regulate growth as much as to act as a public body for supervising improvement of civic services and beautification. City planning commissions were more or less restricted from planning future growth due to their inability to force property owners to comply with plans they might develop.

In 1916, the first serious efforts were made to create and enforce zoning ordinances. The garment industry in New York City was about to expand into the exclusive Fifth Avenue district. A zoning ordinance was enacted to protect Fifth Avenue property values by prohibiting all but specified property uses in that district. Other cities began to adopt zoning ordinances to create or protect local property values. Many property owners objected to the introduction of zoning laws which dictated what they could do with their property. Most of the objections were raised as a result of zoning ordinances which prohibited owners from using their land to generate profit or income without compensation for the rights lost. In 1926, the Supreme Court of the United States ruled that zoning laws which were legally enacted were constitutional. This ruling by the Supreme Court gave powers of enforcement to those municipalities which had enacted zoning laws for the purpose of regulating future growth. These new controls gave impetus to city planning all across the nation.

Planning Goals

"This year, we need to plan our family budget more carefully." "Here is my long-range plan for becoming a Florida real estate broker."

These are familiar statements to many. "Planning" is deciding in advance the actions needed to achieve desired goals. Every deliberate action to bring about a desired result in the growth process which would be different from uncontrolled and spontaneous growth is a form of planning. What is meant by city planning in the broadest sense is the effort to coordinate and regulate city growth as it occurs in order to achieve four basic goals:

1. To plan future land uses which will permit the maximum number of properties to attain their highest and best use;
2. To reduce the possibility that one type of land use may cause loss of value to neighboring properties;
3. To reduce the cost of present and future growth which must be borne by taxpayers; and,
4. To create an optimum social and economic environment as a result of community growth.

Naturally, the four planning goals are related. If a well-conceived plan of orderly growth is developed, all four goals will be realized to varying degrees. However, if uncontrolled growth is permitted, urban sprawl will result. Widely scattered subdivisions will increase the cost of services and utilities. The cost of new schools, roads, and medical facilities will be increased. Uncontrolled growth would permit open mining of phosphate with its attendant adverse consequences next to a high quality, residential neighborhood. In short, planning increases the chance of goal accomplishment.

Few planning efforts are 100 percent successful. The prospects for success can be increased, however, by systematically searching out available knowledge regarding:

1. What has happened in the past;
2. What the existing situation is; and,
3. What the past and present indicate as a trend for the future.

Since a democratic government can govern itself, there is no reason why it cannot plan for itself. The responsibility for collecting and analyzing information needed to plan is normally assigned to an agency called either the "planning commission" or "planning board," whichever name is preferred locally.

The Planning Commission

There are federal, state, county, and city planning commissions (or boards). The most common levels of government which sponsor planning commissions in Florida are the city and the county. A city or county must be managed and operated on a business-like basis if it is to grow and prosper. Like it or not, a city must compete with other cities, and a county must compete with other counties for new industries, new markets, new residents. While developing plans for attracting new businesses or residents, the work done by planning commissions will often uncover unexpected obstacles to growth. For example, during the course of accomplishing its planning function, a planning commission may discover that the city's economy is almost totally dependent upon one or two industries. Perhaps the economy is based on a military installation, or a large factory, or a university. The Western states offer numerous examples of ghost towns that relied on a single industry for the town's economy. A planning commission can draw up a plan for developing a broader economic base, present the residents with several choices as to the type of growth most desired, and avoid possible economic hardship at a later time.

Composition of Planning Commissions

Planning commissions are most effective when composed of members who represent all walks of life in the community. Members of the planning commission are most often not trained professional planners. The overriding goal in determining membership should be to appoint representatives from each socio-economic level. A planning commission composed entirely of lawyers, for example, could not possibly speak for all the people. The hopes, desires, and goals of all income levels of residents must be considered.

Members of the planning commission are usually appointed, not elected, and serve in a voluntary, unpaid capacity. The primary legislative body of the city or county is the appointing authority. Normally a city commission or a county commission is the appointing authority. Planning commissions vary in size, and the term for which a planning commissioner is appointed may vary from the terms of his colleagues. This assures a staggered rate of replacement and is designed to prevent any one appointing authority from appointing an entire planning commission. The planning commissioners are usually appointed for terms of service longer than the term of the appointing authority. This reduces the obligation of planning commissioners to any single political body and hopefully minimizes political influence within the planning body.

The elimination of political influence is important to effective planning. When a city or county government makes a decision to build a new street, widen an old street, or extend water and sewer networks, it affects the personal fortunes of residents. Planning is one of the most difficult and demanding tasks which a government may set for itself. Thus, it is important that all segments of the population be represented on the planning commission.

Important as the planning function may be to the future welfare of a community, the planning commission is not the final authority in matters related to planning. The commission or board is only an advisory body to the elected city or county government. The planning commission is responsible for planning just as the police department is responsible for law enforcement, but the elected government must make the final decisions based on recommendations from subordinate agencies. In the vast majority of cases, city and county governments accept the advice of the planning commission.

Planning Commission Support Staff

Does it seem realistic to expect a carpenter, a doctor, or a minister appointed to the planning commission to become so expert at planning that they know what information is needed, where it can be found, and what to do with it? No, but while each member of the commission may be expert in his or her own field, they are not often urban planning experts. The function of the planning commission is to make policy decisions regarding the type of city it feels the citizens want in the future, and it sets goals and provides residents with a number of feasible alternative plans for achieving those goals. But the job of collecting, sorting, analyzing, and reporting is done by the planning commission staff.

The planning commission support staff is composed of full-time city or county employees. Staff members are normally college or university trained planners. They have learned how to evaluate the economic base of a city. They know the most productive sources of information regarding population, proper land uses, and support requirements for future growth. It is the planning support staff which collects the raw data, refines it, and produces the basic studies needed to develop a flexible, comprehensive plan for future growth.

Basic Background Studies

Before any well-conceived plan can be prepared, the planning commission and its support staff must have a good idea of what has happened in the past, what the present situation is, and what developing trends indicate for the future.

Normally, the planning support staff will attempt to apply the past, present, and future criteria to six separate areas of concern:

1. Population
2. Area economic base
3. Existing land uses
4. Physical or physiographic analysis
5. Community facilities
6. Thoroughfare network

1. Population Background Study. Because the population study concerns people, it is the most basic and most important of all the planning studies. Florida is approaching a population level almost sufficient to produce growth internally which feeds on itself. In October, 1976, planners from all over the state met

in Orlando to discuss growth and the problems it might produce. A state comprehensive plan was discussed at that meeting. The state planning document noted that Florida's population had increased 37 percent during the 1960's alone. Then between 1970 and 1974, the state's population increased another 20 percent. The planning document conservatively estimated that another 20 percent increase in population would occur by 1990. When the estimated 1990 population is compared with the 1960 population, it indicates that the population in Florida will almost triple in size during those 30 years. No wonder real estate is a fascinating business! This is especially so when one goes deeper into the population background study and discovers from the state planning document that in the 1960's 74 percent of the population increase was due to in-migration. Some 88 percent of the population growth between 1970 and 1973 was due to in-migration. In 1973 alone, in-migration accounted for almost 95 percent of Florida's population increase. However, not all of Florida's new citizens stayed. Some left during the 1974-75 recession, but the adjustment necessary was negligible when compared to the population growth statistics.

But a population background study for planning must be concerned with more than raw numbers. It must also identify the structure of the population, the number of households and their approximate incomes, the numbers and locations of different ethnic groups, occupations of residents, and educational levels. With this information, predictions can be made for the future. In rapidly growing areas, predictions will normally be limited to periods of 5 to 10 years into the future. In those parts of the country where growth is slow, or no growth is occurring, the planning predictions may be projected for 15 to 20 years into the future. In Florida, the shorter planning periods are more appropriate.

The population study developed to assist planners has important implications for everyone in the real estate business. For example, when the population background study is completed, it will give planners an indication of the number of new households expected to move into an area. Further, a relatively good idea of employment and income levels will be available from the study. This information can assist builders and developers in planning their future markets and the type of homes most suitable for new residents.

The real estate business and many mortgage lending firms have used a rule of thumb which says that a homebuyer should not pay more than two and one-half times his annual net income for a home. Assume the population study predicts a population increase of 2,200 new households per year for the next five years. Suppose the study also identifies the estimated income levels as: 500 households with incomes of $10,000 per year; 1,500 households at $14,000 per year; and, 200 households at $20,000 per year. It now becomes clear for those who take the trouble to consult the population study that, in this example, the best housing market over the following five years will probably be in the $30,000 to $40,000 price range ($14,000 x 2.5 = $35,000).

2½ times - rule of thumb

The population study also reveals other important information. It will show changes in the size of an average household. To illustrate, prior to the turn of the century, the average household consisted of 4.6 people. This meant that 100 houses would shelter 460 people. Today, the size of the average household is down to 3.6 people. Now the same 100 houses shelter only 360 people. It will require almost 28 additional houses to shelter the 460 people which formerly occupied 100 houses. In Florida, which has a higher proportion of elderly residents than most other states, the difference may be even greater.

The population study will also be of great assistance in estimating the cost of social services for a larger population. Planners can alert cities and counties to the number of additional policemen, firemen, teachers, medical facilities, and the like which will be required to handle the new residents.

2. Area Economic Base Background Study. Next in importance to the population background study is the area economic base study. Many questions about the economic activity in the area must be answered: What have the primary economic activities been in the area? Have they changed? Do the residents in the area desire change? What types of industries are most prevalent? Does the city or county have enough diversification in basic industries to avoid economic recession if individual industries suffer a setback?

Part of the area economic base background study will analyze the effect of basic industry employment in the area. "Service" industries are those such as grocery stores, barber shops, retail stores, etc., whose customers are primarily local residents. These industries keep money already in the area circulating, but they do not account for a great amount of outside money coming into the area. "Basic" (base) industries, on the other hand, are those industries which attract outside money into the area.

The area economic base study will reveal whether an area is principally tourist-oriented, industrial, commercial, educational, or even political in character. Perhaps it will disclose that the area is a combination of several economic activities. The more diversified the economic base, the stronger the area economy will tend to be. This contributes to growth and stable property values.

When the area economic base background study is completed, it will serve as a good cross-check on the population study. Obviously, something is wrong if the population study predicts a large increase in population and the economic base study predicts a reduction in economic activity. The predictions of the two studies should support each other, or a logical explanation should be presented.

3. Existing Land-use Background Study. In order to plan for a future land use, an inventory of all public and private land uses is taken. One of the results of any land-use plan should generally be an arrangement of land uses which locates future residential areas near existing residential districts, future commercial areas near present commercial zones, and future

industry near present industry.

To accomplish these objectives, one of the first steps toward completing the land-use background study is usually a complete land survey with detailed maps plotting each separate land parcel. Individual lots and tracts will be identified on land-use maps with colors or codes to indicate the present use of the land. Once completed, the existing land-use patterns will dictate, to a great degree, where future land uses should be.

Generally, professional planners use five basic land-use categories:

1. Residential
2. Commercial
3. Industrial
4. Agricultural
5. Public

All five basic land-use classifications are further separated into individual subcategories. For example, a county might use:

1. Residential: single-family, one- to four-family, cluster-residential, and multi-family
2. Commercial: neighborhood shopping, community business, professional offices, shopping center, central business district
3. Industrial: component assembly, light manufacturing, heavy industry, warehousing.

No uniform standard of land-use classification applies in all parts of the state. Each planning commission or zoning authority can establish any system desired to prevent encroachment of incompatible uses.

Once the land-use study is complete and all of the current uses of individual parcels are accounted for, it is a relatively simple matter to determine the number of acres being utilized for residential, commercial, etc. This information can then be coordinated with findings from the population study to develop a preliminary land-use plan for the future.

To illustrate, assume the population growth example referred to earlier. Some 2,200 households are predicted to be added to the population each year for the next five years. This means 11,000 new households in the next five years. By dividing the present population into the number of acres currently used for residential purposes, each household is using .4 (4/10) acre of land (an overall average). Professional planners would check to see if that figure had been fairly constant over a period of years. Assume that no perceptible change in average residential land allocation has occurred. If the planners count on .4 acre for each of the 11,000 households expected to be added to the area, a requirement is established for at least 4,400 additional acres of land to be zoned residential. It is not uncommon for planners to add an additional 10 - 20 percent as a safety factor. As a result of the information developed from the basic population study and the basic land-use background study, the planners in this example would be justified in recommending that 5,000 additional acres be zoned residential for accommodating anticipated new residents.

The problem of deciding where the 5,000 additional acres of future residential development should be located is somewhat dependent upon where existing residential areas are located. Normally, residential growth along established access routes will persist in the same direction until some barrier is encountered. By using the map showing current land uses and by consulting the physiographic study (see below), planners usually can readily determine where future residential growth should occur.

4. Physiographic Study. Many newcomers to Florida have encountered unforeseen development costs due to lack of knowledge regarding the subsurface conditions of land. Sinkholes and subsurface muck are but two of the problems which can cause the unwary landowner to exceed budgeted construction costs.

The physiographic study will help to avoid unexpected problems with soil conditions. It is a study of the physical structure of the land within a county or city. All of the various soil types will be catalogued and then plotted on a map. Each soil type is coded to indicate recommended usage. For example, some soil types have poor weight-bearing capacities. Areas where these types of soil are found would not be suitable for heavy, high-rise buildings. Some soils do not drain properly. Anyone planning to develop these areas would need to budget for drainage systems. The county or city physiographic study with accompanying maps will frequently be the dominant factor in determining future uses for specific tracts of land. Many of the flooded homes and subdivisions in Florida could have been avoided if developers had consulted the physiographic study prior to acquiring selected tracts for development.

5. Recreation and Community Facilities Study. This study must be closely coordinated with the population study. It begins with an inventory of all municipal facilities such as community centers, convention centers, parks, playgrounds, and recreation facilities existing at the time the study is prepared. The location of each facility is plotted on an area map and a relationship established with the number and type of population served. For example, a playground serves little purpose if located among nursing homes or retirement centers. Small parks in areas where senior citizens tend to cluster are a more practical land use.

When the existing community facilities are located and plotted, plans can be made for the location of similar facilities in those areas where future growth is planned. Projections can be made for the number and location of additional parks, playgrounds, and community recreation facilities needed to service planned residential areas.

6. Thoroughfare Background Study. This last of the six basic background studies is also closely related to the population study, and to the economic study as well. A background analysis of this type is no longer optional for cities with populations of more than 50,000 people. Federal and state laws require that cities of 50,000 people or more do an urban area thoroughfare

study to reflect present and future transportation networks. Because cities of that size have an effective market area much larger than that contained within the city limits, this plan must include the surrounding urban areas which are considered part of the metropolitan market area.

Thoroughfare studies are normally a joint venture involving city, county, and state transportation departments and regional planning commissions. These studies must anticipate requirements for access and egress to future residential areas which may be still in the planning stage. They must also anticipate increased amounts of roadway and pedestrian traffic generated by new residents. In addition, the transportation requirements of neighboring cities and counties must be considered. The transportation problems of most counties are shared with their neighbors. Dade - Broward, Pinellas - Hillsborough, and Orange - Seminole - Osceola Counties are but a few of the counties in the state sharing mutual transportation problems as well as water, drainage, and other concerns. Thus, they share the need for joint planning efforts.

Goals Formulation

When the six basic background studies are completed, the planning support staff will have provided the planning commission with the information needed to enter the next phase of city planning -- goals formulation.

Before the data from the basic background studies is converted into a single comprehensive plan for future growth, the planning commission will attempt to find out what type of city the residents want. Do they desire more or less industry? If more, what kinds of industry? Do the residents prefer to forego fast economic growth in order to preserve their present life style? Various methods are used to obtain indications of the desires of the people. Some cities mail each resident a questionnaire; some use inserts in local newspapers; some call public hearings; others have members of the planning commission make presentations to social and civic clubs. The methods for obtaining feedback from the public are almost infinite. The main purpose of this phase of city planning is to identify broad planning objectives which the people in the community want to achieve.

Many people feel that the professional planners who constitute the planning support staff should determine planning goals. But time and time again, experience has demonstrated that the desires of the population must be included if a comprehensive plan is to be effective. This is one of the reasons why the composition of a planning commission should include representatives from various occupations and income levels. In any event, the desires of the people must be known before the basic background studies can be converted into a comprehensive plan for future development and growth.

Zoning

With the six basic background studies as a guide and the desires of the community made known through the broad planning goals to be accomplished, the planning commission is in a better position to prepare a plan for attaining those objectives. Controls must be established to regulate future land uses so that the public interest will be served. To ensure that property owners adhere to the type of land use planned for particular areas, zoning ordinances are enacted. Zoning ordinances are one of the most important and effective tools available to city planners. Furthermore, no other land-use control affects the citizens of a community to a greater degree.

Aside from providing city planners an effective tool, the more widely accepted and popular objective of zoning is to stabilize and protect property values of single-family homeowners. The legal right of municipalities to enact zoning laws is derived from federal and state constitutional rights called "police powers." Police powers include the right to regulate the use of private real property if done to protect the health, safety, morals, and general welfare of the public.

A zoning ordinance is a law legally enacted by a municipality or county which authorizes the dividing of the city or county into districts or zones. Each zone is assigned a specific land-use classification. Only the assigned land use is permitted in a particular zone unless an exception is granted by the zoning authority. This protects against encroachment by other land uses which might detract from existing values. Zoning laws regulate the size and height of structures, the purposes for which a structure may be used, the proportionate area of a lot which the structure may occupy, the set-back requirements, and even the number of people or households that can occupy a structure. Most zoning ordinances include a zoning map, often in various colors, to indicate different zoning categories. They not only regulate land use but also land coverage and appearance, height of buildings, and population densities.

In order to be legal, zoning laws must meet a set of criteria designed to protect the rights of property owners. The Fourteenth Amendment to the United States Constitution requires that zoning ordinances, or any other law, cannot be destructive, confiscatory, unreasonable, or arbitrary. Most zoning authorities have found that the best way to comply with these standards is to base zoning laws on a comprehensive plan for the city wherein the various zoning districts are established and incorporated into the plan as a means of achieving community goals.

Various zoning categories are designed to accomplish different purposes. For example, residential zoning is intended to regulate density of units per acre, meaning the number of homes per acre. To accomplish this purpose, several subcategories will establish different minimum sizes for lots to fit each subcategory. For example, imagine that in your county residential zone R-1A requires all lots in that subcategory to contain at least 9,000 square feet of land. This would automatically restrict the number of lots per acre a developer could create from each acre in a subdivision. Every acre of land contains 43,560 square feet. A given developer is going to develop 100 acres. In the process of turning raw land into a subdivision, between 20 and 25 percent of the land is commonly utilized for streets for recreational purposes. Wider streets and neighborhood recreation facilities add quality but reduce the amount of land available for lots. Using 25 percent loss for streets and recreation, the developer can determine the number of lots per acre (density) permitted by R-1A zoning in your county. The number of acres involved will determine the total number of lots available.

Solution:		
	Square feet per acre	43,560
	Land available for lots	x .75
	Square feet available per acre	32,670
	Minimum square feet per lot	÷9,000
	Lots per acre (density)	3.63
	Number of acres available	x 100
	Total subdivision lots	363.00 = 363

In the same county, residential zoning subcategory R-1AA might require one-acre lots and R-1B may only require a minimum of 8,000 square feet per lot. Zoning authorities may create as many zoning subcategories as needed. They can also fix the criteria for each subcategory.

While the objective of residential zoning is to control density, the purpose of commercial zoning is to regulate intensity of use. Intensity is determined by the type and amount of pedestrian and vehicular traffic generated by a commercial enterprise. Businesses which generate a great deal of traffic, such as a service station, are normally less desirable next to quiet residential areas. On the other hand, a doctor's office or an attorney's office does not create the same degree of threat to residential values. Zoning ordinances will normally recognize these conditions by creating a buffer zone between residential areas and high-intensity commercial zones. Frequently, the buffer zone will allow multi-family zoning (for example, apartments) next to single-family residential areas, then a professional business zone, then higher-intensity zones.

Industrial zoning is also intended to regulate intensity of use. In addition, various industrial zoning subcategories are used to control the amount and location of industrial offshoots resulting from different kinds of industrial activity. A city with a wide industrial base may have many subcategories of industrial zoning, whereas a city more oriented toward agriculture, tourism, or education might have only one or two industrial subcategories.

One of the most recent innovations in industrial activity has been the development of industrial subdivisions, often called industrial parks. Creation of these well-planned, landscaped, and architecturally controlled industrial areas has done much to improve the reputation and character of industrial zoning. In industrial parks, only industrial activities are normally allowed, and the types of industries in such areas are carefully selected. Almost every city in Florida with a population of 50,000 or more can point with pride to one of these new industrial subdivisions.

Although the county property appraiser may be interested in knowing exactly which level of government owns what property, for zoning purposes most zoning authorities consider all property owned by all levels of government as public. Public zoning includes, for example, city parks, county courthouses, and federal post office buildings. This zoning category is not usually divided into subcategories and is exempt from local zoning regulation.

The agricultural zoning classification is also an all-inclusive category which is not divided into subcategories. If the existing use of the property is for some type of agriculture, no zoning controls will attempt to regulate the type of agriculture permitted. If the owner should fail to qualify with the county property appraiser for an agricultural classification, his property could then be rezoned into another zoning category.

Board of Adjustment

In attempting to provide the greatest good for the greatest number, individual property owners are sometimes hurt by strict application of zoning ordinances. Most zoning laws provide a set of procedures for appealing the enforcement of zoning provisions in cases where strict compliance would cause undue hardship or reduce property values. To handle appeals and requests for relief, most zoning authorities have established a semi-judicial body called the Zoning Board of Adjustment, or simply Board of Adjustment. These boards must take all possible precautions to render objective, unbiased decisions since their quasi-judicial powers give them some of the characteristics of a court. Once the Zoning Board of Adjustment renders a decision, most zoning laws will allow a property owner only one avenue of appeal, which is litigation in the courts. The primary function of the Zoning Board of Adjustment is to provide property owners some degree of relief from otherwise rigid zoning codes.

Two of the most frequently encountered problems (requests) handled by a Zoning Board of Adjustment are variances and special exceptions. Anyone considering real estate as a vocation should know what each of these problems is and how each is handled.

The title alone gives a clue as to what a variance is supposed to accomplish: to be allowed to vary from strict compliance with all or part of a zoning code. In order for a property owner to be granted a variance from existing zoning requirements, two conditions must be met:

1. The property owner must show that a hardship exists or will be created by strict compliance with zoning requirements. The owner must also show that he or she did nothing to cause the hardship.
2. The Zoning Board of Adjustment must use the same standards of established criteria to judge the validity of all requests for variance.

The reasons for requiring these two conditions to be met are fairly obvious. The first condition will prevent a property owner or developer from taking some action designed for private benefit only to expect the Zoning Board of Adjustment to correct the situation the property owner or developer created. The second condition is to ensure fair and impartial treatment for each property owner requesting a variance. If the Zoning Board of Adjustment must use the same criteria or standards in deciding all requests, this helps to develop and ensure objectivity in making decisions. A stranger to or a friend of a board should theoretically have to meet the same standards in order to be granted a variance.

Many people have trouble with the word "hardship." It has nothing to do with economic or personal hardships. It is related to land use, and the hardship must be involved with use of the property. For example, suppose you bought a nice lot on a river where zoning restrictions require set-back distances of 25 feet from the front of the lot and 30 feet from the river or rear of the lot. Then suppose you are about to start construction of a new house designed to fit precisely the above set-back requirements when a survey reveals that erosion by the river over time has carried away 10 feet from the river side of your lot. The maximum set-back distance possible is now only 20 feet. Since zoning requires 30 feet, you will be in violation if you go ahead with construction. Violation of zoning laws can cause removal of the offending structure. In order to prevent potential trouble, you would request a variance. The hardship exists and you did nothing to cause the hardship. You would have met the hardship requirement for a variance (condition Number 1 above).

The Zoning Board of Adjustment is authorized to issue special exceptions for controlling the location of particular land uses. For example, suppose you live in a county where one of the industrial zoning subcategories allows paper mills to operate (for purposes of illustration, this shall be termed industrial subcategory I-M). Now suppose there are two large areas zoned I-M just outside the city limits of your city: one is located on the southwest corner of the city, and the other on the northeast corner. One of the characteristics of paper mills has always been the distinctive odors which they produce. If the prevailing winds in your area (in this example) are from the south or west, the paper mill could cause considerable irritation and even loss of property values for nearby properties. The Board of Adjustment could issue a special exception permitting the paper mill to operate in the northeast I-M industrial zone where the prevailing winds would take the odors away from the city but prohibiting the paper mill from operating in the southwest I-M zone where the odors would be carried into the city.

Nonconforming Uses

Whenever zoning ordinances are first introduced into a community, it almost invariably results in scattered incidents of nonconforming use. Before zoning came into use, it was not uncommon, for example, to find a small neighborhood gas station located within a large residential area. When the entire area was later zoned residential, the small gas stations within the district zoned residential became nonconforming uses of land (a kind of "grandfathering," in effect).

The United States Constitution prohibits a property owner from being deprived of property without due process or fair compensation. Local governments cannot employ eminent domain powers to correct nonconforming uses unless the purpose for which the property is taken is for a public use. The methods used to correct a nonconforming land use vary around the state. Most zoning authorities will include in zoning ordinances a designated time period long enough for nonconforming property owners to recapture their investment in the property. After the expiration of the designated period, the property owner must convert the use of his property to that use for which the area is zoned. If, during the designated period, the structure on the property is damaged or destroyed by more than 50 percent, the property must be converted to a use conforming with area zoning. Further, nonconforming use properties usually will not be permitted to be increased in size or to undergo structural changes. Most zoning authorities restrict repairs and maintenance of such properties to those needed for sanitation and safety purposes. These procedures are designed to result in all properties eventually becoming conforming uses.

From what has been said, it is apparent that planning commissions and planning support staffs have a wide spectrum of responsibilities. City and urban planning has been called both an art and a science by different authorities. Perhaps it is a combination of both.

It is important to understand that the results of the planners' work affect everyone. As the state grows, planning assumes an ever-increasing role of importance and responsibility. Regional planning groups are becoming more instrumental in controlling growth. In fact, no planned development of sufficient size to impact surrounding areas can be approved without regional planning approval. Developments of Regional Impact (DRI's) have become the subject of a separate statute in Florida to ensure better control of the environment, today and tomorrow.

Regional planning commissions, sometimes called regional planning councils, are organized in much the same manner as county or city planning groups. The commission members are appointed, and a trained professional support staff is provided to assist with administrative and technical matters.

Both the regional and local planning commissions are advisory in nature. This means that the appointing authorities will make the decisions to implement, reject, or modify recommendations submitted by the planning groups. However, there are several areas of responsibility for which city planning commissions are commonly delegated final authority. These areas are: (1) subdivision plat approval; (2) site plan approval; and (3) sign control.

1. Subdivision plat approval. As a result of unethical promotion of "boom and bust" subdivisions in the 1920's, most Florida counties initiated strict subdivision controls to prevent a recurrence. When a developer plans to create a subdivision, the subdivision plat must be submitted to the planning commission for approval. The plat will show for record purposes the name of the subdivision, the sizes and dimensions of all lots, street widths and locations, proposed easements, public-use lands, and usually deed restrictions. In Florida, developers of subdivisions are now required to show that costs related to street paving and installation of utility conduits will be paid by the developer.

They are not issued a building permit until final approval is granted by the planning commission. When the approval is received, the developer can proceed to record his plat in public records and receive a building permit.

2. Site plan approval. The term site plan indicates a project of greater than average size. Examples would be a proposed shopping mall, a condominium complex, or a high-rise office building. The site plan serves the same function that a subdivision plat serves for a subdivision. It is a detailed plan of how the project is to be developed, how traffic and parking will be dealt with, and what impact may be expected on neighboring properties. This is another area in which the expertise of the planning commission's support staff can be of great assistance. Reviewing and checking site plan proposals requires painstaking attention to detail and a well-rounded background of information. Again, the builder/developer of a large project may not be granted a building permit until approval of the site plan is obtained from the planning commission. This ensures compliance with all physical, economic, and environmental requirements.

3. Sign control. Some cities do not consider it necessary to regulate the size, location, and lighting of signs. As time provides an accumulating inventory of evidence, more and more cities are beginning to exercise control over signs. Frequently, the planning commission is given the task of sign control, which means some section of the planning support staff will be delegated the task. The primary aims of sign control are to minimize distraction to motorists and to eliminate actual safety hazards created by signs at blind corners, lighted signs which glare into the eyes of drivers at night, and the like. Any aesthetic improvement resulting from sign control is a welcomed by-product.

It appears that planned, controlled development with maximum flexibility offers the best hope for the rapid growth Florida will experience over the next 10 or so years. There is no valid reason for growth not occurring. If a wall 20 feet high were built from Mobile, Alabama to Jacksonville, Florida, it would only slow the growth, not stop it. Planning offers an opportunity to exercise mastery over coming events.

CHAPTER 14

PLANNING and ZONING

1. City planning in the U.S. is an innovation of the last century. T F

2. One of the major reasons for the increased emphasis on city planning in the 1800's was the philosophy of laissez faire. T F

3. The first serious effort to create and enforce zoning ordinances was in New York. T F

4. The impetus to city planning in the early 1900's came from a California Supreme Court ruling. T F

5. The responsibility for city or county planning is usually vested in a planning commission or planning board. T F

6. A planning commission is normally composed of trained professional planners. T F

7. Members of a planning commission are elected to serve different terms of office. T F

8. In municipalities with planning commissions, the commission is the final authority in planning matters. T F

9. The primary function of a planning commission is to make policy recommendations to an elected governmental body. T F

10. The basic background studies involved in planning cover eight separate areas of concern. T F

11. The most basic and important of all the basic planning studies is the:
    a. Economic base study
    b. Land-use study
    c. Community facilities study
    d. Population study

12. An existing land-use study will:
    a. Show where future land uses should be
    b. Involve a detailed land survey
    c. Require an inventory of public and private land uses
    d. All of the above

13. The basic population study will indicate:
    a. The number of new households expected to move into the area
    b. The best housing markets of the future
    c. The future cost of social services
    d. "a" and "b" above
    e. All of the above

14. The basic background study used to cross-check the population study is the:
    a. Community facilities study
    b. Economic base study
    c. Land-use study
    d. Physiographic study

15. Basic industries contribute to stability and growth; service industries are the businesses which:
    a. Do not attract much outside money to the area
    b. Attract outside money to the area
    c. Manufacture and export products
    d. Create and export service assistance

16. If 2,000 households are expected to move into the area in the next 5 years, and present land use shows each household uses .5 acre, what will the future residential land-use requirement be if a 10% safety factor is added?
    a. 1,100 acres
    b. 1,000 acres
    c. 10,000 acres
    d. 11,000 acres

17. If the annual net income levels of the above 2,000 households are: 300 households earn $5,000; 600 earn $10,000; and, 1,100 earn $15,000, then the best future housing markets will be in which price range?
    a. $12,000 to $18,000
    b. $35,000 to $40,000
    c. $20,000 to $30,000
    d. $40,000 to $50,000

18. The physiographic background study will reveal the:
    a. Physical location of shopping centers and subdivisions
    b. Transportation network structure
    c. Surface and subsurface structure of land
    d. Density and intensity structure of population

19. A thoroughfare background study is normally a:
    a. City project
    b. County project
    c. State project
    d. Joint venture

20. The most effective tool available to planning for land-use control is:
    a. Zoning
    b. A land-use map
    c. A variance
    d. An economic background study

21. In order for a property owner to be granted a variance, he must provide evidence that:
    a. The same treatment has been afforded other owners
    b. A hardship related to land use exists
    c. The variance, if granted, will be for his use only
    d. The land use existed prior to zoning laws

22. Residential zoning is designed to regulate:
    a. Intensity
    b. Frequency
    c. Density
    d. All of the above

23. Commercial zoning is designed to regulate:
    a. Intensity
    b. Frequency
    c. Density
    d. All of the above

24. A small general store around which a new subdivision was developed would be an example of a:
    a. Special exception
    b. Variance
    c. Site plan
    d. Nonconforming use

25. Both regional and local planning commissions are generally advisory in nature; however, an example of an area where they have final authority would be:
    a. Zoning codes
    b. Building code approval
    c. Comprehensive plan approval
    d. Subdivision plat approval + site plan approval + sign control

CHAPTER 15

FEDERAL HOUSING LAWS and FLORIDA LANDLORD AND TENANT ACT

Major Trends in Real Estate Legislation:

Year	Law
1866	Civil Rights Act
1934	National Housing Act (Federal Housing Administration created, FHA-insured loans)
1944	Veterans Administration created (VA-guaranteed loans)
1948	Federal National Mortgage Association (FNMA) (secondary market for FHA and VA loans)
1968	Fair Housing Act (part of the Civil Rights Act of 1968)
1968	Interstate Land Sales Full Disclosure Act
1968	Truth-in-Lending Act (effective 1969)
1974	Real Estate Settlement Procedures Act (RESPA) (amended in 1975, amendment effective in 1976)
1973	Florida Residential Landlord and Tenant Act (FRLTA) (as amended 1974, 1975, 1976)

Many federal, state, and local housing laws which have a bearing on the day-to-day practice of real estate are often ignored and frequently misunderstood by practitioners. Nearly everyone in the business is familiar with the expression that, "Ignorance of the law is no excuse." But, the laws which have a direct bearing on real estate are staggering in number. No one person can hope to become expert in the interpretation and application of all of them. Thus, the purpose of this chapter is to select from countless laws some of the more important ones which Florida real estate practitioners need to be knowledgeable about in order to serve the public better and to ensure that they themselves comply with the laws. The explanation of these laws follows the above-listed sequence.

Although real estate as an organized industry is regarded as a product of the 20th century, one of the oldest federal laws which applies to current real estate practices is the Civil Rights Act of 1866. This statute prohibits discrimination on the basis of race by providing that, "All citizens of the United States shall have the right, in every State and Territory, as is enjoyed by white citizens thereof to inherit, purchase, lease, sell, hold, and convey real and personal property." In 1968, the U.S. Supreme Court upheld the 1866 Act, in the case of Jones vs. Mayer, as still the law of the land. Not only was the law upheld, but

HANDBOOK, Appendix I

16.09

also the Supreme Court ruling clearly states that all racial discrimination, whether private or public in the sale or rental of property, is prohibited and illegal. This decision does not exempt the private owner of a single-family dwelling.

After the Civil Rights Act of 1866, the next legislation of importance to this discussion is the National Housing Act of 1934. This was actually emergency legislation enacted to assist in the recovery of the national economy from the terrible depression of the early 1930's. Congress created the Federal Housing Administration (FHA) and authorized government mortgage insurance for long-term home mortgages in an attempt to stimulate home buying and to create jobs within the construction industry. Since 1934, the FHA has probably played a larger role in making the U.S. a nation of homeowners than any other single element. It is still one of the most important influences in modern real estate activity.

Several additional laws affecting real estate were passed by Congress in the late 1930's and early 1940's, but the next milestone for the purposes herein was the creation of the Veterans Administration (VA) in 1944. Intended as a gesture of gratitude to returning veterans of the military services who had participated in World War II, the VA was authorized to guarantee mortgages made to veterans by private lenders. This guarantee by the government was intended to reduce the lender's risk to the point that, in most cases, no cash down payment would be required of the veteran. The law which was passed in 1944 provided for a 50 percent guarantee, up to a maximum of $2,000, and the interest rate was not to exceed 4%. In 1977, the guarantee was either 60 percent of the mortgage or $17,500, whichever was less, and the interest rate was 8½%. Like the FHA, the VA has played a major role in homeownership.

In 1948, Congress legislated into existence the Federal National Mortgage Association (FNMA) for the purpose of establishing a formal secondary market for FHA and VA loans. Until that time, lenders contended that while government-backed mortgages were good security for the money invested in such loans, the lenders were reluctant to tie up large amounts of money in long-term loans because of lack of liquidity. If they wanted to recover their money by selling the mortgages, it was often difficult to do. Creation of FNMA ("Fannie Mae") helped to alleviate this problem. It brought money into the mortgage market and the building boom was underway.

In 1968, the Fair Housing Act was passed as a part of the Civil Rights Act of 1968. This legislation went much farther than did the 1866 Act: any discrimination is illegal in the sale, leasing, financing, or brokerage services if such discrimination is based on race, color, religion, sex, or national origin. Both single-family and multi-family housing are covered by the provisions of the Civil Rights Act of 1968.

HANDBOOK, Chapter IV

Categories of housing in the 1968 Act include:

A. Single-family houses:

1. All houses not privately owned
2. All privately owned houses if a broker or salesperson is employed to sell, rent, or lease
3. All houses owned by a person who owns three or more houses
4. Any house owned by a person who, in any two-year period, sells more than one of which he was not the most recent owner.

B. Multi-family housing:

1. All multi-family dwellings of five or more units
2. All multi-family dwellings of four or less units, if none of the units is occupied by the owner.

The following discriminatory acts are all prohibited by the Civil Rights Act of 1968 if any are based on race, color, religion, sex, or national origin:

1. Refusing to rent to, sell to, negotiate, or deal with a person.
2. Quoting different terms or conditions for buying or renting.
3. Advertising that housing is available only to people of a certain race, color, sex, religion, or national origin.
4. Making any false statement concerning the availability of housing for inspection, rent, or sale.
5. Making statements that minority groups might move into a neighborhood in order to persuade an owner to sell or rent.
6. Statements or practices by any lending institution which present different terms or conditions for home loans, or which deny loans for discriminatory reasons.
7. Denying membership in, or use of, any real estate service, broker's organization, multiple listing service, or any organization concerned with sale or rental of housing.

Actions not covered by the Civil Rights Act of 1968 are covered by the Civil Rights Act of 1866 if based on racial discrimination.

Also in 1968, the Interstate Land Sales Full Disclosure Act was passed. The purpose of this law is to protect consumers from misrepresentation by unscrupulous land developers. This law applies to subdivisions with 50 or more lots for sale as part of a common promotional plan in interstate commerce. No developer is permitted to sell or lease any lot in a subdivision of 50 or more lots unless he has filed a "Statement of Record" with the U.S. Department of Housing and Urban Development (HUD). The land, its physical characteristics, the condition of the title, and identification of owners must be provided. In addition, this act requires that each purchaser be furnished a "Property Report" before signing a purchase contract or lease. The Property Report must contain items extracted from the Statement of Record as specified by HUD.

HANDBOOK, Chapter IV

Truth-in-lending laws were passed via several acts in 1968 and went into effect in 1969. The overall purpose of these laws is to inform consumers of exact credit costs prior to making a purchase. When the laws became effective, this caused advertising of credit associated with a real estate purchase to be placed under the supervision of the Federal Trade Commission (FTC). One immediate result was to make "bait-and-switch" type advertising a federal offense. For example, if a subdivision developer advertises homes for sale with a down payment of $1,000, the seller must accept $1,000 as the complete down payment or this would be a violation of the law.

The truth-in-lending (TIL) laws, including Federal Reserve Regulation Z which implements the law, require that the annual percent of interest charged consumers must be clearly and accurately stated. Also required is that any other charges listed by some other name must be included if such charges are legally defined as interest. The law does not attempt to regulate interest rates charged as this is within each individual state's area of responsibility. The most important objectives of the truth-in-lending laws are disclosures of finance charges and the annual percentage rate. Finance charges on residential property need not be stated as a total figure; however, if credit terms for residential property are advertised, the words "annual percentage rate" must be spelled out and identified in those terms. It is not uncommon to see an ad which states "mortgage interest rates at 8½%" followed by a parenthetical statement like "(annual percentage rate 8 3/4%)". The difference between the mortgage interest rate and the annual percentage rate (APR) might be due to a charge for FHA mortgage insurance premium (MIP), or private mortgage insurance (PMI), or some other expense legally definable as interest.

In 1974, the Real Estate Settlement Procedures Act (RESPA) was enacted to ensure that buyers are informed regarding the amount and type of charges which they will be expected to pay at closing. In its original form, the implementation of the Act was so cumbersome that it caused numerous complaints and opposition from real estate brokers and mortgage lenders. As a result, the law was revised in 1975, with the revisions becoming effective in 1976. The amendments to RESPA were actually an attempt by Congress to compromise between those who wanted to establish maximum costs for all closing items and those who advocated disclosure of only those costs which would allow consumers to shop for the most favorable closing costs. As amended, RESPA now designates six areas which are of interest to real estate registrants in Florida:

HANDBOOK, Chapter IV

1. Uniform settlement statement
2. Borrower's special information booklet
3. Advance estimate of settlement costs
4. Selection of title closing agent
5. Kickbacks and referral fees
6. Purchase of title insurance.

1. Uniform settlement statement. RESPA now requires the use of a uniform settlement statement by the closing agent for any and all loan closings which are not exempt from the law (see transactions exempt from RESPA below). The same form, published by HUD and

called "Disclosure/Settlement Statement," is used for all closings which come under the provisions of RESPA. The form is explained in the special information booklet provided each borrower (item 2 above and below). Although the settlement, or closing, agent must use the form at closing, responsibility for the preparation of the form lies with the mortgage loan lender. RESPA does not prohibit the use of other closing statements also, but the uniform HUD settlement statement must be made available to the borrower at or before closing, unless waived by the borrower. If requested by the borrower, the closing agent must allow the borrower to examine the costs included on the settlement statement, to the extent they are known, one business day before the closing. If an escrow agent is used for closing (closing in escrow), the uniform settlement statement is not required.

2. Borrower's special information booklet. As part of the consumer protection under RESPA, lenders are required to provide all prospective borrowers with a copy of the special information booklet as prescribed by HUD. This booklet must be furnished to a potential borrower at the time a written loan application is made, or within three business days thereafter. It defines and gives illustrations of closing costs on a line-by-line basis, which aids the borrower in making a better judgment regarding his or her individual transaction. The booklet also describes the roles and functions of all parties usually involved in the sale/purchase of real estate, and covers the fees the borrower may be charged.

3. Advance estimate of settlement costs. At the time of application for a loan, the lender is required to provide the borrower good faith estimates of probable closing costs related to those items for which information is available from past experience or from knowledge of current costs. Generally, these costs include loan closing service fees, recording fees, attorney's fees, title search, and title insurance fees. Any standard settlement charges or fees known to the lender are to be included. As a means for making closing items known, members of local Boards of REALTORS in Florida provide prospective purchasers of real property with a list of some 15 or so major closing items which may be costs to the buyer. However, brokerage commissions, advance hazard insurance costs, or escrow items like taxes and insurance are not required to be included.

4. Selection of title closing agent. If a lender designates that a particular attorney, title company, or person must be used to conduct the closing of the transaction, the lender is required by law to give the borrower an estimate of the closing agent's charges and a statement indicating any business relationship between the lender and closing agent. This requirement does not apply if the borrower is not required to pay any part of the closing costs.

5. Kickbacks or referral fees. Under RESPA, no person or business may give or accept:

a. Any fee, kickback, or thing of value in exchange for business relating to a real estate loan transaction; or

For lender—or lawyer—

b. Any portion, split, or percentage of charges made for rendering a service, unless the service was actually performed.

Specifically exempted from, and not considered in this category of payments, are payments made:

a. To cooperating brokers or other referral arrangements between real estate agents or brokers
b. By the lender to its employee or agent for services actually performed
c. By a title company to its employee or agent for services performed
d. To attorneys-at-law for services actually performed.

Caution: Real estate brokers and salespersons must be sure that any fees collected, other than commissions, are for specific services actually performed. Violators are subject to both criminal and civil penalties. Civil penalties include triple damages.

6. Purchase of title insurance. No seller of real property can legally require that title insurance be purchased from any particular company as a condition of sale. The purpose of this prohibition is to prevent situations where developers might obtain a very low title insurance rate on undeveloped land with the understanding that future lot buyers, or home buyers, would be required to obtain title insurance from the same company. Here also, triple damages may be awarded for violation.

Transactions exempt from RESPA:

1. Loans to finance the purchase of 25 acres or more
2. Loans for home improvement, or to refinance, or any other type of loan, if the purpose is not to purchase or transfer title
3. Loans to finance the purchase of a vacant lot, if none of the loan proceeds will be used to place a residential structure or mobile home on the lot
4. Sale or transfer of property involving only assumption of an existing loan or sale subject to an existing loan
5. A construction loan unless it is intended to be converted into a permanent loan
6. Permanent loans to finance construction of a one- to four-family structure when the lot is owned by the borrower
7. Loans to finance the purchase of property when the primary purpose is resale of the property.

Florida Residential Landlord and Tenant Act

The remainder of this chapter deals with this important law which was passed in 1973 and amended in 1974, 1975, and 1976. The intent of the "Landlord and Tenant Act" was to place the landlord and tenant on a more equitable basis in their legal relationship. The law applies only to the rental of a dwelling unit or a mobile home lot. It does not apply to commercial leases, medical facilities, transient accommodations (motels and hotels), cooperative apartments, or condominiums. 83.40-63, F.S.

A "dwelling unit" is defined as "a structure that is rented for use as a home, residence, or sleeping place by one person, or by two or more persons who maintain a common household; or a mobile home rented by a tenant; or a mobile home lot that is rented for occupancy by one or more persons who own the mobile home located on the lot." For the purposes of this law, a "tenant" is defined as "any person entitled to occupy a dwelling unit under a rental agreement." This definition does not conflict with but is a narrower definition of the term than is contained in 13.01 of the Commission HANDBOOK. Under recent Florida law, an 18-year old is vested with the rights of majority and is thus entitled to enter into a rental agreement.

Section 83.45 contains a prohibition of "unconscionable rental agreement or provision." Such an incident could occur if the tenant was forced to sign a rental agreement containing a clause or provision which caused an unreasonable hardship for the tenant. This part of the law is aimed at correcting those instances where rental agreements contain "fine print" which binds a tenant to unreasonable conditions. It may help to make future rental agreements become simplified. The prohibition of unconscionable agreements is reinforced by a later part of the law which states that any portion of a rental agreement which tries to limit or preclude the liability of a landlord to his tenant would be unenforceable. The reverse would be true also if a tenant attempted to limit his responsibility to the landlord.

Deposits. One of the most controversial topics in this entire Florida statute has to do with deposit money and advance rents. Summarized, the law requires that when money is given to a landlord as a security deposit, or for advance rent, the landlord is obligated to account for such deposits in different ways, depending on prevailing conditions: 14.12

> If security deposits, or advance rents, are to be held in excess of three months, the total amount of such funds held by the landlord are to be kept in a separate account on behalf of the tenants. These funds cannot be co-mingled with other funds; or,
>
> the landlord may post a surety bond with the Clerk of the Circuit Court, in the county where the dwelling is located. The surety bond must equal the total amount of all tenant deposits and advance rents, or $50,000, whichever is less.
>
> If the landlord requires a security deposit, or advance rent, which is to be held in excess of six months, different requirements apply. If the funds are held in a separate account on behalf of the tenants and not co-mingled or made use of by the landlord until they legally become his property, no interest on the funds need be paid to the tenants. But if the funds are deposited in an interest-bearing account, they must be deposited in a Florida banking institution. The landlord must inform each tenant of the name and address of the bank and the amount of money deposited on behalf of the tenant. Thusly, the landlord must pay to the tenant at least 75 percent of any interest earned by such deposits; or,

the deposits and advance rents may be held by the landlord or his agent in a co-mingled account. If the funds are held in such an account, the landlord is required by law to pay his tenants interest at the rate of 5 percent per annum, simple interest.

The Florida Residential Landlord and Tenant Act (FRLTA) requires that the landlord must inform tenants in writing, within 30 days from the receipt of advance rent or security deposit, of the manner in which the tenant's funds are being held. In the notice to the tenant, the landlord must also show the rate of interest, if any, and the date that interest payments will be made to the tenant. The landlord is required either to pay the interest or to credit the interest to the tenant at least one time each year.

The parts of the law dealing with security deposits and advance rents have been changed several times since the law was enacted. There is no doubt that some confusion and hardship on the part of landlords has resulted from time to time. For such cases, professional counsel should be obtained.

Landlord's obligation to maintain premises. In Florida, a landlord is required to maintain any rented dwelling unit in a condition which meets all building, housing, and health codes in that community. If no codes have been established in that particular area, the law requires landlords to maintain rented premises in "good repair and capable of resisting normal forces and loads." The wording of the law in this instance may require corrective action by the courts to eliminate some of the existing vagueness. 14.11

In addition to the landlord's obligation to maintain, he is also required to provide exterminating service to get rid of bugs and rodents, to provide garbage receptacles and pickup, and to provide heat plus running hot water. The landlord is allowed to charge his tenants for any or all of the services provided. If the dwelling unit rented is either a single-family home or a duplex, the landlord is not legally obligated to provide exterminating service, garbage pick-up, etc.

It should perhaps be pointed out that the obligation of a landlord to provide insect extermination, garbage pick-up, etc. can be altered or set aside by a written agreement between the tenant and landlord. However, this is not true regarding the landlord's obligation to maintain the dwelling unit in a condition which will meet existing building, housing, and health codes. This latter requirement is created by the law and the statute prohibits alteration by agreement.

The landlord cannot be held responsible for conditions caused or created by any negligent or wrongful acts of the tenant, or for an omission on the part of the tenant or his guests. Also, landlords are not required to maintain mobile homes when a tenant is renting the landlord's lot.

Tenant's obligations. The act also imposes an obligation on the tenant to maintain the rented premises by complying with existing building, housing, and health codes. The law specifically requires the tenant to maintain the dwelling unit in a clean and sanitary condition and to maintain interior plumbing fixtures in a clean and sanitary manner. The tenant is further required to be reasonable in the use and operation of all plumbing, electrical, heating, and air-conditioning equipment.

The responsibility for conduct of the tenant and/or his guests is also stipulated in the law. The tenant, his family, and guests are legally obligated to conduct themselves so as not to disturb the peace of other tenants.

Landlord's access to premises. The Landlord and Tenant Act identifies the purposes and conditions which create a legal right for the landlord to enter rented premises. The law states that a tenant shall not unreasonably withhold consent for a landlord to enter rented premises from time to time in order to: 14.10

1. Inspect the premises
2. Make necessary or agreed upon repairs, decorations, alterations, or improvements
3. Supply agreed-upon services
4. Exhibit or show the apartment.

In case of emergency or when necessary to protect or preserve the premises, a landlord is entitled to enter a dwelling unit at any time. However, the law prohibits a landlord from abusing his right of access in order to harass a tenant. Except in emergencies, landlords are obligated to enter rented premises at times reasonable and convenient for the tenant.

Another little known aspect of the law deals with access during absence of the tenant from the premises for extended periods of time. If a tenant is to be absent from his rented dwelling for a period of time equal to one-half the time for normal periodic rent payments, new conditions apply to landlord access. If the rent is current and the tenant notifies the landlord of an intended absence, the landlord cannot enter the premises during the period of absence except with the tenant's consent, or in an emergency for protection or preservation of the dwelling unit. This section of the law emphasizes that landlords do not have the right to snoop during a tenant's absence.

Vacating premises. Another important area of the Landlord and Tenant Act is how and when rented premises are vacated. If a tenant vacates rented premises at the end of a lease or tenancy agreement, the landlord is required by law to notify that tenant within 15 days if he, the landlord, intends to claim a part or all of the tenant's security deposit. This is one reason why all knowledgeable landlords attempt to obtain a forwarding address when a tenant leaves. The law requires that the landlord's notification must be in writing and sent by certified mail to the tenant's last known mailing address. If the landlord fails to give the required notice to the tenant within a 15-day period, he forfeits his right to claim part of the deposit. The deposit must then be returned to the tenant with any accrued interest.

If a tenant is properly notified of the landlord's claim on the security deposit, the tenant is allowed 15 days after receipt of the landlord's notice to file an objection. The date which is established by delivery of the notice by certified mail begins the tenant's 15-day period. If a dispute should arise which must be settled in court, the law states that the prevailing party in the litigation is entitled to receive from the other party reimbursement for his court costs plus reasonable attorney fees.

When a tenant vacates or abandons rented premises before the expiration of the agreed term, he must give at least 7 days notice to the landlord by certified mail, unless the terms of a written lease exempt the tenant from this obligation. It makes no difference if the duration of tenancy is week to week, month to month, or year to year. If the landlord is not given written notice by certified mail at least 7 days prior to vacating or abandoning the premises, the landlord is excused from notifying the tenant of the landlord's claim on the security deposit.

Termination of rental agreements. If a landlord fails to maintain rented premises, or fails to comply with the terms and conditions of the rental agreement, the tenant may terminate the agreement by following the procedure below:

1. The tenant must first give written notice to the landlord citing the noncompliance and stating his intent to cancel the agreement if the noncompliance is not corrected.
2. Thereafter, the landlord has 7 days to correct the noncompliance and resolve the problem.
3. If the noncompliance is not corrected within 7 days after delivery of the tenant's complaint to the landlord, the tenant is entitled to terminate the agreement.

In those cases in which a tenant does not desire to terminate his rental agreement but does want to correct a landlord's noncompliance, the law provides alternative courses of procedure:

1. If the dwelling unit is not rendered untenantable by the landlord's failure to comply, the tenant can remain in occupancy of the premises, and the law states that the rent shall be reduced in proportion to the loss in rental value caused by the noncompliance.
2. If the dwelling unit is rendered untenantable due to the landlord's noncompliance, the tenant cannot be liable for the rent during the period the premises remain untenantable. This is a departure from the procedure in a non-residential lease agreement. In the case of a non-residential lease, the landlord has no obligation to repair damaged premises unless the obligation is specifically contained in the lease agreement.

If a tenant fails to comply with a lease or rental agreement, the landlord can terminate the agreement by following the above three-step procedure. The same time period of 7 days is allowed for compliance by the tenant. However, if the tenant's noncompliance is failure to pay rent when due, the following procedure is required for a landlord in order to terminate the agreement:

1. The landlord must give the tenant written notice demanding payment of rent within 3 days or possession of the premises.

The delivery of a written notice can be by mail or by personal delivery. If the tenant is absent from his place of residence when the notice is delivered, the person delivering the notice may attach the notice to the door of the dwelling. It is always advisable to take a person to witness delivery of the notice. The 3-day time limit begins from the time the notice is posted by mail or delivered at the residence.

2. The tenant has 3 days to pay the rent or surrender the premises. If the tenant continues to default in payment of rent after the allotted 3 days have lapsed, the landlord must resort to judicial action to have the tenant evicted.
3. If the rental agreement is terminated and the tenant vacates the premises, then the landlord is required to give the tenant written notice by certified mail of any claim on the tenant's security deposit or advance rent held by the landlord as described previously.

Eviction requirements. From time to time, a landlord finds it necessary to evict tenants from rented dwelling units. In any eviction process, the landlord must adhere to the following procedure: 14.16

1. The landlord must notify the tenant in writing of his demand for possession of the premises. The notice may be by mail or by attaching a copy of the notice to the door of the tenant's residence. The landlord should always keep a copy of the notice with an indication of the date mailed or delivered.
2. If the tenant does not surrender the premises to the landlord within 3 days after notification, the landlord must file a complaint in the county court where the dwelling is located. This complaint will identify the premises and cite the reasons that justify recovery. A member of the sheriff's department will usually deliver the complaint to the tenant.
3. The tenant will be allowed 5 days to file an answer defending himself against the complaint. If the tenant decides to defend his continued possession, the courts must decide the case.
4. If the tenant merely continues to occupy the premises without answering the landlord's complaint, the landlord must obtain a final judgment from the court. A landlord is entitled to have his motion for final judgment advanced on the court's calendar.
5. After the landlord has received a final judgment against the tenant, he still must obtain a "writ of execution" in order to have the sheriff physically evict the tenant.
6. To evict the tenant, the sheriff must first give notice to the tenant that he will be evicted unless he surrenders possession within 24 hours. After the 24 hours have lapsed, the sheriff and his representatives will physically remove the tenant and his belongings from the premises.

When a tenant refuses to vacate, it sometimes may take one or two months to complete the entire eviction procedure. While the law permits a landlord to seek advancement of his case on the calendar of the court, the court is allowed to exercise its discretion in deciding whether to approve such a request.

No one chapter of a book can possibly include all the details and applications of federal and state laws pertaining to the entire field of real estate. This chapter has addressed only a few of the most important laws with which persons new to real estate in Florida need to be familiar. The extracts from various laws contained herein are intended for educational purposes only and do not qualify a reader to initiate legal action without seeking counsel from qualified attorneys.

CHAPTER 15

FEDERAL HOUSING LAWS and
FLORIDA LANDLORD AND TENANT ACT

1. The federal statute which prohibits a private homeowner from discriminating on the basis of race if selling, renting, or leasing is:
   a. 1968 Fair Housing Act
   b. 1866 Civil Rights Act
   c. 1934 National Housing Act
   d. 1968 Interstate Land Sales Full Disclosure Act

2. In 1948, the Federal National Mortgage Association was created for the purpose of:
   a. Insuring mortgage loans
   b. Guaranteeing mortgage loans
   c. Establishing an informal loan screening agency
   d. Establishing a formal secondary mortgage market

3. The 1968 Fair Housing Act prohibits discrimination based on:
   a. Race, color, religion, sex, or national origin
   b. Race, color, sex, or age
   c. Religion, weight, or height
   d. Race, color, religion, creed, or national origin

4. The Truth-in-Lending Law:
   a. Does not affect real estate financing credit
   b. Attempts to regulate maximum interest rates charged consumers
   c. Requires disclosure of finance charges as well as annual percentage rates of interest
   d. All of the above

5. The Real Estate Settlement Procedures Act (RESPA) was enacted to:
   a. Establish a maximum cost for all closing items
   b. Require disclosure of only those costs that would allow buyers to shop for closing arrangements
   c. Attempt to compromise between "a" and "b" above
   d. Establish a minimum cost for all closing items

6. If requested by the borrower, and if available to the closing agent, the borrower must be provided with which of the following at least one day before closing:
   a. Uniform settlement statement
   b. Borrower's special information
   c. Advance estimate of settlement costs
   d. Notice of title closing agent selection

7. As part of the preparation for a closing, a listing broker referred a property owner to an appraiser. The appraiser completed the appraisal and charged the owner $250 which was entered on the RESPA settlement statement. The appraiser gave the listing broker $50 for the referral. According to RESPA:
   a. The listing broker has violated the law
   b. The appraiser has violated the law
   c. Both the broker and the appraiser have violated the law
   d. The arrangement is entirely legal

8. Which of the following is exempt from RESPA requirements:
   a. The sale of a house where the only financing is assumption of an existing loan
   b. A construction loan which will become a permanent loan only after the building is completed
   c. A loan to purchase a new house in a new subdivision
   d. All of the above

9. The intent of the Florida Residential Landlord and Tenant Act is to:
   a. Give the tenant a legal advantage in his relationship with the landlord
   b. Make the landlord-tenant relationship more equitable
   c. Provide landlords the legal assistance needed to create an advantageous relationship
   d. None of the above

10. When security deposits, or advance rents, are held by a landlord in Florida for more than three months:
    a. Such funds must always be kept in a separate account
    b. Such funds may be deposited in the landlord's account if he posts a $50,000 bond with the Circuit Court
    c. Such funds must bear interest at the rate of 6%
    d. Such funds must bear interest at the rate of 7%

11. When a landlord requires security deposits, or advance rents, which will be held in excess of six months:
    a. No interest need be paid if the funds are held in a separate tenant account and not co-mingled or used by the landlord
    b. The landlord must pay the tenant one-half of all interest collected if deposited in an interest-bearing account
    c. The landlord must pay the tenant 6% interest if deposited in a co-mingled account
    d. All of the above

12. If a landlord rents a duplex to two tenants, he is obligated to provide:
    a. Pest extermination service
    b. Garbage pick-up service
    c. Garbage receptacles
    d. None of the above

13. A landlord is excused from notifying a tenant of any claim on the tenant's deposit if not given the minimum notice required by law when a tenancy is terminated prior to the agreed term. Unless the tenant is exempt by a written lease, the minimum notice is:
    a. Two weeks notice by certified mail
    b. Seven days notice by certified mail
    c. Ten days notice by certified mail
    d. Fifteen days notice by regular mail

14. If a tenant vacates rented premises promptly when a lease or tenancy expires:
    a. The landlord must inform the tenant within 45 days if the landlord claims part of the security deposit
    b. The landlord must return the tenant's security deposit within 30 days or explain any exception
    c. The landlord must inform the tenant within 25 days if part of the tenant's deposit will be claimed
    d. The landlord must inform the tenant within 15 days if part of the tenant's deposit will be claimed

15. A tenant is obligated to:
    a. Ensure that his or her guests do not disturb the peace
    b. Be reasonable in operating air-conditioning equipment
    c. Maintain interior plumbing in a clean and sanitary way
    d. All of the above

16. If a tenant's rent is current and he notifies the landlord of an intended absence, the landlord:
    a. Cannot enter the tenant's rented premises except with the tenant's consent
    b. Can enter in an emergency for preservation of the premises
    c. Neither "a" nor "b" above
    d. Both "a" and "b" above

17. How long does a landlord have to correct a noncompliance that is brought to his attention by written notice from a tenant?
    a. 7 days
    b. 10 days
    c. 2 weeks
    d. 30 days

18. A landlord must follow designated procedures in evicting tenants. The first step in a legal eviction is to:
    a. Request the sheriff to deliver an eviction notice to the tenant
    b. Notify the tenant by mail of the landlord's demand for possession
    c. Attach a notice to the door of the premises that possession of the premises is demanded
    d. Either "b" or "c" above

CHAPTER 16

COMPUTATIONS and CLOSING STATEMENTS

Section 15, FREC HANDBOOK, imposes a duty on the broker handling a real estate transaction to account accurately for all money entrusted to him. The customary manner of performing this duty is by providing both parties a complete and accurate closing statement. Also, a federal statute, the Real Estate Settlement Procedures Act (RESPA), assigns new disclosure obligations and responsibilities for brokers, salesmen, and mortgagees regarding costs to both buyers and sellers. Thus, brokers, and all salesmen who might one day become brokers, must not only understand the closing statement, but must also be capable of computing the various simple arithmetic problems to be solved in arriving at the figures finally entered on the closing statements and disclosed to contracting parties. 15.01 15.02

In addition, real estate is a business involving percentages. Commissions are based on a percent of the selling price; a salesman's income is based on a percentage of the brokerage commission; interest rates on mortgages are based on percentages; and, many more everyday situations require an ability to work simple percentage problems.

This chapter will attempt to explain simple methods which may be used to help those who have not worked with numbers for some time. It will suggest methods and procedures for solving problems associated with the following:

1. Fractions
2. Decimals
3. Mortgage amortization
4. Prorating expenses
5. Closing statements

Review of Fractions

Many adults have had no occasion to work with fractions and percentages for years. This chapter assumes little or no prior knowledge about fractions.

When a whole unit, or number, is divided into equal parts, each of the parts is a fraction, and a percentage, of the whole unit. For example, if a city block is divided into two equal parts, each of the parts is ½ of a city block. Each of the parts is also 50 percent of a city block. But for now, just the subject of fractions will be dealt with to get the terminology straight.

When dealing with fractions, the number below the line is called the denominator. The denominator always indicates the total equal parts in a whole unit. In the example of the city block above, each part was ½. The lower number (denominator) indicates the total number of equal parts in the entire city block. If the fraction ¼ had been used, the denominator would have indicated that the city block was divided into four equal parts.

The number in a fraction which appears above the line dividing the numbers is called the numerator. The numerator indicates how many of the equal parts, which make up a whole unit, one is concerned with. For example, in the fraction 3/4, the numerator indicates three equal parts and the denominator shows a total of four equal parts, so you are talking about all but one equal part of something (all but ¼).

Changing Fractions to Decimals

The line which is located between two numbers of a fraction means "divided by." Thus, ¼ means 1 divided by 4; ½ means 1 divided by 2, etc. If you divide the bottom number (denominator) into the top number (numerator), you will get a percentage which indicates what percent of the whole unit the fraction represents. For example, in the fraction ½, divide the denominator into the numerator and your answer will be .50 or 50 percent. You have now converted a fraction (½) into a decimal number which tells you what percent of a whole unit the fraction represents.

Changing Percent into Decimals

Assume you are told that a property you want to list has increased 34 percent in value. Do you recall how to change percent into a decimal number for ease in computation? To change any percent into an equivalent decimal, simply place a decimal point two places to the left of the number and drop the percent sign. Thus, 34% becomes .34, and 150% becomes 1.50. If only one number is involved, add a zero to the left to permit moving the decimal point two places to the left. For example, you want to calculate the sales commission on a house and the sales commission is 7%. Simply place a zero left of the 7 and move the decimal two places left. Thus .07 is the answer.

Decimal Place Values

A great deal of the basic math required to compute routine real estate problems involves decimal numbers. This review of decimals will be more meaningful if you refresh your memory on the decimal system of place values and the importance of the decimal point in separating whole numbers from fractional parts of whole numbers. The following chart of decimal place values should be memorized if you do not already know the place values.

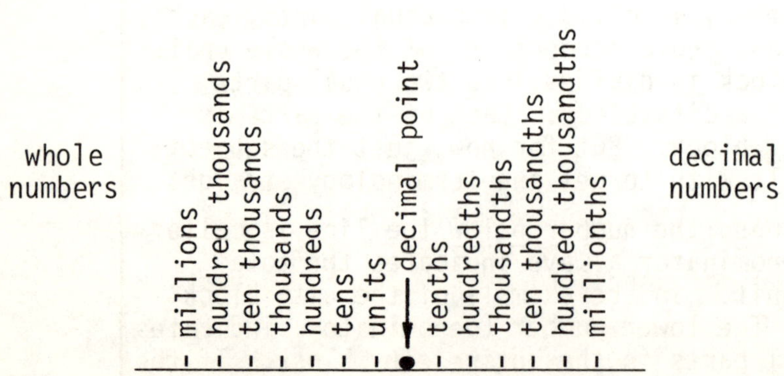

Notice that the whole numbers are on the left of the decimal point. The decimal numbers of a whole number are on the right side of the decimal point.

In those situations requiring one to convert percentage figures into decimals, remember that the word "percent" has two syllables. The first syllable, "per," is from the Latin and means "through." The second syllable, "cent," is from the Latin word "centum" and means "hundred." Perhaps this helps to remember that when converting (changing) numbers with a percent sign to a decimal figure, you actually convert the number to hundredth parts of a whole number. For example, 8% converted into decimal figures is 8/100 or .08.

Percentage Figures	Decimal Numbers
100%	1.00
70%	.70
50%	.50
10%	.10
6%	.06
1%	.01
½%	.005
¼%	.0025

Working With Decimals

In computing Consumer Price Index (CPI) problems or calculating the sale price for a net listing, you will need to know how to divide decimal numbers into whole numbers. A good way to avoid errors is to first make the decimal (the divisor) a whole number by moving the decimal as many places to the right as is needed to make the decimal a whole number. For example, you want to divide 1.80 into 41,500. First, move the decimal two places to the right making 1.80 become 180. But you must keep the same ratio between the divisor and dividend, so the second step is to place two zeros to the right of the number you are dividing (the dividend); 41,500 now becomes 4,150,000. When you divide 180 into 4,150,000, you will obtain the answer (quotient). What you have done is to move the decimal point the same number of places in both numbers. It is always necessary to add zeros to the number being divided (dividend) in order to be able to move the decimal point toward the right.

Now, assume you have just concluded a net listing agreement for a ranch. The owner has told you he must have $435,000 net and has agreed you can add your commission and legitimate expenses to his net amount to arrive at a sales price. Your knowledge of the law and local customs tells you that you are entitled to a 10% commission plus expenses. What will the amount of your sales commission be? Did you say $43,500? Wrong! A sales commission is based on the selling price. If you take $43,500 as your commission, you would be accepting 10% of the net listing price, not the 10% of the sales price to which you are entitled. So the solution involves dividing decimals into whole numbers again.

If you are allowed a .10 sales commission, then the net listing price of $435,000 represents .90 of the sales price, disregarding expenses which will be added later. The correct way to find the sale price, before expenses, is to divide .90 into $435,000. By doing so, you are saying $435,000 is 90% of some amount, and this will tell you what that amount is:

Solution:

$$.90\overline{)\$435{,}000}$$

$$90.\overline{)43500000.}$$

$$\begin{array}{r} 483333.33 \\ 90.\overline{)43500000.00} \end{array} \text{ rounded to } \$483{,}333.$$

Sale price before expenses	$483,333
Net amount required by owner	435,000
Your .10 commission	$ 48,333
.10 of $435,000	43,500
Possible loss if not computed correctly	$ 4,833 !

To the initial sale price of $483,333 you would now add estimated expenses to determine total sale price. If all of the estimated expenses are not required, the difference would be returned to the owner.

The point of this illustration is to demonstrate the monetary value of knowing how to use decimals correctly!

As previously mentioned, a real estate salesman or broker must be able to compute percentage problems in order to survive in the business of real estate. Many people have had learning experiences associated with percentages which have caused them to regard percentage problems as difficult. Actually, percentage problems are extremely simple. Everyone knows that half of anything is 50%, and one-fourth of anything is 25%. Also, 100% of something is the entire thing, and a figure of 125% represents one-fourth more than one complete item. To illustrate, suppose you are discussing the number of houses built last year in your county. All the new houses, totaled together, make 100% of the houses built. Further, at the end of this year, suppose you say that the houses built this year were 125% of the houses built last year. In other words, one-fourth more houses have been built this year than were built last year.

Computing Sales Commissions

Many brokers use production plateaus as the criterion for increasing their salesmen's commissions. For instance, a salesman may be paid 50% of the broker's commission up to a total production plateau of $200,000 of property sold by the salesman. From $200,001 to $350,000, the salesman may be increased to 55%. All salesmen need to understand, and be familiar with, the process for converting dollars and percentages into earned income.

Suppose the broker's listing agreement specified that 6½% sales commission was to be paid on the sales price of a parcel. Then assume that a salesman who has passed the $200,000 plateau sold the property. The salesman is to receive 55% of the 6½% sales commission. Disregarding listing commissions, and Multiple Listing Service (MLS) fees, how much would the salesman earn if he sold the property for $62,000?

```
1st Step:        $62,000 = sales price
                 x .065 = sales commission rate
                 310000
                372000
              $4030.00 = total commission

2nd Step:          $4030 = total commission
                   x.55 = salesman's commission rate
                  20150
                 20150
              $2216.50 = earned by salesman
```

Often a broker who lists a property with higher than normal value will agree to a graduated sales commission. This provides an incentive for the broker to get the seller the very best price possible. For example, suppose a broker lists a relatively new office building for sale. He agrees to accept a 5% sales commission on the first $200,000 of the actual sales price, 7½% on the next $500,000, 8½% on the next $500,000, and 10% of anything greater (over $1,200,000, in other words). What would the broker's total sales commission amount to if he sold the office building for $2,200,000?

```
1st Step:      $200,000 = first increment of sales price
               x    .05 = first increment of commission
             $10,000.00 = total first increment commission

2nd Step:      $500,000 = second increment of sales price
               x   .075 = second increment commission
               2500000
              3500000
            $37500.000 = total second increment commission

3rd Step:      $500,000 = third increment of sales price
               x   .085 = third increment of commission
               2500000
              4000000
            $42500.000 = total third increment commission

4th Step:      $200,000 = first increment of sales price
                500,000 = second increment of sales price
              + 500,000 = third increment of sales price
             $1,200,000 = total of first 3 increments

5th Step:    $2,200,000 = total sales price
             -1,200,000 = total first 3 increments
             $1,000,000 = amount to apply 10% sales commission

6th Step:  $1,000,000   = last increment of sales price
           x        .10 = last increment of sales commission
           $100,000.00  = last increment total commission
```

There is one step remaining -- to determine the total of the commission increments.

7th Step:

$10,000	=	1st increment commission
37,500	=	2nd increment commission
42,500	=	3rd increment commission
+100,000	=	last increment commission
$190,000	=	total sales commission (Wow!)

Suppose the salesman who actually negotiated the transaction had been promised 63% of the total sales commission. How much would the salesman have earned?

$190,000	=	total sales commission
x .63	=	salesman's portion
570 000		
11400 00		
$119700.00	=	$119,700 amount earned by salesman!

Mortgage Amortization

Mortgages used to purchase residential property usually call for regular, uniform payments which will include both interest payments and payments on the unpaid balance of the debt (principal). This type of mortgage is called the "level-payment plan" because the regular, periodic payments remain the same, although the amount of the payment which goes for interest gradually decreases while the amount assigned to amortizing the debt (principal) gradually increases.

To calculate how much money is to be regarded as interest and how much is to be paid on the principal, only three facts are needed in this type of problem:

1. The outstanding amount of the debt (principal)
2. The rate of interest
3. The amount of the payment per period (usually monthly)

Interest rates for mortgages are expressed as annual interest rates. Thus, when a $30,000 mortgage was secured at 7½%, this simply means that the interest rate is 7½% per year. To find the monthly interest actually paid, first determine what 7½% of $30,000 will amount to for the entire year. Dividing this amount by 12 (the number of months) gives the amount of monthly interest, as long as the unpaid balance is $30,000. If the principal amount changes, the calculations must be done over again, based on the new amount.

Example: You sell a home with a mortgage of $30,000 at 8% interest. The prospect wants you to explain how much of his monthly payment will go for interest, and how much for principal, during the first three months. His monthly payment is $220.20.

1st Step:

$30,000	=	unpaid balance
x .08	=	annual rate of interest
$2,400.00	=	interest as if paid annually

2nd Step:	$200	= first month's interest
	12 ⟌ $2,400	
	2 4	
	00	

3rd Step:	$220.20	= total monthly payment
	-200.00	= interest
	$ 20.20	= payment on principal

Prospect's answer for <u>first</u> month: Interest $200.00
Principal $ 20.20

But the prospect wanted to know about the first three months. So you take credit for the $20.20 paid on the principal by subtracting that amount from the $30,000:

4th Step:	$30,000.00	= principal first month
	- 20.20	= principal paid first month
	$29,979.80	= unpaid balance

Now you simply repeat the steps you did above to determine the answers for the second and third months:

5th Step:	$29,979.80	= unpaid balance
	x .08	= annual interest rate
	$2,398.3840	= interest as if paid annually

6th Step:	$ 199.865	= second month's interest
	12 ⟌ $2,398.3840	(round to $199.87)

7th Step:	$220.20	= monthly payment
	-199.87	= second month's interest
	$ 20.33	= second month's principal

8th Step:	$29,979.80	= unpaid balance
	- 20.33	= second month's principal
	$29,959.47	= new unpaid balance

9th Step:	$29,959.47	= new unpaid balance
	x .08	= annual interest rate
	$2,396.7576	= interest as if paid annually

10th Step:	$ 199.7298	= third month's interest
	12 ⟌ $2,396.7576	(round to $199.73)

11th Step:	$220.20	= monthly payment
	-199.73	= third month's interest
	$ 20.47	= third month's principal

So the answer to your prospect's question is:

First month:	Principal = $20.20; Interest = $200.00
Second month:	Principal = $20.33; Interest = $199.87
Third month:	Principal = $20.47; Interest = $199.73

Frequently, it becomes necessary to calculate the amount of interest paid over an extended period. For example, suppose your principal has been making a monthly payment on his mortgage for fourteen years and is informed by the mortgagee that 22% of the mortgage has been paid. He asks you to calculate the total amount of interest he has paid on the loan during the 14 years he has been making payments.

First you find the total amount of money paid by your principal during the 14 years that he has been paying on the mortgage. From this total amount paid, you subtract 22% of the original loan. The difference is all interest.

In order to solve this problem, you must know four things: the amount originally borrowed, the amount of each monthly payment, how many payments have been made, and the amount already paid back on the original loan (usually expressed as a percent of the borrowed amount).

When you learn that payments have been made for 14 years, you also know that 168 monthly payments have been made (12 months x 14 years = 168 monthly payments). You need only multiply the total number of monthly payments made times the amount of the monthly payment required in the mortgage to determine the total amount paid during the 14-year period. From this total amount, you subtract the number of dollars paid on the principal. The difference is interest.

Example: You have paid $196.45 on your mortgage each month for ten years. You learn that your mortgage is only seventeen percent paid off after ten years. If the original amount borrowed was $25,900, how much total interest have you paid to date?

1st Step:	12	= months in a year
	x 10	= years paid on mortgage
	120	= months paid on mortgage to date
2nd Step:	$196.45	= monthly mortgage payment
	x 120	= months paid on mortgage to date
	$23,574.00	= total amount paid to date
3rd Step:	$25,900	= amount originally borrowed
	x .17	= percent of loan repaid to date
	$4,403.00	= principal repaid on loan to date
4th Step:	$23,574	= total amount paid to date
	- 4,403	= principal repaid on loan to date
	$19,171	= total interest paid to date

Prorating Expenses

It is customary when transferring title to have the seller's ownership interests cease on the day of closing when title is delivered and to have all prorated items determined as of midnight prior to the date of closing. This means that the seller is not charged for taxes on that day and the buyer's insurance will begin on that day. Prorating is usually required when rents are paid in advance, taxes are paid in arrears, and interest on mortgages may be overdue or prepaid. To account for these circumstances, all items which are to become a credit or a debit (charge) to either the seller or the buyer are "apportioned" or "prorated." The following items are normally prorated since the expenses or income usually apply to both buyer and seller:

1. Prepaid rent
2. Interest on mortgages
3. Hazard insurance
4. Property taxes

Frequently, additional items will be prorated so as to account accurately for all income and expenses to both parties. Utilities, for example, may be prorated. Fuel oil, special assessments, or practically any item agreed upon by the two parties may be prorated.

In figuring prorated costs, two methods may be used: the 15.10
"average month-day combination method"; and, the "365-day method." Both methods are acceptable to the Florida Real Estate Commission; however, the Commission prefers the 365-day method due to its greater accuracy.

<u>Average Month-Day Combination Method</u>. The objective of both methods is to arrive at a daily cost figure for the month during which title closing is to occur. Using the average month-day combination method, simply determine the average monthly cost of the item, then divide the average monthly cost by the number of days in the closing month.

Example: Closing date is June 15. The annual insurance premium is $180 and has been paid by the seller. How much is the buyer to pay the seller for the prepaid insurance remaining if the policy is to expire at midnight on November 30?

Solution:

$$\$180 \div 12 \text{ months} = \$15 \text{ per month}$$
$$15 \div 30 \text{ days} = \$.50 \text{ per day}$$

The buyer will receive insurance coverage for 5 complete months (July through November) and 16 days in June:

1st Step:

$$\begin{array}{rl} \$15 & \text{per month} \\ \underline{\times\ 5} & \text{months} \\ \$75 & \end{array}$$

2nd Step:

$$\begin{array}{rl} 16 & \text{days in June} \\ \underline{\times .50} & \text{per day} \\ \$8.00 & \end{array}$$

3rd Step:

$$\begin{array}{rl} \$75 & \\ \underline{+\ 8} & \\ \$83 & = \text{credit to seller; debit to buyer} \end{array}$$

<u>365-Day Method</u>. Using the 365-day method, first divide 365 into 15.10
the annual cost of the item in question to find the exact daily rate. Then multiply the number of days involved times the daily

rate. (The primary difference between the two methods lies in the fact that months are not used in the 365-day method, only days!) With the same problem information as used in the above example, apply the 365-day method:

Solution: $180 ÷ 365 days = $.4931 or $.49 per day

The exact number of days remaining in the insurance policy = June 15-30; July 1-31; August 1-31; September 1-30; October 1-31; and, November 1-30. Total number of days remaining = 169.

169 days
x.49 cost per day
$82.81 = credit to seller; debit to buyer

If the full .4931 (cost per day) had been used instead of rounding to the nearest penny, the result would have been $83.33 (169 days x $.4931 per day = $83.33). Therefore, it is apparent that the average month-day combination method is a good compromise between the precise and rounded results produced by the 365-day method. For this reason, the average month-day method is sometimes employed unless large sums of money are involved. c
Where large sums are involved, the more precise 365-day method is utilized without rounding to the nearest penny.

Prorating rent. Normally, any income collected in advance is considered as belonging to the new owner as of the date of closing. In other words, the unused portion of advance rent belongs to the buyer. The total rent amount should be divided by the number of days involved in the rental period and allocated on a daily basis. For example, assume that a property rents for $260 per month. The closing date is on the 21st day of a 30-day month. The method of prorating would be as follows:

$260 ÷ 30 = $8.67 per day

$8.67 x 10 = $86.70 (due buyer)

$260 - $86.70 = $173.30 (due seller)

On the closing statements, you credit the buyer with $86.70 and debit the seller $86.70. The $173.30 was earned by the seller before closing and is not mentioned on either closing statement.

In computing dollars and cents for prorating purposes, all decimals should be carried to three places. If the third decimal number is "5" or above, it should be dropped and the second decimal number changed to the next highest number. If the third decimal number is "4" or below, simply drop the third number altogether and leave the second number as is. For example, in the above prorating of rent, when you divided the number of days in a month (30) into the monthly rent amount ($260), the answer was $8.666. You drop the third decimal number and change the second decimal to "7." This practice is common in computing all prorations.

Interest on mortgages. Since mortgage payments are normally made 15.09
each month, one month is usually the period used to calculate interest owed. Interest is paid at the end of the period ("in

arrears," or in other words, after having the use of the money). It is, therefore, charged to the seller up to the date of closing. This item is prorated in the same manner as property taxes. Interest is figured from the last date for which interest was paid. The exact number of days in each month is used, and interest is figured on a daily basis.

Hazard insurance. Unlike property taxes and mortgage interest, hazard insurance is paid in advance. Therefore, the seller will have already paid the insurance premium. It is often more economical for the buyer to assume the remaining portion of the insurance than to arrange for new insurance. In such a case, the cost of the insurance is prorated between seller and buyer. The prorated cost is figured on a daily basis for a 365- or 366-day year. The buyer pays for each day remaining in the policy year normally beginning with the date of closing and ending at the date prior to the anniversary date. The amount resulting from this calculation is shown on the buyer's statement as a debit. On the seller's statement, it is shown as a credit since he is being reimbursed for something for which he has already paid. Insurance prorations are figured to the end of the policy period and do not include the anniversary date of the policy. Thus, if the insurance anniversary date is on September 16, and the date of closing is June 1, the prorated amount to be paid by the buyer would be only 107 days, beginning with June 1 and including September 15. 15.12

From time to time, other items such as cost of utilities and outstanding special assessments may be considered as prorated cost items. When this occurs, and in the absence of any agreement to the contrary, prorating is done on a daily basis and is computed as of the date of closing.

Closing Statements

All real property sales or exchanges must eventually be concluded by a transfer of title. This normally occurs at what is called the "closing." In an earlier chapter entitled "Contracts," the point was made that the date and place of title closing should be specified in the sales contract. The period of time between signing of the sales contract and the title closing is designed to allow the buyer, seller, and broker an opportunity to prepare for the actual closing. The buyer is afforded an opportunity to have the boundaries of the property surveyed and have the public records checked for condition of the title and determination of existing liens, judgments, or other encumbrances. The seller has an opportunity to bring his abstract up to date and to remove any encumbrances on the property which he may have contracted to clear. He may also feel inclined to use the time to check the credit rating of the buyer if a purchase money mortgage is involved. The broker, attorney, or title company will have an opportunity to allocate expenses (debits) and credits associated with the title transfer. While the law designates primary responsibility for specific items, theoretically any and all closing costs are negotiable. 15.01

The Florida real estate license law places the responsibility upon the broker for an accurate accounting and delivery of all monies, deposits, drafts, abstracts, mortgages, conveyances, leases, or other documents entrusted to him by the parties to the transaction. The customary method of discharging this responsibility, and the simplest and most satisfactory, is by ensuring that complete and accurate closing statements are prepared and delivered to the buyer and the seller. Also, information from the closing statements can be helpful in fulfilling responsibilities created by RESPA, the federal Real Estate Settlement Procedures Act. The primary considerations in the preparation of closing statements are clarity and accuracy, regardless of the form used.

In order to show clearly and completely the several facets of expense, income, and other items relating to the transaction, it is customary to prepare a closing statement for both the seller and the buyer, plus a resume which reconciles all the debits and credits involved. To the new practitioner, this may at first appear to be a formidable task; however, as one becomes familiar with the items involved, it becomes clear that proper organization of information is the key to successful preparation of closing statements. Once the debits and credits are properly assigned to the appropriate parties, it becomes a simple matter to set them down on the closing statement form. For this purpose, a copy of the authors' "Work Organizer for Closing Statements" is provided at the end of the regular portion of this chapter to assist in organizing the entries which may appear in various property transactions. In addition, a sample closing is shown using the organizer and appropriate closing forms.

The sales contract should designate responsibility for payment of closing cost items. It is of major importance that the real estate broker or salesman carefully explain the approximate cost of such items to both the buyer and the seller, before an agreement is reached and the contract signed. It is obvious, therefore, that in order to explain the closing cost items, a broker or salesman must first understand them himself. 15.02

Closing Statement Items

State Documentary Stamp Tax on Deeds. (See Chapter 6 also.) 15.03
The State requires the payment of a tax on deeds and other conveyances. This tax is called the "State documentary stamp tax" and is assessed at the rate of $.30 for each $100, or any fraction thereof, on the entire purchase price of the property. In cases involving exchange of property, the tax is based on the values of the properties involved in the exchange. The State documentary tax is paid by buying documentary stamps at the recorder's office and placing them on the deed or conveyance. They are cancelled by writing the date and initials of the person doing the cancelling across the face of the stamps. Where property between joint owners is being divided with no difference in value, or where the consideration is love and affection, no tax is payable except the minimum tax allowable, which is $.30. On normal sales or exchanges, the State documentary stamp tax is paid by the grantor (seller) and is shown as a debit to the seller on the closing statement. (See "Seller's Closing Statement" at the end of this chapter for an example.)

State Documentary Surtax on Deeds. (See Chapter 6 also.) The Florida Legislature continued the federal documentary stamp tax when it was repealed. In its new form, the tax is called the "State documentary surtax," and a minimum of $.55 is chargeable 15.03
to all deeds. It is still based on $.55 for each $500, or fraction thereof, but it does not apply to the entire purchase price of the property conveyed. It only applies to "new money," that is, the amount of the purchase price remaining after existing mortgages are deducted. However, any new mortgages created at the time of property transfer are included in the amount on which the documentary surtax is calculated. This tax is usually paid by the seller and is shown as a debit to him on the Seller's Closing Statement.

For example, suppose a residence is sold for $30,000. The buyer will assume an existing $20,000 mortgage and create a new second mortgage in the amount of $5,000 while paying $5,000 cash. The State documentary surtax would be figured on $10,000, which is what remained of the total sales price when the existing mortgage was deducted. Therefore, the surtax on this transaction would be $11 ($.55 x $10,000 ÷ $500). If the surtax had been based on $10,001, the amount of tax to be paid would have been $11.55 because of the fractional part of $500 represented by the added $1.

State Documentary Stamp Tax on Notes. Florida requires the pay- 15.04
ment of a documentary stamp tax on any instrument containing a 201.07, F.S.
promise to pay money. The tax rate is $.15 per $100, or fraction 201.08, F.S.
thereof, and is figured on the face value of the note. This tax is not considered a real estate tax but is a tax on obligations to pay. Since the mortgagor is the person creating the debt, this tax is normally paid by the mortgagor and is shown as a debit to the buyer (mortgagor) on the closing statement.

State Intangible Tax on Mortgages. The State requires an intan- 15.06
gible tax to be paid on all new mortgages. This tax, like the preceding three taxes, is a one-time tax and is not paid annually. The tax rate is two mills (.002) per dollar of indebtedness. This tax is paid to the county tax collector, and the mortgage must be endorsed to show payment of the tax before it can be recorded. Since a mortgage is regarded as a "Class C" security belonging to the mortgagee, this tax is paid by the mortgagee unless the mortgagor agrees to pay the tax in order to obtain the loan. In the surtax example shown previously, the new second mortgage would require payment of an intangible tax in the amount of $10 (.002 x $5,000 second mortgage). The intangible tax charge would then be shown as a debit against the seller unless an agreement to the contrary had been arranged.

County and/or City Property Taxes. In Florida, property taxes 15.10
are paid on a calendar-year basis, as mentioned earlier. They are assessed as of January 1 each year, become due and payable on November 1, and become delinquent on the following April 1. Thus, property taxes are paid in arrears. The seller will have had the possession and use of the property for some portion of the year, unless the transfer of title is effective on January 1, which is highly unlikely. In order to apportion the property

taxes fairly, they are prorated on the basis of a 365-day year, or a 366-day year (leap year). The total tax assessment is divided by the number of days in a year to determine the actual cost per day. Then the property tax chargeable to the seller, on departure from the property, is easily calculated by multiplying the cost per day by the number of calendar days before title was conveyed. The resulting amount is shown on the Seller's Closing Statement a a debit. It is also shown on the Buyer's Closing Statement, but as a credit. The buyer's share of property taxes is not reflected on either closing statement because he will not be required to settle his tax bill at closing. The buyer will pay the entire year's property tax after November 1 to include the amount paid him by the seller.

In addition to the various mandatory taxes involved with title closing, several other charges are associated with preparation and recording of legal instruments, broker's commission, title insurance, etc.

Attorney's Fees. The customary method of handling an attorney's fees, for preparation of documents, is to require the person who must sign the document to pay the fee for its preparation. This means that the seller, or grantor, pays for preparation of the deed, and the buyer, or mortgagor, pays for preparation of the mortgage and note. The charges resulting are shown as a debit on the closing statement of the person required to pay. An attorney's charges shown on the seller's statement will not be shown on the buyer's statement in any manner, and vice versa.

Recording Fees. Several of the legal instruments signed at closing should be recorded in order to give adequate notice of new ownership and debt status. Charges associated with recording these documents are usually paid by the person who wants a particular document recorded. For example, the grantee (buyer) will want his deed recorded and will pay for this service even though the grantor (seller) paid for its preparation by an attorney. The various recording fees are shown on the appropriate party's closing statement but will not appear on both statements. 15.07

Broker's Commission. The person who employed the broker is required to pay his commission. Usually, the seller is the broker's principal (employer). The broker's commission is listed on the employer's closing statement as a charge but, of course, does not appear on the other party's closing statement. 15.08

Abstract Continuation or Title Insurance. Under Florida law, the seller of property is not required to provide an abstract of title, unless he agrees to do so. Nor is he required to provide any form of title insurance or an opinion of title. It is the broker's duty to recommend that the buyer protect his interests by obtaining an up-to-date abstract and title insurance, or an attorney's opinion of title. However, the broker is duty bound to reflect the cost of an abstract or title insurance as a charge against the party who instructed him to take such action. If the seller refuses to be responsible for delivery of an abstract and the buyer instructs the broker to obtain one, then the buyer's closing statement will show the cost of such an item as a debit and no mention will be made on the seller's closing statement. 15.14

It should be pointed out, however, that the normal procedure is for the seller to deliver an abstract and accept the cost, while the buyer may require title insurance and accept that cost. Each cost is shown on its individual closing statement.

Special Assessments. All special assessments become liens on property as soon as their amount is known and assessed against the property. An owner is sometimes allowed to pay the assessment costs over a period of years as installments. Therefore, a mistaken assumption is often made that the buyer of such a property will take over any remaining installments. This can be arranged in the contract of sale, but unless agreed upon between the seller and the buyer, the seller can be forced to pay the entire outstanding amount at or prior to closing. If the special assessment costs are to be paid by the seller, but the seller does not want to pay the entire cost out of pocket in one lump sum, one way of handling the matter at closing would be to show the outstanding amount as a credit to the buyer on the Buyer's Closing Statement, and as a debit to the seller on his statement. Thus, the buyer would get credit, for the seller's entire special assessment owed, by the withholding of money otherwise due the seller at closing. 15.11

Liens. As may be realized from the above paragraph, the seller is responsible for all existing or pending liens against the property. At the time of closing, all liens must have either been already satisfied by the seller or have been reached by agreement between the buyer and the seller regarding their disposition. 15.11

Cash Reconciliation Statement (Resume)

When the closing statements for both the seller and the buyer have been completed, the broker, or closing agent, is prepared to summarize the entire transacton in a "resume" or Cash Reconciliation Statement. This will clearly and accurately show the amount of money deposited by the buyer, plus the balance due from him. It will also show the expenses chargeable to each party, including the brokerage commission and the amount due the seller at closing. Normally the broker, or person making out the closing statements, will have prepared the checks to be disbursed. After examination by the seller and the buyer, each should be requested to sign his copy of the closing statement. 15.16

Rules of Thumb

Before leaving the subject of closing statements, a few general rules of thumb may help the person who is not familiar with the proper preparation of these instruments:

1. On the seller's statement, the only entries in the credit column are the overall purchase price and any prepaid items. That's all! The total of these items is entered at the bottom of the statement under "Credits." The total amount of charges (debits) plus the amount due the seller at closing must equal the amount shown at the bottom of the seller's credit column.

2. On the buyer's statement, the total purchase price plus all charges and expenses are entered under the debit column. The

resulting total sum is the key to the buyer's statement. When all entries under the credit column are totaled, the difference between total credits and total debits is the amount the buyer must pay at closing. When the amount due from the buyer at closing is added to the total credits, it will, naturally, balance with the buyer's debit column.

3. All expenses (attorney's fees, documentary stamps, etc.) are shown only on the statement of the appropriate person and are not "double entry items." Double entry items are those which are shown as a credit to one party and a debit to the other.

4. All entries from the total purchase price down through prorated items, with the single exception of the buyer's deposit, are double entry items and appear on the closing statements of both parties.

5. Any expense or item is subject to negotiation between contracting parties. In the absence of a negotiated agreement, Florida Statutes will normally regard parties responsible as follows:

a. Checklist of items credited to seller:

Total purchase price
All prepaid items

b. Checklist of items debited to seller:

Mortgages assumed
Mortgages newly created
Recording the mortgage
Prorated taxes, interest, rent
Security deposits
State documentary stamps on the deed
State documentary surtax stamps on the deed
State intangible tax on the mortgage
Broker's commission
Abstract continuation (if appropriate)
Attorney's fees (deed)

c. Checklist of items credited to buyer:

Earnest money deposit
Mortgages assumed
Mortgages newly created
Prorated property taxes (city and county)
Prorated unpaid interest
Prorated rent
Security deposits

d. Checklist of items debited to buyer:

Purchase price
Prorated insurance
State documentary stamp tax on the note
Recording of the deed
Attorney's fees (mortgage and note)

As mentioned previously, a copy of the authors' "Work Organizer for Closing Statements" follows. In addition, a closing problem is posed, and completed samples are provided of the Organizer, a Buyer's Closing Statement, a Seller's Closing Statement, a Composite Closing Statement, and a Cash Reconciliation Statement (Resume or Broker's Statement). The authors have chosen these formats with the full knowledge that many versions exist and some are not used in certain situations (e.g., the Cash Reconciliation Statement).

Sample Closing Statement Problem

Mr. Bravo and his wife have decided to buy Lot 14, Block C, Page 641, public records of Foam County, Florida. They are buying from Mr. and Mrs. Sierra and have given the sellers a $2,000 binder deposit, to be held in escrow until closing of the transaction. The contract stipulates that the Bravos will pay a total purchase price of $42,500. An existing first mortgage of $31,400 will be assumed by the Bravos as part of the purchase price. The Bravos are also to give the Sierras a $6,100 second mortgage and pay for the taxes created by the second mortgage. Also, the Bravos are to purchase the Sierras' interest in a one-year, prepaid insurance policy which runs from March 1, 1973 to March 1, 1974 with a premium of $264. (The 365-day method of prorating is used on the opposite pages.)

Mr. and Mrs. Sierra are to deliver an up-to-date abstract of title which will cost them $48, convey title with a general warranty deed, and pay for the required taxes on the deed. The sales contract specifies that the property taxes shall be prorated on the basis of 1972 taxes which were $360 for the city and $756 for the county. The Sierras have agreed to pay the broker who negotiated the transaction a commission of $2,975.

The closing is scheduled for July 1, 1973 with proration time midnight, June 30, 1973. Attorneys for the sellers and buyers have agreed to charge $50 for preparation of the instrument of conveyance and $75 for the mortgage instrument and note. Recording fee for the mortgage is $7.50, and $4 for recording the deed.

Beginning with the Work Organizer for Closing Statements, the various applicable items from above are computed and listed. The Buyer's, Seller's, and Broker's Closing Statements are also completed to show their use.

Note: Do not try to make the seller's and buyer's statements balance out with each other -- they are not supposed to do this. The closing statements for both seller and buyer are supposed to balance with the Cash Reconciliation Statement.

WORK ORGANIZER FOR CLOSING STATEMENTS

DEBIT BUYER	CREDIT BUYER	DEBIT SELLER	CREDIT SELLER
Purchase Price $________ Prorated Ins. ________ ________ ________ Doc. Stamps on Note ________ Intang. Tax on Mortgage ________ Atty. Fees ________ Record Deed ________ Title Ins. ________ TOTAL BUYER DEBITS $________	Deposit $________ 1st Mortgage ________ 2nd Mortgage ________ Prorated: City Taxes ________ County Taxes ________ Rent ________ Security Deposit ________ Total Credits ________ Total Debits ________ less Total Credits ________ BALANCE DUE BUYER $________	1st Mortgage $________ 2nd Mortgage ________ Doc. Stamps on Deed ________ Surtax Deed ________ Intang. Tax on Mortgage ________ Prorated: City Taxes ________ County Taxes ________ Rent ________ Abstract ________ Atty. Fees ________ Record Mort. ________ Commission ________ TOTAL SELLER DEBITS $________	Purchase Price $________ Prorated Ins. ________ ________ Total Credits ________ less Total Debits ________ BALANCE DUE SELLER $________

INSURANCE	CITY TAXES	COUNTY TAXES
Premium cost ÷ 365 = daily cost Daily cost x no. of days to Buyer (DEBIT BUYER; CREDIT SELLER)	Annual taxes ÷ 365 = daily cost Daily cost x no. of days used by Seller (DEBIT SELLER; CREDIT BUYER)	Annual taxes ÷ 365 = daily cost Daily cost x no. of days used by Seller (DEBIT SELLER; CREDIT BUYER)

PREPAID RENT	1st MORTGAGE INTEREST	2nd MORTGAGE INTEREST
Amt./period ÷ days in period Days owned by Buyer ________ x amount per day ________ (DEBIT SELLER; CREDIT BUYER)	Balance due x % = annual int. Annual int. ÷ 12 = monthly int. Monthly int. ÷ 30 = daily int. (DEBIT SELLER; CREDIT BUYER)	Balance due x % = annual int. Annual int. ÷ 12 = monthly int. Monthly int. ÷ 30 = daily int. (DEBIT SELLER; CREDIT BUYER)

DOC. STAMPS DEED	SURTAX DEED	DOC. STAMPS NOTE	INTANG. TAX MORT.	COMMISSION
$.30 x $100 on purchase price (debit seller)	$.55 x $500 on new money (debit seller)	$.15 x $100 on note face value (debit buyer)	.002 (mills) x $1 mort. face val. (debit lender)	Purchase price x __ % (debit employer)

DEBIT BUYER		CREDIT BUYER		DEBIT SELLER		CREDIT SELLER	
Purchase Price	$42,500.00	Deposit	$ 2,000.00	1st Mortgage	$31,400.00	Purchase Price	$ 42,500.00
		1st Mortgage	31,400.00	2nd Mortgage	6,100.00		
		2nd Mortgage	6,100.00	Doc. Stamps on Deed	127.50		
Prorated Ins.	176.00	Prorated:				Prorated Ins.	176.00
		City Taxes	178.00	Surtax Deed	12.65		
		County Taxes	375.00	Intang. Tax on Mortgage			
Doc. Stamps on Note	9.15	Rent		Prorated:			
		Security Deposit		City Taxes	178.00	Total Credits	42,676.00
Intang. Tax on Mortgage	12.20	Total Credits	40,053.00	County Taxes	375.00	less	
				Rent			
				Abstract	48.00	Total Debits	41,273.65
Atty. Fees	75.00	Total Debits	42,776.35	Atty. Fees	50.00		
Record Deed	4.00	less		Record Mort.	7.50		
Title Ins.		Total Credits	40,053.00	Commission	2,975.00		
TOTAL BUYER DEBITS	$42,776.35	BALANCE DUE BUYER	$ 2,723.35	TOTAL SELLER DEBITS	$41,273.65	BALANCE DUE SELLER	$ 1,402.35

INSURANCE	CITY TAXES	COUNTY TAXES
Premium cost ÷ 365 = daily cost Daily cost x no. of days to Buyer (DEBIT BUYER; CREDIT SELLER)	Annual taxes ÷ 365 = daily cost Daily cost x no. of days used by Seller (DEBIT SELLER; CREDIT BUYER)	Annual taxes ÷ 365 = daily cost Daily cost x no. of days used by Seller (DEBIT SELLER; CREDIT BUYER)
365) $264.000 = .723 $.723 x 243 DAYS = $175.689 ROUND TO $176.	365) $360.000 = .986 $.986 x 181 DAYS = $178.466 ROUND TO $178.	365) $756.00 = 2.07 $2.07 x 181 DAYS = $374.67 ROUND TO $375.

PREPAID RENT	1st MORTGAGE INTEREST	2nd MORTGAGE INTEREST
Amt./period ÷ days in period Days owned by Buyer ______ x amount per day (DEBIT SELLER; CREDIT BUYER)	Balance due x % = annual int. Annual int. ÷ 12 = monthly int. Monthly int. ÷ 30 = daily int. (DEBIT SELLER; CREDIT BUYER)	Balance due x % = annual int. Annual int. ÷ 12 = monthly int. Monthly int. ÷ 30 = daily int. (DEBIT SELLER; CREDIT BUYER)

DOC. STAMPS DEED	SURTAX DEED	DOC. STAMPS NOTE	INTANG. TAX MORT.	COMMISSION
$.30 x $100 on purchase price (debit seller)	$.55 x $500 on new money (debit seller)	$.15 x $100 on note face value (debit buyer)	.002 (mills) x $1 mort. face val. (debit lender)	Purchase price x __ % (debit employer)
$100) $42,500. = 425. $425 x .30 = $127.50	$42,500 − 31,400 = $11,100 $500) $11,100.00 = 22.20 23 x .55 = $12.65	$100) $6,100. = 61. 61 x .15 = $9.15	$6,100 x .002 = $12.200	$42,500 x .07 = $2,975.00

BUYER'S CLOSING STATEMENT

DATE OF CLOSING: July 1, 1973	DEBITS	CREDITS
Purchase Price	$ 42,500.00	$
First Mortgage - Balance		31,400.00
Second Mortgage		6,100.00
Binder Deposit		2,000.00
Prorations:		
Rent		
Interest: 1st Mortgage		
2nd Mortgage		
Insurance	176.00	
Taxes: City		178.00
County		375.00
Expenses:		
Abstract Continuation		
Attorney's Fee	75.00	
Documentary Stamps:		
Mortgage-Note	9.15	
State on Deed		
Florida Surtax		
Intangible Tax - Mortgage	12.20	
Recording:		
Mortgage		
Deed	4.00	
Brokerage		
Total Debits and Credits	$ 42,776.35	$ 40,053.00
Balance Due from Buyer		2,723.35
GRAND TOTALS	$ 42,776.35	$ 42,776.35

SELLER'S CLOSING STATEMENT

DATE OF CLOSING:
July 1, 1973

	DEBITS	CREDITS
Purchase Price	$	$ 42,500.00
First Mortgage - Balance	31,400.00	
Second Mortgage	6,100.00	
Binder Deposit		
Prorations:		
Rent		
Interest: 1st Mortgage		
2nd Mortgage		
Insurance		176.00
Taxes: City	178.00	
County	375.00	
Expenses:		
Abstract Continuation	48.00	
Attorney's Fee	50.00	
Documentary Stamps:		
Mortgage-Note		
State on Deed	127.50	
Florida Surtax	12.65	
Intangible Tax - Mortgage		
Recording:		
Mortgage	7.50	
Deed		
Brokerage	2,975.00	
Total Debits and Credits	$ 41,273.65	$ 42,676.00
Balance Due Seller	1,402.35	
GRAND TOTALS	$ 42,676.00	$ 42,676.00

COMPOSITE CLOSING STATEMENT

Seller's Statement Debit	Seller's Statement Credit	Item	Buyer's Statement Debit	Buyer's Statement Credit
		PURCHASE TERMS:		
	$42,500.00	Total Purchase Price	$42,500.00	
		Binder Deposit		$ 2,000.00
$31,400.00		First Mortgage Balance		31,400.00
6,100.00		Second Mortgage		6,100.00
		PRORATIONS & PREPAYMENTS:		
		Rent		
		Interest: First Mortgage		
		Interest: Second Mortgage		
		Prepaid: First Mortgage		
		Prepaid: Second Mortgage		
	176.00	Insurance	176.00	
178.00		Taxes: City		178.00
375.00		Taxes: County		375.00
		Other ____________		
		EXPENSES:		
48.00		Abstract Continuation		
50.00		Attorney's Fees	75.00	
2,975.00		Brokerage		
		Title Insurance		
		DOCUMENTARY STAMPS:		
127.50		State Tax on Deed		
12.65		State Surtax on Deed		
		State Tax on Note	9.15	
		State Intangible Tax on Mortgage	12.20	
		RECORDING:		
7.50		Mortgage		
		Deed	4.00	
		Miscellaneous ____________		
		TOTALS:		
$41,273.65	$42,676.00		$42,776.35	$40,053.00
To:		**BALANCE DUE:**	From:	
1,402.35				2,723.35
		GRAND TOTALS:		
$42,676.00	$42,676.00		$42,776.35	$42,776.35

BROKER'S CLOSING STATEMENT*

	RECEIPTS	DISBURSEMENTS
Deposit	$ 2,000.00	$
Check from buyer at closing	2,723.35	
Brokerage fee		2,975.00
Check to seller at closing		1,402.35
Seller's expense (less brokerage)		245.65
Buyer's expense		100.35
TOTALS	$ 4,723.35	$ 4,723.35

*It is assumed that the broker will handle the recording of all instruments and the payment of the abstract, attorney's fees, stamps, recording fees, etc.

CHAPTER 16

COMPUTATIONS and CLOSING STATEMENTS

(This quiz is intended to review not only Chapter 16 but also much of the preceding information requiring various computations.)

1. Change the following percentages to decimals:

   a. 39½% ______ c. 75% ______
   b. 2% ______ d. 145% ______

2. Change the following percentages to fractions:

   a. 50% ______ c. 25% ______
   b. 20% ______ d. 40% ______

3. Change the following fractions to decimals:

   a. 1/8 ______ c. 1/16 ______
   b. 3/5 ______ d. 1/20 ______

4. Divide the following:

   a. $1.72\overline{)44,032}$ b. $.60\overline{)493.8}$ c. $25.5\overline{)18,768}$ d. $.17\overline{)7,735}$

5. A senior salesman receives 55% of all sales commissions earned. His broker has listed a motel for $1,450,000. The listing contract specifies a 6½% sales commission for the first $600,000 of selling price, 7% for the next $800,000, and 8% commission on all of the actual sales price exceeding $1.4 million. What will the salesman's commission be if he sells the motel for the listed sales price?

   a. $99,000 c. $95,000
   b. $54,450 d. $44,550

6. You sell a $48,000 home to a buyer who uses a mortgage of $40,000 at 8½% for 30 years as part of the purchase money. His monthly payments for principal and interest are $307.60. How much of the second monthly payment will be used to amortize the debt?

   a. $24.27 c. $34.72
   b. $37.24 d. $24.44

7. You have been paying on a 30-year mortgage for 20 years. The original mortgage was for $25,000 with an interest rate of 6%. Your monthly payments have been $150.50. At the end of 20 years, your mortgage is 38% paid. How much interest have you paid in 20 years?

   a. $30,000 c. $26,620
   b. $13,725 d. $24,275

8. What would the tax rate be for a city with an expected expenditure of $7,001,000, a non-property tax income of $1,100,000, and a total assessed property valuation of $292,000,000 which includes 2,200 properties eligible for normal homestead exemption?

   a. 2 mills b. 3 mills c. 21 mills d. 31 mills

9. What must the seller pay in Florida documentary and surtax stamp charges on a property which sold for $41,500 with a $10,000 down payment, a second mortgage of $11,500, and assumption of a $20,000 existing mortgage?

	Doc.		Surtax
a.	$124.50	and	$23.65
b.	$228.00	and	$12.90
c.	$228.00	and	$34.20
d.	$168.40	and	$28.95

10. In order to get a mortgage of $31,000, a buyer has agreed to pay all state tax costs incurred by creation of the new mortgage. What will total cost be?

a. $155.00 c. $ 96.80
b. $ 84.60 d. $108.50

11. You have a mortgage of $28,000 at 7% with a 30-year term. The monthly payment is $186.30. What portion of the second month's payment will apply to amortization of the mortgage? c

a. $22.97 c. $23.29
b. $23.10 d. $23.42

12. In the mortgage cited in Question 11 above, what would the monthly payments amount to if your property taxes were $840 and your annual insurance $176?

a. $277.97 c. $274.97
b. $267.97 d. $270.97

13. With the same mortgage used in Questions 11 and 12 above, you have paid off approximately 18% of your mortgage at the end of 10 years. How much interest have you paid during the 10-year period?

a. $17,316 c. $44,996
b. $27,476 d. $14,674

14. The Florida surtax required on an all-cash sale of $31,000 is:

a. $17.05 c. $18.60
b. $34.10 d. $28.60

15. Determine the interest and principal portions of the second month's payment on a mortgage of $26,000 at 7% with a payment of $202.10.

	Interest		Principal
a.	$151.67	and	$50.43
b.	$151.02	and	$51.08
c.	$151.94	and	$50.16
d.	$151.37	and	$50.73

16. Closing date for a property sale is August 15. The annual insurance premium is $198 with March 31 as its anniversary date. The seller has paid the annual premium in advance. What will be owed by the buyer at closing if computed by the 365-day method?

a. $ 73.70 c. $ 74.25
b. $123.12 d. $125.70

17. What is the required FHA down payment for a home selling at $31,000?

a. $3,750 c. $2,750
b. $3,200 d. $1,350

Practice Closing Statement Problem

Mr. and Mrs. Will B. Sellers sold their home, described as Lot 12, Block A, Pine Scent Subdivision, to Mr. and Mrs. Hap E. Byer for $41,400 on September 2, 1978. The closing date is October 15, 1978. Mr. Byer paid an earnest money deposit of $2,000 which you, the real estate salesperson, promptly gave to your broker to be held in escrow. Mr. and Mrs. Byer will assume an existing mortgage of $29,400 with an interest rate of 8%. Monthly payments for principal and interest are $240.49. The mortgage interest for October has been computed to be $196, rounded to the nearest dollar. The Sellers have agreed to take back a $5,000 purchase money second mortgage.

Mr. and Mrs. Sellers have prepaid the annual homeowner's insurance at a cost of $212. The anniversary date of the policy is May 1. City property taxes are estimated to be $470; county and school board taxes are estimated to be $864.

Mr. Sellers' attorney's fees will be $50, and Mr. Byer's attorney's fees will be $75 for preparation of the new mortgage and note. Recording fee for the deed will be $7, and recording fee for the mortgage will be $11. Mr. Byer has agreed to assume all costs related to the new second mortgage. Mr. Sellers is to provide an up-to-date abstract at a cost of $45, and Mr. Byer is to pay $390 for title insurance. An appraisal fee of $75 is to be paid by the Sellers. All prorations are to be computed as of midnight prior to the date of closing. The brokerage sales commission is 7% of the selling price. c

1. How much will Mr. and Mrs. Sellers pay for the required tax stamps on the deed?

   a. $124.20 c. $143.70
   (b.) $137.40 d. $154.20

2. If interest on the mortgage is paid in arrears each month, who will owe whom how much for interest in October?

   (a.) Sellers will owe Byers $88.48
   b. Sellers will owe Byers $101.12
   c. Byers will owe Sellers $101.44
   d. Byers will owe Sellers $196.00

3. How much will the Byers be required to pay for taxes related to the new mortgage?

   a. $15 (c.) $17.50
   b. $10 d. $ 7.50

   on 5,000.– .002 = 10.00, .15 × 50 = 7.50, 17.50

4. How much will the Byers need to reimburse the Sellers for homeowner's insurance?

   a. $ 96.86 c. $120.56
   (b.) $114.84 d. $106.12

5. How much will the Sellers need to give credit to the Byers for property taxes?

   a. $680.19 c. $ 285.48
   b. $370.23 (d.) $1,050.42

(Note: There are 125 multiple choice questions which follow. Obviously, fewer than 125 may be used. If the student achieves a score of 80% or better for any number of questions over 100 which are answered correctly without using any reference material, the student should be in a strong position relative to subsequent examinations. It is recommended that 2½ hours or more of uninterrupted time be budgeted to take this exam.)

1. A defendant named in an administrative complaint is required to file an answer to the allegations contained therein. The time for filing such an answer must be:

   a. Not more than 20 days from mailing
   b. Not less than 30 days from mailing
   c. Not more than 30 days from mailing
   d. Not less than 20 days from mailing

2. A former lessee has become a tenant at will and pays his rent monthly. He must be given how much notice to vacate?

   a. No notice
   b. 15 days
   c. 45 days
   d. 30 days

3. Disregarding debts and taxes, which one of the following percentages of real property would a widow with one child receive after her husband's death, if they had owned the property as tenants by the entireties?

   a. 30%
   b. 100%
   c. 33 1/3%
   d. 50%

4. A separate instrument used in Florida as personal evidence of a debt secured by a mortgage is a:

   a. Promissory note
   b. Mortgage for deed
   c. Debtor's agreement
   d. Mechanic's lien

5. A broker's registration was revoked. The registration of all salesmen working for him are, as a result, automatically:

   a. Cancelled
   b. Revoked
   c. Denied
   d. Suspended

6. A broker received a $5,000 deposit from a buyer on Tuesday at 8:00 a.m. His principal will not be available until Friday. The broker's normal banking day is Wednesday. He should:

   a. Deposit the $5,000 at his earliest convenience in his escrow account
   b. Deposit the money on his regular banking day
   c. Deposit the money in his escrow account on Tuesday
   d. Wait until his principal returns and find out if the owner is willing to accept the buyer's offer

7. A syndicate or business trust is given life by registration with:

   a. The Attorney General
   b. The State Securities Commission
   c. The Department of Banking and Financing
   d. The Department of State

8. Mr. Brown wanted to build a hotel. A broker showed him three choice sites zoned for hotels. Brown promised to decide on a site in three weeks, so the broker took a two-week vacation. On his return, Mr. Brown bought the site. The broker sold the site not knowing that the zoning on that site had been changed to industrial zoning.

   a. The broker is guilty of culpable negligence.
   b. The broker is not guilty of wrongdoing.
   c. The property owner is guilty of fraud.
   d. The broker is guilty of fraud.

9. A salesman's registration is revoked. The resulting effect on his certificate is:

   a. The certificate is of no use to him
   b. It should be retained for reissue in the future
   c. It should be retained so that he may operate
   d. It should be retained for renewal

10. An oral agreement was concluded between two parties calling for a three-year lease at $200 per month, with the first year's lease fee paid in advance. Which is most correct?

    a. The lease is not a lease but a tenancy at will.
    b. The lease is invalid because the period is longer than two years.
    c. The lease is invalid due to lack of a consideration.
    d. All of the above.

11. An owner directs a broker to show his property to any prospect except those belonging to two races. The broker should:

    a. Report the incident to FREC
    b. Comply with the owner's request
    c. Report the incident to the police
    d. Withdraw from the relationship

12. A broker has a listing priced at $20,000. An uninformed buyer offers him $25,000. The broker buys the property for $20,000, then sells it for $25,000. Which is most correct?

    a. The $5,000 profit is called an "overage."
    b. The $5,000 profit is called a "secret profit."
    c. Both buyer and seller can legally recover $5,000 from the broker.
    d. All of the above.

13. In Florida, the legal concept regarding mortgages on real property is:

    a. Title theory
    b. Lien theory
    c. Foreclosure theory
    d. Defeasance theory

14. A broker has a property listed at $55,000. A buyer indicates he will pay $55,000 if forced to do so, but will give the broker $2,000 if the broker will convince the owner to sell for $50,000. The owner is satisfied with $50,000, but the owner learns of the above agreement before closing. The seller should:

a. Cancel the sales contract he signed
b. Take $2,000 from the broker's commission
c. Sue both the buyer and the broker
d. Go through with the sale but pay no sales commission

15. Which one of the following is not absolutely essential to make a contract valid:

a. Competent parties
b. In writing and signed
c. Offer and acceptance
d. Binder deposit

16. To obtain an active broker's license in Florida, one:

a. Must have been an active salesman for 12 months
b. Must take and pass four examinations
c. Need not first complete a period of designated apprenticeship
d. All of the above

17. The administrative power of FREC to enact rules and regulations is: c

a. Executive power
b. Quasi-judicial power
c. Administrative power
d. Quasi-legislative power

18. A registered real estate salesman sued an owner, whose property he sold, for his commission instead of suing his broker. The salesman may be penalized by:

a. Fine
b. Payment of damages
c. Suspension
d. All of the above

19. A broker pays motel clerks $10 for each couple referred to him. Which is correct?

a. The motel clerks have violated F.S. 475.
b. The broker has violated F.S. 475.
c. Both the broker and the motel clerks have violated F.S. 475.
d. The motel clerks are entitled to the customary reward in that area.

20. Mr. Delta and Mr. Echo bought 180 acres of land with undivided interests. Neither partner was a broker, but Mr. Echo agreed to sell the land at a profit. Mr. Delta was so grateful that he decided to allow Mr. Echo to take 65% of the profit and he, Mr. Delta, would take his original investment plus 35% of the profit.

a. Since Mr. Echo sold his land, he does not need to be registered.
b. F.S. 475 has been violated.
c. Mr. Echo had Mr. Delta's consent, so no violation occurred.
d. None of the above.

21. A broker was found to be mentally incompetent and confined to the state asylum for the mentally ill. The Florida Real Estate Commission will:

a. Take no action since he cannot use his certificate in the asylum
b. Suspend his registration
c. Require the broker to show cause why he should not be suspended
d. Revoke the broker's registration

22. When a buyer purchases mortgaged property and takes title with no responsibility for the note, he has purchased:

a. By assumption of the mortgage
b. Subject to the mortgage
c. Utilized a wrap-around mortgage
d. By refinancing

23. Which of the following business relationships cannot be registered as a real estate broker?

a. Corporation for profit
b. Partnership
c. Limited partnership
d. Corporation sole

24. A real estate broker's sales commission is regulated by:

a. Negotiated agreement
b. Local custom and tradition
c. Florida Real Estate Commission
d. Florida Association of REALTORS

25. A securities broker was hired to sell stock in a land development corporation. Later, he bought and sold mineral rights and oil leases for the corporation. He was paid in corporation stock and not in cash. Which is correct?

a. He need not register with FREC.
b. He should register with the SEC.
c. He should register with the Florida Securities Commission.
d. He should register with both "c" above and FREC.

26. A broker paid $600 for a 7-month option on a $6,000 lot. Six months later, the broker finds a buyer ready, willing, and able to pay $9,000 for the lot. The broker can:

a. Be reported for collecting an overage
b. Be suspended for making a secret profit
c. Collect a commission on $9,000 only
d. Compel the owner to sell for $6,000

27. A customer asks a broker about buying a specific house. The broker states that he does not have the house listed but takes the customer to talk with the owner, who refuses to deal through a broker. The next day, the owner sells the house to the customer directly.

a. The broker is due a commission.
b. The broker should sue the owner.
c. The buyer is obligated to pay the broker.
d. The broker is not due a commission.

28. A real estate salesman can legally be paid his earned sales commission by:

a. The seller of the property
b. The buyer of the property
c. His employer
d. Any of the above

29. Title to real property is technically conveyed when the deed is:

a. Recorded in the public records
b. Voluntarily delivered and voluntarily received
c. Signed and witnessed
d. None of the above

30. A couple who answered a broker's classified .. regarding a property for sale are the:

a. Broker's principals
b. Broker's employers
c. Broker's agents
d. Broker's customers

31. A form of joint business relationship which <u>cannot</u> be registered as a real estate broker is a:

a. General partnership
b. Limited partnership
c. Joint venture
d. Sole proprietorship

32. A broker received an offer on a listed property at the seller's price and terms. Before he could inform the seller, he received a higher offer. He submitted the first offer and the seller, his principal, accepted it. The broker:

a. Is guilty of fraud
b. Has done nothing wrong
c. Is guilty of negligence
d. Earned his commission

33. Two brokers arrange the exchange of their principals' properties. Although the properties are of different values, both brokers are to receive 6% sales commissions, and they agree to pool their commissions and divide them equally. No mention of this is made to their principals. Which is correct?

a. The courts will force the principals to pay.
b. The brokers are entitled to the amount of commission a sale would produce.
c. One, but not both, brokers may collect.
d. The brokers have violated 475, Florida Statutes.

34. A sales contract involving real property will usually contain a provision that in case of breach by the buyer, the earnest money deposit will be treated as:

a. Liquidated damages to the seller
b. Unliquidated damages to the broker
c. Liquidated damages to the broker
d. Unliquidated damages in escrow

35. Commissioners of the Florida Real Estate Commission are appointed by the:

a. Governor and confirmed by the Cabinet
b. Governor and confirmed by the Secretary of State
c. Governor and confirmed by the Attorney General
d. Governor

36. Local government exercises its greatest effect on the real estate business by:
a. Creation of tax shelters for those developing low-income housing
b. Use of zoning, taxation, and the planning process
c. Providing financing where justified
d. None of the above

37. The fiduciary relationship between a broker and his principal creates a relationship which is:

a. Not to be disclosed
b. A temporary relationship
c. Based on confidence and trust
d. All of the above

38. To open his own real estate business, a registrant must qualify for and obtain which type of registration certificate?

a. Broker
b. Salesman-broker
c. Non-active broker
d. Any of the above

39. Homestead rights provide which of the following protection?

a. Neither spouse can sell the homestead without the consent of the other.
b. Afford protection against attack by personal creditors of either spouse
c. Protect widows and children against improvidence by the husband/father
d. All of the above.

40. A complete and comprehensive title search would not require:

a. Search of judgment docket
b. Issue of title insurance
c. Investigation of tax records
d. Review of wills

41. Which of the following is not one of the primary general property rights?

a. Disposition
b. Use
c. Exclusion
d. Discrimination

42. A city's legal authority to enact zoning ordinances:

a. Is specifically and explicitly mentioned in the U.S. Constitution
b. Has its origin in constitutional police power
c. Is a right which cannot be denied by the state
d. All of the above

43. Eminent domain is the governmental right to:

a. Restrict the use of property without compensation to the owner
b. Establish tax rates and levy assessments
c. Take property for public purpose in exchange for fair compensation
d. Create zoning and health ordinances

44. What authority originates from the U.S. Constitution and relates to protection of health and welfare of citizens at local levels?

a. Escheat
b. Eminent domain
c. Police power
d. Community protection power

45. Which of the following is not an essential element in a valid contract?

a. Legal objective or purpose
b. Competent parties
c. Grantor (part of deed)
d. Consideration

46. Which of the following is not an essential element in a real estate sales contract?

a. Names of contracting parties
b. Survey of the property
c. Meeting of the minds
d. Mutual consideration

47. The statute of limitations is the authority which outlines the:

a. Requirement for real estate sales contracts to be in writing
b. Essential elements of a contract
c. Remedies available in case of breach
d. Period of time a contract may be enforced

48. The statute of frauds will invariably apply to:

a. Options, listings, and leases
b. The transfer of personal property
c. Instruments of conveyance of real property
d. Legal documents

49. The Florida surtax is calculated on the basis of the:

a. Sales price of the property
b. Amount of the mortgage loan
c. Amount of the new mortgage
d. New money involved in the transaction

50. To qualify as a tenancy by the entireties:

a. Four unities must be established
b. Seven unities must be satisfied
c. Property must be owned by husband and wife
d. The deed must specifically state an intent to create such a tenancy

51. Actual notice is:

a. Not as legal as constructive notice
b. Established by physical possession
c. The act of recording in the public records
d. More practical and convenient than constructive notice

52. Restrictions on private rights of property ownership are divided into two main categories with several different names applied. They are:

a. Public restrictions and private restrictions
b. Government restrictions and deed restrictions
c. Government restrictions and private restrictions
d. All of the above

53. At least one warrant or covenant will always be included in a:

a. Quit-claim deed
b. Chattel deed
c. Bargain-and-sale deed
d. Title insurance deed

54. When compared to actual notice, constructive notice is:

a. More practical for most people
b. Just as legal, no more, no less
c. Provided by recording in the public records
d. All of the above

55. In a deed, the warrant of "quiet enjoyment" pertains to:

a. Peace and tranquility on and around the property
b. Peaceful possession of the property
c. Guaranteed satisfaction with the property
d. Property is completely vacated

56. The vertical area between the principal meridian and the parallel line running north and south at a six-mile distance from the principal meridian is called a:

a. Township
b. Range
c. Tier
d. Check

57. The geographical areas created by the intersections of two parallel range lines and two parallel township lines are called:

a. Ranges
b. Sections
c. Townships
d. Plats

58. One acre contains how many square feet?

a. 42,650
b. 44,620
c. 41,356
d. 43,560

59. In the figure shown, the legal description and amount of acreage in the darkened parcel is:

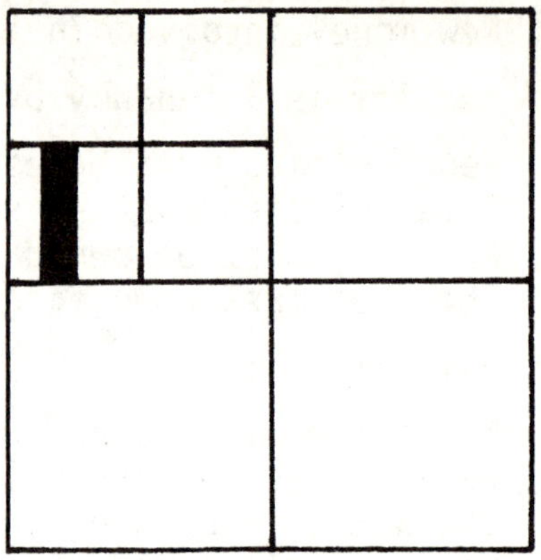

a. W½ of SW¼ of NW¼: 20 acres
b. E½ of W½ of NW¼ of SW¼: 10 acres
c. W½ of E½ of NW¼ of SW¼: 10 acres
d. E½ of W½ of SW¼ of NW¼: 10 acres

60. The government survey method of legal description is:

a. The most accurate method
b. Was used in the 13 original colonies
c. Has as a basis a principal meridian and a base line
d. Used to describe properties of different sized sections and townships

61. The financial institution which is the most important source of single-family mortgage loans is:

a. Life insurance companies
b. Commercial banks
c. Savings and loan associations
d. Mutual savings banks

62. If a buyer obtains a mortgage which covers the purchase of real property, plus a refrigerator, dishwasher, carpets, and drapes, he has a:

a. Blanket mortgage
b. Construction mortgage
c. Equitable mortgage
d. Package mortgage

63. A package mortgage will usually be of greatest benefit to:

a. A just-married couple
b. An elderly, retired couple
c. A middle-aged couple with growing children
d. Empty-nesters

64. A title theory state is a state in which a mortgage will:

a. Transfer title to the lender, until the loan is paid
b. Create an encumbrance on title to a property
c. Create a tenancy in common, until the loan is paid
d. Create a joint tenancy for the lender, until the loan is paid

65. The mortgage broker acts as a middleman between:

a. The borrower and the lender
b. The mortgage banker and the mortgagor
c. The mortgagee and the mortgagor
d. All of the above

66. If you make level monthly payments on an amortized loan, which is most correct?

a. Initially, interest is the smallest portion of the payment.
b. Initially, principal and interest are approximately equal.
c. Initially, interest is the largest portion of the payment.
d. Level monthly payment means the same amount of principal paid each month.

67. In the mortgage money market:

a. Demand always exceeds supply
b. Money is not actually a commodity
c. Interest rates to the lenders usually remain stable
d. The price of money is called interest

68. FHA has agreed to insure a mortgage for $38,000 at 8½% for 30 years. FHA mortgages are at 94. On this mortgage, what will the real yield be to the lender?

a. 8½%
b. 8 3/4%
c. 9¼%
d. 9½%

69. An area designated as a "capital deficit" area is one in which:

a. Economic growth has come to a halt due to lack of funds
b. Savings are plentiful but there is no economic growth
c. Business firms have stopped adding to their capital assets
d. Economic growth is so great that outside financing must be obtained

70. The Property Appraisal Adjustment Board is composed of:

a. 3 county commissioners and 2 school board members
b. 2 county commissioners and 3 school board members
c. 2 county commissioners and 2 school board members
d. None of the above

71. You have a $30,000 mortgage at 8% for 30 years with monthly payments of $220.13. You have paid off approximately 18% of your mortgage at the end of 10 years. How much interest have you paid during the 10-year period?

a. $17,316.40
b. $21,015.60
c. $24,000.00
d. $14,647.95

72. A farmer who feels that his farm has been assessed excessively high for tax purposes should first:

a. Seek the advice and assistance of the Florida Farm Bureau
b. Appeal to the county property appraiser
c. Appeal to the Property Appraisal Adjustment Board
d. Appeal to the county tax collector

73. The tax which produces the major portion of local government revenue in Florida is the:

a. Sales tax
b. Gasoline tax
c. Excise tax
d. Property tax

74. Normally, hazard insurance on real property is:

a. Paid in advance
b. Paid in arrears
c. Not involved in closing costs
d. Paid as the service is provided

75. Florida Statute 475 requires a registered broker to:

a. Maintain a sign at or near his office
b. Refrain from locating his office in the proximity of a doctor's office
c. Keep records of his real estate transactions
d. All of the above

76. A property listing available to all interested real estate brokers is:

a. A general listing
b. An open listing
c. A standing listing
d. An exclusive listing

77. In real estate transactions involving licensed real estate registrants, consumers' interests are protected best by:

a. The Code of Ethics
b. State statutes called statute of fraud and statute of limitations
c. State licensing laws
d. Professional and ethical standards of real estate organizations

78. Residential zoning is intended to regulate:

a. Intensity of use
b. Intensity of traffic
c. Density of traffic
d. Density of units /# of units per acrea

79. A planning commission is <u>not</u> normally responsible for:

a. Computation of the property tax rate
b. Sign control
c. Site plan control
d. Environment and ecology protection

80. The purpose of Florida's Green Belt Laws is to:

a. Ensure that green areas are incorporated into city planning
b. Protect remaining natural areas around towns and cities
c. Protect natural wildlife areas
d. Protect farmers' interests

81. You have been hired to appraise the local public library building. The approach to value most appropriate would be the:

a. Market comparison approach
b. Cost approach
c. Public land approach
d. Income approach

82. The income approach to value does <u>not</u> include:

a. Reproduction value of the building
b. Vacancy and collection losses
c. Estimated gross income
d. Capitalized net income

83. Real estate appraisers are primarily concerned with:

a. Highest and best use
b. Comparison with other properties
c. Real estate market trends
d. Market value

84. A property has been appraised at $27,800. Two separate lenders have established an 85/15 loan-to-value ratio for the property. What will the amount of the down payment be using the 85/15 loan-to-value ratio?

a. $2,780
b. $4,170
c. $ 1,030
d. $23,630

85. The cost approach to value includes:

a. The estimate of potential gross income
b. The estimate of property expenses
c. The estimate of reproduction cost
d. All of the above

86. A secondary market is one in which:

    a. Commodities are originated for sale
    b. Other than basic necessities are sold for the first time
    c. Independent brokers only may exchange goods
    d. Items originated elsewhere are for sale

87. When a registrant is involved in "qualifying the buyer," the salesperson:

    a. Checks on the credit rating of the buyer
    b. Finds out what the buyer can afford and what the buyer wants
    c. Determines how long the buyer worked in his previous job(s)
    d. None of the above

88. You have sold a house under the following conditions:

Sales price:	$56,000	Second mortgage:	$ 9,500
Cash paid:	$14,500	Existing mortgage:	$32,000

    The Florida surtax will be:

    a. $168.00 c. $61.60
    b. $ 50.60 d. $26.40

89. What would the total required tax stamps cost for a deed conveying a $47,500 tract which sold with $10,000 cash down, a second mortgage of $15,500, and an assumed mortgage of $22,000?

    a. $167.50 c. $174.25
    b. $170.55 d. $142.50

90. You have a level-payment plan, amortized mortgage of $32,000 at 8½% for 30 years. The monthly payment is $245.06. What amount of interest will be paid from the second monthly payment?

    a. $116.66 c. $225.18
    b. $226.54 d. $174.36

91. Your principal owns a home which has been appraised at $52,500. He still owes $32,760 on the first mortgage, and $4,200 on a second mortgage. Your sales commission will be $3,640. What is your principal's equity in the home?

    a. $13,589 c. $11,900
    b. $19,740 d. $15,540

92. The city has decided to pave the streets of a recently incorporated community. Property owners will be assessed 70% of the cost of paving which is found to be $25 per running foot. The 70% assessment tax will be apportioned between owners on both sides of the streets. What will the special assessment costs be for a property with 80 feet of frontage?

    a. $1,400 c. $700
    b. $2,000 d. $350

93. You plan to buy a house with FHA financing. FHA mortgages are at 94. The house has been appraised at $42,000, and the FHA interest rate is 8½%. What amount will the seller pay as a discount for the loan?

    a. $2,280
    b. $2,424
    c. $1,426
    d. $2,139

94. In order to obtain a $39,000 mortgage loan, a buyer has agreed to pay all State taxes incurred by creation of the new loan. What will his total tax costs be?

a. $136.50
b. $ 78.00
c. $ 58.50
d. $117.00

95. A property has been assessed at $40,000. The city tax rate is 10 mills, the county tax rate is 9 mills, and the school board tax rate is 8 mills. The owner has qualified for and received regular homestead exemption. How much will the owner save from his county taxes as a result of homestead exemption?

a. $135
b. $ 45
c. $50
d. $40

96. The city of Funshine, Florida estimates that the total expenditures for the next year will amount to $12,000,000. A total of $3,000,000 is anticipated from non-property tax sources. The total assessed valuation of all taxable property in the city amounts to $930,000,000. Records indicate that 6,000 properties have qualified for and been granted regular homestead exemptions. What will the city tax rate be if it is based solely on the data provided above?

a. 10 mills
b. 1 mill
c. 100 mills
d. 9.6 mills

97. The Florida real estate license law exists:

a. To protect the registrant from the public
b. To protect the public from the registrant and to regulate the activities of all persons engaged in the real estate business
c. To punish owners who fail to pay a commission earned by a registered real estate broker
d. To regulate those engaged in the real estate profession and to protect the public

98. The Governor of Florida appoints (circle the <u>incorrect</u> answer):

a. One new commissioner each year
b. Commissioners to a three-year term of office
c. Commissioners who have been active real estate brokers in Florida for five years
d. Commissioners who elect, among themselves, a chairman and a vice-chairman

C

99. A corporation for profit doing business as a real estate broker must (circle the <u>incorrect</u> answer):

a. File a charter with the Secretary of State
b. Have one officer who is an active real estate broker
c. Register with the Commission as a broker
d. Register all stockholders as non-active brokers with the Commission

100. A salesman accepts employment with a broker at 45% of sales commissions earned as a result of his sales efforts. The broker lists a property for $48,000, with a 7% sales commission agreed to by the owner. The salesman sells the property at the listed sales price. What is the broker's share of the commission?

a. $1,512
b. $3,360
c. $1,848
d. $1,884

101. A prospect is legally entitled to rely on any statement made by a broker regarding the:

a. Amount of last year's taxes
b. Size of the closets
c. Location of schools
d. Type of insulation in the walls

102. In Florida, a female over 18 years of age is legally:

a. An adult
b. An adulteress
c. Competent to sign contracts
d. Only "a" and "c" above

103. The 1968 Fair Housing Law prohibits discrimination based on:

a. Race only
b. Race, religion, and national origin
c. Race, color, religion, sex, or national origin
d. All of the above

104. The Civil Rights Act of 1866 prohibits discrimination in housing based on:

a. Race only
b. Race, religion, and national origin
c. Race, color, religion, sex, or national origin
d. All of the above

105. What is the required FHA down payment for a house appraised at $43,500?

a. $4,350
b. $5,340
c. $3,450
d. $2,750

106. A salesman who accepts a real estate commission from someone other than his employer, without his employer's consent, can be:

a. Fined
b. Imprisoned
c. Suspended
d. All of the above

107. The term "real estate" or "real property" includes:

a. Land and improvements
b. Leaseholds
c. Subleaseholds
d. All of the above

108. All final orders of FREC, revoking or suspending registration of a broker, become effective:

a. When the time for filing an appeal has expired
b. When entered into FREC records
c. On the date stated in the final order

109. A final order of the Commission:

a. Cannot be appealed
b. Can be appealed to the District Court of Appeals
c. Can be appealed to the Circuit Court of Appeals
d. Can be appealed to the County Court of Appeals

110. A corporation for profit is normally managed by:

a. Directors of the corporation acting through the executive officers
b. Stockholders of the corporation acting through the directors
c. Executive officers acting through the directors
d. Member stockholders acting through the executive officers

111. When partnerships register with FREC as real estate brokers, the registration is issued in the name of:

a. The individual partners
b. The partnership
c. The active broker whose license is the basis for registration
d. All of the above

112. The first Florida real estate licensing law was enacted in:

a. 1913
b. 1919
c. 1923
d. 1925

113. The executive powers and duties of the Commission include:

a. Conducting hearings
b. Publishing rules and regulations
c. Granting of registration
d. All of the above

114. In the exercise of its quasi-judicial power, FREC is empowered by law to:

a. Levy fines up to, but not more than, $500
b. Impose prison sentences up to 60 days
c. Assess damages resulting from breach of contract suits
d. None of the above

115. If a principal refuses to pay a broker his sales commission after the property is sold, the broker may:

a. File a mechanic's lien on the owner's property
b. File a suit in the courts for his commission
c. Refuse to permit the closing to occur
d. All of the above

116. An exception to the normal maximum administrative and criminal penalties authorized by F.S. 475 is:

a. Filing a false affidavit for the purpose of acquiring registration
b. Filing a false affidavit to place a lien on property
c. Filing a false affidavit to disqualify a commissioner
d. All of the above

117. After a sales contract has been signed by both buyer and seller, but before the date of closing, the contract is a/an:

a. Bilateral contract
b. Expressed contract
c. Executory contract
d. All of the above

118. It is important that a buyer's wife join her husband in executing a sales contract because:

a. This indicates a willingness to convey her ownership rights
b. It will help to avoid difficulties at closing
c. It indicates her agreement to the price and terms
d. "a" and "b" above
e. "b" and "c" above

119. If you have located a township numbered T1N, R1E, the township due north of that township is:

a. T1N, R2E
b. T1S, R1E
c. T2N, R1E
d. T2N, R2E

120. In Florida, real property is assessed on January 1 of each year and becomes a lien on the property on:

a. November 1, the same year
b. April 1, the next year
c. January 1, the same year
d. December 31, the same year

121. Closing date for a property sale is June 14. The annual insurance premium is $157 with May 22 as its anniversary date. The seller has paid the annual premium in advance. What will be owed by the buyer at closing if computed by the 365-day method?

a. $ 11.70
b. $147.06
c. $ 10.32
d. $148.40

122. A broker should not accept the task of appraising a parcel if:

a. He has no financial interest in the property
b. The appraisal report is to be in a form report
c. He has sold the property before
d. His fee will be contingent on the appraised value

123. A broker may be awarded the designation of Certified Property Manager by the:

a. Institute of Real Estate Management
b. Local Board of REALTORS
c. Building Owners and Managers Association
d. National Association of REALTORS

124. The State statute requiring that all conveyances of real estate must be in writing to be valid is the:

a. Statute of limitations
b. Statute of frauds
c. Statute of descent
d. Statute of validity

125. Mr. Zebra is a registered real estate broker and an experienced appraiser. He has a prospect who is interested in investing in income property. Mr. Zebra finds a property which is producing a net income of $21,000 per year. The prospect informs Mr. Zebra that he will buy the property if he can get it for a price which will return him 14% per year on his investment. If the desired 14% rate of return is regarded as a 14% capitalization rate, what will Mr. Zebra's prospect be willing to pay for the property?

a. $150,000
b. $148,000
c. $ 15,000
d. $ 14,800

112 abandonment: a surrender of rights; point when a broker makes no effort to service or sell listed property; failure to perform.

66 able (as in "ready, willing, and able"): financial ability to produce the money required to purchase a property. (see Ready)

85,282 abstract of title: condensed history of title to property consisting of a summary of the links in the chain of title extracted from documents bearing on the title status.

159 acceleration clause: stipulation in a mortgage that the entire unpaid balance of the debt may become due and payable if a default of expressed conditions should occur.

108 acceptance: voluntary receipt of an item offered by another.

115 acknowledgment: certification of a document by a notary public; formal declaration of an act before a competent official.

85 actual notice: informing any interested party of a right, title, or interest in property by possession of the property.

22 administrative complaint: written summary of charges against either an applicant for registration or a registrant. (formerly called an "information")

96 administrator's deed: a deed signed by a court-appointed "personal representative" to act for a deceased owner.

217 ad valorem: according to value; in proportion to worth.

56 advance fee: collection of a fee prior to a transaction actually closing or prior to the performance of a service.

60 adverse interest: a purpose in opposition to the interest of another party (as, for example, with a buyer and a seller).

83 adverse possession: a method of obtaining title to real property by occupying it in an open and hostile manner contrary to the interests of the owner.

58 advisory opinion: a course of action for determining the disposition of a contested deposit.

2,59 agency: express or implied authorization for one person to act for another; one of the divisions of the real estate business.

76 allodial system: a theory of ownership of land which states that individuals may own land free of the rights of an overlord.

166,274 amortization: payment of a debt by regular, installment payments.

22 answer: a defendant's reply to an administrative complaint giving his view of the facts.

8,138 appraisal: an estimation of property value by a competent person.

222 assessed value: worth established by county property appraiser for each unit of real property.

114 assignee: person to whom a right or interest is transferred.

99,114 assignment: written instrument which serves to transfer the rights or interests of one person to another.

114 assignor: person who gives his legal rights or interests to another person.

170 assumption of mortgage: the taking over of an existing mortgage by a buyer.

103 attachment: a legal writ obtained to prevent removal of property which is expected to be used to satisfy a judgment.

115 attorney, power of: designation of another person to act in and for a principal as though he were present.

38,46 BAR SALE: term used as a memory device for the seven services of real estate.

128 base line: in land description, a line running in an east/west direction and separating the various townships (tiers).

110 bilateral contract: an agreement wherein both parties are legally obligated to each other to perform.

57 bill of interpleader: a course of action when two contesting parties cannot reach an arbitrated agreement.

56 binder: a memorandum given subject to the writing of a formal contract for sale, usually acknowledging receipt of a portion of the down payment for purchase of real property.

55 blind ad: an advertisement providing only a telephone number, a post office box, or an address with no other identification.

30 bona fide: without deceit or fraud; genuine; in good faith.

40,54 branch office: a business location other than the principal place of business for a real estate broker's office.

112 breach: failure to do or perform what has been promised.

building code: a local government ordinance regulating construction practices and materials.

149 capitalization rate: the relationship between the net income from a real estate investment and the present value.

17,60 Caveat emptor: "Let the buyer beware!"

23,220 certiorari, writ of: an order to bring from a lower court to an appellate court an action or record of proceedings in a case.

78 chattel: any item of personal property.

128 check: a square measuring 24 miles on each side and representing the largest unit of measure in the government survey system.

93 clause: a distinct provision in a written document.

269,279 closing: final settlement between buyer and seller; the date on which title passes from seller to buyer.

86 cloud on title: any defect, valid claim, or encumbrance which serves to impair the title or curtail an owner's rights.

collateral: real or personal property pledged as security on a debt.

collusion: two or more parties jointly attempting to defraud a third party.

272,282 commission: compensation paid to a broker or salesman for successfully concluding a transaction.

17-26 Commission: short form for Florida Real Estate Commission (FREC).

common law: unwritten law which developed from customs, tradition, and related court decisions.

82 community property: real property acquired during a marriage.

210 condominium: a multi-unit project consisting of individual ownership of a dwelling unit and partial ownership of common areas.

108,118 consideration: an inducement offered to conclude a contract.

85 constructive notice: the recording of a document or instrument in the public records designed to give adequate notice to all.

140,271 Consumer Price Index (CPI): a measurement of average price changes of goods and services using a base year (also called the "cost-of-living index").

107 contract: an agreement between two or more competent parties to do, or not do, some legal act for a legal consideration.

161,166 conventional loan (mortgage): real estate loan granted which is neither FHA insured nor VA guaranteed.

48 conversion: unauthorized use or retention of money or property which rightfully belongs to another person.

92,97 conveyance: written instrument which serves to transfer an interest in real property from one party to another.

41 cooperative association: an organization owned collectively by members who share the profits and losses.

41 corporation: an artificial or fictitious person formed to conduct specified types of business activities.

41 corporation not for profit: an artificial or fictitious person organized for purposes other than conduct of commercial affairs.

41 corporation sole: an artificial or fictitious person formed by an ecclesiastical body.

10 counseling: one of the component activities of the agency division of the real estate business.

court of equity (court of chancery): a court in which suits based on fair and just collateral rights may be brought, as distinguished from a common-law court.

92 covenant: a warranty, guarantee, or promise formally given in a legal document.

292 credit: an entry or balance on the right side of an account. As a verb, to make an entry on the right or credit side of an account. As a noun, positive information reflecting an increased allowance of money, and entered under the credit heading of a statement.

49 culpable negligence: inadequate attention to duties and obligations by one who knows, or should know, what is required of him.

81 curtesy: the interest a husband acquires in his wife's property by operation of the law (see Elective share).

64 customer: one with whom the broker or salesman hopes to be successful in accomplishing the purpose of employment; a prospect.

112 damages: losses incurred as a result of a breach of contract or some other cause. (see also Liquidated and Unliquidated damages)

292 debit: an entry or balance on the left side of an account. As a verb, to make an entry on the left or charge side of an account which reflects the amount of decrease in assets to be recorded. As a noun, positive information reflecting a decrease in money, and entered under the debit heading or column of a statement.

101 decedent: a deceased person, usually used to refer to one who has recently died.

45 declaration of trust: a formal instrument filed by a business trust with the Dept. of State as a prerequisite for creating the trust.

57,112 declaratory judgment: a course of action declaring rights claimed under a contract or statute intended to prevent loss or guide performance by the party or parties affected.

83,92 deed: a type of conveyance; a written instrument to transfer title to real property from one party to another.

default: failure to comply with the terms of an agreement or to meet an obligation when due.

159 defeasance clause: a provision in a mortgage which specifies the terms and conditions to be met in order to avoid default and thereby defeat the mortgage.

86 defect: an imperfection or deficiency; a flaw in a title to real property. (see also Cloud on title)

defendant: the accused person at a trial or hearing.

170 deficiency decree: judgment brought when a mortgage is foreclosed and the foreclosure sale does not produce enough money to pay completely the costs of the sale, taxes, and the unpaid balance of the mortgage.

142,207 demand (principle of demand and supply): the quantity of goods or services wanted by consumers.

245 density: the number of homes or lots per acre.

260 deposit: earnest money or some other valuable consideration given as evidence of good faith to accompany an offer to purchase or rent. (see also Binder and Earnest money)

25 deposition: written testimony of a witness under oath.

147,205 depreciation: a loss of value usually related to age of the item.

83 devise: a gift of real property by a will.

83 devisee: one who receives real property under a will.

190 discounting: a practice designed to make FHA and VA mortgages competitive with conventional mortgages. (see also Point, discount)

185 disintermediation: a disengagement process when depositors withdraw money from savings accounts for direct investment in stocks, bonds, and other securities.

document: any written paper which provides information or evidence.

documentary stamps: (see State documentary stamps)

domicile: the place where one establishes his legal residence or permanent home.

81 dower: an interest in real property granted a wife by operation of the law as a result of her marriage to an owner of real property (see Elective share).

down payment: a portion of a purchase price paid prior to closing the transaction. Earnest money (binder deposit) may be a part of the down payment, or the entire down payment may be considered earnest money.

56 earnest money: a sum which, if a contract is executed, is applied against the down payment, or part of a down payment. (see also Binder and Deposit)

99 easement: a right, privilege, or interest in real property which one individual has in lands belonging to another; a legal right to trespass; rights of way authorizing access to or over land.

148 economic life: the period of time a property may be expected to be profitable or productive.

81 elective share: an estate defined as consisting of 30 percent of the decedent's personal property and Florida real property, except homestead-exempt property and claims.

87 eminent domain: the constitutional right given a unit of government to take private property involuntarily if taken for public use and a fair price paid to the owner.

encroachment: unauthorized use of another person's property.

encumbrance: any lien, claim, or liability affecting the title or attaching to real property.

94 encumbrance clause: a provision in a deed to real property which warrants that no liens, claims, or liabilities exist on the property being conveyed, except as specified.

equity: the interest or value an owner has in property over and above all mortgages against the property; a system of legal rules administered by a court of chancery (see also Court of equity).

88 escheat: reversion of property to a sovereign state when an owner dies without leaving a will or any known heirs.

56 escrow account: an account in a bank, title company, or trust company having trust powers, which may not be used for deposit of personal funds by any person (see Trust account).

56 escrow agent: trustee; a disinterested party appointed by two or more interested parties to hold and account for funds, papers, documents, or property until a transaction is concluded.

77 estate: tenancy; the interest one holds in real property; the total of one's property and possessions.

79 estate by the entireties: a tenancy created by husband and wife jointly owning real property with instant and complete right of survivorship.

78 estate for life (life estate): a tenancy with a duration limited to the life of some person whose lifetime is used to measure the estate.

78 estate for years: a tenancy measured from a starting date to a termination date (may be for a few days or longer than any natural life, e.g., a leasehold is an estate for years).

77 estate in fee (fee simple, fee simple absolute): the most comprehensive and complete interest one can hold in real property.

estate in sole: real property owned by a corporation sole.

78 estate, joint: an interest or tenancy owned by more than one person, each having equal rights to possession and enjoyment; the interest a deceased tenant conveys to surviving tenants by specific wording in the deed establishing the joint estate.

78 estate of freehold: an estate for the life of the owner, or an estate which can be inherited by the heirs of an owner.

78 estate of remainder: an estate which can only become effective after another estate has terminated.

estate of reversion: an estate which comes back to the original estate.

83 estoppel: a principle of law which prohibits (stops) a person from defending himself against his own acts, or his lack of required action.

17 ethics: the moral obligations and duties which a member of a profession or craft owes to the public, to a client, or to other members of the profession or craft.

23 examiner: a person appointed by the Commission, or its chairman, to conduct hearings, administer oaths, receive evidence, and transcribe complete reports regarding denial, suspension, or revocation proceedings.

116 exclusive agency: a listing given to one real estate broker as the sole agent for sale of an owner's property.

116 exclusive right to sell: a listing given to one real estate broker as the sole agent for sale of an owner's property, with the commission going to the broker regardless of who sells the property during the listing contract period.

83 executor (executrix): a "personal representative" designated in a will to carry out the provisions of the will.

110 executory contract: an agreement containing some act or condition which remains to be completed.

82,222 exempt property: a right to property which has been decreed to be excluded from taxation or claim by others.

FHA: (see Federal Housing Administration)
FHLMC: (see Federal Home Loan Mortgage Corporation)
FNMA: (see Federal National Mortgage Association)
FREC: (see Commission)

201 factor market: a resource pool representing the four major elements (factors) of production which are bought and sold.

178 Federal Home Loan Mortgage Corporation (FHLMC)("Freddie Mac"): a secondary mortgage market institution authorized to buy and sell conventional, FHA, and VA loans.

161,255 Federal Housing Administration (FHA): insures mortgage loans made by FHA-approved lenders on homes which meet FHA standards in order to make mortgages more desirable investments for lenders.

177,255 Federal National Mortgage Association (FNMA)("Fannie Mae"): a private institution in the secondary mortgage market which buys and sells mortgages.

189 Federal Reserve System ("the Fed"): a central banking authority which works closely with the U.S. President and Treasury to influence the cost, availability, and supply of money.

59 fiduciary relationship: an alliance of trust and confidence which creates a moral and a legal obligation when extended by one person and accepted by another.

final order: the written form of a decision rendered by FREC.

74,168 fixture: object which was once considered to be personal property but which has become real property because of attachment to, or use in, an improvement to real property.

Florida Land Sales and Condominiums, Division of: a division of the Florida Department of Business Regulation, created to implement the Florida Land Sales Act and to provide reasonable protection for all who might desire to invest or live in Florida.

Florida Real Estate Commission: (see Commission)

259 Florida Residential Landlord and Tenant Act: legislation to place a landlord and tenant on an equitable basis in their legal relationship.

157 foreclosure: a court process to transfer title to real property used as security for a debt as a means of paying the debt by involuntary sale of the property.

109 formal contract: any agreement which contains all the essentials of a contract, in writing, and under seal.

fraud: any deception, or intent to deceive, for the purpose of acquiring an unfair advantage of another party.

78 freeholder: one who owns an interest in real property which may be measured by the life of the owner, or which can be sold, conveyed, or inherited. (see also Estate of freehold)

95 further assurance: a provision in a deed containing a covenant or warranty to perform any further acts which the grantee (buyer) might require to perfect title to the property.

GNMA: (see Government National Mortgage Association)

177,235 Government National Mortgage Association (GNMA)("Ginnie Mae"): a federal government corporation designed to handle special assistance functions for certain loans and securities.

125,128 government land survey system (rectangular method): a type of land description, developed by the federal government for subdividing lands utilizing surveying lines.

92 grantee: party who receives a deed or grant; buyer.

93 granting clause (premises clause): the provision in a deed which specifies the names of the parties involved, the words of conveyance, and a description of the property.

92 grantor: party who signs and gives a deed; seller.

225 Green Belt Law, Florida: legislation which authorizes county property appraisers to assess land used for agricultural purposes to be assessed according to its value as agricultural land.

94 habendum clause: provision in a deed to real property which stipulates the estate or interest the grantee is to receive and the type of title conveyed.

202 highest and best use: a principle of value which focuses on the most profitable likely use to which a property can be put.

80,223 homestead: term used to describe three separate but related situations: (1) a statutory condition designed to protect the interests of a widow and lineal descendants; (2) a tract of land limited in size; and, (3) a tax exemption.

207 household: an occupied dwelling unit (may consist of a family or bachelors, divorced persons, widows, etc.).

39,40 ineffectual (ineffective): status of a certificate while registration is suspended.

information: (see Administrative complaint)

25 injunction: a writ or order by a court forbidding a party from doing something.

instrument: any legal or formal writing, such as a will, option, lease, contract, or deed.

159 insurance clause: a provision in a mortgage which requires the mortgagor to obtain and keep current a hazard insurance policy.

281 intangible tax, State (on mortgages): tax on new mortgages charged at the rate of two mills (.002) per dollar of face value.

246 intensity: the concentration of activity (pedestrian and vehicular traffic) used as the means for designating land for commercial zones.

189 interest: the price paid for the use of borrowed money.

56 intermingle: failure to place earnest money in a separate trust account, or actually mixing together (co-mingling) money or a deposit with personal funds.

interpleader, bill of: (see Bill of interpleader)

83 intestate: without a will.

41 joint adventure (joint venture): two or more parties in an arrangement confined to only one or a limited number of business deals.

41 joint business relationship: two or more parties joined together for business purposes (9 such recognized in Florida).

joint estate: (see Estate, joint)

judgment: decree of a court which not only declares that one party owes another party a debt but also fixes the amount of the debt.

218 just value: the fair market value.

236 laissez faire: allow to act; noninterference by government in trade, industry, and individual action generally.

land contract: an agreement for the sale of real property on an installment plan.

125 land description (legal description, legal): a definite and positive written identification of a specific parcel of land and its location without additional oral testimony.

99 lease: an estate for years; an agreement which does not convey ownership but does convey possession and use for a period of time and for compensation.

leasehold: an estate in real property held under a lease arrangement.

99 lessee: a tenant or leaseholder; party to whom a lease is given.

99 lessor: the landlord or owner; party who grants a lease to another.

167,274 level-payment plan: a method for amortizing a mortgage whereby the borrower pays the same amount each month.

29,37,39 license: in Florida, the proper name for a real estate license is a "registration certificate." Denotes a privilege or right granted by the State to operate as a real estate broker, broker-salesman, or salesman.

100,283 lien: a claim on property for payment of some obligation or debt.

156,158 lien theory: a legal concept which regards a mortgage as a just claim on specific property pledged as security for the mortgage debt.

57,112 liquidated damages: the amount of valuable consideration specified in an agreement as a penalty for default. (see also Damages)

114 listing: an oral or written employment agreement between a broker (or a salesman employed by a broker) and the owner of real property; authorization to sell, rent, or exchange.

187 loan correspondent: generally a mortgage banker or company which provides services for lending institutions.

156,166, 180 loan-to-value ratio: the proportion of a mortgage loan on property to the value of the property (usually expressed as a percentage).

125,134 lot and block numbers: a type of legal description of land.

31 major: a person who has attained adulthood; majority (18 in Fla.).

24 mandamus, writ of: an order of a superior court directing a lower court or body to do some specified act.

83,120 marketable title (merchantable title): rights to real property which are so reasonably clear that a buyer may have peaceful and quiet enjoyment of the property free of litigation.

138 market value: the estimated highest price a property will bring from a fully informed buyer, willing but not compelled to buy, and the lowest price a fully informed seller will accept if not compelled to sell.

157 Master in Chancery: an appointed representative of a court, such as a sheriff, used to auction foreclosed property.

102 mechanic's lien (materialman's lien): a type of claim based on the principle of "unjust enrichment." It exists in favor of parties who have performed labor or delivered material or supplies for the repair or construction of an improvement on real property.

meeting of the minds: point when two people thinking of the same thing reach an agreement through an offer and acceptance.

83,120 merchantable title: (see Marketable title)

meridian: any of the lines of longitude on the earth's surface; in land description, the vertical lines running in a north/south direction parallel to the principal or prime meridian and separating the various ranges. (see also Principal meridian)

125 metes and bounds: a type of land description ("metes" means distance; "bounds" means direction or boundaries).

226 mill: a unit of money used to specify a property tax note ($1 for each $1,000 of assessed value).

226 millage: a tax rate, expressed as number of mills to be applied.

134 monuments: a type of land description using physical features of the land.

49 moral turpitude: an act of corruption, vileness, or moral depravity; a disgraceful action or deed.

9,156,175 mortgage: a written agreement which pledges property as security for payment of a debt.

9,176 mortgage banker: one who makes mortgage loans with the expectation of reselling them to an institutional lender.

9,176 mortgage broker: one who finds a mortgage lender for a potential borrower, and vice versa.

101,157 mortgagee: a lender who holds a mortgage on specific property as security for the money he has loaned to a borrower (mortgagor).

101,157 mortgagor: a borrower who gives a mortgage on his property to obtain a loan from a lender (mortgagee).

23 motion to quash: a formal proposal filed by a defendant along with his answer to an administrative complaint.

Multiple Listing Service (MLS): an arrangement among members of a real estate board or exchange which allows each member broker to share his listings with other members so that greater exposure is obtained and greater chance of sale will result.

17 NAREB: abbreviation for National Association of Real Estate Boards; now named National Association of REALTORS.

12,13,17 National Association of REALTORS: (formerly the National Association of Real Estate Boards); only broker members of a local board affiliated with the Association are authorized to call themselves "REALTORS." Salesman members are REALTOR-ASSOCIATES.

116 net listing: an agreement or contract to sell or rent a property for a specified minimum net amount for the owner (the broker must add his commission and expenses to the owner's specified minimum in order to arrive at a purchase price).

248 nonconforming use: continuing land use which is not in compliance with zoning ordinances.

157 note: the legal evidence of a debt which must accompany a mortgage in Florida; a legally executed pledge by the borrower to pay a stipulated sum of money.

notice: (see Actual and Constructive notice)

obligee: a lender or mortgagee.

obligor: a borrower or mortgagor.

111 offeree: one who receives an offer, usually the seller.

111 offeror: one who makes an offer, usually the buyer.

65 opinion of title: a formal statement by an attorney regarding the status of a title after examination of the chain of title.

118 option: a right or privilege to purchase or lease real property at a specified price during a designated period based on a sufficient consideration.

110,120 optionee: the party who takes an option and pays a consideration.

110,120 optionor: the party who gives an option and receives a consideration.

193 origination fee, loan: a charge by a lender for taking a mortgage.

43 ostensible partnership: one or more parties cause a third party to be deceived into believing a partnership exists when no such arrangement does exist.

63,67 overage (secret profit): retaining more than the agreed amount, or more than the customary sales commission, without the express knowledge and consent of the parties involved; a form of fraud.

141 overimprovement: an addition or change to property not in line with its highest and best use, or a betterment which exceeds that justified by local conditions.

156,168 package mortgage: (see Mortgage)

109 parol contract: an agreement which is not under seal.

41 partnership: two or more competent individuals each of whom contracts or agrees to be responsible for the actions of other partners and to share in the profits of the venture.

160 penalty clause: a provision in a mortgage which requires the borrower to pay a penalty in the form of money if the mortgage payments are made in advance of the normal due date, or if the mortgage is paid in full ahead of schedule.

19 per diem: by the day; an allowance of a specific amount for each day.

112,117 performance: point when a party or parties to a contract fulfill the promises or obligations in the contract.

74 personalty: personal property; chattel or moveable property; any property which is not real property.

plaintiff: the person or party bringing suit or charges of violation against another in a court or semi-judicial body; the complaining party.

235 planning: devising ways and means for achieving desired goals.

134,249 plat (plat map): a plan of a tract of land subdivided into lots and showing required or planned amenities.

190 point, mortgage: a charge of one percent of the mortgage value; assessment by a lender to increase the interest yield from the mortgage loan to a position competitive with the interest yield from other types of investments; the difference between the current actual interest rates and the maximum interest rates allowed by the FHA and VA (paid by the seller of a home when the buyer secures an FHA or VA mortgage).

87,245 police powers: the authority of government to protect the property, life, health, and welfare of its citizens.

power of attorney: (see Attorney, power of)

159 prepayment clause: a provision in a mortgage which allows the mortgagor to pay the mortgage debt ahead of schedule without penalty.

prescription: a method of acquiring an interest in real property through long and continued use.

29 prima facie evidence: at first view; requiring no further proof; acceptable by the face of; a presumption of fact unless overruled by some other evidence.

prime meridian: (see also Meridian and Principal meridian)

59,120 principal: the party employing the services of a real estate broker; amount of money borrowed in a mortgage loan, excluding interest and other charges.

128 principal meridian: a line designated by the U.S. Land Office as the primary reference line for a specific geographical area; principal or prime meridians are named to indicate the point of intersection with the base line designated for the same area.

probate: the process of proving or authenticating a will.

67,117 procuring cause: the person whose efforts were the cause of an executed sales contract, regardless of who actually writes the contract.

157 promissory note: a written promise to pay a specific amount to a lender. (see also Note)

73 property: a bundle of legal rights.

7 property management: one of the component activities of the agency division of the real estate business.

276 prorate: to divide or assess proportionate shares of charges and credits between the buyer and seller according to their individual period of ownership.

64 prospect: the customer with whom a broker or salesman hopes to be successful in accomplishing the purpose of employment.

102,168 purchase money mortgage (purchase money): any new mortgage given as part of the purchase price of real property.

quash: to annul; set aside. (see also Motion to quash)

quasi: as if; of a similar nature; seemingly.

95 quiet enjoyment: a warrant in a deed guaranteeing that the buyer may enjoy possession of the property in peace and without disturbance by reason of other claims on the title by the seller or anyone else.

93 quit-claim deed: a type of deed which will effectively convey any present interest, claim, or title to real property which the seller (grantor) may own (mostly used to clear title defects and to give property to deserving recipients).

257,269 RESPA: Real Estate Settlement Procedures Act.

130 range: in the government survey system of land description, any vertical strip of land six miles wide located between two consecutive sub-meridians or range lines.

130 range line: a sub-meridian which encloses a six-mile wide vertical column of property (the areas enclosed between the meridians are ranges).

66 ready (as in "ready, willing, and able"): indicates that the prospect is in a position and of a mind to complete the transaction; "willing" implies that the prospect desires to do so at the price and terms agreed; and, "able" refers to the prospect's financial ability to produce the required sum of money when necessary.

73 real estate: land, including the air above and the earth below, plus any permanent improvements affecting the utility of the land, and every interest in ownership of real property; real property; any property which is not personal property.

8,138 real estate appraiser: one who has the expertise to determine value and recommend use of real property for others, for compensation.

real estate business: a commercial activity in which the sale, purchase, leasing, rental, exchange, or management of real property is conducted by qualified and registered parties either acting for themselves or for others for compensation.

real estate profession: actually, still a semiprofession requiring knowledge of real estate values, experience in dealing with the public, plus exceptional personal integrity and character as qualifications to act as advisors and agents for members of the public.

73 real property: land, including the air above and the earth below, with all the permanent structures and improvements to the land. (synonymous with real estate and realty -- see Real estate)

13,59 REALTOR: a real estate broker who is a member of a local board of REALTORS which is affiliated with the state association and the National Association of REALTORS. (not synonymous with the term real estate agent)

74 realty: a synonym for real estate and real property.

reasonable time: a variable period of time which may be affected by: market conditions, desires of the owner, supply and demand, fluctuation of values, discovery of mineral or petroleum deposits, etc.

160 receivership clause: a provision in a mortgage, related to property which is income-producing, which is designed to require that income derived shall be used to make mortgage payments in the event the mortgagor defaults.

recording: to place any document or instrument affecting title or an interest in real property in the public records of the county wherein the property is located.

rectangular method: (see Government survey system)

94 reddendum clause (reserving clause): a provision in a deed used to reserve some right or restriction for the grantor (seller).

161 redemption: to repurchase, to buy back, to recover property which is used as security for a mortgage by paying the debt.

29 registrant: an individual who has qualified for, and been registered with, the Florida Real Estate Commission as a broker, broker-salesman, or salesman (a registrant may or may not be qualified to receive a registration certificate).

29 registration: authorization by the Florida Real Estate Commission to place an applicant's name, business address, and in the case of a salesman, the name and business address of an employer, on the Commission list of officially recognized brokers and salesmen. Registration is a status and does not authorize a person to operate as a broker or salesman.

29 registration certificate: a license to operate and indicates that the registrant named on the certificate is in good standing with the Commission for the period shown by the issue date.

160 **release clause**: a provision in a blanket mortgage covering more than one unit of real property which provides for the mortgagor to obtain freedom from the mortgage, for each unit, when a designated amount has been paid to the mortgagee for each unit to be released and free.

remainder, estate of: (see Estate of remainder)

78 **remainderman**: the party designated to receive an estate in remainder. Two types: vested remainderman (one who is known and named); and, contingent remainderman (one whose identity is not certain or one to be selected by the occurrence of some event).

112 **renunciation**: to abandon an acquired right without transferring that right to another.

30 **resident**: an individual who has renounced his intention of retaining residence in another state and is physically present in Florida with a sincere intention of remaining in the state indefinitely.

86,98 **restriction**: any device or action which controls or limits the use of real property.

reversion, estate of: (see Estate of reversion)

47,113 **revocation**: to cancel, annul, rescind, or make void; the permanent cancellation of a person's registration.

riparian rights: private ownership rights extending to the normal high-water mark along a river or stream and including access rights to water, boating, bathing, and dockage in accordance with state and federal statutes.

secret profit: (see Overage)

128,130 **section**: one of the primary units of measurement in the government survey system of legal descriptions of land. A section is one mile square and contains 640 acres.

94 **seizen clause**: a covenant in a deed which warrants that the grantor (seller) is seized of the property by virtue of a fee simple title and has a complete right to dispose of same.

250 **site plan**: a document which indicates the improvement details for a project of greater-than-average size.

101,228, 283 **special assessment**: a tax levied against property to pay for all, or part of, an improvement which will benefit the property being assessed.

111 **specific performance**: a remedy for an injured party obtained through a court of equity which requires exact and specific accomplishment of the terms of a contract by a defendant.

100 **specific lien**: a claim which affects only the property specified in the lien instrument or agreement.

97,280 **State documentary stamp tax on deeds**: stamps required to be placed on all deeds or other documents used as conveyances; the charge is based on the total purchase price at the rate of $.30 per each $100, or fraction thereof.

281 **State documentary stamp tax on notes**: stamps required to be placed on all documents which contain a promise to pay money; the charge is based on the entire face value of the debt at the rate of $.15 per $100, or fraction thereof.

97,281 **State documentary surtax on deeds**: tax paid on the amount remaining after subtracting all existing liens and mortgages which will remain; the rate is $.55 per $500, or fraction thereof.

statute: an established rule or law passed by a legislative body.

107 statute of frauds: an act which requires that certain real estate instruments and contracts affecting title to real property must be in writing in order to be enforceable.

113 statute of limitations: an act which prescribes specific time restrictions for enforcement of rights by action of law.

statutory lien: a claim which is created by operation of law (tax lien, special assessment lien, etc.).

11,249 subdivide: to segment acquired large tracts of real property in order to create small tracts for the purpose of resale.

99 sublease: a lessee leasing a property to a third party for a period of time less than the original lease (also referred to as subletting).

145 substitution, principle of: an economic law of value: no sensible buyer will pay more for a property than the cost of an equally desirable replacement property.

207,210 supply (principle of demand and supply): the quantity of goods or services offered for sale to consumers.

125 survey: the procedure used to measure and describe a specific tract of real property for the purpose of determining exact boundaries and the area contained therein.

78 survivorship, right of: a legal concept whereby the surviving owners of a joint interest in real property are entitled to the interest formerly owned by one or more deceased owners of that property.

47 suspension: to cause to cease or bring to a stop for a time of operation; the temporary withholding of a person's registration.

41 syndicate (business trust): a group of people who associate with each other for the purpose of purchasing shares or units at a specified amount per unit, with the money raised to be used to purchase real property, often for subdividing and resale.

177 tandem plan: a method used to accomplish GNMA's special assistance goals.

217,221 tax: compulsory payment paid by a citizen to a unit of government.

160 tax clause: a provision in a mortgage which requires the borrower to pay all legitimate property taxes.

217,226 tax rate: the percentage of value which is used to determine the amount of tax to be levied against each individual unit of property; ad valorem (according to the value).

77 tenancy: the estate or rights of a tenant.

80 tenancy at sufferance: an estate which was lawfully acquired for a temporary period of time but retained after the period of lawful possession has expired.

80 tenancy at will: an estate which may be terminated by either party at any time upon proper notice as prescribed by law.

tenancy by the entireties: (see Estate by the entireties)

79 tenancy in common: the interest in real property owned by two or more parties who are not husband and wife.

tenancy, joint: (see Estate, joint)

254 tenant: a person or party with rights of occupancy or possession of real property.

93 tenendum clause: a provision in a deed designed to specify those improvements or other rights which are being transferred in addition to the land itself.

83 testator (testatrix): a person who makes a will.

83,156, 158 title: the group of rights which represent ownership of real property and the quality of the estate owned; evidence of ownership of property.

86,259, 282 title insurance: a policy of insurance which protects the holder for any loss resulting from defects in the title.

128,130 township: a square tract of land measuring six miles on each side and including 36 sections (formed by the crossing of range and township lines).

46 trade name: any adopted or fictitious name used to designate a business concern.

41 trust: a right of property, either real or personal, held by one party for the benefit of another.

56 trust account (escrow account): an account in a title or trust company, or a bank with trust powers, opened and utilized solely for safekeeping deposits for customers.

trustee (escrow agent): a person or party, either appointed or required by law, to administer or manage another's property.

254,256 truth-in-lending laws: legislation passed which serves the purpose of ensuring that consumers know the exact costs of credit prior to making a purchase.

110,118 unilateral contract: an agreement in which only one party promises to perform without receiving a reciprocal promise to perform from the other party.

112 unliquidated damages: the amount of valuable consideration awarded by a court to an injured party as a result of default. (see also Damages)

180 usury: charging a rate of interest greater than the legal one; unlawful interest.

VA: (see Veterans Administration)

262 vacate: to set aside, cancel, or annul.

108 valid: capable of binding force; sufficient to be legally binding.

108 valid contract: an agreement binding on both parties and legally enforceable against all parties to the agreement.

247 variance: an exception to zoning regulations or ordinances granted to relieve a hardship.

102,119 vendee: the buyer or purchaser of real estate under an agreement.

102 vendee's lien: a claim created against property for the money paid under a contract for sale by the purchaser if the seller defaults.

102,119 vendor: the seller of real estate in an agreement of sale.

102 vendor's lien: a claim against property giving the seller the right to hold the property as security for any unpaid purchase money.

161,164, 255 Veterans Administration (VA): guarantees mortgage loans to encourage private lending agencies to give liberal mortgages to veterans and their widows.

39,40 void: invalid; without force; no longer effective.

92 warrant: a guarantee or covenant, as in a warranty deed.

93 warranty deed (general warranty deed): a type of deed containing the strongest and most comprehensive promises of further assurance possible for a grantor (seller) to convey to a grantee (buyer).

83 will: any written document legally executed and containing the essentials of a "last will and testament" by which an individual disposes of his or her estate, effective after his or her death.

willing (as in "ready, willing, and able"): (see Ready)

93 witness: a person who gives testimony; one who observes and attests to the signing or executing of a document.

writ of certiorari: (see Certiorari, writ of)

writ of mandamus: (see Mandamus, writ of)

235,244 zoning: classification of real property for various purposes; the government power to control and supervise the utilization of privately owned real property (actually the exercise of police powers granted by federal and state constitutions to regulate the use of land in order to promote the health, safety, and general welfare of the citizens).